INDIGENOUS CHILDREN'S SURVIVANCE IN PUBLIC SCHOOLS

Indigenous Children's Survivance in Public Schools examines the cultural, social, and political terrain of Indigenous education by providing accounts of Indigenous students and educators creatively navigating the colonial dynamics within public schools. Through a series of survivance stories, the book surveys a range of educational issues, including implementation of Native-themed curriculum, teachers' attempts to support Native students in their classrooms, and efforts to claim physical and cultural space in a school district, among others. As a collective, these stories highlight the ways that colonization continues to shape Native students' experiences in schools. By documenting the nuanced intelligence, courage, artfulness, and survivance of Native students, families, and educators, the book counters deficit framings of Indigenous students. The goal is also to develop educators' anticolonial literacy so that teachers can counter colonialism and better support Indigenous students in public schools.

Leilani Sabzalian (Alutiiq) is an Assistant Professor of Indigenous Studies in Education at the University of Oregon.

INDIGENOUS AND DECOLONIZING STUDIES IN EDUCATION

Series Editors: Eve Tuck and K. Wayne Yang

INDIGENOUS CHILDREN'S SURVIVANCE IN PUBLIC SCHOOLS

Leilani Sabzalian

Routledge
Taylor & Francis Group

NEW YORK AND LONDON

First published 2019
by Routledge
52 Vanderbilt Avenue, New York, NY 10017

and by Routledge
2 Park Square, Milton Park, Abingdon, Oxon OX14 4RN

Routledge is an imprint of the Taylor & Francis Group, an informa business

© 2019 Taylor & Francis

Library of Congress Cataloging-in-Publication Data
Names: Sabzalian, Leilani, author.
Title: Indigenous children's survivance in public schools / Leilani Sabzalian.
Description: New York, NY : Routledge, 2019. | Includes bibliographical references and index.
Identifiers: LCCN 2018044652| ISBN 9781138384514 (hardback : alk. paper) | ISBN 9781138384507 (pbk. : alk. paper) | ISBN 9780429427503 (ebook)
Subjects: LCSH: Indians of North America--Education. | Indian school children--Services for--United States. | Culturally relevant pedagogy--United States. | Education, Urban--United States.
Classification: LCC E97 .S23 2019 | DDC 371.829/97--dc23
LC record available at https://lccn.loc.gov/2018044652

ISBN: 978-1-138-38451-4 (hbk)
ISBN: 978-1-138-38450-7 (pbk)
ISBN: 978-0-429-42750-3 (ebk)

Typeset in Bembo
by Taylor & Francis Books

To my sons Jahan and Khalil.
They tried to write me out of existence,
but I have written my way back in.
I did this for you.

CONTENTS

SERIES EDITORS' INTRODUCTION

Leilani Sabzalian has created a book that does something that we wish all tellings about the lives of Indigenous children and families would do: emphasize the long histories and even longer futures of Indigenous peoples by attending to the complexity and sovereignty of Indigenous communities. The stories that Sabzalian shares here do an important kind of work in the world—they reveal the ways that Indigenous people, indeed, have experienced inestimably cruel genocidal violences in the establishing of settler colonial nation states, and in their continued enactments on Indigenous lands and waters. But more, Sabzalian writes into the stories the ways that, "Native courage, creativity, intelligence, determination, and artfulness—acts of Native survivance—are our inheritance and our legacy as Indigenous peoples" (from the Introduction). In telling these stories and in offering survivance stories as an Indigenous research method, Sabzalian has rendered a profoundly ethical corrective to the way that stories get told about Indigenous people: the survivance of Indigenous children and families cannot be ignored.

In 2012, we had the opportunity to interview Gerald Vizenor—a citizen of White Earth Nation, a professor, author of more than 30 books, and the person who coined the term survivance—in his home. Sitting together in his living room, we asked him to reflect on his own use of the term, and the widespread life and proliferation of the concept of survivance across many disciplines. He told us that "Survivance is an intergenerational connection to an individual and collective sense of presence and resistance in personal experience and the world, or language, made particularly through stories," (Vizenor with Tuck & Yang, 2014, p. 108). He told us that "survivance stories are much richer than mere descriptive or moral stories. They last longer, and are not commercial" (ibid.) Later in the conversation, describing how language and intervening on the ways that things are usually said is a mainstay of his approach to resistance, he told us, "To resist, tease, and change language is a serious responsibility" (p. 111).

Sabzalian, in describing the survivance in the everyday acts of students, families, and educators, shows what it means to fully embrace this responsibility. Through the stories in this book, we learn how some policies—incompletely conceived and incompletely implemented as they can often be—can still be used by Indigenous families to create spaces to define meaningful educational practices and priorities. In the context of the many humiliating ironies of schooling, people continue to make pathways toward more Indigenous presence, more interruption of colonial discourses, and more attention to the futurity of Indigenous peoples, *as Indigenous peoples.*

Towards these efforts, Sabzalian details the practices of survivance storytelling, especially those which "give space to think and feel," and idea Sabzalian brings forth from the work of Jo-Ann Archibald, a notable scholar from Sto:lo First Nation. Sabzalian generously provides a series of conceptualizations meant especially for teachers, in order to begin shifting what teachers know about Indigenous citizenship, nationhood, and sovereignty. This is what it will take, Sabzalian tells us, for curriculum and pedagogy in mainstream schools to meet the needs of Indigenous students.

We are so fortunate that *Indigenous Children's Survivance in Public Schools* has found a home in our book series, Indigenous and Decolonizing Studies in Education. Still in its early years, this series brings together the central concerns of Indigenous and decolonizing studies with the innovative contributions of social justice education. The books in this series have a commitment to social change with a specific material politics of Indigenous sovereignty, land, and relationships. Because the material politics of decolonization and Indigeneity connect and sometimes abrade with social justice educational research and practices, the books in this series will engage the political incommensurabilities that generate possibilities for education

"There is no way to know the outcome of survivance," Gerald Vizenor told us that afternoon in his living room. Survivance as a concept requires us to keep open, to keep attending, to keep connecting across generations. Survivance storytelling as a practice helps us to remember our many responsibilities and obligations to ancestors, to our future ancestors, and to one another. We are grateful for the tellings and re-tellings that Leilani Sabzalian has offered to all of us in this gem of a book.

Series editors

Eve Tuck is Associate Professor of Critical Race and Indigenous Studies and Canada Research Chair of Indigenous Methodologies with Youth and Communities at the Ontario Institute for Studies in Education (OISE), University of Toronto.

K. Wayne Yang is Provost of Muir College and Associate Professor in Ethnic Studies at UC San Diego.

Reference

Vizenor, G., Tuck, E., & Yang, K. W. (2014). Resistance in the blood. In E. Tuck & K. W. Yang (Eds.), *Youth resistance research and theories of change* (pp. 107–117). New York: Routledge.

PREFACE

Much has happened since I began my research that led to this book. Recently and most notably, hundreds of Native nations and thousands of Indigenous and allied people engaged in collective resistance to the Dakota Access Pipeline, an underground pipeline designed to carry hundreds of thousands of barrels of crude oil each day through the Dakotas and Iowa to Illinois. This proposed pipeline, initially slated to go through Bismark, North Dakota but deemed too dangerous for the resident population's water source, was rerouted to go through Standing Rock traditional territory and under the Missouri River, directly threatening the water of Indigenous peoples, destroying sacred and culturally important sites, and making visible in practice the hidden curriculum of policy decisions that some lives matter more than others.

In December of 2016, the Army Corps of Engineers denied Dakota Access Pipeline the easement they needed to drill under the Missouri River, a decision that was not the result of institutional or corporate benevolence, but rather, due to the collective and courageous organizing and resistance on the part of Water Protectors. To achieve this, Indigenous peoples and allies withstood freezing temperatures, a foreboding militarized police presence, and state violence via attack dogs, mace, water cannons, tear gas, sound cannons, and concussion grenades for months to block the pipeline and protect Standing Rock lands and waters. The victory, however, was short-lived. In January 2017, the President signed an executive order, expediting the construction of the pipeline which became fully operational that June, and now transports hundreds of thousands of barrels of crude oil through it each day. Yet Water Protectors continue their resistance in courts, some filing a federal class action lawsuit alleging excessive use of force by law enforcement, while hundreds of others battled individual charges, some federal, such as Civil Disorder. Resistance has taken the form of prayer walks, writing letters to those, such as Red

Fawn Fallis (Oglala Lakota), who are currently in federal prison, and supporting efforts by the Water Protector Legal Collective, which continues to provide legal support for those in need.

Standing Rock reflects one of the greatest, though not the only, struggles for Indigenous self-determination and sovereignty of this era. Idle No More, for example, is another notable example of an Indigenous-led movement for self-determination and a prominent example of Native survivance. As an Indigenous-led movement that began in Canada and spread worldwide, Idle No More focused on protecting Indigenous sovereignty, lands and waters, and fostering Indigenous resurgence. Though rooted in centuries of Indigenous resistance, the Idle No More movement specifically was initiated by four women—Nina Wilson, Sylvia McAdam, Jessica Gordon, and Sheelah McLean—who were concerned about legislation in Canada (bill C-45) that would effectively erode First Nations' treaty rights, lands, and waters, and decided to hold a teach-in in Saskatoon. The movement gained considerable visibility with the public hunger strike from Chief Theresa Spence of the Attawapiskat First Nation and elder Raymond Robinson from the Cross Lake First Nation in Manitoba. The movement continued with teach-ins, panel sessions, public protests, marches, and round dance flash mobs, among other forms of creative resistance.[1] And like Standing Rock, there has not been a clear end, victory, or sense of relief for the movement. As colonial discourses and tactics have continued to shift, Indigenous resistance has needed to stay alert and active.

The ongoing, collective struggles at Standing Rock and Idle No More to protect sacred lands and waters and the vehement and violent encroachment by the State, corporations, or the US federal or Canadian governments exemplify both settler colonialism (Tuck & Yang, 2012; Veracini, 2011a; Wolfe, 2006) and survivance (Vizenor, 1999) writ large. These struggles also exemplify the relentless, shapeshifitng nature and processes of colonial tactics. During the struggle to protect Standing Rock, Enbridge Energy Inc., a Canadian corporation with a large share in DAPL, began construction on the Line 3 pipeline that would begin in Alberta, Canada and carry hundreds of thousands of crude oil through Anishinaabe and treaty territory to Superior, Wisconsin. Colonial forces were not stopped, just deterred and redirected. Line 3 also reflects the fleeting and tenuous nature of Indigenous victories against corporate extraction. Four years of Indigenous and grassroots organizing had successfully blocked the Sandpiper pipeline slated to go through the same territory. When Sandpiper was blocked, Line 3 took its place, one black snake replacing another.[2] Standing Rock is real, but also a metaphor for the ever-present threat of colonial dispossession—when one pipeline is shut down, another surfaces, and the struggle continues across Indigenous lands. In Oregon, my home state, Indigenous Water Protectors and allies have fought to protect Cascade Locks from Nestlé, fought to undam the Klamath River, and fought to protect the West Coast from the Pacific Connector Pipeline and Jordan Cove Liquified Natural Gas Project. These examples emphasize the relentless nature of colonialism, but equally important, they also represent the tenacity and enduring nature of Indigenous survivance. Important, too, are the ways these examples underscore coloniality and survivance as localized and experiential, rather than universal or abstract, phenomena.

Given this current climate of both epic violence and resistance, the subtle and everyday ways Native students, families, and educators confront colonial contexts and engage in practices of survivance may feel irrelevant, an inadequate challenge to the vast social, economic, and political issues that face Native peoples and nations within the United States. But settler colonialism and survivance do not only surface in epic moments of public politics; they also surface in subtle, unremarkable, and everyday ways.

The struggles at Standing Rock epitomize settler colonialism—understood here as a triadic structure of settler supremacy, chattel slavery, and Indigenous erasure designed to expropriate and acquire Indigenous lands (Arvin, Tuck, & Morrill, 2013; Wolfe, 2006)—as Indigenous lands are recast by the State, the Army Corps, and corporations as both property and commodity, and Indigenous peoples cleared out of the way for resource extraction. Similarly, schools have been massive instruments of colonization, most evident in the overt practices of assimilation when Native students were forcibly placed in boarding schools, removed from their homes, punished for speaking their languages, and indoctrinated into white culture (Adams, 1995). Yet settler colonialism surfaces and is reproduced in schools in quieter, subtler ways as well—through "legitimized racism" (Robertson, 2015) toward Indigenous students, state standards that direct attention primarily to Native history (Shear et al., 2015), settler colonial orientations and "grammars" of curriculum (Calderón, 2014b), processes of schooling rooted in the deep structures of the colonialist consciousness (Grande, 2015), and non-Native modes of being, affect, and commonsense (Rifkin, 2014), among others. Thus, the logic of Indigenous erasure that constituted the Dakota Access Pipeline and Army Corps of Engineers' oversight of Indigenous peoples' concerns and treaty rights, or the more epic moments of Indigenous erasure and assimilation where schools sought to erase and replace Native students' cultural identities, are discursively linked to and continual with the ways erasure surfaces in everyday educational policy and practice. Indigenous dispossession and erasure—writ large in federal policies of extermination, annexation, civilization, removal, assimilation, or termination, for example—also manifest in quieter ways in public schools as teachers disregard Indigenous students' perspectives, privilege Eurocentric curriculum, commodify and objectify Native culture, absorb Indigenous students into multicutural frameworks, or encode Indigenous erasure into educational policy. Indeed, settler colonialism manifests in curricular silences, what is not taught and not said in classrooms.

As an example, the day after Water Protectors were assaulted by militarized police, the Los Angeles Times reported a story about an annual "5th Grade Feast" at La Cañada Elementary School in California. This longstanding tradition "invites participants to dress in wide, white pilgrim-style collars and buckles or fringed and beaded wardrobes inspired by America's first natives as they break proverbial bread and reflect on what the holiday [Thanksgiving] means to them" (Cardine, 2016). Two days later, the National Council for Social Studies (NCSS) circulated a "smart brief," a "3x-weekly snapshot of news on best practices, curriculum, and professional development for social studies educators" (NCSS, 2016), that featured the school feast. At a time when actual Indigenous peoples were recovering from extreme violence at Standing Rock, the premier national social studies organization promoted "playing Indian" (Deloria, 1998; Green, 1988) as a best practice. NCSS aims to support social studies educators to "teach students the content knowledge, intellectual skills, and civic values necessary for fulfilling the duties of citizenship in a participatory democracy" (NCSS, 2017)—yet the smart brief promoted a form of symbolic violence that, akin to the corporate encroachment onto Indigenous lands, sought to erase Indigenous peoples and assert settler entitlement. Teaching students to dress up as "Native Americans" for the feast (which generalizes, commodifies, objectifies, and romanticizes Indigenous peoples and cultures), was not only acceptable; it was promoted as an exemplar social studies activity. This book does not suggest a causal link between these events. Rather, I am suggesting that their meanings and investments are technically and discursively linked through Indigenous erasure, a core practice of settler colonialism rooted in a "logic of elimination" (Wolfe, 2006, p. 387). As Tuck and Gaztambide-Fernández (2013) argue, "settler colonialism's logic of elimination requires the removal of Indigenous peoples of a territory, 'but not [just] in any particular way' (p. 388); by any means necessary" (p. 77). The epic and violent conflicts in North Dakota, in Canada, or along the Line 3 pipeline are discursively linked to the persistent silence in public schools around these very issues. The State's, the Army Corps,' the federal and Canadian governments,' and corporations' routine oversight of Indigenous rights is linked to the silence in public schools regarding Indigenous citizenship, sovereignty, governance, and treaty rights.

This book is an attempt to link the epic violence that threatens Indigenous peoples and lands to the everyday colonial violence Indigenous students, families, and educators face in schools. My intention is not to create a taxonomy of colonial violence nor imply causality. Rather, this book is an attempt to document various sets of colonial relations that undermine Indigenous self-determination in schools, many which surface in small and everyday acts erasure, silence, and marginalization that are continuous with and foreground more epic colonial violence. I see the violence in Standing Rock and the violence in schools as interrelated, as simultaneous and entangled, as continuous. This book attempts to document resistance to that colonial violence so that educators can unlearn colonizing school practices and policies and learn how to "work in productive opposition to a system that has failed and continues to fail" Native youth (Paris, 2016, p. 8).

Though addressing a small, urban school district in the Pacific Northwest, this study examines the types of socializing processes that educate students, Native and non-Native, in ways that undermine self-determination and sovereignty. But this book is not only about colonialism. As the collective resistance at Standing Rock has shown, Native people defy colonial contexts and engage in creative practices of survivance (Vizenor, 1999) that forward Indigenous theorizations of the present and future. Just as settler colonialism can operate in both extraordinary and ordinary ways, stories and practices of survivance simultaneously surface in the epic and the everyday.

Survivance, a semantic combination of the words survival and resistance, exceeds either of those words alone. Survivance describes "Indigenous creative approaches to life beyond genocide, beyond the bareness of survival" (Morrill, 2017, p. 15), signifying "a sense of native presence over absence, nihility, and victimry" (Vizenor, 2007, pp. 12–13). The collective action at Standing Rock and the movement and moments it has inspired is undoubtedly a metastory of survivance. Survivance is epitomized by Native women who have been at the heart and frontlines of this movement, the women who birthed the next generation of protectors or led resistance through prayer. Survivance is embodied by the Native youth who ran from their homelands to Washington DC to challenge decisions made by the Army Corps of Engineers and the State, or reflected in the leadership of Chairman Dave Archambault III who led his nation by criticizing policies that threaten his peoples' lifeways and elevating this issue to an international audience. The countless Indigenous people who heeded the call from Ladonna Brave Bull and left their jobs or families to stand in solidarity at Standing Rock, the Native veterans who took up the call to stand on the frontlines, or the people who prayed in the face of armed guards despite outright threats and physical assault are striking acts of survivance by extraordinary individuals and communities. Yet survivance is also embodied by the father on food stamps who donated $25 to the Sacred Stone Legal Defense Fund, the mother who could not go to Standing Rock, but told her children stories of the movement, the Native students who created signs and distributed them at a solidarity rally. Survivance characterizes the everyday ways Indigenous peoples have reframed imposed narratives, using social media to remind the public they are #ProtectorsNotProtestors. More than just a no (though this movement was cleary grounded in #NoDAPL), these hashtags were small shifts in language that forwarded Indigenous futurities—#KeepItInThe-Ground, #RezpectOurWater, #MniWiconi, #WaterIsLIfe.

Survivance in Indigenous education follows a similar pattern. While passing legislation in Montana, Washington, or Oregon that requires Indigenous education for all, or a community-led effort to open a language- and culture-based charter school exemplify metastories of survivance, traces of survivance are also visible in the small, everyday, and future oriented acts of Native students, families, and educators negotiating the colonial contexts of public schools—a 7-year old student who contests stereotypical images of Indigenous people presented him as curriculum, a Native high school student who decides to pursue a project on her own time because it was deemed unimportant by her teacher, a Native educator who works quietly, but strategically, to make her way into schools and classrooms, or a Native youth group that keeps meeting, despite being shuffled around, even shut out of, various spaces in the district. Each of these small acts exemplifies self-determination and survivance in action.

My hope is that the survivance stories in this book demonstrate the nuanced intelligence, courage, artfulness, and survivance of Native students, families, and educators as they negotiate the colonial contexts of urban Indigenous education in a public school district. Bearing witness, not just to these small acts of survivance, but to the colonial contexts that constrain Native educational self-determination in public schools, will not disrupt the complex, omnipresent structures of colonialism endemic to US society (Brayboy, 2005). But bearing witness is also necessary, a way to disrupt the normalizing logics of education (Moreton-Robinson, 2016) in order to imagine education otherwise. I hope this book, in a small way, contributes to spaces of possibility, real or imagined, for Native youth in public schools.

A Note on Terminology and Audience

Throughout this book, I interchangeably use the terms Native/Indigenous when referencing Indigenous people, the discipline Indigenous studies, or when referring to Indigenous education. I recognize that any such terms (Native American, American Indian, Alaska Native, Native, Indigenous) gloss over and collapse the rich linguistic, cultural, spiritual, geographic, and political diversity of Native peoples and nations; yet I use these overarching terms, recognizing limitations in such a task. As Cherokee author Thomas King (2012) writes, "the fact of the matter is there has never been a good collective noun because there never was a collective to begin with" (p. xiii). As a citational practice, when possible, I purposefully utilize the specific affiliations of the Indigenous scholars, authors, and artists I cite, deferring to Indigenous peoples' own referents when possible. However, to protect the confidentiality of students, families, and educators in this project, I refer to them only as Native/Indigenous, or Indian when used as a self-referent. As this book will show, "Indian" is a complex, and yet highly circulated term (e.g., Indian Education, Indian Country, urban Indian). Some chapters, such as Pilgrims and Invented Indians, attempt to address the complexity of that term. I recognize the term holds diverse connotations, ranging from a source of identity and pride to an offense. Some scholars have gone to task on the word (Vizenor, 1999; Vizenor, Tuck, & Yang, 2014), referring to it as a "colonial enactment" and "simulation" that has sustained dominance and "superseded tribal names" (Vizenor, 1999, p. 11). For others, it remains the common and preferred referent used in homes and homelands. I utilize Indian when referring to "Indian Education" programs or policies, or as it is used by individuals and the literature; however, I also use Indian when speaking of society's dominant representation of Indigenous peoples (Berkhofer, 1979), which should hopefully be clear throughout the book.

I also use the word settler in reference to non-Indigenous peoples. As previously discussed, the term settler comes from the literature on settler colonialism. Some argue that "settler" and "settlement" are too benign of words to use to describe the people who initially colonized Indigenous lands, or whose ancestors continue to benefit from the dispossession of Indigenous lands. Others may feel uncomfortable with the referent, a similar response perhaps to the ways pointing out whiteness prompts "white fragility" (DiAngelo, 2011). But as Kanaka Maoli scholar Maile Arvin offers, to identify oneself as a non-Indigenous settler can be discomforting, but also productive, inviting self-reflection about our roles and responsibilities to Indigenous peoples and lands (Aikau, Arvin, Goeman, & Morgensen, 2015). This book asks educators to consider the different trajectories of knowledge, relationships, and responsibilities that become available when openly identifying as non-Indigenous settlers.

Writing a book also inevitably forces questions regarding my intended audience. I want to be clear that while white women and non-Indigenous educators continue to represent the majority of the teaching force (Leonardo & Boas, 2013; U.S. Department of Education, 2016) and are an important audience for this book, this book is intended to inform and inspire all educators, some of whom I presume to be Indigenous. As Linda Tuhiwai Smith (2012) states, "What is more important than what alternatives indigenous peoples offer the world is what alternatives indigenous peoples offer each other" (p. 110).

Thus, to the Indigenous educators and researchers striving to create space for Native presence in public schools, I hope this book is helpful to you. Even if you are already familiar with experiences and literature in this book, I hope this book serves as an affirmation. To the courageous community of Indigenous students, families, and educators in particular, who interrupted their long-standing marginalization by reclaiming Native space in the district, I write to say that I see you. I recognize the labor of love you have undertook—often on your own time and your own dime—to make that vision a reality. To those who fearlessly and relentlessly continue to advocate, volunteer, and show up in small and big ways for Native youth, I write to let you know my hands go up to you. To Native youth here and everywhere—I write to tell you that I see you. I recognize what you are up against. I also recognize your power. I see the big and small ways that you make schools and classrooms better, carving out space for your presence, your future, and those who will follow you. To the Indigenous artists, authors, and scholars of Indigenous studies, I write to thank you for giving me tools and analytics to understand and intervene into settler colonial schooling. Finally, to all educators, administrators, researchers, and teacher educators, I hope this book is helpful to you and enlists you in the ongoing project of creating space for Indigenous self-determination and sovereignty in public schools. We need you.

I also hope it is clear throughout this book that I am writing against the ways settler colonialism constrains educational practice, not against individual teachers.

Like Patel (2016), "I both assume and pay little attention to good intentions" (p. 33). My focus here "is less on intentions than on institutional discourses, less on 'goodness' and 'badness' than on historically configured relations of power" (Shohat & Stam, 2014, p. 3). I should also be clear that these stories are not intended to promote sympathy or even empathy for Indigenous students. As critical race scholars have noted, empathy, and in particular "false empathy (Delgado, 1990; Duncan, 2002; Vaught, 2011), can be superficial, shallow, and often "excuses White structural domination" (Vaught, 2011, p. 21). Empathy "has power dimensions and can be a dangerous force if it is not genuine" (Duncan, 2002, p. 89). Without attention to such dimensions, it "exists inside a supremacist framework that cannot disrupt it" (Vaught, 2011, p. 20). Instead of fostering empathy, these stories are intended to "distort" (Ohito, 2016) the unexamined ways whiteness and colonialism surface in educational policy and practice. They are meant to puncture, to disrupt, to cause discomfort (Boler, 1999; Kaomea, 2003; Ohito, 2016), inviting reflection, perhaps even anger. "Where is the rage?" asks critical theorist bell hooks (1995). Similarly, Acoma Pueblo author Simon Ortiz, replying to an audience member's apology at one of his talks, said, "Instead of apologizing, you should get pissed off. Get angry so that some real change can be acted out" (as cited in Robbins, 2011, p. xiv).

These stories are not intended to provoke empathy or apologies. Rather, my hope is that they provoke discomfort, indignation, and a sense of urgency and responsibility, here defined as a commitment to disrupting colonialism and teaching in service of Indigenous self-determination and sovereignty. Citing Delgado's character Rodrigo, Vaught (2011) writes, empathy "is always more attractive than responsibility"; but "responsibility is the transformational alternative to liberal and oppressive empathy" (p. 23).

For some of you, making explicit the ways colonial discourses function in schools will be new knowledge; for others, this knowledge is already recognizable, and so the book may function as an affirmation and form of validation (Delgado, 1990). My hope is that whether these insights are new or already understood, bringing educational experience into conversation with Indigenous studies scholarship will help you identify, articulate, and disrupt the normalizing logics of educational practices (Moreton-Robinson, 2016) for Indigenous students and help you envision Indigenous education in ways that resist, or even unmake, settler colonial relations and practices (Aikau, Goodyear-Ka'ōpua, & Silva, 2016, p. 158).

Notes

1 More information can be found at the Idle No More website (http://www.idlenomore.ca/).
2 For more information on Line 3 and other issues facing Indigenous communities and lands, visit Stop Line 3 (https://www.stopline3.org/) and Honor the Earth (http://www.honorearth.org/).

References

Adams, D. W. (1995). *Education for extinction: American Indians and the boarding school experience, 1875–1928*. Lawrence, KS: University Press of Kansas.

Aikau, H. K., Arvin, M., Goeman, M., & Morgensen, S. (2015) Indigenous feminisms roundtable. *Frontiers: A Journal of Women Studies*, 36(3), 84–106.

Aikau, H. K., Goodyear-Kaʻōpua, N., & Silva, N. E. (2016). The practice of kuleana: Reflections on critical Indigenous studies through trans-Indigenous exchange. In A. Moreton-Robinson (Ed.), *Critical indigenous studies: Engagements in first world locations* (Critical issues in indigenous studies) (pp. 157–175). Tucson, AZ: The University of Arizona Press.

Arvin, M., Tuck, E., & Morrill, A. (2013). Decolonizing feminism: Challenging connections between settler colonialism and heteropatriarchy. *Feminist Formations*, 25(1), 8–34.

Berkhofer, R. (1979). *The white man's Indian: Images of the American Indian, from Columbus to the present*. New York, NY: Vintage Books.

Boler, M. (1999). *Feeling power: Emotions and education*. Hoboken, NJ: Taylor & Francis.

Brayboy, B. M. J. (2005). Toward a tribal critical race theory in education. *Urban Review: Issues and Ideas in Public Education*, 5, 425–446.

Calderón, D. (2014a). Speaking back to manifest destinies: A land education-based approach to critical curriculum inquiry. *Environmental Education Research*, 20(1), 24–36.

Calderón, D. (2014b). Uncovering settler grammars in curriculum. *Educational Studies: Journal of the American Educational Studies Association*, 50(4), 313–338.

Cardine, S. (2016). La Cañada Elementary School 5th-graders dress the part for traditional Thanksgiving feast. *La Cañada Valley Sun*, November 21. Retrieved from www.latimes.com/socal/la-canada-valley-sun/news/tn-vsl-me-feast-20161123-story.html.

Delgado, R. (1990). When a story is just a story: Does voice really matter? *Virginia Law Review*, 76(1), 95–111.

Deloria, P. (1998). *Playing Indian*. New Haven, CT: Yale University Press.

DiAngelo, R. (2011). White fragility. *International Journal of Critical Pedagogy*, 3(3), 54–70.

Duncan, G. (2002). Critical race theory and method: Rendering race in urban ethnographic research. *Qualitative Inquiry*, 6(1), 85–104.

Grande, S. (2015). *Red pedagogy: Native American social and political thought* (2nd ed.) Lanham, MD: Rowman & Littlefield.

Green, R. (1988). The tribe called Wannabee: Playing Indian in America and Europe. *Folklore*, 99(1), 30–55.

hooks, b. (1995). *Killing rage: Ending racism*. New York: Henry Holt and Company.

Kaomea, J. (2003). Reading erasures and making the familiar strange: Defamiliarizing methods for research in formerly colonized and historically oppressed communities. *Educational Researcher*, 32(2), 14–25.

King, T. (2012). *Inconvenient Indian: A curious account of Native people in North America*. Minneapolis, MN: University of Minnesota Press.

Leonardo, Z., & Boas, E. (2013). Other kids' teacher: What children of color learn from White women and what this says about race, whiteness, and gender. In M. Lynn and A. Dixson (Eds.), *Handbook of critical race theory in education* (pp. 313–323). New York, NY: Routledge.

Moreton-Robinson, A. (2016). *Critical indigenous studies: Engagements in first world locations*. Tucson, AZ: The University of Arizona Press.

Morrill, A. (2017). Time traveling dogs (and other Native feminist ways to defy dislocations). *Cultural Studies ↔ Critical Methodologies*, 17(1), 14–20.

National Council for Social Studies. (2016). NCSS SmartBrief, November 23.

National Council for Social Studies. (2017). About National Council for Social Studies (NCSS). Retrieved from www.socialstudies.org/about.

Ohito, E. (2016). Making the emperor's new clothes visible in anti-racist teacher education: Enacting a pedagogy of discomfort with White preservice teachers. *Equity & Excellence in Education*, 49(4), 454–467.

Paris, D. (2016). On educating culturally sustaining teachers. TeachingWorks working papers: University of Michigan. Retrieved from www.teachingworks.org/images/files/TeachingWorks_Paris.pdf.

Patel, L. (2016). *Decolonizing educational research: From ownership to answerability*. New York, NY: Routledge.

Rifkin, M. (2014). *Settler common sense: Queerness and everyday colonialism in the American Renaissance*. Minneapolis, MN: University of Minnesota Press.

Robbins, C. (2011). *All Indians do not live in teepees (or casinos)*. Lincoln, NE: University of Nebraska Press.

Robertson, D.W. (2015). Invisibility in the color-blind era: Examining legitimized racism against Indigenous peoples. *American Indian Quarterly*, 39(2), 113–153.

Shear, S. B., Knowles, R. T., Soden, G. J., & Castro, A.J. (2015). Manifesting destiny: Re/presentations of Indigenous peoples in K-12 U.S. history standards. *Theory & Research in Social Education*, 43(1), 68–101.

Shohat, E., & Stam, R. (2014). *Unthinking Eurocentrism: Multiculturalism and the media*. New York, NY: Routledge.

Smith, L. T. (2012). *Decolonizing methodologies: Research and indigenous peoples* (2nd ed.). London: Zed Books.

Tuck, E. & Gaztambide-Fernández, R.A. (2013). Curriculum, replacement, and settler futurity. *Journal of Curriculum Theorizing*, 29(1), 72–89.

Tuck, E., & Yang, K. W. (2012). Decolonization is not a metaphor. *Decolonization: Indigeneity, Education and Society*, 1, 1–40.

U.S. Department of Education. (2016). *The state of racial diversity in the educator workforce*. Washington, DC: U.S. Department of Education, Office of Planning, Evaluation and Policy Development, Policy and Program Studies Service.

Vaught, S.E. (2011). *Racism, public schooling, and the entrenchment of White supremacy: A critical race ethnography*. Albany, NY: SUNY Press.

Veracini, L. (2011a). Introducing settler colonial studies. *Settler Colonial Studies*, 1, 1–12.

Veracini, L. (2011b). On settlerness. *Borderlands e-journal*, 10(1), 1–17.

Vizenor, G. R. (1999). *Manifest manners: Narratives on postindian survivance*. Lincoln, NE: University of Nebraska Press.

Vizenor, G. R. (2007). *Literary chance: Essays on Native American survivance*. València: Universitat de València.

Vizenor, G., Tuck, E. & Yang, K.W. (2014). Resistance is in the blood. In E. Tuck & K. W. Yang (Eds.), *Youth resistance research and theories of change* (pp. 107–117). New York, NY: Routledge.

Wolfe, P. (2006). Settler-colonialism and the elimination of the native. *Journal of Genocide Research*, 8(4), 387–409.

ACKNOWLEDGEMENTS

All books are a collective effort and I am so very grateful for the community that has supported me and this project. This book was made possible and stronger because of each of you. Quyanaasinaq to my partner Hadee, my sons Jahan and Khalil, and the rest of my family who stood by me, encouraged me, and were patient throughout these past few years as I tried to balance my roles as a mother, partner, daughter, writer, and teacher. Quyanaasinaq to the Native youth, families, and educators who have so graciously and generously shared their time and stories with me. Quyanaasinaq to Dawn Malliett for her dedication to me and the community. Quyanaasinaq to my dissertation advisor, Jerry Rosiek, and my committee members, Kirby Brown, Joanna Goode, and Scott Pratt, for their academic and professional mentorship and their faith in me as a scholar. Quyanaasinaq to my dear friend Angie Morrill for generously reading my work and providing unwavering friendship, mentorship, and inspiration throughout this process. Quyanaasinaq also to Odo and Meh for allowing me to use their brilliant artwork for the cover, which embodies the book's theme of survivance in public schools. Quyanaasinaq to Spirit Brooks for her encouragement and support in editing this manuscript, and to Lani Teves and Jennifer O'Neal for motivating me during our writing circles. Quyanaasinaq to the National Academy of Education/ Spencer Foundation for providing funding for the research upon which this book is based, and to the fellows I met there—Rosa, Nicole, Django, Nolan, Jessica, Zat, Nicole, Ilana, Michael, and Adrienne—who supported and inspired me. Quyanaasinaq to the editors at Routledge, in particular Catherine Bernard, Hélène Feest, Rachel Dugan, and Peter Stafford, for their support in making this book possible. Lastly, quyanaasinaq to Eve Tuck and Wayne Yang for their generous mentorship, and the critical and generative feedback they offered me on this manuscript.

INTRODUCTION

The stories of *survivance* are elusive, obscure, and rightfully imprecise by ordinary definitions, translations, and catchword histories, but survivance is invariably true and just in native practice. The nature of survivance is unmistakable by native storiers, and the stories create a sense of presence, natural reason, active traditions, narrative resistance, and continental liberty, clearly observable in personal attributes, such as humor, spirit, cast of mind, and moral courage. The character of survivance necessitates an active sense of native presence over absence, nihility, and victimry.

Gerald Vizenor, 2007, pp. 12–13

...*survivance* subtly reduces the power of the destroyer. [Vizenor] seizes on *survivance's* older sense of *succession*, orienting its connotations not toward loss but renewal and continuity into the future rather than memorializing the past.

Karl Kroeber, 2008, p. 25

Mainstream media and dominant discourses routinely and stubbornly portray Indigenous peoples as vanished, as victims, or as broken and damaged (Tuck, 2009), yet Native survivance is a persistent feature of Indigenous communities. Native courage, creativity, intelligence, determination, and artfulness—acts of Native survivance—are our inheritance and our legacy as Indigenous peoples. I typically resist generalizations about Indigenous peoples because, as Mvskoke Creek scholar Tsianina Lomawaima (1999) states, "so many stereotypes rest on the mistaken assumption that all Indians are alike" (p. 5); but here—because I believe it is true, and also because I believe Indigenous peoples deserve, perhaps even need, to hear it—I draw from Anishinaabe scholar Gerald Vizenor's work to emphasize survivance as "invariably true and just in native practice," and "unmistakable by native stories." Saying this does not mean all Indigenous peoples are the same. The active, creative, future-oriented practices and praxes of Indigenous peoples are as diverse Indigenous peoples themselves. But saying Native survivance is a fact—whether in its enactment or its potential—provides an important antidote to the erasure and deficit narratives that chase and displace Indigenous peoples. At times, survivance is practically imperceptible: a desire about the world, a feeling or instinct one follows, a refusal to let something go unnoticed. On other occasions, survivance is momentous: the resistance at Standing Rock, for example, which was a reminder to the world and each other of our presence, power, and creativity as Indigenous peoples. As this book will show, survivance is a diverse, yet persistent feature of Indigenous education. It surfaces in Native students' observations about their curriculum, or Native educators' creativity as they circumvent institutional resistance. Survivance emerges in the everyday acts of Native students, families, and educators as they create spaces of possibility within public schools. Survivance surfaces in my own writing and storytelling as I try to imagine more promising practices of Indigenous education. It is said that intergenerational trauma is inherited, a colonial legacy passed on through our DNA. This book posits that whether or not this is true, survivance is a legacy we inherit as Indigenous peoples. Indigenous children, and those who teach them, should know this.

Recognizing Native survivance means recognizing the various ways Indigenous peoples continue to chart meaningful futures for ourselves in spite of colonial violence, and telling stories of how Native youth, families, and educators carve out spaces of survivance within and in spite of US Indian policy, in spaces such as Indian education.[1] Indian education has often meant colonial education *for*, not *by*, Native peoples (Lomawaima, 2002)—federal boarding schools, on-reservation day schools, or mission schools, for example, that sought to assimilate Indigenous children into colonial values, practices, and ideals. But even within assimilative colonial policies and institutions, Indigenous survivance has persisted. "Indian self-education has survived under tremendous duress" (Lomawaima, 1999, p. 5). Further, Indigenous peoples have consistently demanded more from public educational institutions. The Indian Education Act of 1972 and the Indian Self-Determination and Education Act of 1975, for example, exemplify movements and acts of survivance, and were important shifts in Indian education. Countless Indigenous educators, families, and allies testified to the Special Senate Subcommittee on Indian Education about the travesty of Indian education, a travesty recognized in 4,077 pages of hearings and 450 pages of committee print that were distilled into the Kennedy Report.[2] Such advocacy led Senator Kennedy to call Indian education a "national disgrace" (U.S. Congress, 1969, p. 3) and to advocate strongly for Indigenous control of education. The Indian Education Act established the Office of Indian Education and the National Advisory Council on Indian Education, as well as the template for the Indian Education formula grant program to support Native students in public schools. As this book will show, the act has not guaranteed the type of education Indigenous educators advocated for, yet the movement nevertheless made stark the devastating impact of prior colonial forms of education, and provided a formal mechanism for Indigenous families and educators to provide input to shape educational priorities and processes. And despite the routine marginalization of Indian education in public school districts,

Native educators and families continue to leverage this movement in service of educational self-determination.

It was within a space made possible by the Indian Education Act that a group of us—Indigenous families, students, and educators—in a small, urban school district, began reclaiming space for Indigenous students. In 2012, we started a weekly after-school youth group within the Title VI/Indian Education program, a space where Indigenous students and families could be in community together and define our own educational priorities and practices. It wasn't long before we could see clear benefits to our group and to the program. Students involved had opportunities to form healthy relationships with their peers, develop positive cultural identities, engage with Native literature, sharpen their critical literacy skills, and participate in meaningful place- and culture-based education. The program also provided the opportunity for participating Indigenous parents and family members to meet each other and network. Importantly, it was this net-working that enabled organizing that led to securing further grant funding to establish a Native youth center, a necessity given the roadblocks we faced as a community without a permanent home. Since the establishment of the center, the Indian Education program has grown considerably, and now includes a weekly preschool program that integrates Native language into literacy activities, a culture camp for students during summer and winter breaks, and a first foods program where students learn to harvest, prepare, and preserve traditional foods. The program growth has been promising and exciting.[3]

As programs expanded, students and parents would comment on how they appreciated the opportunities afforded by the after-school programs and the center. However, I also heard more frequent reports about patronizing representations of Indigenous people in curriculum, racist microaggressions with teachers and school parents, and moments of exclusion and silence. The increasing frequency of these reports was not a surprise. We had created a space with a majority of Indigenous students and families where it was "safe to be Indigenous on *Indigenous terms*" (Lomawaima & McCarty, 2014b, p. 9). People felt comfortable expressing experiences in these spaces they would not elsewhere. It was natural that we would be hearing such stories. Because stories helped me understand the contexts and contestations of colonialism students and families negotiated, it felt natural to represent the issues facing Indigenous students, families, and educators via stories. To do so, I drew from a longstanding Indigenous tradition of storytelling, complemented by critical race scholarship.

Survivance Storytelling

Survivance storytelling is my attempt to engage in a practice of critical and responsible storytelling. Survivance stories are both descriptive and interventive. My hope is that by documenting the racial and colonial dynamics Native students and families navigate, as well as the nuanced intelligence, courage, artfulness, and survivance they employ as they navigate those dynamics, educators will critically examine what it means to teach in colonial contexts and teach toward Indigenous self-determination.

The stories families began sharing of their educational experiences were laced with colonialism and survivance. Thus, survivance stories are characterized by their attention to colonialism but also to the varied practices of survivance within those experiences. Survivance draws attention to Indigenous peoples' "active sense of presence" (Vizenor, 1999, p. vii) and creative negotiations amidst colonial dispossession. As Vizenor offers, Native survivance is "not a mere reaction, or a survivable name. Native survivance stories are renunciations of dominance, tragedy and victimry. (p. vii). Survivance stories intervene into discourses that have long pathologized Indigenous lives—savage, primitive, vanishing, damaged, victim—and instead reflect Indigenous peoples' "active resistance and repudiation of dominance" (Vizenor, 2008, p. 11). Survivance—Native peoples' power to refuse colonial scripts of erasure or victimization, and instead creatively confront, resist, decenter, disrupt, and transform those scripts in various ways, big and small—is a central theme of this book.

Survivance describes our communal self-determination to reclaim space in a school district and create a Native youth center, an effort rooted in "fierce Native advocacy for 'places of difference' within and outside of schools where the profound range of diversity that characterizes Native America could be appreciated, nurtured, and recognized" (Lomawaima & McCarty, 2014b, p. 4). But survivance can also manifest in small ways—a Native educator's commitment to educate teachers and students in the district regardless of her routine marginalization, a light-skinned Native student's desire for recognition in her classroom, even my own methodological commitment to a "Native feminist reading practice" of "reading survivance from a place of survivance" (Morrill, 2017, p. 15). Each survivance story in this book is an attempt to reflect back the courage, commitment, and continuity of Native students, educators, and community members that I have witnessed.

My practice of survivance storytelling borrows theories and methods from the field of Critical race theory (CRT), and in particular, counterstorytelling methodologies (Delgado, 1989; Solórzano & Delgado Bernal, 2001; Solórzano & Yosso, 2002), however the stories, practices, and theories of survivance existed long before this. Survivance storytelling is akin to counterstorytelling, a theoretically grounded approach to research rooted in Critical Race Theory (Solórzano & Yosso, 2002), yet survivance storytelling is aspirational in a distinct way—it specifically foregrounds colonization and aims to further Indigenous self-determination and sovereignty.

Though indebted to the work of critical race scholarship, survivance stories are more explicitly grounded in Lumbee scholar Bryan Brayboy's (2005) theory of Tribal Critical Race Theory (hereafter TribalCrit), which calls for approaches to research that center Indigenous issues, knowledges, aims, and methods. Like CRT, TribalCrit challenges the neutrality of the field of education and centers the experiences and stories of those marginalized by educational systems. However, TribalCrit revises a central assumption of CRT—that racism is endemic to society—by recognizing that colonization precedes and produces race. TribalCrit recognizes that racism impacts Indigenous students, but "colonization and its debilitating influences are at the heart of TribalCrit; all other ideas are offshoots of this vital concept" (Brayboy, 2005, p. 431). Importantly, TribalCrit also centers Indigenous knowledges, Indigenous political identities, and Indigenous aims of self-determination and sovereignty. A brief summary of TribalCrit's nine central tenets include the following:

- Colonization is endemic to society.
- US policies toward Indigenous peoples are rooted in imperialism, White supremacy, and a desire for material gain.
- Indigenous peoples occupy a liminal space that accounts for both the political and racialized natures of our identities.
- Indigenous peoples have a desire to obtain and forge tribal sovereignty, tribal autonomy, self-determination, and self-identification.
- The concepts of culture, knowledge, and power take on new meaning when examined through an Indigenous lens.
- Governmental policies and educational policies toward Indigenous peoples are intimately linked around the problematic goal of assimilation.
- Tribal philosophies, beliefs, customs, traditions, and visions for the future are central to understanding the lived realities of Indigenous peoples, but they also illustrate the differences and adaptability among individuals and groups.
- Stories are not separate from theory; they make up theory and are, therefore, real and legitimate sources of data and ways of being.
- Theory and practice are connected in deep and explicit ways such that scholars must work towards social change. (Brayboy, 2005, pp. 429–430)

Survivance storytelling, rooted in TribalCrit, engages a practice of counterstorytelling that takes into account the important affordances of Indigenous traditions of thought and Indigenous studies. Storytelling is a longstanding Indigenous tradition (Archibald, 2008; Brayboy, 2005; Drabek, 2012; Million, 2014). As Million (2014) writes, "Story *is* Indigenous theory" (p. 35). Survivance storytelling, grounded in "the power of our everyday stories, the theory of stories as theory, and Indigenism as theory" (Million, 2014, p. 32), recasts counterstorytelling within a longstanding tradition of Native resistance discourse (LaRocque, 2010) and "writing back" (Smith, 2012).

Like counterstories, survivance stories aim to disrupt, decenter, and destabilize "master narratives" of education (Solórzano & Delgado Bernal, 2002).[4] They also "seek to challenge the assumptions of power and Eurocentric notions of normativity" and the "taken-for-granted assumptions of racial neutrality with/in the world" (Atwood & López, 2014, pp. 1144–1145). Like counterstories, they also aim to "cast doubt on the validity of accepted premises or myths, especially ones held by the majority" (Delgado & Stefancic, 2012, 159). Beyond these "destructive" (Delgado, 1989) functions, survivance stories, like counterstories, are also intended to be generative, creative, and pedagogical. Survivance storytelling describes our practice at the Native youth center of sharing stories and experiences that contest, decenter, or defy colonial norms and expectations. "Storytelling and counterstorytelling these experiences" Solórzano and Yosso (2002) argue, "can help strengthen traditions of social, political, and cultural survival and resistance" (p. 32). Among those marginalized by dominant discourses, counterstories can foster a sense of community, reduce isolation, and function as a form of healing and liberation (Delgado, 1989; Solórzano & Delgado Bernal, 2001; Solórzano & Yosso, 2002).

While borrowing from counterstorytelling methodologies, my method of storytelling is situated within the longstanding tradition of Native counterstorytelling from educational activists like Zitkala-Ša (Yankton Dakota). Her writing featured in the *Atlantic Monthly* in the late 19th and early 20th century, as well as her book *American Indian Stories* (1921) provided counterstories to Richard Henry Pratt's *Indian Helper* and *The Red Man* columns, that advertised boarding schools as education that "transformed the Indian from savage to civilized" (Enoch, 2002, p. 126). Zitkala-Ša's writing reversed the "white = civilized, Indian = savage script" (p. 126), and she "used her essays to erase this script and inscribe her own version of this narrative" (p. 124). In some instances, she reversed this narrative to tell "civilized" narratives of her "savage" home life. In others, she rescripted the school's "civilizing" techniques as cruel and savage, highlighting "the hypocrisy and injustice that she witnessed" as both a student in a boarding school, and later "as a teacher at Carlisle" (Enoch, 2002, p. 133). Importantly, however, Zitkala-Ša was not just engaged in a practice of resistance, but also what Leech Lake Ojibwe scholar Scott Lyons (2000) refers to as "rhetorical sovereignty," a literary practice of Native survivance and presence that contests colonialism and creates space for Indigenous self-determination. My work draws from rhetorical models like hers to point out the colonial assumptions and contradictions that underpin policies and practices purportedly designed to serve Native children. I do so while also trying to imagine and infuse other educational trajectories that such policies and practices foreclose.

Survivance stories draw specific attention to the intersections of education and colonization (Brayboy, 2005; Brayboy & Castagno, 2009; Castagno & Brayboy, 2008) while also recognizing "there is a danger in allowing *colonization* to be the only story of Indigenous lives" (Alfred & Corntassel, 2005, p. 601). There is a tendency in research, warns Unangax̂ scholar Eve Tuck (2009), that overemphasizing "historical exploitation, domination, and colonization to explain contemporary brokenness, such as poverty, poor health, and low literacy" (p. 413) can lead to the idea that "oppression singularly defines a community" (p. 413). This is not only an ineffective and unreliable theory of change, but can lead to "the long-term repercussions of *thinking of ourselves as broken*" (p. 409). To navigate the ethical and representational decisions inherent in my desire to make visible colonial dynamics while also telling stories responsibly, I draw from Indigenous theories of refusal (A. Simpson, 2007; Tuck & Yang, 2014a) and desire (Tuck, 2009).

Refusal marks the context, and limits, through which I recognize Native survivance and the impetus for drawing attention to the structures, discourses, and practices that sustain settler colonialism. Drawing from Kahnawake Mohawk scholar Audra Simpson's (2007) foundational questions—"Can I do this and still come home; what am I revealing here and why? Where will this get us? Who benefits from this and why? " (p. 78)—refusal has prompted me to consider how I invite research participants to speak in these stories, which stories to responsibly share, and whether my research, as opposed to other interventions, would be valuable to this community (p. 224). Survivance stories navigate the tension between honoring students' voices and maintaining a focus on the structural phenomenon of racism and colonialism (Vaught, 2011). They are concerned with questions, such as, "How do we learn from and respect the wisdom and desires in the stories that we (over) hear, while refusing to portray/ betray them to the spectacle of the settler colonial gaze?" (Tuck & Yang, 2014a, p. 223). In response to these questions and axioms, my research has been an attempt to "study up" (Nader, 1972). At times Native students and families' voices are present, but I have included them only when I have felt they "contribute to our sovereignty or complicate the deeply simplified, atrophied representations of ... Indigenous peoples that they have been mired within anthropologically" (A. Simpson, 2007, p. 78). By refusing to focus on the pain, loss, or damage of Native students (the "scars" that make bodies "more interesting") (Sherril Jaffe, as cited in Tuck & Yang, 2014a, p. 229), or even overemphasize individual survivance (an approach which risks falling into a trap of humanizing Indigenous students to invoke "false empathy") (Delgado, 1996), refusal analytically "shifts the gaze from the violated body to the violating instruments," a move which "helps move us from thinking of violence as an event and toward an analysis of it as a structure" (p. 241). Refusal guides my writing of survivance stories to focus on the particular actions, values, and philosophies of educators and administrators, and through them, to the historical trajectories and discursive regimes that enable such educational practices.

Coupled with refusal is an emphasis on desire. Desire, Tuck (2009) argues, is an important "antidote" to damage-based narratives that position Native students as damaged/at-risk. When taken up uncritically, these research representations can lead to interventions that posit the problem with fixing our children, rather than the oppressive systems that they somehow, despite relentless dehumanization, ignorance, and erasure, still engage and contest with courage. "Depathologizing studies" and desire-based frameworks resist "all-too-easy, one-dimensional narratives of damage in order to expose ongoing structural inequity" (p. 417). This does not mean ignoring the challenges that Native youth experience in schools, but rather, striving to "account for the loss and despair, but also the hope, the visions, the wisdom of lived lives and communities" (p. 417). Desire is "concerned with understanding complexity, contradiction, and the self-determination of lived lives" (Tuck, 2009, p. 416).

A desire-based approach to storytelling helps account for the contradictions of working within and against colonial contexts. Such an approach disrupts "the dichotomized categories of reproduction and resistance" and points to the ways our actions can embody a "thirding ... neither/both/and reproduction and resistance" (Tuck, 2009, pp. 419–420). Colonialism implicates all of us (Kaomea, 2003). None of us can escape hegemony (Boler & Zembylas, 2003). As an Indigenous educator and researcher, I am not immune to this entanglement with coloniality, even as I set out intentionally to disrupt colonial practices and relations. Rooted in desire, the stories in this book attempt to move "beyond familiar tales of colonial villains and colonized victims or heroes" ... to "uncover more complicated, nuanced stories of (post)colonial complicity and entanglement" (Kaomea, 2003, p. 23). Desire, Tuck (2009) offers, "is about longing, about a present that is enriched by both the past and the future ... It is not only about the painful elements of social and psychic realities, but also the textured acumen and hope" (p. 644).

To attend to both the violence of normative coloniality as well as hope, I employ a practice of "disruptive daydreaming" (Dion, 2008; 2012; Simon, 1992) in which I attempt to infuse more promising and imaginative educational approaches that serve Indigenous students and are of service to Indigenous aims of self-determination and sovereignty. Dion draws from Simon (1992) to describe disruptive daydreaming:

> Education and disruptive daydreaming share a common project: the production of hopeful images. That is, the production of "images of that which is not yet" that provoke people to consider, and inform them in considering, what would have to be done for things to be otherwise. (as cited in Dion, 2008, p. 11)

To attend to the question of "what would have to be done for things to be otherwise," I often interweave questions and theories throughout these empirically based stories. At times, I ask within the stories what poet Adrienne Rich (1993) considers "the first revolutionary question—What if?" (pp. 241–242). What if a teacher's curriculum or a school policy were rooted, not in Indigenous erasure, but in self-determination or sovereignty? Within the stories I imagine alternatives to the education offered Indigenous students. At other times, I put Indigenous studies scholarship in conversation with educational practice as a way to historicize, contextualize, or juxtapose what is with what has been and what could be. I theorize within the stories in this explicit way to respect and recenter Indigenous knowledge, but also to avoid the "hegemonic pitfall" that "counterstories alone will likely be absorbed into dominant ideology" (Vaught, 2011, p. 22). For example, I read a teacher's social studies curriculum in light of the anthropological practice of "salvage ethnographies" (Gruber, 1970), an attempt to recover "authentic" culture before Indigenous people, according to colonial logics, inevitably disappear. Or I question the ways a principal's efforts to invite a Native dancer to perform at an elementary school for Native Heritage Month resembles prior colonial performances such as The World's Fairs, exhibitions that literally put Native people on display, as if they were animals in a zoo, to physically depict the savage to civilized continuum of progress. In each instance, I trace "the legacies of colonial education" (Lomawaima, 1999, p. 21) and unsettle deep-seated Eurocentrism that often goes undetected. As educators, we didn't invent the cultural narratives we inherited and (often unintentionally) reproduce (which includes our subject positions as teachers within settler colonial institutions); nevertheless, we are responsible for our positionalities within the historical trajectory of these discourses. These stories, rooted in desire, are "time warping" (Tuck & Yang, 2014a, p. 231). They are not concerned with linear sequences of events, but draw from the past and future (not necessarily in that order), to engage in a critical and hopeful relationship with the present.

Finally, survivance stories dovetail with and contribute to the field of teacher knowledge research, a field which respects the complex and contextual professional knowledge required of teachers, and argues for equally complex and robust theories of inquiry and professional development (Chang & Rosiek, 2003; Connelly & Clandinin, 1999; Dibble & Rosiek, 2002; Sconiers & Rosiek, 2000; Shulman, 1986; Shulman, 2004). Storytelling often "feels new" (Clandinin & Rosiek, 2007) to educational researchers, but it is an ancient practice that can help people make sense of the world and provide a complex and context-rich affective, imaginative, and discursive space to examine life and the futures that can stem from it (Delgado, 1989; King, 2005; Vizenor, 1990). Indigenous studies and CRT scholars appear to share assumptions with narrative researchers that stories are both politically and pedagogically valuable (Atkinson & Mitchell, 2010; Chang & Rosiek, 2003; Sconiers & Rosiek, 2000; Clandinin & Rosiek, 2007; Connelly & Clandinin, 1999). Survivance stories, when situated at the intersections of critical narrative research and Native resistance discourse, can inform teachers' professional knowledge landscapes (Clandinin & Connelly, 1995; Connelly, Clandinin, & He, 1997) so they can teach in ways that disrupt colonialism and support self-determination and sovereignty. Survivance stories can cultivate what Wahpetunwan Dakota scholar Waziyatawin Angela Cavender Wilson (2006) terms the "sensibilities" necessary to detect anti-Indianism (Cook-Lynn, 2001) in policy and practice: "Indeed," she writes "anti-Indian educational and ideological hegemony is so firmly established, most Americans cannot recognize it even when it appears before their eyes" (p. 68). Survivance stories can also illuminate how teacher knowledge is often influenced by ideologies, like settler colonialism, that are "so pervasive that few if any practitioners may be thinking outside of it," and so, contribute to the call for more "narrative research ... that generates new counterhegemonic understanding of teaching practice" (Chang & Rosiek, 2003, p. 252). Although written primarily as a form of community recognition, my hope is that survivance stories also develop educators' sensibilities to detect the nuanced ways colonial dynamics play out in educational policy and practice, fostering educators' *anticolonial literacy*. We need educators who can analyze colonial discourses in educational policy and practice and who are committed to countering coloniality at every turn. Such literacy and commitments are necessary if we are to better serve Native students in public schools.

Indian Education as Containment

The survivance stories in this book emerged out of my work in an Indian Education program in a small urban public school district in the Pacific Northwest, which I refer to as Oakfield. The school district is located in the forcibly ceded homelands of Kalapuya peoples, the Indigenous peoples who were here prior to settlement, and who continue to maintain cultural and political relationships to this place. The City of Oakfield has about 60,000 people, the racial makeup of which is 85.9% White, 12% Hispanic/Latino, 1.4% American Indian/Alaska Native, 1.3% Asian, 1.1% Black, 0.3% Native Hawaiian, and 4.8% who identify as multiracial (U.S. Census Bureau, 2010). Oakfield school district, which spans 15.7 square miles, has 22 schools that enroll nearly 11,000 students. As in most urban locales, the Indian education program serves students from Native nations within the state, as well as students who are citizens and descendants of various Native nations from throughout the US.

As I worked in the Indian Education program, the experiences students and families shared with me underlined the limitations of such add-on forms of educational intervention. Indian Education formula grant programs are funded by the Department of Education and are the "principal vehicle for addressing the particular needs of Indian children" in public schools (Office of Indian Education, 2017). These programs, however, are intended to supplement, not supplant, general services and supports for Indigenous students. According to the Office of Indian Education,

> Grant funds supplement the regular school program by meeting the culturally related academic needs of Indian children. Projects help Indian children sharpen their academic skills, assist students in becoming proficient in the core content areas, and provide students an opportunity to participate in enrichment programs that would otherwise be unavailable. Funds support such activities as culturally-responsive after-school programs, Native language classes, early childhood education, tutoring, and dropout prevention. (2017, n.p.)[5]

Each program is "designed to address the unique cultural, language, and educationally related academic needs of American Indian and Alaska Native students" (Office of Indian Education, 2014) and should be tailored to the needs and desires of the particular local educational agency (LEA) that applies for the formula grant in consultation with a parent committee. In this district, grant funds supported a program coordinator who served as an advocate and liaison for Native students and families. The coordinator also designed after-school programming that included tutoring, cultural programming, and community events, such as the annual pow wow.

The creation of special places and times where the needs of Indigenous students can become a central programmatic focus is important in a colonial context where there are no such spaces. However, it also reproduces the problematic dynamics of the creation of reservations, which designates some land the sovereign territory of Native peoples, and thereby legitimizes the erasure of the entitlement of Native people to all the lands on this continent. Similarly, the Indian Education programs in our district marked a very limited portion of curriculum and time as a place to attend to Indigenous students' experience K–12 schooling. This in turn brought into high relief the geography of neglect, caricature, and disrespect born of ignorance in which students traversed throughout the rest of their school day and days.

The program's positioning within the district reverberates with the logic of containment that Lomawaima and McCarty (2006; 2014a; 2014b) have described as the "safety zone." Drawing from curricular and pedagogical patterns in federal boarding schools, the safety zone theory (SZT) describes a persistent pattern of delimiting "safe" and "dangerous" forms of Indigenous difference. Boarding schools forcibly sought to erase Indigenous identities, and replace them with more "civilized" ones: "Replace heritage languages with English; replace 'paganism' with Christianity; replace economic, political, social, legal, and aesthetic institutions" (Lomawaima & McCarty, 2006, p. 4). Yet even in these spaces of outright assault on Indigenous children, some forms of cultural difference were allowed, even promoted—Native children were allowed to construct miniature tipis on the school playgrounds or read bilingual books written in their languages, for example (Lomawaima & McCarty, 2006; 2014b). The SZT sought to explain why some forms of difference are tolerated, even desirable, while others are deemed too threatening to include or support. As Lomawaima and McCarty (2006) argue, "[t]he federal government has not simply vacillated between encouraging or suppressing Native languages and cultures but has in a coherent way ... attempted to distinguish safe from dangerous Indigenous beliefs and practices" (p. 6). These decisions were not arbitrary, but pivoted on whether Indigenous beliefs and practices were deemed "safe, innocuous, and tolerable," or "too dangerous, different, and subversive of mainstream values" (p. 5).

A similar pattern of control and containment can be seen in the district's understanding of cultural difference. Some forms of cultural difference, for example, are promoted—for instance, Indigenous students are frequently invited to drum or dance at multicultural assemblies and fundraising events, or asked to make dreamcatchers for school board members. Yet when the expression of cultural difference threatens school policy—as in a Native student's desire to wear regalia to graduation despite a school's "no adornment" policy"—cultural difference becomes threatening and intolerable. The same logic of containment can also be seen in the district's approach to Indigenous education. As a committed group of Indigenous families and educators, we created "windows of opportunity" for Indigenous education by "chipping out spaces to express Indian-ness within institutions controlled by others" (Lomawaima & McCarty, 2006, p. 14), "zones of sovereignty" for ourselves (Lomawaima & McCarty 2014a). Yet these efforts did little to disrupt the "business as usual" (Castagno & Brayboy, 2008) approach to schooling Indigenous students faced in public schools day in and day out. Despite our efforts to create zones of sovereignty, Indigenous education was equivocated with the Indian Education program, domesticated, safe, and innocuous on the margins. Framing Indigenous education in such a way—as supplemental, as what happens on the margins, on weekends or after school, as what Indigenous educators do for Indigenous students—seemed to alleviate administrators and educators from viewing their everyday educational practices in schools *as* Indigenous education.

As I began to think about this research, I realized that it was not enough to analyze, celebrate, critique, and refine the kind of Indian Education programs in which I was working. While such work is important, I did not want to cede the rest of the K-12 education to settler colonial schooling that would erase and ignore our Native children. I turned my attention, therefore, to what the work of resistance and transformation looks like outside of those safe spaces. I wanted to examine what was involved in bringing unsafe Indigenous views of education into mainstream, what Quechua scholar Sandy Grande (2015) terms *whitestream* educational spaces. My goal wasn't certainty, a desire to articulate what Indigenous education should look like in this space. Instead of seeking a new form of certainty about Indigenous what education should be, I chose instead to ask what forms of understanding might enable educators to stand with Indigenous students and families in the space of some of the impossibilities created in a settler colonialist contexts? What sorts of knowledge and practices might challenge the safety zone of Indigenous education in a small, urban public school district?

Although I can now describe this research design in retrospect with some degree of clarity, while I was conducting the research it was never that clear to me. I did have plans and questions, but they changed as my understanding evolved. My research responded to the stories that Indigenous students, families, and educators shared with me. This lack of a prescribed program of research was not, I do not believe, a retreat from my responsibility as a researcher to be clear with myself and others about what I was doing. Instead, it felt like being responsive, responsible, and "of use" (Fine & Barreras, 2001) to the community and concerns and experiences being expressed, by refusing to be encapsulated in any single conception of what we need to know about Indigenous education. During the field work and subsequent write up, I tried to come back to some basic questions about my work and its purpose.

Survivance Stories as Indigenous Research Method

As a youth group coordinator and parent advocate, my role initially was to help support and grow the program. Over time, and with the support of the program coordinator and parent committee, my involvement also included two years of fieldwork for my doctoral research from which this book is based. When I began my study, the Indian Education program served approximately 150 students, a consistent number over the years, though with targeted recruitment, enrollment has grown and the program currently serves over 260 students.

The primary means of data collection for this study were participant observation, semi-structured interviews (both individual, and with families), and document analysis. My observations and field notes came from program, school, and community events, classroom observations, and various public meetings. My role varied throughout the research, as I observed, participated, and often led programs. I led the Native youth group, for example, helped organize community events, taught at summer school, and served on the parent committee. However, I also sat in the back of classrooms, schools, and community events and observed. While much of the data comes from field notes, I also conducted 25 interviews with students, families, program staff, teachers, and administrators. Additionally, I reviewed and analyzed various documents, including websites, program materials, district and policy documents, student work, other archival records, and physical artifacts.

From this data, a methodology of constructing stories emerged that reflected back the dynamics and experiences I observed and that were relayed to me. While in the beginning my observations and interviews were broad, I began to listen *for* stories (Lawrence-Lightfoot, 2005) of Indigenous students' and families' experiences in schools. I would then follow these stories, interviewing parents, families, or teachers about the experiences to construct a survivance story around the particular issue a Native student, family member, or educator expressed. My aim was to write stories that denaturalized, problematized, and unsettled deeply entrenched and over-simplified conceptions of how to best serve Native students and teach Native-related content (Kaomea, 2003). To be responsible, as well as have a more direct impact in the issues I witnessed, beyond telling the stories I would also offer informal professional development to the teachers and administrators involved. This, coupled with my involvement and commitment to the program, was my way of enacting responsibility as a researcher, by undertaking research that is "relevant and address[es] the problems of the community." As Brayboy (2005) continues, "there is little room for abstract ideas in real communities" (p. 440).

The method of listening for and writing survivance stories is meant to be answerable to urban Indigenous communities. In her book *Decolonizing Education Research* (2016), Patel calls on educational researchers to be answerable to several core questions—Why this? Why me? Why now and why here? (pp. 57–60). Positioning my work in relation to her call is my way of enacting responsibility for the decisions I have made as an educational researcher, the historical and disciplinary trajectories I find myself within, and the communities of which I am a part and serve.

Why This?: Survivance, Settler Colonialism, and Story

In response to *Why This?*, I offer this book as an attempt to address an important gap in teacher knowledge, and to prompt a reconsideration of the types of knowledge currently expected of teachers. My argument is that knowledge of Native survivance, settler colonialism, and Native studies should be requisite teacher knowledge to counter deficit thinking, detect and interrupt settler colonial discourses in educational policy and practice, and imagine and enact anticolonial and decolonial educational alternatives in public schools. There is an acute need for teacher knowledge of Indigenous studies (Battiste, 2013; Brayboy & Castagno, 2009; Castagno & Brayboy, 2008; Kaomea, 2005). This need exists in part due to the lack of sustained attention teacher education programs give to Indigenous studies and Indigenous education, as well as the inattentiveness of individual teachers who don't often imagine themselves teaching Indigenous students (Dion, 2007, 2008; Haynes Writer, 2002; Higgins, Madden, & Korteweg, 2013) (despite the fact that most Indigenous students attend public schools and are educated by non-Indigenous teachers). Preparing educators to support Indigenous students and incorporate Indigenous studies into their curriculum should be part of a systemic effort to support Indigenous education within teacher education programs, efforts which Madden (2015) has highlighted can look a variety of ways—learning from Indigenous traditional models of teaching, pedagogy for decolonizing, Indigenous and anti-racist education, and Indigenous and place-based education. This book is intended to complement such systemic approaches by couching some of the knowledge teachers need within stories, an approach that attends to the complexity, as well as contextual, discursive, and narrative dimensions of teacher knowledge (Chang & Rosiek, 2003; Rosiek & Atkinson, 2007; Shulman, 1986; Shulman, 2004). Because settler colonial discourses are subtle and often difficult to detect (Calderón, 2014b; Grande, 2015; Rifkin, 2014; Veracini, 2011a), my claim is that stories are well-suited to develop teachers' ability to critically analyze colonial discourses in educational policy and practice, what I refer to as anticolonial literacy. By embedding Indigenous studies theoretical frameworks and conceptual tools within empirically based case studies, my aim is to tell stories that make visible colonial dynamics in policy and practice, what I refer to as anticolonial literacy, an intervention into what Gloria Ladson-Billings (1998) has referred to as "a *nice* field like education." My aim is also to recognize Native practices of survivance.

A focus on survivance is essential to counter deficit theories that have historically and contemporarily frame discussions of Indigenous students (Deyhle & Swisher, 1997). By reading and representing Native students and families as actively engaged in survivance, my hope is to reframe (Smith, 2012) and re-present (Enoch, 2002) Native students and communities who are typically pathologized by educational discourse. Indeed, the tradition of pathologizing Indigenous children is embedded in the history and foundation of colonial systems of education (Lomawaima, 1999), systems that ignored longstanding "conscious" Native educational systems (Lomawaima, 2002, p. 425), and instead, proposed "appropriate" methods to civilize, Christianize, and Americanize Native children and divest Native peoples of their lands (Adams, 1988).[6]

For the most part, schools no longer overtly declare students' homes as savage, force students to cut students hair, or explicitly punish them for speaking their native languages (though there are exceptions),[7] yet cultural or economic deficit frameworks persist "that emphasize what a particular student, family, or community is lacking to explain underachievement or failure" (Tuck, 2009, p. 413). These contemporary framings are more nuanced—such as recent interventions geared toward developing students' "resilience" or "grit" (Thornton & Sánchez, 2010; Duckworth et al., 2007)—which individualize systemic issues and locate the educational problem (and corresponding intervention) within the students themselves. My argument that educators recognize Native survivance is *not* an endorsement of survivance as the latest coping mechanism for Native students. The focus on individual students is seductive. When weighing the time, energy, and collective efforts it would take to transform complex, systemic issues to better support an individual student against the more immediate and satisfying project of adequately equipping that student to tolerate such a system, the allure of such theories makes sense. It is individual students who negotiate the daily dynamics of school, and who will continue to negotiate those dynamics throughout their schooling and professional endeavors. Focusing on what constitutes resilience or grit and nurturing those traits might appear more manageable, especially when locating these challenges in larger social processes can leave a teacher or researcher with feelings of despair. However, when read in light of historical trajectories of colonial schooling, educational interventions geared toward "arming children of color for the life they will face" (Sue et al., 2007, p. 283), however consciously strategic, function as contemporary iterations of the "Indian problem." Whereas earlier approaches explicitly aimed to "kill the Indian, save the man" (Pratt, 1973, p. 261), contemporary approaches are subtler as they seek to develop the agency of Indigenous students to cope with hostile educational environments. I have no intention of fueling such an approach to educational reform; instead, while recognizing that survivance can counter deficit thinking, the primary purpose of this book is to draw attention to the settler colonial discourses and practices Native students continue to confront in public schools.

This book responds to a call that educators

> pay more attention to the ways colonization, racism, and power matter in educational settings and work towards more effective and longer-term preservice and in-service training that helps educators understand and strategize about their role as agents for social change and greater educational equity. (Brayboy & Castagno, 2009, p. 49)

As Calderón (2009) argues, "Education in the United States today is not merely a legacy of the colonial project—it is a functionary arm of colonialism that acts to absorb even progressive educational movements" (p. 53). This book aims to make explicit the ways colonization *continues to* shape the educational experiences of Indigenous youth in public schools (Brayboy, 2005; Brayboy & Castagno, 2009;

Castagno & Brayboy, 2008), focusing not on *whether* colonization configures educational experiences, but on *how* colonialism continues to organize and impact Native students' educational experiences, and undermine education for self-determination and sovereignty.

To define colonization, I draw from Indigenous studies and settler colonial studies scholarship (Byrd, 2011; Kauanui & Wolfe, 2012; Tuck & Yang, 2012; 2014; Veracini, 2011a; 2011b; Wolfe, 2006) who recognize settler colonialism as a "structure, not an event" (Wolfe, 2006). Commonsense understandings of colonization (also typically reproduced in textbooks) often distance the discourse and practice temporally and/or spatially—colonization is what occurred during the early years of exploration, contact, and settlement of the US and ended with the American Revolution (Kauanui & O'Brien, 2012), or colonization is what happens in far-away places by foreigners, such as the colonization of India by the British (Tuck & McKenzie, 2015). Yet these temporal and spatial framings obscure the ways colonization is both *contemporary and local*. Veracini (2011b) suggests the distinction between classic colonialism and settler colonialism be thought of in terms of *circles* and *lines*: classic or external colonialism functions in a circular form "consisting of an outward movement followed by [an often violent] interaction with exotic and colonized 'others' in foreign surroundings, and by a final return to an original location" (p. 205), whereas settler colonialism functions in a linear fashion "where the traveler moves forward along a story line that can't be turned back" (p. 206). There is no distinction in settler colonialism between past and present, precisely because "there is no spatial separation between metropole [the imperial center of power] and colony [the territory under control]" (Tuck & Yang, 2012, p. 5).

Thus, it is imperative that educators recognize that colonization is not historic, nor a phenomenon that happens elsewhere, but a structure materially, economically, and discursively embedded into the fabric of the US and other nation-states like Canada, Australia, and New Zealand. This structure is premised on the pursuit of Indigenous land, which settler colonizers need, because there is no return for the settlers who came or that continue to come here (Veracini, 2011b). Instead, as Wolfe (2006) has argued, "settler colonizers come to stay" (p. 388).

Staying—both on Indigenous lands and atop the racial and economic hierarchy of the US—requires a triadic structure of Indigenous dispossession and erasure (to remove Indigenous peoples from desired lands and disavow prior and legal claims to them), chattel slavery (to ensure productivity and profit from those lands), and settler supremacy (to maintain the fiction that settlers are the rightful inheritors and owners of those lands) (Dunbar-Ortiz, 2014; Glenn, 2015; McCoy 2014; Tuck & Yang, 2012; 2014; Wolfe, 2006). Beyond the attempted elimination of actual Indigenous peoples, settler colonialism also erases itself from view making the structures of settler colonialism practically invisible when they are most effective (Veracini, 2011a). Said another way, settler colonialism "covers its tracks" (Veracini, 2011a, p. 3).

While the practices of colonialism are "wide and varied" (Tejeda, 2008, p. 30), the goal has always remained the same—to erase Indigenous peoples, and lay claim to and profit from Indigenous lands. Once violent and forcible means of Indigenous erasure—extermination, civilization, removal, annexation, dispossession, assimilation, termination, and relocation—have, with time, grown subtler.[8] Cities were "founded" and "named" atop Indigenous lands and communities that were already lived in, loved, and had their own languages. Far from historic, the erasure of Indigenous peoples continues to be rehearsed in public commemorations of city and state anniversaries and their pioneer founders, displacing Indigenous creation stories with settler origin stories, processes that White Earth Ojibwe scholar Jean O'Brien (2010) has termed "firsting," "replacing," and "lasting." Rather than naturalizing Indigenous presence as a feature of such commemorations and the self-image and identify of these new communities, processes like firsting subtly erase Indigenous peoples by asserting "that non-Indians were the first people to erect the proper institutions of a social order worthy of notice" (p. xii). Great emphasis was placed on various *firsts*: "first settlers, births of first white children (especially males), first marriages, first town meetings and town officers, first meetinghouses and ministers (numbered on into the present), first divisions of land, first newspapers, first schools, first bridges, mills, and other public works that symbolized modernity" (p. 11). Through emphasizing these particular firsts, settlers began to reinscribe themselves as modern, a practice that also relegated Indigenous peoples to "prehistory." Replacing Indigenous names with settler institutions, names, histories, and practices subtly asserted the legitimacy and supremacy of settler presence. And such practices were reinforced by what O'Brien refers to as lasting, "a rhetorical strategy that asserts as a fact the claim that Indians can never be modern" (p. 107). Referring to particular Indigenous peoples as the "last" of their race, or Indigenous peoples as a "vanishing race" altogether are examples of such rhetoric. More subtly, using blood quantum as a means of authenticating Indigeneity (a colonial construction that posits Indigeneity as equivalent with blood, and full-bloodedness as the purest and most authentic means of Indigeneity) is another example of lasting, a way of positioning Indigeneity and Indigenous peoples on path of inevitable disappearance and extinction.[9]

Schools have been central in reinforcing colonial narratives of firsting, replacing, and lasting. Firsts are routinely emphasized in social studies education—curriculum that focuses on the Pilgrims who established the first colony in New England or Columbus and his discovery of the Americas are two common examples. Indigenous names are also routinely replaced with settler names—Plymouth has replaced the Indigenous place name Patuxet, and the terms Indians or Native Americans often stand in for specific Indigenous peoples or nations such as Wampanoag or Taíno. The firsting and replacing in this curriculum is also closely coupled with curriculum that emphasizes lasting—Indigenous peoples in the curriculum are framed as vanished or vanishing, a narrative reinforced by the lack of attention to Indigenous peoples in the 20th or 21st century (Shear et al., 2015). At a broader level, Indigenous peoples are made to disappear by organizing social studies standards and content into precontact and contact, an ideological move that positions Indigenous peoples as prehistory, and settler history as the beginning of modernity.

Thus, structures, discourses, logics, and practice of colonialism are embedded into the very fabric of schooling. Colonialism surfaces in educational policy and practice through the erasure of Indigenous peoples from contemporary curricula (Shear et al., 2015, Journell, 2009), the characterization of Indigenous life as primitive or exotic (Kaomea, 2005), the assumption that Native culture is an appendage to the curriculum, rather than a way of knowing that would systematically reorganize the ways schools operate (Hermes, 2005), the widespread acceptance of non-Native interpretations of Native stories (Iseke-Barnes, 2009), or through Eurocentric curriculum that reinforces settler histories and ideologies (Calderón, 2014b), imposing a "colonizer's model of the world" (Blaut, 1993, p. 10). Indigenous erasure is also encoded into entire domains of knowledge (science, literature, art, etc.) and ideals of educated citizens, each based on white, Eurocentric norms (Patel, 2016; Urrieta & Reidel, 2008). Subtle racialized logics of civilization also undergird discourses of academic achievement. Indian education program goals, for example, are tacitly assimilative in the ways they use "culture" as a way to support dominant discourses of academic achievement, measured by mastery of state content standards (Jacobs, 2006). No longer are schools overtly advertised as the most efficient means of moving students along the path "to intelligent citizenship, to civilization, and to Christianization" '(Gates, 1897, p. 33), a way to "condense nature's methods" (p. 35); but Eurocentric "proof"—state content standards, academic achievement scores, AP or SAT exam scores—is still "self-serving" as Eurocentric criteria continue to determine the success (or civilization) of Indigenous students (Patel, 2016).

My intent here is not to argue that Indigenous students and families do not want to be academically successful, nor that academic success is proof of assimilation. On the contrary, Native youth and families value education and have long expressed desires for Native students to be successful in schools (Brayboy et al., 2012; Castagno & Brayboy, 2008). This is intended only to draw attention to the ways Eurocentric criteria continue to be the standard against which Native success is measured, rather than other possible educational outcomes (e.g., knowledge of place, fluency in one's Native languages, literacy of one's own history and culture, ability to meaningfully contribute to one's community, etc.). For many Indigenous families and educators, the goal is that Indigenous students "are successful in school while developing *as Indigenous peoples*" (Goulet & Goulet, 2014, p. 5, emphasis added).

In summary, colonization must be understood as a contemporary feature of settler society and schooling. And while the practices described above may appear benign, "more legal and more genteel" perhaps than the outright violence

Indigenous peoples have experienced throughout the history of US–Indian relations and schooling, the outcome Wolfe argues, "remains consistent with elimination" (as cited in Kauanui & Wolfe, 2012, p. 241).

As teachers, and in particular social studies teachers, it is our responsibility to understand the dark history of schooling and the intentionally assimilative practices of educators. Civics and citizenship education, for example, explicitly aimed to absorb Indians "into the national life, not as Indians, but as Americans" (Morgan, 1890, p. clxvii). But the stories in this book do not document such overt assimilative expressions or practices by educators. No longer are Indigenous people forced into naturalization ceremonies where they adopt white names, shoot their last bow, accept the plow or the purse, and pledge to live the life of a white person, a gendered colonial process that naturalized agrarian labor for Indigenous men and domestic labor for Indigenous women (Woman's Board of Home Missions of the Presbyterian Church, 1916; Valencia-Weber, 2004). Colonial gender norms are no longer rigidly reinforced by federal officials who require Indigenous girls and young women to renounce their tribal allegiance and hold a purse, declaring, "This means you have chosen the life of the white woman-and the white woman loves her home. The family and home are the foundation of our civilization" (Valencia-Weber, 2004, p. 334). Instead, settler colonialism surfaces in silence around Indigenous citizenship, sovereignty, and nationhood in civics education (Charleston, 1994; Haynes Writer, 2010; Sabzalian & Shear, 2018; Wilmore, 1998), or in the tacit ways US citizenship is rooted in "colonialnormativity" (Brandzel, 2016, p. 25) and functions as "a discourse of belonging that requires the elimination of Indigenous peoples" (p. 27). It surfaces not in the overt declarations of gender norms, but in the subtle reinforcement of heteropatriarchy and heteronormativity.

As teachers, it is also our responsibility to learn about the history and legacy of federal boarding, mission, and day schools that sought to eradicate Indigeneity and framed young Native children as beings in need of fixing (McCoy, 2017), a history and legacy with which Native peoples have had complex and contradictory experiences with, ranging from appreciation to contempt, hatred, and resentment of the experience (Adams, 1995; Child, 1999; 2014; Johnston, 1988; Lomawaima, 1994).[10] But the stories in this book do not document overt practices of assimilation by educators. Instead, the cultural and political tools of domination and assimilation today are more refined, and circulate as commonsense, as silence, as affect, as denial, as multiculturalism, or even as best practices. They are systemic, as Mi'kmaq educator and scholar Marie Battiste (2013) observes, because "the modern educational system was created to maintain the identity, language, and culture of a colonial society" (p. 30). As Aileen Moreton-Robinson (Geonpul) (2016) observes, "It takes a great deal of work to maintain Canada, the United States, Hawai'i, New Zealand, and Australia as white possessions" (p. xi). This book argues that the practices of Indigenous erasure are subtle, yet schools remain deeply implicated in the logic of elimination and the "work" of settler colonial maintenance.

In returning to "why this?," I offer that understanding the ways schools reproduce racialized and colonial discourses, in subtle and not so subtle ways, is necessary in order to serve Indigenous students in schools and teach toward Indigenous self-determination and sovereignty. Rather than considering these policies and practices as historic events, settler colonialism as an analytic questions the ways Indigenous erasure is still encoded into educational discourse, policy, and practice. As Saito (2014) argues, "By understanding settler strategies of elimination, subjugation, subordination and manipulation—the ways in which colonization is effectuated—we can begin to develop, envision, and implement strategies to counter those processes" (p. 104). For a paradigmatic shift in Indigenous education, settler colonialism must be recognized by educators as a "structural fact" (Wolfe, as cited in Kauanui & Wolfe, 2012). Only through this recognition can educators unsettle the normativity of such discourses, and begin to imagine and teach in anticolonial ways.

As Plains Cree scholar Emma LaRocque (2010) argues, "colonization is not abstract, it is an experience" (p. 100). Stories are an effective way to attend to the contexts, anomalies, complexities, and messiness of experience. Attending to experiences, rather than abstract knowledge, can also support educators cultivate the "sensibilities" (Wilson, 2006) necessary to detect anti-Indianism (Cook-Lynn, 2001) in policy and practice, and to develop anticolonial and decolonial literacy. My intent in this book is not to posit a new pedagogical framework that will address educators' interactions with Indigenous students everywhere. The assumption that one framework can serve all Indigenous students is one I am trying to resist. This is, in part, because there are many current frameworks that effectively help teachers think through conceptually and practically what it means to serve marginalized students generally, and Indigenous students in particular. For example, culturally sustaining pedagogy (Paris, 2012), revolutionary/critical pedagogy (Freire, 1970; McLaren, 2005; Duncan-Andrade & Morrell, 2008), culturally responsive pedagogies (Villegas & Lucas, 2002; Gay, 2010), culturally relevant pedagogies (Ladson-Billings, 1995; 2014); anti-oppressive education (Kumashiro, 2000), multicultural education (Nieto & Bode, 2012); or ethics of care (Valenzuela, 1999)—are all important contributions that theorize curriculum and pedagogy within a sociopolitical contexts of cultural difference. Scholars like Lee (2011), have shifted the paradigm of culturally responsive pedagogy to "socioculturally responsive education" (SCR) to recognize that "Native youth's lives are also inclusive of social influences not solely defined by their Native culture, such as mainstream media, family income and occupations, trial economic development, off-reservation residence, and peer influences" (p. 277). Moreover, scholars, such as Grande (2015) and McCarty and Lee (2014), have moved forward this body of work by interrogating the Western assumptions that underlie theories of curriculum and pedagogy and foregrounding Indigenous aims of self-determination and sovereignty. Indigenous scholars invested in understanding, implementing, and justifying cultural-based education (CBE) and culturally responsive schooling (CRS) have also made invaluable contributions to this field, and provided models for better serving Indigenous students (see Castagno & Brayboy, 2008, Brayboy & Castagno, 2009, and Demmert & Towner, 2003 for comprehensive reviews of this work).

Conversations within and between these frameworks have pushed the field of education and Indigenous education in generative directions. My project is indebted to each of these frameworks and the shifts in my own theorizing and practice they have generated. I offer these stories, not as a way to supplant the importance of frameworks, but as a complementary means of thinking through this work as it is lived in schools. Frameworks open up possibilities to think through the values, theories, and principles that might ground and guide our work. Stories, on the other hand, provide experiences through which to understand, expand, or contest the possibilities within those theories.

Stories can also be a particularly effective intervention into essentialized conceptions of how to teach Indigenous students and oversimplified theories of integrating Native "culture" in the curriculum, some of which has been based on scholarship that relied on and reproduced essentializations about Native students (Castagno & Brayboy 2008; Deyhle & Swisher, 1997; Hermes, 2005). Despite the intention of such scholarship, which has often included explicit caveats that Native students represent distinct rather than monolithic cultures, titles such as *Teaching the Native American* (Gilliland, 1995), or concepts like a Native American "learning style" risk reducing Native students to "one-dimensional proportions" (Lomawaima & McCarty, 2006). As Castagno and Brayboy (2008) note,

> Much of the learning styles literature risks either implicitly or explicitly making broad generalizations and essentializing what is actually an incredible range of variation. This work and the way it is often read perpetuate racist beliefs and schooling practices. (p. 961)

This scholarship has played an important role in countering deficit thinking that specifically pathologized Native students as cognitively inferior. As Deyhle and Swisher (1997) note, the research on cultural difference "challenged prevailing beliefs of cultural deprivation as an explanatory model for school failure" (pp. 150–151). The impetus was to identify Native students' cultural differences and adapt instruction accordingly in order to facilitate Native students' success. Yet given the context of racism, colonialism, and deficit thinking that has characterized relationships between Native students and schools, it is little wonder this body of research has been read in ways that justify cultural inferiority and mediocre schooling for Indigenous youth. From this body of research, Native students have been simplistically framed as spatial, visual, holistic, cooperative, silent, or right-brained (Deyhle & Swisher, 1997). As Chrisjohn and Peters (1986) argue, the assertion Native students use the right hemisphere of their brain became a dangerous form of "science fiction" that was used to justify not only a right-brained industry full of right-brained experts who develop and sell right-brained curricula, but also to justify remedial, nonacademic curriculum for Indigenous students. This body of research on cultural differences also tended to ignore broader political, social, and economic dynamics, such as institutional racism or the power dynamics in schools and classroom (perhaps more compelling explanations for why some Native students were "silent") (Deyhle & Swisher, 1997; Lomawaima, 1999).

Deyhle and Swisher (1997) recognized the danger in this body of research being "used to both further stereotypes and locate the problem in 'them'" (p. 154). A conversation with an elementary principal I worked with about her conception of cultural competency illustrates a link to the ways this line of thinking can inform an educator's schema:

> I have one [Native staff member] who I hired this year and ... just to have her say, "Yeah, I'm Cherokee. It wasn't a big part of me growing up, but the older I get, the more I realize that part of the reasons I like to gather in circles versus line up is because part of the Native American culture is that we gather together in circles; we don't line up linearly." And she goes, "And probably part of my thinking is I'm a circular thinker because I'm not just a straightforward thinker." And so, recognizing those things and honoring them, and being able to ... that's part of our cultural competency is being able to claim it, name it, and frame it, so that it gives people context.

Having no interaction with the Cherokee staff member, it is unclear whether she described herself in that way; however, Indigenous peoples are not immune to the ways these discourses function and get reproduced within Native communities (Chrisjohn & Peters, 1986; LaRocque, 2010; Lomawaima, 1999; Lyons, 2010; Nelson, 2014; Womack, 2008). Taken up uncritically, at times by Native people themselves, the search for Indigenous characteristics can lead to over-simplified and problematic beliefs such as "Indians think in circles" (Nelson, 2014), or "Indian time is 'circular' rather than 'linear," a conception that Ojibwe scholar Scott Lyons (2010) denounces as "a characteristic we apparently share with Disney's *The Lion King*" (p. 9). That the principal uncritically accepted and "honored" her employee's cultural difference as part of her cultural competency repertoire is equally, if not more, problematic given her position of power within the school. Given this, I seek to move from documenting a set of characteristics, to documenting the complexities of working within settler colonial contexts through story.

In answering why this, I also offer that these narratives are not meant to pre-scribe simple solutions to the dilemmas of teaching within a context of racialized and colonial discourses. Rather than deploying narratives that *solve* dilemmas, these narratives are meant to provoke radical commitment to reflection and to critical work within and against these dominant and pervasive discourses. Richardson and Villenas (2000) specifically use the metaphor of "*dancing* with, within, and against whiteness as a trope in explaining the complexities of this endeavor" (p. 268); a metaphor that wonders about the values and consequences of our frameworks and actions, and questions the possibilities and limits of our work. These stories are meant to prompt reflection, discomfort, growth, and action. As Kanaka Maoli scholar Maile Arvin suggests, "uncomfortability can be productive" (as cited in Aikau, Arvin, Goeman, & Morgenson, 2015, p. 90).

Rather than offering prescriptions for what teachers should think and feel, it is my hope these stories provide *space* to think, to feel, to reflect, to imagine, and to act (Archibald, 2008). These stories are intended to refine teachers' professional knowledge landscapes, what Connelly and Clandinin (1999) refer to as territories comprised of personal, conceptual, curricular, ethical, and intuitive dimensions. The knowledge base required of teachers, as Dibble and Rosiek (2002) argue, isn't always about "discrete pedagogical problems," but teacher practical knowledge [often] deals with more diffuse issues—such as the meaning of racial identity in a classroom." As such, these stories surface tensions, but do not resolve them (Chang & Rosiek, 2003). They are intended to invite educators to reflect on their teaching, and dwell "on uncomfortable feelings that support educators in living with the tensions that contain kernels of insight that eventually grow into deeper understanding," a process which "ends not with the teacher articulating a neat solution to a profound challenge, but with the teacher demonstrating a greater appreciation of difference in the classroom and its implications for teaching" (Dibble & Rosiek, 2002).

Why Me?: Experiences Lived and Learned

As Patel (2016) clarifies, the question *why me?* is not meant to be "misconstrued as a prompt for exceptionality or destiny," but rather, meant to invite "a humble pause and reflection on the specifics of individuals' experiences that make them appropriately able to craft, contribute, and even question knowledges" (pp. 57–58). In this pause, I offer that my personal and educational experiences, coupled with my engagement with Native studies scholarship, provided me a particular vantage point from which to perceive and unsettle normative educational discourses. While Indigenous identity and experience are not freely available to everyone, engagement with Indigenous studies scholarship is, and as I argue in this book, should become a central component of teacher knowledge. I offer a brief story to share why I undertook this particular project, but also to suggest that there are costs to continuing with business as usual approaches to schooling.

I come to this work as an Alutiiq woman who grew up outside of my birth home and my ancestral homelands in Alaska. After moving in and out of several foster homes and a long legal battle, I was adopted into a white family. I also attended predominately white schools. As a result, I grew up in close proximity to whiteness. Placing Native children in close proximity to whiteness has a long history in Indian policy and colonial education. Settler colonial schooling has always been deliberately place-based. When Captain Richard Henry Pratt and his accomplice Estelle Reel developed their "outing program" for Carlisle Industrial Indian School, they recognized the power of place-based education. Native students were placed in white homes, "preferably in the country, during a portion or all of the year, where they will be treated as one of the family, made to attend the public school of the district while it is in session, and paid a small sum for their services" (Reel, 1901, p. 189). As Reel (1901) argued,

> Association with good white people is the best civilizing agency that can be devised. Through it the Indian youth unconsciously imbibe the traits of character of those with whom they associate, and continue to be more like them the longer they remain in their society. (p. 190)

Pratt and Reel were consciously crafting spaces of assimilation in middle class white homes where Indigenous children would "soak up" white values. This practice of removing Native children from their homes continued throughout the 20th century, and although slowed by the Indian Child Welfare Act (1978), remains an issue today (NICWA, 2015).

I draw attention to this aspect of my upbringing because whiteness continues to be one of the unmarked backdrops of public schooling. Homes and schools today may not be maliciously crafted as spaces in which Native children imbibe dominant culture, no longer intentionally rooted in the practice of, as noted in an editorial in the 1891 newspaper *The Indian's Friend*, getting "one Indian family away from another and to get them mixed up with white people" (as cited in Jacobs, 2009, pp. 26–27). Nevertheless, they often remain assimilative by default. Rooted in colorblindness and liberal multiculturalism, my own K-12 schooling experiences resonate remarkably with the practices I document in this book— making masks and tipis, reading Native "legends" written by white authors, learning of the courage and heroism of Western explorers—a disheartening realization as my elementary education ended nearly 30 years ago.

To be clear, I grew up in a very loving home and had teachers who loved me. I was surrounded by good intentions. My upbringing and education weren't deliberately assimilative. My proximity to whiteness also afforded me particular privileges, access to economic privilege and dominant cultural capital, for example, that likely contributed to my academic success. But my upbringing was also marked by contradictions: a discourse of rescue and feelings of resentment, a loving home and feelings of alienation, access to privilege and but also to racial bias and bigotry. Even in a house full of love and successful in school, I grew up feeling out of place and achingly unfulfilled. My experience involved what W.E. B. Du Bois (1961) has called a sense of "two-ness" (p. 17). As a young child steeped in Eurocentrism and socialized into settler colonial scripts and subjectivities, I was vulnerable to erasure; but I also had a deep longing that would not let me be erased.

My initial entryway into this scholarship stemmed from that particular longing to redress issues of identity and belonging that I felt growing up. This is not a longing rooted in imperialist nostalgia (Rosaldo, 1989), one that reaches for some timeless and authentic past (ironically, a past the colonist has destroyed). Rather, I understand Indigenous longing as a resistance to erasure, and a catalyst for Native resurgence (McCarty & Lee, 2014). For me, then, this research has been an important, personal project of remembrance, reclamation, and connection (Smith, 2012); I have even literally re-membered (Absolon & Willett, 2005) my way back into my relations and my community. I have also used the resources of the academy—access to books, journals, conferences—to understand my lived experiences. Native studies, and in particular Native feminisms, have been a lifeline for me. Native feminist conceptions of home, land, place, identity, and recognition (Goeman, 2009; Hernández-Ávila, 1995; Million, 2011; Ramirez, 2007; L. Simpson, 2015) have helped me locate my experiences within discourses of settler colonialism and survivance, rather than personal pathology. They also motivated me to keep finding my family. It was Koyukon Athabascan poet Mary TallMountain who wrote to me, "I tell you now. You *can* go home again" (1987, np).

I tell this story because as Battiste (2013) offers, telling stories can be an "act of resistance. Speaking in and through stories then becomes a way to engage in self-transformation" (p. 17). I tell this story because the Native children who are asked to make tipis and masks, who are taught to regurgitate colonial myths, grow up and can speak back to such miseducation. Unlike my experience, and as some of the chapters in this book show, some Native students have knowledge from their homes and communities that already contests such miseducation. Others, like myself, have had to find and fight our ways back. Survivance can be a long, slow, and arduous process. It may require immense courage (cold-calling a village and various relatives to see if anyone remembers who you are); labor (to read Native literature, often in addition to our required studies); conviction (not only to withstand Eurocentrism, but also judgment and alienation from Indigenous peoples); and humility (to reflect on our lives and worldviews and unlearn the language of conquest) (Jacobs, 2006). I tell this story, further, to complicate the idea of what it means for a Native student to be "successful." I worry, for example, that recent findings from the National Indian Education Study—that extracurricular American Indian/Alaska Native (AI/AN) activities are correlated with reduced achievement, or Native students' preference for non-AI/AN authors correlates with increased achievement—will fuel justifications for assimilative forms of schooling. Counter to these results, my experiences and this book argue that Native children *need* Native studies and that these extracurricular spaces can benefit Native students.

This short story, and the stories in this book, are a testament of survivance. They are also a cautionary tale for educators to consider the unintentional ways education might socialize Native children, as well as what Indigenous children may have to unlearn as a result of public schooling. Given my experiences, I am personally driven to wonder how schools are still positioned as spaces which tacitly seek to erase Native students. However, the tools I have used to question the normative logics of schooling are not instinctual, nor do they come from my socialization into Indigenous knowledge systems. They stem from my labor and engagement with Native studies. This story, then, is a call for teacher education programs to make systemic efforts to address Native studies. As Native students and scholars, we often undertake such labor, often on our own time. Teacher education programs and educators must make equal efforts to respect and engage Native studies scholarship, and to share in this labor of reading, resisting, and relearning.

Why Now and Why Here?: Locally Responsive Research

> The first principle is that we must localize the struggle before scaling up the analysis to a regional or global scale—Jeff Corntassel calls this the need to resist the "free Tibet" syndrome where progressive, decolonial activists and researchers are eager to work in solidarity to free "fill in the blank with the third-world colonized country of your choice" but yet are blind to the decolonial struggles happening where they work and live. (Hokulani Aikau, as cited in Aikau, Arvin, Goeman, & Morgensen, 2015, p. 85)

In response to *why now and why here?*, I offer that understanding the ways colonization, racism, and power matter in my "own backyard" (Aikau et al., 2015, p. 85) is my way of being locally responsive. The most visible programs of research on Indigenous K-12 education takes place in reservation schools, tribally controlled schools, or schools with large numbers of Indigenous students. However, the majority of Indigenous students attend public schools, many of which have small percentages of Indigenous students (NCES, 2012). As a result, urban Indigenous students and their families are constantly in danger of being ignored by educators, policy makers, and researchers. Moreover, educators often view their practice as education, not Indigenous education, a phenomenon that is not unique to this particular area. Tsalagi scholar and teacher educator Jeannette Haynes Writer (2002) documents similar dynamics of erasure and evasion in New Mexico:

> Through conversations with numerous students in the required Multicultural Education courses that I have been responsible for in the last several years, most of the preservice teachers disclose that they do not plan to teach on or near Indian reservations or in areas with significant Native populations. These same preservice teachers have the impression that Native people live only on reservations and do not move outside their historical areas of location. This misconception is problematic ... In addition, many of my preservice teachers believe that they do not have to address Native issues because American Indian students will not be in their classrooms. (p. 10)

In the district in which this research is based, less than 2% of the district's 11,000 students identify as American Indian/Alaska Native. Each of the 22 schools in this district, then, is what the National Council for Education Statistics (NCES) (2012) refers to as "low density" schools, meaning that less than 25% of the student population are American Indian/Alaska Native. Despite the statistical minority of Indigenous students in this district—which is not an inevitable historical fact, but the result of policies and practices of genocide, removal, dispossession, termination, and assimilation (Berg, 2007)—I believe *each and every Native student in this district is precious.*

Research on Indigenous education in public school districts is important, as approximately 90% of AI/AN students attend public schools; moreover, 50% of AI/AN 4th graders and 56% of AI/AN eighth graders attend "low density" schools (NCES, 2012, p. 11). While a vast literature base for Indigenous education exists,[11] research that examines the more successful models of Indigenous education, are, as Dorer and Fetter (2013) note, "particularly pertinent to tribally owned, private, or charter schools that are characterized by relative flexibility, autonomy, and cultural homogeneity in their schools (p. 7). To address this, there is a growing number of scholars committed specifically to urban Indigenous education (Amerman, 2010; Bang et al., 2013; Bang et al., 2014; Dion & Salamanca, 2014; Friedel, 2011; Gray 2011; Martinez, 2010; Powers, 2006). However, much of this research often, and understandably, focuses on after-school education, or Indigenous education at community centers. This book complements this body of work by addressing Indigenous education efforts in a low density, yet highly intertribal, public school district where Indigenous students are a statistical minority in their schools, and at times, perhaps the only Native student in their class. In low density schools and districts, Indigenous education is not often a priority. Yet despite the "density" of Indigenous students, the education of Indigenous students remains a "treaty right" (Tribal Nations Education Committee, 2016) and an educational "trust responsibility" (Charleston, 1994), one of the many "promises which were given [to Indigenous peoples] in exchange for land"(Deyhle & Swisher, 1997, p. 114). This book and the research upon which it is based is thus intended to remind educators of our educational trust responsibility, and to contribute to the broader conversation on how to better support Indigenous education in public schools.

Writing about Indigenous education in this place has been challenging. I often feel caught between the promising and generative literature in Indigenous studies on the one hand, which articulates theories and practices of Indigenous education, self-determination, sovereignty, and cultural resurgence, and the constraints and compromises of settler colonial practices as they are lived day to day in schools on the other. In such stifling spaces, Indigenous theorizations of education and decolonization feel at times practically impossible. I try to imagine the possibilities if Indigenous students—their identities, lands, bodies, values, families, communities, and desires—were recognized and supported. I try to imagine what success could mean for Indigenous students in this space—a "holistic" notion of success, inclusive not only of "*academic* success," but also "meaningful integration of Native *cultural content* into the curriculum, student *self-concept*, and in-depth *community engagement*" (Ewing & Ferrick, 2012, p. 4). Yet at times success feels like tearing a tipi off of the wall. Success has meant getting librarians to realize that redsk*n and sq*w are derogatory terms that have no place in children's literature, or getting teachers to talk about Indigenous peoples in the present tense. Success has meant getting a teacher to realize that Indigenous students don't all have dark skin, or even just that Indigenous education matters. In such moments, when these become my measures of success, I question my investments and theories of change. I worry about who I am investing in and where I am locating the power to transform Indigenous education. I see the promise in Indigenous community-based charter schools and Indigenous teacher preparation programs. Yet I also worry about abandoning the Indigenous students who have few options but to be educated in these spaces. My work in these spaces often feels compromising, but so too does the thought of conceding the terrain of public schooling. Doing so feels like another form of removal and erasure.

It remains an open question for me whether the public schools in this district and in general are capable of educating for democracy, self-determination, and sovereignty. It also remains open whether teacher education programs and individual teachers will care enough to take Indigenous educational issues and priorities seriously. Nevertheless, by "assert[ing] a Native gaze on a racially contested landscape" (Deyhle, 2013, p. 6) of public schools and "counterimagining" (Kroeber, 2008, p. 29) educational possibilities from within, my goal is to pry open possibilities for educators and enlist them in anticolonial and Indigenous education efforts in mainstream public schools and classrooms. By bringing Native studies theories and frameworks to bear on a particular set of educational experiences in this district, these stories are a "strategic contestation" (LaRocque, 2010, p. 24) of what I have both participated in and witnessed, my attempt to address both "the *not yet* and, at times, the *not any-more*" (Tuck, 2009, p. 417).

To summarize, survivance storytelling is a method I constructed as I negotiated my role, relationships, and responsibilities as an Indigenous researcher working with Indigenous youth and families in this district. Writing survivance stories has been my way of contesting colonialism, reflecting and affirming the Native survivance that I witnessed in my research, and connecting to the long legacy of Native survivance of which I am a part. As I mentioned earlier, my emphasis on survivance is not intended to be the latest iteration of grit. My aim in sharing this method is not to arm a new generation of researchers who now seek to inquire into and document Native survivance. I do hope, however, that Indigenous students, educators, and researchers find this description useful, and draw from this or develop their own methods to reflect, affirm, and make connections to our shared legacy.

Outline of Chapters

Each survivance story in this book documents a particular educational experience and the chapters stand alone. However, to facilitate reading these stories, I have divided the book into two parts, and included a section description that provides a brief overview each chapter.

Part I, "Colonialism in the Classroom," includes three chapters, each of which addresses educational experience at the classroom level. Chapter 1, "Pilgrims and Invented Indians," documents a 7-year old Native student's experience of and resistance to the conventional Pilgrims and Indians curriculum in an elementary classroom. Chapter 2, "Halloween Costumes and Native Identity," represents a Native youth group's organizing around issues of representation during Halloween, and in particular, one Native youth's attempt to bring that knowledge to her classroom teacher. Lastly, Chapter 3, "Native Sheroes and Complex Personhood" is about contemporary Indigenous peoples and identity.

Part II, "Colonialism in the Culture of Schools," includes three chapters that each take a broader view of curriculum by attending to school-wide and community-based curricular efforts. Chapter 4, "Little Anthropologists" tackles the Native American Unit typically taught in schools across the United States, and questions the type of knowledge students gain from this type of curriculum. Chapter 5, "Native Heritage Month," documents a school assembly that takes place during Native Heritage Month, and interrogates the value of Native performances. Finally, Chapter 6, "Education on the Border of Sovereignty," represents a high school mural project created in consultation with Native nations.

Taken together, these chapters point to various forms of knowledge teachers need to better serve Native students and families. A theme that comes up clearly, particularly in the first few chapters, is that teachers should know better and do better by Native students. Building on this assumption, the chapters then move to how educators might more responsibly educate Native students, and draw from Indigenous studies to inform their curriculum and pedagogy. Although these stories are particular to this place, my hope is that educators make connections to their own contexts and practices, reflect on how their own teaching reproduces colonialism, and enlist themselves in the struggle to support Indigenous self-determination in schools. We need *all* educators to see themselves as responsible for this work. As Vaught (2011) argues, "It should not be an accident or stroke of good fortune that a Black or Brown [or Native] child receives a good education. It should be a systemic, structural guarantee" (p. 209).

The final chapter, "Interventions for Urban Indigenous Education," summarizes some of the more general insights and recommendations that emerge from the survivance stories for schools and districts, teacher education programs, educational policy, and research. The book ends with a brief vignette, documenting a community effort premised on survivance, exploring the ways that survivance is often improvisational, using the resources at hand to support Native students despite, at times, dire circumstances.

Notes

1 Over the years, Indian Education has been located under various "Title" programs. In 1994, Indian Education was reauthorized as Title IX Part A of the Elementary and Secondary Education Act (ESEA). Under the 2001 No Child Left Behind Act (NCLB),

Indian Education was reauthorized as Title VII Part A of ESEA and most recently, as Title VI under the Every Student Succeeds Act (ESSA) of 2015. I refer more generally to the efforts of Indigenous educators or the community as "Indigenous education."

2 The formal report was entitled "Indian Education: A National Tragedy - A National Challenge."

3 For a more in-depth account of this community organizing and the development of the Native Youth Center, see *Native Feminisms in Motion* (Sabzalian, 2016).

4 These are also referred to as "stock stories" (Delgado, 1989) and "majoritarian" stories (Delgado, 1993; Solórzano & Yosso, 2002) within CRT literature.

5 The references to "language" and "culturally responsive" are new additions to the program's purpose and description, as a result of ESSA.

6 Importantly, Indigenous students have always engaged in acts of overt and covert resistance and survivance within these institutions (Adams, 1995; Lomawaima, 2002). Students met in secret, continued speaking their languages, resisted teacher authority by hiding, marching off beat, burning down schools, or running away (Child, 1999; Lomawaima, 1994; 2002; Fear-Segal, 2007). Despite the attempted assaults on their identities and livelihoods, "students devised strategies to assert independence, express individuality, develop leadership, use Native languages, and undermine federal goals of homogenization and assimilation" (Lomawaima, 2002, p. 423).

7 In 2012, a Menominee girl in Wisconsin was chastised for speaking Menominee and suspended from school (ICMTN, 2012). In 2014, a Navajo student in Texas was reportedly sent home from school and ordered to cut his long hair because it violated school dress-code policy (Moya-Smith, 2014). This year a Choctaw student in Oklahoma was forced to choose between keeping his long hair or playing sports (Phillips, 2018).

8 To be clear, the logic of elimination has been official US policy for centuries. The Indian Wars (from Wars with the Powahtan Confederacy in 1622 to Wounded Knee in 1890), the Civilization Fund Act (1819), the Indian Removal Act (1830), the Dawes Act (1887) the overthrow of Queen Lili'uokalani (1893) and later annexation of Hawai'i (1898), and mission, and later state-run off-reservation Indian boarding schools designed to assimilate Native children (late 19th and early 20th century), Indian termination (1953) and the Indian Relocation Act (1956) are but a few of methods of legalizing Indigenous dispossession.

9 Although often the first association with Indigeneity, establishing Indigenous identities via blood is only one of the many ways to construct Indigeneity. Ancestral ties and kinship relations, cultural knowledge, residency or community involvement, or a combination of various forms are other ways Indigenous peoples determine Indigenous identity and community membership.

10 For children's literature to support teaching about boarding are residential schools, see Campbell (2005), Chiori (1998), Loyie (2005), Sterling (1992), and Ends/Begins (Robertson & Henderson, 2010) and The Pact (Robertson & Henderson, 2011).

11 See for example: Barnhardt, 2009; Brayboy & Castagno, 2009; Cajete, 1994; Castagno & Brayboy, 2008; Deloria & Wildcat, 2001; Demmert & Towner, 2003; Deyhle & Swisher, 1997; Kawagley & Barnhardt, 1998; Lee, 2011; Lipka et al., 1998; McCarty, 2002; McCarty & Lee, 2014.

References

Absolon, K. & Willett, C. (2005). Putting ourselves forward: Location in Aboriginal research. In L. A. Brown & S. Strega (Eds.), *Research as resistance: Critical, indigenous and anti-oppressive approaches* (pp. 97–126). Toronto, ON: Canadian Scholars' Press.

Adams, D. W. (1988). Fundamental considerations: The deep meaning of Native American schooling, 1880–1900. *Harvard Educational Review*, 58(1), 1–29.

Adams, D. W. (1995). *Education for extinction: American Indians and the boarding school experience, 1875–1928*. Lawrence, KS: University Press of Kansas.

Aikau, H. K., Arvin, M., Goeman, M., & Morgenson, S. (2015) Indigenous feminisms roundtable. *Frontiers: A Journal of Women Studies*, 36(3), 84–106.

Alfred, G. (1999). *Peace, power, righteousness: An indigenous manifesto*. Don Mills, ON: Oxford University Press.

Alfred, T., & Corntassel, J. (2005). Being Indigenous: Resurgences against contemporary colonialism. *Government and Opposition*, 40(4), 597–614.

Alim, H. S. (2012). #demographobia, the irrational fear of a changing demographic, & the #asianamerican vote & #endofwhiteidentitypolitics. November 11. http://tv.msnbc. com/2012/11/10/white-identity-politics-doomed-2012-republican-effort/... [Tweet]. Retrieved from https://twitter.com/hsamyalim/status/267754880372965376.

Amerman, S. (2010). *Urban Indians in Phoenix schools, 1940–2000*. Lincoln, NE: University of Nebraska Press.

Archibald, J. A. (2008). *Indigenous storywork: Educating the heart, mind, body, and spirit*. Vancouver: UBC Press.

Atkinson, B., & Mitchell, R. (2010). "Why didn't they get it?" "Did they have to get it?": What reader response theory has to offer narrative research and pedagogy. *International Journal of Education & the Arts*, 11(7). Retrieved from www.ijea.org/v11n7.

Atwood, E. & López, G. R. (2014). Let's be critically honest: Towards a messier counterstory in critical race theory. *International Journal of Qualitative Studies in Education*, 27(9), 1134–1154,

Bang, M., Curley, L., Kessel, A., Marin, A., SuzukovichIII, E. S., & Strack, G. (2014). Muskrat theories, tobacco in the streets, and living Chicago as Indigenous land. *Environmental Education Research*, 20(1), 37–55.

Bang, M., Marin, A., Faber, L., & Suzukovich, E. S. (2013). Repatriating Indigenous technologies in an urban Indian community. *Urban Education*, 48(5), 705–733.

Barker, J. (2005). *Sovereignty matters: Locations of contestation and possibility in indigenous struggles for self-determination*. Lincoln, NE: University of Nebraska Press.

Barnhardt, R. (2009). Alaska Native Knowledge Network: Connecting education to place. *Connect Magazine*. Synergy Learning International Incorporated.

Battiste, M. (2013). *Decolonizing education: Nourishing the learning spirit*. Saskatoon: Purich Publishing Limited.

Berg, L. (2007). *The first Oregonians* (2nd ed.). Portland, OR: Oregon Council for the Humanities.

Berkhofer, R. (1979). *The white man's Indian: Images of the American Indian, from Columbus to the present*. New York, NY: Vintage Books.

Biolsi, T. (2005). Imagined geographies: Sovereignty, Indigenous space, and American Indian struggle. *American Ethnologist*, 32(2), 239–259.

Blaut, J. (1993). *The colonizer's model of the world: Geographical diffusionism and Eurocentric history*. New York, NY: Guilford Press.

Boler, M. (1999). *Feeling power: Emotions and education*. Hoboken, NJ: Taylor & Francis.

Boler, M., & Zembylas, M. (2003). Discomforting truths: The emotional terrain of understanding difference. In P. Trifonas (Ed.). *Pedagogies of difference: Rethinking education for social change* (pp. 110–136). New York, NY: RoutledgeFalmer.

Brandzel, A. (2016). *Against citizenship: The violence of the normative* (Dissident feminisms). Urbana, IL: University of Illinois Press.

Brayboy, B. M. J. (2005). Toward a tribal critical race theory in education. *Urban Review: Issues and Ideas in Public Education*, 5, 425–446.

Brayboy, B., & Castagno, A. (2009). Self-determination through self-education: Culturally responsive schooling for Indigenous students in the USA. *Teaching Education*, 20(1): 31–53.

Brayboy, B. M. J., Fann, A. J., Castagno, A. E., & Solyom, J. A. (2012). *Postsecondary education for American Indian and Alaska Natives: Higher education for nation building and self-determination*. San Francisco, CA: Wiley Subscription Services.

Byrd, J. A. (2011). *The transit of empire: Indigenous critiques of colonialism*. Minneapolis: University of Minnesota Press.

Cajete, G. (1994). *Look to the mountain: An ecology of indigenous education*. Durango, CO: Kivakí Press.

Calderón, D. (2009). Making explicit the jurisprudential foundations of multiculturalism: The continuing challenges of colonial education in US schooling for Indigenous education. In A. Kempf (Ed.), *Breaching the colonial contract: Anti-colonialism in the U.S. and Canada* (pp. 53–77). New York, NY: Springer.

Calderón, D. (2014a). Speaking back to manifest destinies: A land education-based approach to critical curriculum inquiry. *Environmental Education Research*, 20(1), 24–36.

Calderón, D. (2014b). Uncovering settler grammars in curriculum. *Educational Studies: Journal of the American Educational Studies Association*, 50(4), 313–338.

Campbell, N. (2005). *Shi-shi-etko*. Toronto: Groundwood Books.

Castagno, A. E., & Brayboy, B. M. K. J. (2008). Culturally responsive schooling for Indigenous youth: A review of the literature. *Review of Educational Research*, 78(4), 941–993.

Champagne, D. (2007,). Self-government's roots: Communities. *Indian Country Media Today Network*, January 19. Retrieved from https://indiancountrymedianetwork.com/news/self-governments-roots-communities.

Chang, P., & RosiekJ. (2003). Anti-colonial antinomies: A case of cultural conflict in the high school biology curriculum. *Curriculum Inquiry*, 33(3), 251–290.

Charleston, M. G. (1994). Toward true Native education: A treaty of 1992. Final report of the Indian Nations At Risk Task Force. *Journal of American Indian Education*, 33(2), 7–56.

Child, B. (1999). *Boarding school seasons: American Indian families, 1900–1940*. Lincoln, NE: University of Nebraska Press.

Child, B. (2014). The boarding school as metaphor. In B. J. Child, & B. Klopotek (Eds.), *Indian subjects: Hemispheric perspectives on the history of Indigenous education* (pp. 267–284). Santa Fe, NM: SAR Press.

Chiori, S. (1998). *Home to Medicine Mountain*. San Francisco: Children's Book Press.

Chrisjohn, R., & Peters, M. (1986). The right-brained Indian: Fact or fiction? *Journal of American Indian Education*, 25(2), 1–7.

Clandinin, D., & Connelly, M. (1995). *Teachers' professional knowledge landscapes*. New York, NY: Teachers College Press.

Clandinin, D. J., & Rosiek, J. (2007). Mapping a landscape of narrative inquiry: Borderland spaces and tensions. In D. J. Clandinin (Ed.), *Handbook of narrative inquiry: Mapping a methodology* (pp. 35–75). Thousand Oaks, CA: Sage.

Cobb, A. (2005). Understanding tribal sovereignty: Definitions, conceptualizations, and interpretations. *American Studies, 46*(3/4), 115–132.

Connelly, F., & Clandinin, J. D. (1999). *Shaping a professional identity: Stories of educational practice*. New York, NY: Teachers College Press.

Connelly, F. M., Clandinin, D. J., & He, M. F. (1997). Teachers' personal practical knowledge on the professional knowledge landscape. *Teaching and Teacher Education*, 13(7), 665–674.

Cook-Lynn, E. (1996). American Indian intellectualism and the new Indian story. *American Indian Quarterly*, 20(1), 57–76.

Cook-Lynn, E. (2001). *Anti-Indianism in North America: A voice from Tatekeya's earth.* Urbana, IL: University of Illinois Press.

Corntassel, J. (2003). Who is Indigenous? Peoplehood and ethnonationalist approaches to rearticulating Indigenous identity. *Nationalism and Ethnic Politics,* 9(1), 75–100.

Corntassel, J. (2012). Re-envisioning resurgence: Indigenous pathways to decolonization and sustainable self-determination. *Decolonization: Indigeneity, Education, & Society,* 1(1), 86–101.

Coulthard, G. (2014). *Red skin, white masks: Rejecting the colonial politics of recognition.* Minneapolis, MN: University of Minnesota Press.

Crenshaw, K., Gotanda, N., Peller, G., & Thomas, K. (1995). *Critical race theory: The key writings that formed the movement.* New York, NY: New Press

Delgado, R. (1989). Storytelling for oppositionists and others: A plea for narrative. *Michigan Law Review,* 87, 2411–2441.

Delgado, R. (1996). Rodrigo's eleventh chronicle: Empathy and false empathy. *California Law Review,* 84(1), 61–100.

Delgado, R., & Stefancic, J. (2000). *Critical race theory: The cutting edge.* Philadelphia, PA: Temple University Press.

Delgado, R., & Stefancic, J. (2012). *Critical race theory: An introduction* (2nd ed.). New York, NY: New York University Press.

Deloria, P. (1998). *Playing Indian.* New Haven, CT: Yale University Press.

Deloria, V., & Wildcat, D. R. (2001). *Power and place: Indian education in America.* Golden, CO: Fulcrum Pub.

Demmert, W., & Towner, J. (2003). *A review of the research literature on the influences of culturally based education on the academic performance of Native American students.* Portland, OR: Northwest Regional Education Laboratory.

Deyhle, D. (2013). Listening to lives: Lessons learned from American Indian youth. In J. Reyhner, J. Martin, L. Lockard, & W. S. Gilbert. (Eds.), *Honoring our children: Culturally appropriate approaches for teaching Indigenous students* (pp. 1–10). Flagstaff, AZ: Northern Arizona University.

Deyhle, D., & Swisher, K. (1997). Research in American Indian and Alaska Native education: From assimilation to self-determination. *Review of Research in Education,* 22, 113–194.

Dibble, N., & Rosiek, J. (2002). White-out: A connection between a teacher's white identity and her science teaching. *International Journal of Education and the Arts,* 5(3). Retrieved from www.ijea.org/v3n5.

Dion, S. D. (2007). Disrupting molded images: Identities, responsibilities and relationships—teachers and indigenous subject material. *Teaching Education,* 18(4), 329–342

Dion, S. D. (2008). *Braiding histories: Learning from Aboriginal peoples' experiences and perspectives.* Vancouver, BC: UBC Press.

Dion, S. D. (2012). Introducing and disrupting the perfect stranger [Video file]. July. Retrieved from http://vimeo.com/59543958.

Dion, S. D., & Salamanca, A. (2014). inVISIBILITY: Indigenous in the city Indigenous artists, Indigenous youth and the project of survivance. *Decolonization: Indigeneity, Education & Society,* 3(1), 159–188.

Dixson, A., & Rousseau, Celia K. (2006). *Critical race theory in education: All God's children got a song.* New York, NY: Routledge.

Dorer, B., & Fetter, A. (2013). *Cultivated ground. Effective teaching practices for Native students in a public high school.* Harvard University and the National Indian Education Association.

Drabek, A. S. (2012). *Liitukut sugpiat'stun (We are learning how to be real people): Exploring Kodiak Alutiiq literature through core values* (Unpublished doctoral dissertation). University of Alaska, Fairbanks.

Du Bois, W. (1961). *The souls of Black folk.* New York, NY: Fawcett Publications, Inc.

Duckworth, A. L., Peterson, C., Matthews, M. D., & Kelly, D. R. (2007). Grit: Perseverance and passion for long-term goals. *Journal of Personality and Social Psychology,* 92(6), 1087–1101.

Dunbar-Ortiz, R. (2014). *Indigenous peoples' history of the United States.* Boston, MA: Beacon Press.

Duncan, G. (2002). Critical race theory and method: Rendering race in urban ethnographic research. *Qualitative Inquiry,* 6(1), 85–104.

Duncan-Andrade, J., & Morrell, E. (2008). *The art of critical pedagogy: Possibilities for moving from theory to practice in urban schools.* New York, NY: Peter Lang.

Enoch, J. (2002). Resisting the script of Indian education: Zitkala-Ša and the Carlisle Indian school. *College English,* 65(2), 117–141.

Every Student Succeeds Act. (2015). Retrieved from https://www.gpo.gov/fdsys/pkg/BILLS-114s1177enr/pdf/BILLS-114s1177enr.pdf.

Ewing, E. L., & Ferrick, M. E. (2012). *For this place, for these people: An exploration of best practices among charter schools serving Native students.* Washington, DC: National Indian Education Association. Retrieved from www.niea.org.

Fear-Segal, J. (2007). *White man's club: Schools, race, and the struggle of Indian acculturation.* Lincoln, NE: University of Nebraska Press.

Feistritzer, C. E. (2011). *Profiles of teachers in the U.S. 2011. National Center for Education Information.* Retrieved September 9, 2015 from www.edweek.org/media/pot2011final-blog.pdf.

Fine, M., & Barreras, R. (2001). To be of use. *Analyses of Social Issues and Public Policy,* 1(1), 175–182.

First Look Media (Producer). (2016). Shaun King on controversy, color, and Kaepernick. Politically Re-Active with W. Kamau Bell & Hari Kondabolu. [Audio podcast]. September 7. Retrieved from https://itunes.apple.com/us/podcast/politically-re-active-w.-kamau/id1125018164?mt=2.

Freire, P. (1970). *Pedagogy of the oppressed.* New York, NY: Seabury Press.

Friedel, T. L. (2011). Looking for learning in all the wrong places: Urban Native youths' cultured response to western-oriented place-based learning. *International Journal of Qualitative Studies in Education,* 24(5): 531–546.

Gates, M. E. (1897). Proceedings of the Board of Indian Commissioners at the Fourteenth Mohonk Indian Conference. *Twenty-eighth annual report of the Board of Indian Commissioners.* Washington: Government Printing Office.

Gay, G. (2010). *Culturally responsive teaching: Theory, research and practice* (2nd ed.). New York, NY: Teachers College Press.

Gillborn, D. (2008). *Racism and education: Coincidence or conspiracy?* New York, NY: Routledge.

Gilliland, Hap. (1995). *Teaching the Native American* (3rd ed.). Dubuque, IA: Kendall/Hunt.

Glenn, E. (2015). Settler Colonialism as Structure. *Sociology of Race and Ethnicity,* 1(1), 52–72.

Goeman, M. (2009). Notes toward a Native feminism's spatial practice. *Wicazo Sa Review,* 24(2), 169–187.

Goeman, M., & Denetdale, J. (2009). Guest editors' introduction: Native feminisms: Legacies, interventions, and Indigenous sovereignties. *Wicazo Sa Review,* 24(2), 9–13.

Goodyear-Ka'ōpua, N. (2013). *The seeds we planted: Portraits of a native Hawaiian charter school.* Minneapolis, MN: University of Minnesota Press.

Gorski, P. C., & Swalwell, K. (2015). Equity literacy for all. *Educational Leadership*, 72(6), 34–40.

Gottesman, I. (2016). *The critical turn in education: From Marxist critique to poststructuralist feminism to critical theories of race.* New York, NY: Routledge.

Goulet, L., & Goulet, K. N. (2014). *Teaching each other: Nehinuw concepts and Indigenous pedagogies.* Vancouver: UBC Press.

Gover, K. (2015). Settler–state political theory, 'CANZUS' and the UN Declaration on the Rights of Indigenous Peoples. *European Journal of International Law*, 26(2), 345–373.

Grande, S. (2015). *Red pedagogy: Native American social and political thought* (10th Anniversary ed.). Lanham, MD: Rowman & Littlefield.

Gray, R. R. R. (2011). Visualizing pedagogy and power with urban Native youth: Exposing the legacy of the Indian residential school system. *Canadian Journal of Native Education*, 34(1), 9–27.

Gruber, J. (1970). Ethnographic salvage and the shaping of anthropology. *American Anthropologist*, 72(6), 1289–1299.

Guinier, L. (2004). From racial liberalism to racial literacy: Brown v. Board of Education and the interest-divergence dilemma. *The Journal of American History*, 91(1), 92–118.

Harris, C. (1993). Whiteness as property. *Harvard Law Review*, 106(8), 1707.

Haynes Writer, J. (2002). "No matter how bitter, horrible, or controversial": Exploring the value of a Native American education course in a teacher education program. *Action in Teacher Education*, 24(2), 9–21.

Haynes Writer, J. (2008). Unmasking, exposing, and confronting: Critical Race Theory, Tribal Critical Race Theory and multicultural education. *International Journal of Multicultural Education*, 10(2), 1–15.

Haynes Writer, J. (2010). Broadening the meaning of citizenship education: Native Americans and tribal nationhood. *Action in Teacher Education*, 32(2), 70–81.

Hermes, M. (2005). "Ma'iingan is just a misspelling of the word wolf": A case for teaching culture through language. *Anthropology & Education Quarterly*, 36(1), 43–56.

Hernández-Ávila, I. (1995). Relocations upon relocations: Home, language, and Native American women's writings. *American Indian Quarterly*, 19(4), 491.

Higgins, M., Madden, B., & Korteweg, L. (2013). Witnessing (halted) deconstruction: White teachers' "perfect stranger" position within urban Indigenous education. *Race, ethnicity, and education*, 18(2), 251–276.

Holm, T., Pearson, D. J., & Chavis, B. (2003). Peoplehood: A model for the extension of sovereignty in American Indian studies. *Wicazo Sa Review*, 18(1), 7–24.

hooks, b. (1995). *Killing rage: Ending racism.* New York: Henry Holt and Company.

ICMTN. (2012). Student suspended for speaking Native American language. Retrieved from https://indiancountrymedianetwork.com/news/student-suspended-/

Iseke-Barnes, J. (2009). Unsettling fictions: Disrupting popular discourses and trickster tales in books for children. *Journal of the Canadian Association for Curriculum Studies*, 7(1), n.p.

Jacobs, D. (2006). *Unlearning the language of conquest scholars expose anti-Indianism in America.* Austin, TX: University of Texas Press.

Jacobs, M. (2009). *White mother to a dark race: Settler colonialism, maternalism, and the removal of indigenous children in the American West and Australia, 1880–1940.* Lincoln, NE: University of Nebraska Press.

Johnston, B. (1988). *Indian school days.* Toronto: Key Porter Books.

Journell, W. (2009). An incomplete history: Representation of American Indians in state social studies standards. *Journal of American Indian Education*, 48(2), 18–32.

Kaomea, J. (2003). Reading erasures and making the familiar strange: Defamiliarizing methods for research in formerly colonized and historically oppressed communities. *Educational Researcher*, 32(2), 14–25.

Kaomea, J. (2005). Indigenous studies in the elementary curriculum: A cautionary Hawaiian example. *Anthropology Education Quarterly*, 36(1), 24–42.

Kauanui, J. K., & O'Brien, J. (2012). Settler logics and writing Indians out of existence: A conversation between J. Kē-haulani Kauanui and Jean M. O'Brien. *Politica & Società*, 2, 259–278.

Kauanui, J. K., & Wolfe, P. (2012). Settler colonialism then and now: A conversation between J. Kē-haulani Kauanui and Patrick Wolfe. *Politica & Società*, 2, 235–258.

Kawagley, O. & Barnhardt, R. (1998). Education Indigenous to place: Western science meets Native reality. Retrieved from: www.ankn.uaf.edu/curriculum/Articles/Barnha rdtKawagley/EIP.html.

Kelting-Gibson, L. & Hopkins, W. (2006). Preparing educators to meet the challenge of Indian Education for All. *Phi Delta Kappan*, 88(3), 204–207.

King, T. (2005). *The truth about stories: A native narrative*. Minneapolis, MN: University of Minnesota Press.

King, T. (2012). *Inconvenient Indian: A curious account of Native people in North America*. Minneapolis, MN: University of Minnesota Press.

Kroeber, K. (2008). Why it's a good thing Gerald Vizenor is not an Indian. In G. Vizenor (Ed.), *Survivance: Narratives of Native presence* (pp. 25–38). Lincoln, NE: University of Nebraska Press.

Kumashiro, K. (2000). Toward a theory of anti-oppressive education. *Review of Educational Research*, 70(1), 25–53.

Ladson-Billings, G. (1995). But that's just good teaching! The case for culturally relevant pedagogy. *Theory into Practice: Culturally Relevant Teaching*, 34(3), 159–165.

Ladson-Billings, G. (1998). Just what is critical race theory and what's it doing in a nice field like education? *International Journal of Qualitative Studies in Education*, 11(1), 7–24.

Ladson-Billings, G. (2014). Culturally relevant pedagogy 2.0: A.k.a. the Remix. *Harvard Educational Review*, 84(1), 74–135.

LaRocque, E. (2010). *When the other is me: Native resistance discourse, 1850–1990*. Winnipeg: University of Manitoba Press.

Lawrence-Lightfoot, S. (2005). Reflections on portraiture: A dialogue between art and science. *Qualitative Inquiry*, 11(1), 3–15.

Lee, T. S. (2011). Teaching Native youth, teaching about Native Peoples: Shifting the paradigm to socioculturally responsive education. In A. F. Ball & C. A. Tyson (Eds.), *Studying diversity in teacher education* (pp. 275–293). Lanham, MD: Rowman & Littlefield.

Leonardo, Z. (2004). The color of supremacy: Beyond the discourse of "white privilege". *Educational Philosophy and Theory*, 36(2), 137–152.

Leonardo, Z. (2013). *Race frameworks: A multidimensional theory of racism and education*. New York, NY: Teachers College.

Leonardo, Z., & Boas, E. (2013). Other kids' teacher: What children of color learn from White women and what this says about race, whiteness, and gender. In M. Lynn and A. Dixson (Eds.), *Handbook of critical race theory in education* (pp. 313–323). New York, NY: Routledge.

Lipka, J., Mohatt, G. V., & the Ciulistet Group. (1998). *Transforming the culture of schools: Yupik Eskimo examples*. Mahwah, NJ: Lawrence Erlbaum Associates.

Lomawaima, K. T. (1994). *They called it prairie light: The story of Chilocco Indian School*. Lincoln, NE: University of Nebraska Press.

Lomawaima, K. T. (1999). The unnatural history of Indian Education. In K. Swisher & J. Tippeconnic (Eds.), *Next steps: Research and practice to advance Indian education* (pp. 3–31). Charleston, WV: ERIC Clearinghouse on Rural Education and Small Schools.

Lomawaima, K. T. (2000). Tribal sovereigns: Reframing research in American Indian education. *Harvard Educational Review*, 70(1), 1–21.

Lomawaima, K. T. (2002). American Indian Education: *By* Indians versus *for* Indians. In P. Deloria & N. Salisbury (2002). *A companion to American Indian history* (Blackwell companions to American history, 4). Malden, MA: Blackwell.

Lomawaima, K. T. (2008). Tribal sovereigns: Reframing research in American Indian education. In M. Villegas, S. R. Neugebauer, & K. R. Venegas (Eds.), *Indigenous knowledge and education: Sites of struggle, strength, and survivance* (pp. 183–203). Cambridge, MA: Harvard Educational Review.

Lomawaima, K. T. (2013). The mutuality of citizenship and sovereignty: The Society of American Indians and the battle to inherit America. *American Indian Quarterly*, 37(3), 333–351.

Lomawaima, K. T., & McCarty, T. L. (2006). *"To remain an Indian": Lessons in democracy from a century of Native American education.* New York: Teachers College Press.

Lomawaima, K. T., & McCarty, T. L. (2014a). Concluding commentary: Revisiting and clarifying the safety zone. *Journal of American Indian Education*, 53(3), 63–67.

Lomawaima, K. T., & McCarty, T. L. (2014b). Introduction to the special issue examining and applying safety zone theory: Current policies, practices, and experiences. *Journal of American Indian Education*, 53(3), 1–10.

Loyie, L. (2005). *As long as the rivers flow.* Toronto, Ontario: Groundwood Books/House of Anansi Press.

Lyons, S. R. (2000). Rhetorical sovereignty: What do American Indians want from writing? *College Composition and Communication*, 51(3), 447–468.

Lyons, S. R. (2010). *X-Marks.* Minneapolis: University of Minnesota Press.

McCarty, T. (2002). *A place to be Navajo: Rough Rock and the struggle for self- determination in Indigenous schooling.* Mahwah, NJ: Lawrence Erlbaum Associates.

McCarty, T., & Lee, T. (2014). Critical culturally sustaining/revitalizing pedagogy and Indigenous education sovereignty. *Harvard Educational Review*, 84(1), 101–124.

McCoy, K. (2014). Manifesting destiny: A land education analysis of settler colonialism in Jamestown, Virginia, USA. *Environmental Education Research*, 20(1), 82–97.

McCoy, M. (2017). Preparing preservice educators to teach American Indian boarding school histories. In S. Shear, C. M. Tschida, E. Bellows, L.B. Buchanan, & E. E. Saylor (Eds.), *Making controversial issues relevant for elementary social studies: A critical reader* (pp. 255–277). Charlotte, NC: Information Age Press.

McLaren, P. (2005). Fire and dust. *International Journal of Progressive Education*, 1(3): 34–57.

Madden, B. (2015). Pedagogical pathways for Indigenous education with/in teacher education. *Teaching and Teacher Education*, 51, 1–15.

Martinez, G. (2010). *Native pride: The politics of curriculum and instruction in an urban public school.* Cresskill, NJ: Hampton Press.

Million, D. (2011). Intense dreaming. Theories, narratives, and our search for home. *American Indian Quarterly*, 35(3), 313–333.

Million, D. (2014). There is a river in me: Theory from life. In A. Simpson & A. Smith (Eds.), *Theorizing Native studies* (pp. 31–42). Durham, NC: Duke University Press.

Moreton-Robinson, A. (2000). *Talkin' up to the white woman: Aboriginal women and feminism.* St. Lucia, Qld: University of Queensland Press.

Moreton-Robinson, A. (2016). *Critical indigenous studies: Engagements in first world locations.* Tucson, AZ: The University of Arizona Press.

Morgan, T. J. (1890). Instructions to Indian agents in regard to inculcation of patriotism in Indian schools. In *United States, Bureau of Indian Affairs. Fifty-ninth annual report of the Commissioner of Indian Affairs to the Secretary of the Interior* (p. clxvii). Washington: Government Printing Office.

Morrill, A. (2017). Time traveling dogs (and other Native feminist ways to defy dislocations). *Cultural Studies ↔Critical Methodologies*, 17, 14–20.

Moya-Smith, S. (2014). Navajo kindergartner sent home from school, ordered to cut his hair. *Indian Country Today Media Network*, August 28. Retrieved from https://india ncountrymedianetwork.com/education/native-education/navajo-kindergartner-sent-home-from-school-ordered-to-cut-his-hair.

Nader, L. (1972). Up the anthropologist: Perspectives gained from studying up. In D. Hymes (Ed.), *Reinventing anthropology* (pp. 284–311). New York, NY: Pantheon Books.

National Center for Education Statistics. (2012). National Indian Education Study 2011 (NCES 2012-2466). Washington, D.C.: Institute of Education Sciences, U.S. Department of Education.

National Indian Child Welfare Association. (2015). Setting the record straight: The Indian Child Welfare Act fact sheet. Retrieved from www.nicwa.org/government/documents/Setting-Record-Straight-About-ICWA_Sep2015.pdf.

Nelson, J. B. (2014). *Progressive traditions: Identity in Cherokee literature and culture.* Norman, OK: University of Oklahoma Press.

Nieto, S., & Bode, P. (2012). *Affirming diversity: The sociopolitical context of multicultural education.* Boston, MA: Pearson Education.

O'Brien, J. (2010). *Firsting and lasting writing Indians out of existence in New England.* Minneapolis, MN: University of Minnesota Press.

Office of Indian Education. (2014).). Indian Education—Formula Grants to Local Education Agencies. Retrieved from https://www2.ed.gov/programs/indianformula/index.html.

Office of Indian Education. (2016). Title VI Indian Education Formula Grant Program School Year 2016–2017. Retrieved December 30, 2016 from https://easie.grads360.org/#program/additional-resources.

Ohito, E. (2016). Making the emperor's new clothes visible in anti-racist teacher education: Enacting a pedagogy of discomfort with White preservice teachers. *Equity & Excellence in Education*, 49(4), 454–467.

Paris, D. (2012). Culturally sustaining pedagogy, a needed change in stance, terminology, and practice. *Educational Researcher*, 41, 93–97

Patel, L. (2016). *Decolonizing educational research: From ownership to answerability.* New York, NY: Routledge.

Pearce, R. (1988). *Savagism and Civilization.* Berkeley, CA: University of California Press.

Pedri-Spade, C. (2014). Nametoo: Evidence that he/she is/was present. *Decolonization: Indigeneity, Education & Society*, 3(1), 73–100.

Phillips, J. (2018). Native students question rule forcing athletes to cut their hair. *KXII News 12*, August 17. Retrieved from www.kxii.com/content/news/Native-stu dents-question-rule-forcing-athletes-to-cut-hair-491162141.html.

Powers, K. M. (2006). An exploratory study of cultural identity and culture-based educational programs for urban American Indian students. *Urban Education*, 1, 20–49.

Pratt, R. H. (1973). The advantages of mingling with Whites. In F. Prucha (Ed.), *Americanizing the American Indians* (pp. 260–271). Cambridge, MA: Harvard University Press.

Raheja, M. (2010). *Reservation reelism: Redfacing, visual sovereignty, and representations of Native Americans in film.* Lincoln, NE: University of Nebraska Press.

Rains, F. V. (2003). To greet the dawn with open eyes: American Indians, White privilege and the power of residual guilt in social studies. In G. Ladson-Billings (Ed.), *Critical race theory perspectives on social studies: The profession, policies, and curriculum* (pp. 199–227). Greenwich, CT: Information Age Publishing.

Ramirez, R. (2007). *Native hubs: Culture, community, and belonging in Silicon Valley and beyond.* Durham: Duke University Press.

Reel, E. (1901). *Course of study for the Indian schools of the United States. United States Superintendent of Indian Schools.* Washington: Government Printing Office. Retrieved from https://books.google.com/books?id=eTYaAAAAYAAJ&source=gbs_navlinks_s.

Regan, P. (2010). *Unsettling the settler within: Indian residential schools, truth telling, and reconciliation in Canada.* Vancouver: UBC Press.

Rich, A. (1993). *What is found there: Notebooks on poetry and politics.* New York, NY: W. W. Norton.

Richardson, T., & Villenas, S. (2000). "Other" encounters: Dances with whiteness in multicultural education. *Educational Theory, 50*(2), 255–273.

Rifkin, M. (2014). *Settler common sense: Queerness and everyday colonialism in the American Renaissance.* Minneapolis, MN: University of Minnesota Press.

Robertson, D., & Henderson, S. B. (2010). *Ends/begins (7 generations).* Winnipeg: High-Water Press.

Robertson, D., & Henderson, S. B. (2011). *The pact (7 generations).* Winnipeg: HighWater Press.

Rosaldo, R. (1989). Imperialist nostalgia. *Representations, 26,* 107–122.

Rosiek, J., & Atkinson, B. (2007). The inevitability and importance of genres in narrative research on teaching practice. *Qualitative Inquiry, 13*(4), 499–521.

Rowe, M. (2008). Micro-affirmations & micro-inequities. *Journal of the International Ombudsman Association, 1*(1). Retrieved from http://ombud.mit.edu/sites/default/files/documents/micro-affirm-ineq.pdf.

Sabzalian, L. (2016). Native feminisms in motion. *English Journal, 106*(1), 23–30.

Sabzalian, L., & Shear, S. (2018). Confronting colonial blindness in civics education: Recognizing colonization, self-determination, and sovereignty as core knowledge for elementary social studies teacher education. In S. Shear, C. M. Tschida, E. Bellows, L. B. Buchanan, & E. E. Saylor (Eds.). *(Re)imagining elementary social studies: A controversial issues reader* (pp. 153–176). Charlotte, NC: Information Age Press.

Saito, N. T. (2014). Tales of color and colonialism: Racial realism and settler colonial theory. *Florida A & M University Law Review, 10*(1), 1–107. Retrieved from http://commons.law.famu.edu/famulawreview/vol10/iss1/3.

Sconiers, Z., & Rosiek, J. (2000). Historical perspective as an important element of teacher knowledge: A sonata-form case study of equity issues in a chemistry classroom. *Harvard Educational Review, 70*(3), 370–404.

Shear, S. B., Knowles, R. T., Soden, G. J., & Castro, A. J. (2015). Manifesting destiny: Re/presentations of Indigenous peoples in K-12 U.S. history standards. *Theory & Research in Social Education, 43*(1), 68–101.

Shohat, E., & Stam, R. (2014). *Unthinking Eurocentrism: Multiculturalism and the media.* New York, NY: Routledge.

Shulman, L. (1986). Those who understand: Knowledge growth in teaching. *Educational Researcher, 15*(2), 4–14.

Shulman, L. (2004). Just in case: Reflections on learning from experience. In L. Shulman & S. M. Wilson (Eds.), *The wisdom of practice: Essays on teaching, learning, and learning to teach* (1st ed.) (pp. 463–482). San Francisco, CA: Jossey-Bass.

Simon, R. (1992). *Teaching against the grain: Texts for a pedagogy of possibility*. New York, NY: Bergin & Garvey.

Simpson, A. (2007). On ethnographic refusal: Indigeneity, "voice," and colonial citizenship. *Junctures*, 9, 67–80.

Simpson, L. B. (2015). The place where we all live and work together: A gendered analysis of 'sovereignty'. In S. N. Teves, A. Smith, & M. H. Raheja (Eds.), *Native studies keywords* (pp. 18–24). Tucson, AZ: The University of Arizona Press.

Smith, L. T. (2012). *Decolonizing methodologies: Research and indigenous peoples* (2nd ed.). London: Zed Books.

Solórzano, D. G. (1998). Critical race theory, race and gender microaggressions, and the experience of Chicana and Chicano scholars. *International Journal of Qualitative Studies in Education*, 11(1), 121–136.

Solórzano, D. G., & Bernal, D. D. (2001). Examining transformational resistance through a Critical Race and LatCrit Theory framework: Chicana and Chicano students in an urban context. *Urban Education*, 36(3), 308–342.

Solórzano, D. G., & Yosso, T. J. (2002). Critical race methodology: Counterstorytelling as an analytic framework for education research. *Qualitative Inquiry*, 8, 23–44.

Solórzano, D., Ceja, M., & Yosso, T. (2000). Critical race theory, racial microaggressions, and campus racial climate: The experiences of African American college students. *Journal of Negro Education*, 69(1), 60–73.

St. Denis, V. (2011). Silencing Aboriginal curricular content and perspectives through multiculturalism: "There are other children here". *Review of Education, Pedagogy, and Cultural Studies*, 33(4), 306–317.

Sterling, S. (1992). *My name is Seepeetza*. Toronto: Groundwood Books.

Sue, D. W., Capodilupo, C. M., Torino, G. C., Bucceri, J. M., Holder, A. M. B., Nadal, K. L., & Esquilin, M. (2007). Racial microaggressions in everyday life: Implications for clinical practice. *American Psychologist*, 62(4), 271–286.

TallMountain, M. (1987). You can go home again: A sequence. Retrieved from http://hhh.gavilan.edu/kwarren/mary1.htm.

Tejeda, C. (2008). Dancing with the dilemmas of a decolonizing pedagogy. *Radical History Review*, 2008(102), 27.

Teves, S., Smith, A., & Raheja, M. (2015). *Native studies keywords* (Critical Issues in Indigenous Studies). Tucson, AZ: University of Arizona Press.

Thornton, B., & Sanchez, J. E. (2010). Promoting resiliency among Native American students to prevent dropouts. *Education*, 131(2), 455–464.

Tribal Nations Education Committee. (2016). *Minnesota Tribes position on education*. Retrieved from www.tnecmn.com/uploads/3/7/9/5/37956795/tnec_2016_position_on_education.pdf.

Tuck, E. (2009). Suspending damage: A letter to communities. *Harvard Educational Review*, 79(3), 409–428.

Tuck, E., & McKenzie, M. (2015). *Place in research: Theory, methodology, and methods*. New York, NY: Routledge.

Tuck, E., & Yang, K. W. (2012). Decolonization is not a metaphor. *Decolonization: Indigeneity, Education and Society*, 1, 1–40.

Tuck, E., & Yang, K. W. (2014a). R-words: Refusing research. In D. Paris & M. T. Winn (Eds.), *Humanizing research: Decolonizing qualitative inquiry with youth and communities* (pp. 223–248). Thousand Oaks, CA: Sage.

Tuck, E., & Yang, K. (2014b). Unbecoming claims. *Qualitative Inquiry*, 20(6), 811–818.

U.S. Congress, Senate Committee on Labor Public Welfare. (1969). *Indian education: A national tragedy—A national challenge. 1969 Report of the Committee on Labor and Public Welfare, United States Senate, Made by its Special Subcommittee on Indian Education.* Washington, DC: Government Printing Office.

U.S. Census Bureau. (2010). American FactFinder. Retrieved from https://factfinder. census.gov/faces/nav/jsf/pages/index.xhtml.

U.S. Department of Education. (2008). *Indian Education: Formula grants to local education agencies.* Retrieved from https://www2.ed.gov/programs/indianformula/awards.html.

Urrieta, L., & Reidel, M. (2008). Citizenship normalizing and White preservice social studies teachers. *Social Justice*, 35(1), 91–108.

Valencia-Weber, G. (2004). Racial equality: Old and new strains and American Indians. *Notre Dame Law Review*, 80(1), 333–376. Retrieved from http://scholarship.law.nd.edu/ndlr/vol80/iss1/9.

Valenzuela, A. (1999). *Subtractive schooling: U.S.-Mexican youth and the politics of caring.* Albany, NY: State University of New York Press.

Vaught, S. E. (2011). *Racism, public schooling, and the entrenchment of White supremacy: A critical race ethnography.* Albany, NY: SUNY Press.

Vaught, S. E., & Castagno, A. E. (2008). "I don't think I'm a racist:" Critical Race Theory, teacher attitudes, and structural racism. *Race, Ethnicity and Education*, 11(2), 95–113.

Veracini, L. (2011a). Introducing settler colonial studies. *Settler Colonial Studies*, 1, 1–12.

Veracini, L. (2011b). On settlerness. *Borderlands e-journal*, 10(1), 1–17.

Veracini, L. (2011c). Telling the end of the settler colonial story. In F. Bateman & L. Pilkington (Eds.), *Studies in settler colonialism: Politics, identity and culture* (pp. 204–219). Basingstoke: Palgrave Macmillan.

Villegas, A. M., & Lucas, T. (2002). Preparing culturally responsive teachers: Rethinking the curriculum. *Journal of Teacher Education*, 53(1), 20–32.

Vizenor, G. R. (1990). *Crossbloods: Bone courts, bingo, and other reports.* Minneapolis, MN: University of Minnesota Press.

Vizenor, G. R. (1999). *Manifest manners: Narratives on postindian survivance.* Lincoln, NE: University of Nebraska Press.

Vizenor, G. R. (2007). *Literary chance: Essays on Native American survivance.* València: Universitat de València.

Vizenor, G. R. (Ed.). (2008). *Survivance: Narratives of Native presence.* Lincoln, NE:

Wilmore, L. (1998). First peoples first. *Poverty & Race*, 7(1), n.p.

Wilson, A. C. (2006). Burning down the house: Laura Ingalls Wilder and American colonialism. In D. T. Jacobs (Ed.), *Unlearning the language of conquest: Scholars expose anti-Indianism in America* (pp. 66–80). Austin, TX: University of Texas Press.

Wolfe, P. (2006). Settler-colonialism and the elimination of the native. *Journal of Genocide Research*, 8(4), 387–409.

Womack, C. (2008). Theorizing American Indian experience. In C. Womack, D. H. Justice, & C. B. Teuton (Eds.), *Reasoning together: The Native critics collective* (pp. 353–410). Norman, OK: University of Oklahoma Press.

Woman's Board of Home Missions of the Presbyterian Church. (1916). Editorial notes. *The Home Mission Monthly*, Vol. XXX, Issue 10, pp. 242–244.

PART I

Colonialism in the Classroom

The stories in this part all focus on moments of teaching and learning in classrooms. Read together, these three stories draw attention to dimensions of teacher professional knowledge that would help educators teach Indigenous students and Indigenous studies in responsible ways, while also calling into question the idea that such a knowledge base is discrete and that mastering it is attainable.

The first story, "Pilgrims and Invented Indians," begins when Zeik, a 2nd grade Native student, resists the classic settler Thanksgiving narrative of hardworking pilgrims and welcoming Indians. By documenting how Zeik courageously speaks up in class to address what he considers a stereotypical portrayal of Indians, this survivance story highlights the unnecessary pressures stereotypical representations place on young children. Moreover, this story demonstrates that Native students—even young children like Zeik who is only 7—often already have knowledge and experience to critique dominant representations of Indianness and challenge the discursive authority of texts. This survivance story also points to the subtler colonial discourses that could be difficult for young children to detect, such as the ways Eurocentrism tacitly permeates the curriculum. From this survivance story, teachers can infer essential concrete and conceptual knowledge about Native representations, history, and social studies orientations they must understand to better serve students like Zeik.

The next story, "Halloween Costumes and Native Identity," documents a high school Native youth group's organizing around issues of cultural appropriation, including a critical literacy activity in which students write a collaborative letter to Spirit Halloween store condemning their sale of Indian costumes. This story then follows one student as she attempts to bring her new knowledge on this topic to her classroom, only to be shut down by her teacher, Sharon, who doesn't understand "what the big deal is." While drawing attention to essential knowledge for teachers, this chapter also highlights how even Indigenous educators versed in Indigenous studies may also miss moments in the process of teaching and learning. By describing an educational moment that I missed when I didn't recognize a Native student's negative experiences with my own curriculum, this survivance story illuminates the pervasiveness of colonial discourses and how they can even distort understanding between Indigenous peoples, particularly around issues of identity and authenticity. Because students have keen insights into their own experiences, this survivance story suggests teachers should provide avenues for students to give them feedback. Further, this story proposes caring and ongoing relationships with students as a form of accountability for the inevitable moments we miss as teachers.

The final story in this part, "Native Sheroes and Complex Personhood," builds on the themes of identity and authenticity. This survivance story describes a Native student's experience with a social studies unit in which she has the opportunity to research a contemporary Native leader. While highlighting the promising pathways this curriculum offered her to learn about a Native shero and bring her own cultural identity into the classroom, this story also draws attention to the complexity of Indigenous identity. By describing how this young, culturally confident, light-skinned student grapples with how to appear "Native" for the final project, the story makes apparent the ways the normalization of whiteness places an unfair burden on Indigenous students.

This survivance story illustrates why educators must not only pursue concrete and conceptual forms of knowledge, but also relational and political commitments to disrupting dominant discourses that constrain Indigenous students' well-being and educational opportunities in schools.

1

PILGRIMS AND INVENTED INDIANS

It was November, a time when most elementary curricula in this district included Thanksgiving-themed curricula and units on Pilgrims and Indians, when I spoke with Zeik, a Native student involved in the district's Title VI/Indian Education program. Zeik relayed an experience he had in his second grade classroom. His teacher, Ms. Billings, had organized a unit on the Mayflower and his class was learning about Pilgrims. Zeik shared that Ms. Billings read a book to the class about Pilgrims and he didn't like the pictures of Native Americans that were included. He recounted the images, which included a Native man with a painted face, and another of a Native man with feathers in his hair. Zeik told me that he raised his hand in class and said to his teacher, "Not all Native people wear feathers. That is only for Chiefs who earned it. And painting your face is for special times."

Whether Zeik knew that the nonspecific "Indians" he saw in the book were likely Wampanoag people is unclear. Knowledge of tribal diversity is often an effective base from which to critique generic representations of Indians. If Zeik had such knowledge, it did not come from his teacher as she had not heard of the Wampanoag people until our interview. Regardless, Zeik spoke from his own base of experience which was enough to disrupt hegemonic constructions of Indianness offered as official knowledge by his teacher.

"I'm Not an Indian": Invented Indians and Dehumanization

Zeik's commentary in class, though brief, reflected what Ojibwe scholar Scott Lyons (2000) terms *rhetorical sovereignty*, "the inherent right and ability of peoples[1] to determine their own communicative needs and desires in the pursuit of self-determination ..." (p. 462). As Lyons continues, "rhetorical sovereignty requires above all the presence of an Indian voice, speaking or writing in an ongoing context of colonization and setting at least some of the terms of debate" (p. 462). Zeik was setting at least some of the terms of debate in his classroom. Zeik mediated the curricular space, carving out classroom space for himself and his humanity. His words also challenged the discursive authority of his teacher's text. His observation "not all Native people wear feathers" not only contested the curricular representations offered to him, but also revealed the partial and constructed nature of the text. Rather than letting the selective processes of curricular erasure, silence, and misrepresentations go undetected, Zeik's interjection destabilized the dominant discourse by implying other possibilities than what he and his classmates were presented.

At the age of 7, Zeik probably wasn't aware his words were doing all this work. When I asked Zeik why he chose to speak up, Zeik commented that he "just didn't like the pictures." For Zeik, the images of the Indians in the book must have been a stark contrast to his daily experiences with actual Native people who looked, according to him, "just sort of normal." It's not that Zeik never saw Native people dressed in feathers or with their faces painted. He had been to many pow wows and other Native community gatherings. Zeik's comment that feathers are "earned" and "painting your face is for special times" suggested to me that he understood particular aspects of the pictures as more than inherently stereotypical markers, and instead part of a cultural and community context in which those items have particular meanings.

I also learned that Zeik had a particular distaste for the word Indian, a referent repeated throughout the book. It's not that Zeik never heard the word Indian either. Indian was frequently used in the Longhouse and Native community and the Title VI program Zeik was involved in was often called the "Indian Education Program." Yet for Zeik, the word Indian also had a negative connotation. Perhaps it was because his family primarily used their tribal affiliation or the word Native, or because the Indian Education Program, despite the official title, frequently used "Native" in its programming (e.g., Native Youth Group, Native Youth Center). Either way, Zeik didn't like that the book the class read that day used the term:

> I don't like being called an Indian. I'm not an Indian. I'm a Native American. It's like being called a girl gets annoying [because of his long ponytail], but being called an Indian gets *really* annoying. Being called an Indian kind of messes with who I am. They use Indian and make them look not smart and I'm Native American and I'm smart. So when they call me Indian they're kinda trying to say I'm not smart.

At the age of 7, Zeik had already experienced and could detect a hostile climate, one in which people try to make Indians look "not smart." Zeik wasn't a victim—*Zeik saw himself as Native American and smart*—but he didn't identify with the Indian that "kind of messes with" who he is. Zeik's rejection of the term Indian was an act of self-care, mirroring a similar act by James Baldwin (1998) relayed in a reflection on his own upbringing in a hostile climate:

> In order for me to live, I decided very early that some mistake had been made somewhere … I had to realize when I was very young that I was none of those things I was told I was. I was not, for example, happy. I never touched a watermelon for all kinds of reasons. I had been invented by white people, and I knew enough about life by this time to understand that whatever you invent, whatever you project, is you! (p. 682)

Like Baldwin, Zeik rejected the imposition of this invention. He didn't identify with the ways he felt some people were trying to make him look or feel. Zeik's comment reminded me of someone else who had a particular distaste for the word *indian*. [2] Anishinaabe scholar Gerald Vizenor (2014) states,

> My argument about Indians all along has been that we just have to change the name, the actual language of reference. Leave the inventions of the Indian to the people who created it, and then we can easily humiliate them for their silly behavior. They invented an Indian, an image that makes them feel good, or not. The invented name, in my view, has nothing to do with Natives … I created the word *postindian*, a theoretical language and a new idea so that people could say, "No, I'm not Indian, but if you insist, you could say I'm *postindian* because I'm not the Indian that's been invented for popular culture. I came after the invention, and the invention is not me. I'm a young person. I'm not obligated to all that stuff. I didn't participate in it. I'm not an invented Indian, but if you like, you could say I'm *postindian*. I'm a different kind of person imagining myself after the popular cultural indulgence in the invented Indian." (p. 111)

Like Vizenor, Zeik was aware that the Indian in the book was a simulation. Such awareness reflected the "double consciousness," or sense of seeing himself "through the eyes of others" (Du Bois, 1961, p. 17), Native students often have as a result of navigating society's misperceptions. Zeik's teacher, lacking such an awareness, unwittingly reproduced invented Indians as curriculum and negatively impacted Zeik's educational experience.

As with Vizenor, names and language for Zeik were also as a site of resistance. When asked what he prefers as a self-referent, Zeik said his tribal affiliation or Native American. Zeik told me another story, however, that indicated he had already understood the issue at hand was more complex than semantics, more than a matter of merely swapping terms:

> My teacher one time asked [the class] "What do you do when you have a problem?" and I raised my hand and said I try to fly high above my problems

like an eagle and [the girl] next to me said "That's such an Indian thing to say." ... So I guess if she said that's such a Native American thing to say, I'd feel a little better, but not really.

Zeik understood that his peer's statement communicated more than the particular word she chose to use. Whether she had said Indian or Native American, Zeik recognized that he still wouldn't have liked what she was trying to tell him. Zeik's awareness and experiences complicate one of the first questions I am often asked in professional development and teacher education courses that I offer: "What is the appropriate term to use: Native American or American Indian?"

Educators should seek out respectful terms, which likely include the names of specific tribal nations or bands within their region, while also recognizing intergenerational or cultural diversity within usage. Educators should also appreciate the political and social significance terms such as Indigenous, Native American, or American Indian can wield as they attempt to address a base of collective experiences with respect to land, people, and colonization; however, they should also recognize the inadequacy, even the risk, inherent in any term that collapses the rich geographic, political, linguistic, cultural, and spiritual diversity of Indigenous peoples. Zeik may not have recognized all of this at the age of 7, but he *could* detect the complexity of a context in which a semantic swap would not have redressed the harmful dynamics he had experienced. Such awareness by a 7-year-old complicates the initial question many teachers often ask.

Good Teachers with Bad Curriculum

In a later interview with Ms. Billings, she recounted the story as Zeik had told it, explicitly praising Zeik for his insight and courage to speak up in class, a supportive attitude that not all teachers express when their curricular choices are questioned. She stated that she had planned on saying something similar to the class about the images in the book, that this was a historic piece and not all Native people look like that today, but that Zeik had "beat her to the punch." She also shared that her teacher preparation program had trained her to use a "multiple perspectives" approach and "critically" examine the perspective underlying a resource (including what she termed a "white man's perspective"). As she spoke, I struggled to make sense of the gap between her professed theory and actual practice, wondering how she could recognize the need to critically interrogate curriculum, while simultaneously using a book based on generic Indians. On the surface, Ms. Billings was articulating a theory of critical pedagogy (Freire, 1970), and a critical multicultural analytic practice of reading within, across, and beyond the texts (Botelho, Young, & Nappi, 2014). She also named whiteness as influencing curriculum with a frankness that many white elementary teachers I worked with could (or would) not; yet naming whiteness didn't lead to detecting the textbook's construction of generic Indians as a construction of whiteness, what Berkhofer (1979) terms "the white man's Indian."

Ms. Billings admitted the curriculum she used often had flaws, but believed having critical conversations about the texts is important, perhaps even more important for students than spending time trying to find the most accurate books. On some level I shared her sentiment that all students, particularly Native students, should develop a critical relationship with curricula since entire domains of knowledge—science, English, social studies, etc.—have been rooted in Eurocentric philosophies and values. But then, Ms. Billing seamlessly reverted to the position many teachers I have worked with in the district take, and expressed the difficulty she has finding good curriculum. This position is always difficult to understand, upsetting even, given the wealth of resources I knew to be available to teachers.

To be fair, teachers have immense pressures on their time. Ms. Billings routinely, however, demonstrates that she goes above and beyond for her students in many other ways. For example, in a Title I school with increasing mandates to standardize curriculum, Ms. Billings still manages to teach project-based science units on catapults, create space for music weekly, and take students to see plays. Zeik loves his teacher, and rightfully so; she is caring, energetic, engaging, and committed. The recurring response that finding better resources is too difficult seems to reflect then, not just a gap in knowledge, but tacit resistance or unwillingness to looking, even an unexpressed desire to remain a "perfect stranger" (Dion, 2008) to Indigenous realities. This position appears to justify and uphold "business as usual" (Castagno & Brayboy, 2008, p. 981) approaches to Indigenous education that have persisted for decades. Further, these comments illustrate that being a "good teacher" in this district doesn't necessarily require an ability to detect bias and Eurocentrism in the curriculum.[3]

As a scholar of Indigenous education, but also as a parent of two Native children in the district, it is upsetting that "good teachers" and "good teaching" continues to be defined in ways that encompass considerable knowledge gaps about Indigenous histories, politics, perspectives, or contemporary issues, making it difficult to support Native students specifically. These "commonsensical" definitions to good teaching perpetuate, rather than challenge, "the oppressive status quo of schools and society" (Kumashiro, 2015, p. 1). Ms. Billings' inability to detect hegemonic constructions of Indianness impeded the dexterity she needed as a teacher to work against colonialism's varied mechanisms. Regardless of her intentions, her curricular decisions positioned Zeik in a way that required him to withstand the bias he found in the curriculum, or to do extra work educating his peers and his teacher, illustrating the everyday colonialism and "racial microaggressions" (Solórzano, 1998; Sue et al., 2007) Native students face in schools. This was not a critique of Ms. Billings as an individual; numerous teachers I had been referred to as good teachers in the district lacked such awareness. Ms. Billings is not the problem per se, but instead the symptom of a system of public schooling and teacher education in which teachers graduate socially unprepared to respond to Indigenous students or issues specifically. The pervasiveness of this socialized unpreparedness reflects a "systemic racial *macro*aggression" (Matias & Liou, 2015) that practically conditions teachers to inflict such microaggressions in their classrooms. Though the particular actions, orientations, and oversights of Ms. Billings reflects individual illiteracy or ignorance of these issues, such ignorance is also systemic and collective.

Benevolent Conquest and Other Ways Eurocentrism Permeates Curriculum

After Ms. Billings showed me the book—a National Geographic book titled *Pilgrims of Plymouth* (Goodman, 2001)—I could see why Zeik spoke up. On the pages he was concerned about, an Indian stood dressed in buckskin and furs, his hair in a mohawk, a red cross painted across his face. He stood stoically next to a Pilgrim. Both were standing in front of a log cabin, posing, the Pilgrim standing in the doorway, the Indian standing with his foot resting on the bench outside. The images weren't necessarily inaccurate; perhaps they were even accurate, historicized portrayals of Wampanoag life at the time (however, the routine use of the generic label "Indian" instead of "Wampanoag" spoke against such specificity). To Zeik, however, these represented narrow images and terms that he had already had hurtful experiences with and felt compelled to address. What concerned me, however, was not the mohawk, buckskin, or face paint, but the caption above: "The Pilgrims got help from their Indian neighbors" (Goodman, 2001, p. 10). Although the representation was disconcerting, I was more concerned with the "settler grammars" (Calderón, 2014b) that positioned the Indians as colonization's helping hand, a problematic colonial pattern of moving "right from the landing to friendly relationships" (Reese, 2008, p. 64). Even if the narrative didn't blatantly misrepresent Native peoples, it nonetheless positioned them in very specific ways to the Pilgrim protagonists, naturalizing the constructedness of the narrative as "given" and rendering invisible alternative challenges to narrative authority.

My concern grew steadily. On the next page, another Indian was kneeling down next to a Pilgrim in a field, a feather dangling from his long, flowing hair, dutifully showing him how to grow corn. Above them was an image showing Pilgrims and Indians trading tools and fur, while the image alongside showcased a lone Indian sitting upright in a canoe, helping the Pilgrims find the best places to fish. Again, I was struck, not by the feather in the young man's hair, nor the Indian in buckskin in the canoe, but the narrative:

> The Pilgrims traded with the Indians. They gave the Indians tools and cloth. They got animal furs in return. The Indians showed the Pilgrims the best places to fish. They also taught them how to grow corn. (Goodman, 2001, p. 11)

The images and narrative portrayed a "benevolent conquest ... rendering colonization a natural and desired process of the domination by a superior civilization over primitive, inferior peoples" (Furniss, 1999, p. 187). In this benign portrayal of mutually helpful relationships, the fact that many of the colonists viewed the Indians as savages or heathens in need of civilizing or conversion was erased. It's not that I expected detailed accounts of "white man's savagery" (Parker, 1916, p. 261). As James Loewen (1998) notes, "The antidote to feel good history is not feel-bad history," but it is at least "honest and inclusive" (p. 80). Zeik deserved honesty. So did his peers.

Flipping to the next page, a detailed image of a Pilgrim settlement was spread across two pages that included a fenced garden with various vegetables and herbs. One man carried a bale of hay while another man tipped his hat to a Pilgrim woman as she wheeled her wheelbarrow. Everywhere in the photo there were busy Pilgrims working in the garden and in the fields, chopping wood and building fences. There were no Indians represented on this page for young Zeik to contest: no feathers, no fur, no face paint to critique. Yet *this* two-page layout as opposed to the prior two was what I found most troubling, violent even. Underneath this image of bustling Pilgrim life was a caption: "The Pilgrims worked hard and their settlement grew" (Goodman, 2001, pp. 12–13). Such passive language effectively erased the active dispossession through disease, encroachment, and colonial violence that made that growth and settlement possible, and overlooked Indigenous resistance to what was, for some, unwanted growth in Patuxet.

While the book framed the Pilgrim's landing in Plymouth as the beginning of the story and history in that area, much had already happened on the lands that were to become the Pilgrim's "new home." The village had a name, Patuxet, before it was renamed Plymouth by the colonists. There was also a thriving community there before a plague, thought to be yellow fever, devastated the community. And numerous Native people had already been abducted and captured nearby. One Wampanoag man, Epanow, had already been captured from the town of Nope in 1611 and infamously outwitted his captor, Captain Edward Harlow, by convincing the captain he knew where to find gold in his homeland and then escaping. Twenty-seven Wampanoag men, including Tsiquantum (who came to be known as Squanto), were captured by Captain Thomas Hunt from Patuxet and Nauset in 1614.[4] But this history of violence and resistance was erased, and the erasure continued as specific Indigenous communities were generically named Indians, and eventually erased from the story altogether.

The omissions and language in the book anesthetized that context of violence, language that historian Howard Zinn (1995) notes is "not a technical necessity, but an ideological choice"; language that "serves—unwittingly to justify what was done" (p. 8). This image representing the industriousness of the Pilgrims and the passive growth of the settlement troubled me most because the Indians were absent, ghosts (Tuck & Ree, 2013), positioned as victims of their own demise, "coincidentally" in the same time and space as the peaceful Pilgrims. With Indigenous peoples no longer in the story, the narrative subtly shifted from one that acknowledged settler-Indigenous contact to one that suggested the area was now "putatively 'settled' and 'postcolonial'" (Veracini, 2011, p. 3). Beyond misinformation, this text was actively *producing* the very ignorance (Calderón, 2011) that made it difficult to read the erasures it contained. A benign settlement and relationship was being constructed during what was a tumultuous time for Native peoples, and actual Native peoples were displaced, establishing Pilgrims as the new natives (Calderón, 2014b).

Zeik already had community experiences and knowledge from which to challenge narrow or stereotypical representations in the curricula, some of which stemmed from important educational counterspaces (Solórzano et al. 2000; Yosso et al. 2009) such as the Title VI program, or his participation in family or community events. Nonetheless, as a 7-year old child, he was vulnerable to Eurocentric narratives offered through mainstream curriculum: narratives that attempted to instill in him a "settler land ethic and identity" (Calderón, 2014a p. 91). He would need more than a critique of the way images of Native people were represented in curricula to resist internalizing the Eurocentric narratives reproduced in his school as official knowledge. Schools need to stop teaching *all* children such problematic "historical myths" (Levstik & Barton, 2015). As Agarwal-Rangnath (2013) states, "When studying history, we must see, hear, and feel the contributions, resistance, and actions of all those who have contributed to our society and world" (p. 40). But for young Native children, the stakes are higher. At stake were missed opportunities for these students to learn about the courageous resistance, continuance, and contributions of their ancestors and other Indigenous peoples. Indigenous voices and perspectives are often "glossed over or minimized in current textbooks," denying Native students the opportunity to "feel empowered and motivated to make change in [their] own communities as [they] learn how [their] ancestors fought for their freedoms and resisted oppression and discrimination" (Agarwal-Rangnath, 2013, p. 40). Moreover, these narratives position young Native children to potentially internalize settler colonial framings that are premised on and further contribute to their own erasure. While on the surface the exclusion of Native perspectives might appear to be bias by omission, positioning Native students to regurgitate colonizers' accounts of history is a profound act of attempted indoctrination and assimilation.

I thought about the harm that could result from the curricular orientation, as well as the missed opportunities. The issue was not only a matter of inaccurate Indigenous representation, though the curriculum should attend to specific Indigenous peoples rather than generic Indians, which in this case might include the Patuxet, Nauset, Mashpee, or other bands of Wampanoag peoples. Rather, the issue was also with the framing upon which the curriculum rested. This unit was clearing "facing West" (Richter, 2001), a story of adventure and determination rooted in a "frontier myth" of exploration, discovery, encounter, and eventual settlement (Furniss, 1999). The Indians in the story were a footnote to English settler progress, an "adjunct to Colonial history" (Agoglia, 1993, p. 6). What if, instead, the unit had faced East (Richter, 2001)? What if Ms. Billings had employed a curricular standpoint (Au, 2012) that foreground the voices, experiences, perspectives, and histories of Indigenous peoples?

Curricular Standpoints can Counter Eurocentrism

A curricular standpoint is not an inclusive, "multiple perspectives" approach that elides questions of power or sociopolitical context (Botelho, Young, & Nappi, 2014), but an approach that explicitly aims to denaturalize and unsettle Eurocentric narratives of progress and expansion that often tacitly frame curricula. Curricular standpoint draws from a legacy of feminist scholarship that argues the standpoints[5] of those marginalized by stratified social systems have a clearer vantage point from which to understand them. Thus, privileging "the standpoint of the least advantaged," which in this case, means "think[ing] through race relations and land questions from the standpoint of indigenous people" (Connell, as cited in Au, 2012, p. 60), is not just a matter of responsibility, but also accuracy as standpoints produce *clearer* insights into social reality (Au, 2012). Educators must, however, question the ways "Indigenous standpoints" might also be complicated by feminist analyses and women's gendered experiences with colonialism (Moreton-Robinson, 2013; Sabzalian, 2018).

Had Ms. Billings employed a curricular standpoint, the focus of the unit would not be on "exploration" or "discovery," but on Wampanoag perspectives of life, land, and the subsequent "encroachment" and "invasion" of their territory. And had she taken up a Native feminist curricular standpoint, she might also have focused on girl's/women's experiences of that era, or their routine erasure or misrepresentation within history. Students could have learned about the kidnapping of young Matoaka (better known as Pocahontas), and explored the continued mis/representation of Pocahontas today—representation, that Green (1975) argues, is carefully filtered through colonial ideologies, placing Indigenous women "between a rock and a hard place" (p. 713) by emphasizing either "her nobility as a Princess and her savagery as a Squaw," both of which "are defined in terms of her relationships with male figures" (p. 703). Students could also have learned of Indigenous women's role in diplomacy and treaty making, such as Pamunkey tribal leader Cockacoesce who negotiated with English settlers in Jamestown, and who was "an uncommonly astute politician, wily negotiator, and staunch defender of her homeland" (Sonneborn, 1998, p. 31).

In light of curricular standpoint theory, the silences and omissions in the curricula become not only inaccurate, but also irresponsible. Indigenous peoples in their initial encounters often *did* welcome settlers, share their food and resources, and teach them how to survive. Yet in nearly every instance, settlers' desires for land and resources strained these diplomatic relationships. This was true in the early 1600s when, despite Chief Powhatan Wahunsenaca's initial hospitality toward settlers in Jamestown, English colonists' thirst for land and minerals to export back to England led to social tensions and violence (Custalow & Daniel, 2007). It remained true in 1621 when Sachem Ousamequin, commonly known as Massasoit, signed the Wampanoag Peace Treaty with settler colonists, a treaty that was violated as settlers continued to expand their territories beyond the boundaries of Patuxet (Plymouth) that Massasoit and English settlers had agreed to earlier.

A curricular standpoint would have placed Massasoit's diplomacy with English settlers seeking mutual peace and protection not only within the context of threats from Native nations like the Narragansett, but also within a stream of earlier settler violence which included the capture and enslavement of Native peoples. A curricular standpoint also wouldn't have ended the story with the Wampanoag people helping the settlers, but continued the story by acknowledging tensions that arose when settler livestock practices threatened Indigenous agriculture or when settler expansion led to tense relations between Indigenous peoples and settlers. The curriculum wouldn't have overlooked the "praying towns" that were later established to assimilate Indigenous peoples to white religious ways, and that this, coupled with settler encroachment into Pequot territory fueled the Pequot war and eventually Metacomet's (also known as King Phillip's) War. And the curriculum would have foreground Pequot perspectives on such events, such as William Apess who argued that in 1620,

> ... the pilgrims landed at Plymouth, and without asking liberty from any one they possessed themselves a portion of the country, and built themselves houses, and made a treaty, and commanded them to accede to it. This, if now done, would be called an insult, and every white man would be called to go out and act the part of a patriot, to defend their country's rights. (Apess & O'Connell, 1992, p. 280)

Perhaps some of these silences and omissions were due to a lack of information. Maybe it is too much to expect elementary educators, especially those teachers of the younger grades, to have such detailed historical knowledge, especially given the breadth of material they are expected to cover. Or perhaps the omissions were purposeful. A teacher might feel that it isn't age-appropriate for 7-year-olds to learn of the capture and enslavement of Native people prior to the Mayflower, or the 700 men, women, and children who were killed or enslaved in the years following the story. Yet given the sanitized narratives and Eurocentric ideologies that were taught, learning of overt settler violence felt less violent to me than subjecting Native children to accounts that privilege the colonizer's story. Colonized and colonizing histories are also not age-appropriate. As Agoglia (1993) noted in her work with seven- and eight-year olds, "Historical bias, prejudice, and racism are not topics to be reserved for older children" (p. 8). Educators needn't expose children to gruesome violence, but with skill could employ standpoints that were not only more honest, but more capable of helping *all students* understand the world "more fully" (Au, 2012, p. 69).

There are numerous resources to support curriculum to counter frontier myths and settler narratives of expansion which could vary in content and character.[6] What if, for example, Ms Billings had taken an emotional rather than informational approach to the content. What if, grounded in a curricular standpoint (Au, 2012), she had provided emotional scaffolding (Rosiek, 2003) for students to understand Indigenous experiences and perspectives. Doing so would not only denaturalize the hegemonic assumption that Eurocentric accounts of history are the sole and true account, but might also invite socioemotional connections to the content: What would it have *felt* like to live on lands that strangers invaded, desired, and stole? A story in the book *Thanksgiving: A Native Perspective* (Seale, Slapin, & Silverman, 1998) takes such an approach. The story asks students to imagine playing freely in their own house and backyard when suddenly,

> a strange object comes slowly into view in the sky. You've never seen anything like it before. It is a strange shape and very large. It lands in your own back yard! Soon very strange-looking people get out; they are dressed in clothes different from yours and talk to each other in a way that you cannot understand. (p. 62)

The story continues, with guided questions asking students to reflect how they would feel seeing people rummaging through their stuff, helping themselves to the food in their garden, and later, building a house in their backyard. Though an admittedly "simplistic" and "melodramatic" activity, the curriculum writers wanted to challenge the routine Eurocentric orientation of expansion and invasion and supplant romanticized activities (Seale, Slapin, & Silverman, 1998).

Supporting students' emotional connections to Indigenous peoples can support inquiry-based approaches to social studies that recognizes the interpretive nature of history and the need to understand multiple perspectives (NCSS, 2013). Moreover, supporting children's emotional connections to other children in history can foster historical thinking skills (Levstik & Barton, 2015). But there are limits to such an approach. Fostering emotional connections might unwittingly individualize structural patterns and practices, possibly leading to what critical race theorists refer to as "false empathy" (Delgado, 1996; Duncan, 2002; Vaught, 2011). The history of white paternalism and maternalism in this country is rooted in such superficial feelings and sympathy, most evident in the practice creating federal Indian boarding schools as a means of "caring" for Indigenous peoples as a more benign intervention than outright violent warfare. Nevertheless, such an orientation might have provided students with an emotional connection with which to identify with the warranted suspicion, fear, and betrayal Indigenous peoples likely felt when settler colonizers first came to New England.

To be clear, Ms. Billings' curriculum *did* provide students with opportunities for emotional connection, however those opportunities were aimed at understanding and empathizing with the plight and humanity of the Pilgrims, reflecting a tendency in children's literature to "readily report Pilgrims' misfortunes" and ignore "Native Americans' calamities" (Bickford III & Rich, 2015, p. 13). These weren't just omissions; they were also constructions. Focusing solely on the difficulties the Pilgrims' faced, even tacitly, served to justify their entitlement to Indigenous lands. Portraying the Pilgrims as those who faced and fled religious persecution but in America could finally "pray in their own way" (Goodman, 2001, p. 3), or portraying the Pilgrims as a homeless, but industrious, people functions to humanize the Pilgrims as well as justify settlement and Indigenous dispossession. These narratives communicated that the Pilgrims were deserving of the right to build "a new home in America" (p. 3), an approach that reflects a pattern in curricula in which "Whites continue to receive the most attention and appear in the widest variety of roles, dominating story lines and lists of accomplishments" (Sleeter, 2011, p. 2). The danger in this narrative, echoing Wahpetunwan Dakota scholar Waziyatawin Angela Cavender Wilson's (2006) critique of *Little House on the Prairie*, is that

> ... the whites in the story are glorified. One of the most dangerous aspects of the book, therefore, is the extent to which the reader develops an affinity with and adoration of the white characters in the story. (p. 72)

Similar to the affinity fostered with the Ingalls family, it is the connection to the humanity of the Pilgrim settlers that is nurtured, an approach emphasized on the last page. Three Pilgrim children hold hands, smiling at the reader beneath a caption that reads, "The Pilgrims were real people, just like us" (Goodman, 2001, p. 16). It felt ironic that the book used "real people," a referent many Indigenous peoples use to distinguish ourselves from the rest of our relations in the world. But this wasn't intended with irony; instead, it affirmed Pilgrim humanity, and framed the Indians in the story as "just another part of the 'natural forces' against which the white settlers had to persevere" (Miller, 2005, p. 222). An intentional effort to foster students' emotional connections with Indigenous communities might have challenged the presumed "us" that was latently and explicitly referred to in this book.

I also considered the value of situating the curriculum within a context of contemporary relationships and issues. Wampanoag peoples, far from a footnote in history, are diverse and thriving. The Mashpee Wampanoag Tribe and the Wampanoag Tribe of Gay Head (also known as the Aquinnah) are both federally recognized Native nations in Massachusetts with thousands of tribal members enrolled between the two nations. What if the story started with the premise of Wampanoag survival, a stance that would disrupt the narrative arc of progress that tacitly implies Wampanoag people have vanished? What if students also explored Wampanoag efforts to rewrite history?

Wamsutta (Frank B.) James, an Aquinnah Wampanoag elder, attempted to do such a thing in 1970 when asked to speak in Plymouth at the 350th anniversary of the voyage; however, his speech, which criticized the mythology of the benign Pilgrim-Indian narrative, was suppressed, never to be given publicly. And since that day, Native people have organized at Plymouth each Thanksgiving Day to the holiday as a National Day of Mourning. Each year, the United American Indians of New England (UAINE) commemorate a Day of Mourning as a "solemn, spiritual, and highly political day" (UAINE, 2016). Oftentimes, the day is also dedicated to contemporary Indigenous political struggles. Even a brief glance at the UAINE website, would communicate to students an important message:

> We Are Not Vanishing.
> We Are Not Conquered.
> We Are As Strong As Ever. (UAINE, 2016)

By learning how some Indigenous peoples continue to observe Thanksgiving as a National Day of Mourning, students would be invited to reexamine the legacy of Plymouth, not as a narrative of "encounter" or American Progress, but as "a site of conscience," "a place of memory—such as a historic site, place-based museum or memorial—that prevents this erasure from happening in order to ensure a more just and humane future" (International Coalition of Sites of Conscience, 2017). Though not officially declared as a site of conscience, student inquiry into UAINE efforts to revisit Plymouth each year to contest their disappearance and victimization could contest Indigenous disappearance often implicit in curriculum, and support students in recognizing Indigenous survivance today.

In an effort to learn about Wampanoag presence today, students could also explore an online exhibit created by Plymouth 400, an organization based in Massachusetts whose purpose is to create interactive exhibits that examine how events, such as the Mayflower voyage of 1620, shaped America. In so doing, students would not only learn about Indigenous peoples today, but also about the diversity of perspectives within Indigenous communities. Working toward a 400-year commemoration of the voyage, the organization's aim is to "highlight the cultural contributions and American traditions that began with the interaction of the Wampanoag and English peoples, a story that significantly shaped the building of America" (Plymouth 400: 1620–2020, n.p.). Plymouth 400 has explicitly sought Wampanoag involvement in the project through an exhibit entitled "Our" Story: 400 Years of Wampanoag History. However, some Wampanoag citizens and tribal leaders have been hesitant to participate, some even refusing. Students could inquire into the legitimate reasons for hesitancy or refusal, while also exploring why some Wampanoag people, such as Paula Peters (Mashpee Wampanoag), have felt participation is important. Peters produced the first chapter in "Our" Story, "Captured: 1614," which commemorates and details the capture of 27 Wampanoag people from Patuxet and Nauset. Students could watch a video from the exhibit which provides historical context for the unit and foregrounds Indigenous perspectives on an often-overlooked historical event.

Inviting contemporary Indigenous perspectives is often an effective way of challenging dominant discourse. Another short film from the exhibit, "Message Runner," details "how members of the Tribe were chosen, based upon their endurance and their capacity for memory, to run to neighboring villages and territories to deliver essential messages" ("Our" Story, 2015). This film follows a runner who is asked by an important Sachem (leader) at Marshpaug (Mashpee) to carry a message 40 miles to the village of Patuxet (Plymouth). The film traces the Native villages the runner passes along the way, following him through the forests of Kitteaumut (Cataumet) and Comassakumkait (Herring Pond), the grasses of Shawme (Bourne), and along the sandy coastline until he arrives in Patuxet. Upon arriving, he opens the package to find a cell phone with a text message from the Wampanoag which reads "WE ARE STILL HERE!" (Plymouth 400 Inc., 2015). This video documents the important role runners have played in Wampanoag society, speaks to the diversity of Indigenous peoples and lands in that region, teases the audience by juxtaposing primitive discourses with modern technologies, and disrupts colonial narratives by asserting ongoing Wampanoag presence.

A Curriculum of Colonial Myths

Given what I knew of Ms. Billings exceptional teaching in other ways, I had a hard time understanding her unremarkable approach to this particular unit. While this approach is commonplace in elementary schools, I have seen the consequences of these units in my preservice teacher education courses in which I educate students who participated in similar units in their elementary schooling. I have witnessed these future teachers' sense of betrayal and disappointment upon learning the Eurocentric (even fictional) basis of such curriculum, or their frustration with the burden of unlearning historical myths and reorienting themselves to the history they will soon teach. Why, given the access to more accurate historical information, would teachers continue to reproduce such simplistic and inaccurate narratives as curriculum?

At a deeper, societal level I knew the answer: schools *have* to keep telling these myths. These myths hold society up and make the United States possible. The symbolic weight of the Mayflower voyage and the industriousness of the Pilgrims, as it is repeated and rehearsed in schools, has a strong social currency, the narrative linked to the "creation and re-creation of [American] national identity" (Furniss, 1999, p. 187). "I told the Thanksgiving story every day that week [of Thanksgiving]" said Helen Simmerer, a mission teacher on the Navajo reservation in 1916, "and how they enjoyed it! I was so glad that that part of history shows such a friendly relation between the white man and the Indian. Did you ever think what a splendid mission story is that part about Squanto, who hoped he could go to the white man's heaven?" (p. 237).

One hundred years later, these myths continue to function as a form soothing and justifying conquest, settlement, and expansion, part of broader system of "elaborate track-covering" that Tuck and Gaztambide-Fernández (2013) argue attempts "to resolve the uncomfortable and precarious dis-location as usurper, and replace the Indigenous people as the natural, historical, rightful and righteous owners of the land" (p. 77). In this sense, schools practically function as the nation-state's public relations department, authorizing and legitimating particular versions of the nation's origin story. This "tradition of remembering," or "mnemonic socialization" (Zerubavel, 1996), socializes patterns of remembering and forgetting that further US nationalism and undermine "Indigenous peoples' histories, experiences, and realities" (Gray, 2011 p. 12). As Cheyenne/Hodulgee Muscogee scholar Susan Shown Harjo notes of the common mythology taught around the Pilgrims' voyage, it's as if "when the Pilgrims arrived they were dragging land behind them [laughter] ... There was no land brought here, the land here was Native nations'" (National Museum of the American Indian, 2015). Truly recognizing the latter half of her statement and teaching beyond these myths would shatter the veneer of entitlement and superiority that have held settler claims to land in place for all these years. And as current debates, tensions, even bans on Mexican American Studies and ethnic studies curriculum show, teaching against the grain of these myths is often viewed as dangerous and met with profound resistance.

Ms. Billings probably could have refused to teach the Pilgrim-Indian myth altogether. There is nothing in the Oregon State Content Standards (2011) or the new Common Core standards that obliged her to teach about the Mayflower or Pilgrims specifically. There is plenty of room within the Common Core standards to embed critical social studies content within literacy activities (Agarwal-Rangnath, 2013). Moreover, the College, Career, and Civic Life (C3) Framework for Social Studies (2013), for example, draws specific attention to the idea that "History is interpretive," and that "Historical understanding requires recognizing this multiplicity of points of view in the past, which makes it important to seek out a range of sources on any historical question rather than simply use those that are easiest to find" (NCSS, 2013, p. 47). Yet the momentum behind these myths is powerful. The stubbornness of the Pilgrims and Indians narrative appears routine, not required, a socialized ideological choice, not a standardized policy directive. These myths circulate and recirculate with the subtle discursive power of commonsense, motivated perhaps by a latent desire to sidestep this nation's unconscionable origins. Ms. Billings told me this was the unit that her teaching team had always taught, and so perhaps she felt obliged as a newer member of the team. Yet her participation in this myth-making process is not an exception; it is the norm in this district. That Zeik had also learned about the Mayflower earlier in first grade, and *again* in third grade, spoke not just of the persistence, but of the pervasiveness of this myth-making and maintenance.

Zeik's Survivance Story: Color Me Pilgrim

Several weeks later, after the unit had culminated, Zeik showed me the completed packet he had worked on at school. On the cover was a brightly colored Mayflower ship. Inside were several worksheets from a Scholastic book called *50 Month-by-Month Draw and Write Prompts*. In one worksheet, students were asked to "draw and write about the Mayflower." In another worksheet titled "Land Ho!" two Pilgrims looked out over the edge of their boat. Students were prompted to write in the voice balloons "what you think the Pilgrim boy and girl are saying to each other." Zeik had colored the Pilgrim's faces with a light peach color. The male Pilgrim had blonde hair. "Shude [should] we land here?" he wrote in the voice bubble of the female Pilgrim. I donte no [don't know]?" he replied in the male Pilgrim's thought bubble. In response to why Zeik projected ambivalence onto the Pilgrims, he responded "I don't know. I just knew that people already lived there."

The worksheets in the packet were an expected (but still disheartening) extension of the teacher's framing. It remains difficult to tolerate the same harmful story taught in schools despite a wealth of material available that provide guidance in how to teach different narratives and orientations. It was the final worksheet, however, that was the most jarring. Whereas I was previously concerned that Native students might internalize settler colonial discourses, this worksheet literally asked Native students in the class to imagine themselves as Pilgrims; to *be* settlers. "If I Were a Pilgrim …" the title of the worksheet read, followed by the prompt, "Imagine that you are a Pilgrim. Then draw a picture of yourself as a Pilgrim." While there is value to simulation activities geared toward understanding multiple perspectives (Agarwal-Rangnath, 2013; Bigelow & Peterson, 1998), it would be hard to see the appropriateness of a worksheet that asked a Black student to imagine herself as a plantation owner, a Jewish student as an SS commander at Auschwitz, or a Japanese student as a director of an internment camp. In a similar dilemma, responding to the pervasiveness of "mission projects" in California, Ohlone-Costanoan Esselen scholar Deborah Miranda (2012) asks,

> Can you imagine teaching about slavery in the South while simultaneously requiring each child to lovingly construct a plantation model, complete with happy darkies in the fields, white masters, overseers with whips, and human auctions? Or asking fourth graders to study the Holocaust by carefully designing detailed concentration camps, complete with gas chambers, heroic Nazi guards, crematoriums? (p. xvii)

A generous reading of this unexamined requirement would be that curriculum writers (and teachers who use these activities) simply presume an American universal subjectivity of their students, "one that is conveniently unmoored from historic race, gender, or other social markers" (Tallie, 2014, n.p.). Nonetheless, presuming students would or could identify with settler subjectivities (without any misgivings or objections) functions as a subtle form of Indigenous erasure. I was troubled by the prompt, yet like most attempts at Indigenous erasure, this one was incomplete. As Seneca scholar Arthur C. Parker (1916) stated, "The white race in its endeavor to take possession of the continent has experimented with three great plans of dealing with the aborigines [extermination, segregation, and absorption] and none of them has so far entirely succeeded" (p. 252). As an extension of this history, this worksheet tried to absorb Zeik's sense of self, tried to force him "to participate in his own erasure" (Dion & Salamanca, 2014, p. 178), but he would not be erased.

In the given box, Zeik had drawn a blue sky with swirly rain falling from above. Standing in the middle on a bed of green grass, outfitted in black and wearing what appeared to be a Pilgrim hat, was a little brown-skinned boy. That Zeik had to draw himself as a Pilgrim at all made me livid, but I couldn't help feeling proud that he had colored his skin brown. He would not be erased. Of course, if Zeik had light-skin, as many of the Native students in the district do, the path of resisting erasure would be less clear. There is no template for these small acts of survivance; the stories and practices are complicated. But for Zeik, it was not that complicated. It was quite simple in fact—he just didn't see himself as a Pilgrim.

"Then why did you choose to draw a Pilgrim in the box?" I asked him.

He looked at me as if I was crazy. "I didn't have a choice," he said. "The worksheet *said* draw a Pilgrim."

"Why did you draw your skin brown?" I asked him.

Again, he stated quite frankly, "Because my skin *is* brown."

Even in Zeik's compliance there are traces of survivance. Zeik's choice *to remain who he was* (Lomawaima & McCarty, 2006)[7] despite the worksheet's prompt that he imagine himself as a Pilgrim, embodied such resistance, illustrating that even as a Native student goes through the colonial motions requested by schools, they can still enact survivance in small ways. I left our interaction wondering whether I was reading more into Zeik's gesture than was there; I wondered, too, if my reading of his gesture was also a tiny act of survivance. Whether Zeik consciously drew himself with dark skin to upset the presumed subjectivity of the worksheet, or whether he did so simply because his skin *is* brown felt less important than recognizing the colonial educational context that demanded such a gesture of a young Native child.

Reverberating through the worksheet's instructions pulsed longstanding attempts by educators to indoctrinate Native children with settler ideologies, and reinforce racial (and racist) hierarchies. The worksheet Zeik was asked to complete didn't appear much different to me than colonial mission and boarding school attempts to indoctrinate Native youth with Eurocentric and racist orderings. These efforts were once explicit, evident in excerpts from student writing in the 19th century:

The Caucasian is the strongest in the world. The semi-civilized have their own civilization, but not like the white race. The savage race kept their own ways, and they have had three occupations: they were hunted, fished, and foughted with other people. They beat, too. The white race have three occupations: agriculture, manufacturing, and commerce.

The white people they are civilized; they have everything, and go to school, too. They learn how to read and write so they can read newspaper. The yellow people they half civilized, some of them know how to read and write, and some know how to take care of themselves. The red people they big savages; they don't know anything. (American Missionary Association, 1888, p. 244)

Well over a century later, long after colonial mission and boarding schools have closed, Native children like Zeik are still being asked to internalize settler ideologies, to think like and imagine themselves as settlers. This history of colonial schooling shaped how I viewed contemporary curricula, not as a departure from, but as a continuation of prior colonial schooling practices. This context was not visible to Ms. Billings until our interview, but when I let her know that I felt proud Zeik drew himself with a brown crayon despite the worksheet's prompt, she noticeably shuddered. Despite her critiques of whiteness, it was clear she hadn't considered the assumptions that underlay the worksheet's instructions.

I have seen teachers ignore those jarring moments, the educative ruptures that disrupt a taken-for-granted thought, value, or practice, but I also knew that Ms. Billings was sincere in her support for Native students like Zeik and felt hopeful that she would carry that experience with her as she planned for next year. But regardless of whether or not Ms. Billings changed, I knew that Zeik would be okay. He knew he wasn't an invented Indian or a Pilgrim settler. He knew how to assert himself and create space for himself and others. And most importantly, in a society and school that continually tried to erase and dehumanize him, Zeik continued to see himself as Native American and smart.

Notes

1 Lyons is explicit in his use of peoples, plural. This attention to the plural *peoples* reflects a conception of collective Indigenous identity, self-determination, and sovereignty. The United Nations Declaration of the Rights of Indigenous Peoples (United Nations, 2007), for example, protects the rights of Indigenous peoples as individuals and *as peoples*. As D'Errico (2006) notes, however, nation-states have been resistant to the idea of collective self-determination, arguing that "collective self-determination exists only through states, and that indigenous people are groups of individuals with shared cultural, linguistic, and social features, but without any internal coherence as 'peoples'" (p. 242). However, this argument "contradicts the US claims that it deals with indigenous peoples on a 'government-to-government' basis" (p. 242).

2 Vizenor purposely chooses to represent *indian* in lowercase letters and italicized. In *Fugitive Poses* (1998) he states,

The simulation of the *indian*, lowercase and in italics, is an ironic name in *Fugitive Poses*. The Indian with an initial capital is a commemoration of absence—evermore that double absence of simulations by name and stories. My first use of the italicized *indian* as a simulation was in *The Everlasting Sky*. The Natives in that book were the *oshki anishinaabe*, or the new people. Since then, Natives are the presence, and *indians* are simulations, a derivative noun that means an absence, in my narratives (p. 15).

3 This has been noted in other ways in my research as well. When I asked a former administrator on leads regarding strong teachers in the district, I was given several names. When asked how they were with respect to equity work and supporting Indigenous students, she replied she wasn't sure about equity work, leaving the impression that equity is unrelated to definitions "strong" or "good" teachers.

4 Tisquantum may have been captured and enslaved in 1605 as well, though there is not historical agreement on this incident.

5 Importantly, feminist scholarship argues that standpoints are not bound to identity locations (i.e., only women peoples can employ feminist standpoints). Rather, as Harding (2004) argues, standpoints are not *ascribed*, but can be *achieved* through collective, ideological struggle.

6 Examples include: *1621: A New Look at Thanksgiving* (Grace, Bruchac, & Plimoth Plantation, 2001); *Thanksgiving: A Native Perspective* (Seale, Slapin, & Silverman, 1998); *Rethinking Columbus* (Bigelow & Peterson, 1998); or numerous other online resources such as *Teaching Tolerance's* (n.d.) lesson "Thanksgiving Mourning" which features "The Suppressed Speech of Wamsutta James."

7 Given Zeik's distaste for the word Indian, I chose not to directly reference the title of McCarty and Lomawaima's book *To Remain and Indian: Lessons in Democracy from a Century of Native American Education*. The phrase, however, is important as it stems from a section in "The Meriam Report" (officially titled *The Problem of Indian Administration*) in which Lewis Meriam wrote "He who wants to remain an Indian and live according to his old culture should be aided in doing so..." (as cited in Lomawaima & McCarty, 2006, p. xxii), a sentiment that directly contested the assimilative purpose of schooling at the time.

References

Agarwal-Rangnath, R. (2013). *Social studies, literacy, and social justice in the common core classroom: A teachers' guide*. New York, NY: Teachers College Press.

Agoglia, R. (1993). Beyond Thanksgiving: Teaching about Native Americans of New England. *The Radical Teacher*, 43, 6–9.

American Missionary Association. (1888). *The American missionary*, volume 42. Congreational Home Missionary Society, Making of America Project.

Apess, W., & O'Connell, B. (1992). *On our own ground: The complete writings of William Apess, a Pequot* (Native Americans of the Northeast). Amherst, MA: University of Massachusetts Press.

Au, W. (2012). *Critical curriculum studies: Education, consciousness, and the politics of knowing*. Hoboken, NJ: Taylor & Francis.

Baldwin, J. (1998). *Collected essays*. New York, NY: Library of America.

Berkhofer, R. (1979). *The white man's Indian: Images of the American Indian, from Columbus to the present*. New York, NY: Vintage Books.

BickfordIII, J. H., & Rich, C. W. (2015). The historical representation of Thanksgiving within primary- and intermediate-level children's literature. *Journal of Children's Literature*, 41(1), 5–21.

Bigelow, B., & Peterson, Bob. (Eds.). (1998). *Rethinking Columbus: The next 500 years* (2nd ed.). Milwaukee, WI: Rethinking Schools.

Botelho, M. J., Young, S. L-B., & Nappi, T. (2014). Rereading Columbus: Critical multicultural analysis of multiple historical storylines. *Journal of Children's Literature*, 40(1), 41–51.

Calderón, D. (2011). Locating the foundations of epistemologies of ignorance in normative multicultural education. In N. Jaramillo & E. Malewski (Eds.), *Epistemologies of ignorance in education* (pp. 105–127). Charlotte, NC: Information Age Pub.

Calderón, D. (2014a). Anticolonial methodologies in education: Embodying land and Indigeneity in Chicana feminisms. *Journal of Latino/Latin American Studies*, 6(2), 81–96.

Calderón, D. (2014b). Uncovering settler grammars in curriculum. *Educational Studies: Journal of the American Educational Studies Association*, 50(4), 313–338.

Castagno, A. E., & Brayboy, B. M. K. J. (2008). Culturally responsive schooling for Indigenous youth: A review of the literature. *Review of Educational Research*, 78(4), 941–993.

Custalow, L., & Daniel, A. L. (2007). *The true story of Pocahontas the other side of history*. Golden, CO: Fulcrum.

Delgado, R. (1996). Rodrigo's eleventh chronicle: Empathy and false empathy. *California Law Review*, 84(1), 61–100.

D'Errico, P. (2006). American Indian sovereignty: Now you see it, now you don't. In E. Stromberg (Ed.), *American Indian rhetorics of survivance: Word medicine, word magic* (238–255). Pittsburgh, PA: University of Pittsburgh Press.

Dion, S. D. (2008). *Braiding histories: Learning from Aboriginal peoples' experiences and perspectives*. Vancouver, BC: UBC Press.

Dion, S. D., & Salamanca, A. (2014). inVISIBILITY: Indigenous in the city Indigenous artists, Indigenous youth and the project of survivance. *Decolonization: Indigeneity, Education & Society*, 3(1), 159–188.

Du Bois, W. (1961). *The souls of Black folk*. New York, NY: Bantam Books.

Duncan, G. (2002). Critical Race Theory and method: Rendering race in urban ethnographic research. *Qualitative Inquiry*, 8(1), 85–104.

Freire, P. (1970). *Pedagogy of the oppressed*. New York, NY: Seabury Press.

Furniss, E. (1999). *The burden of history: Colonialism and the frontier myth in a rural Canadian community*. Vancouver, BC: UBC Press.

Goodman, S. (2001). *Pilgrims of Plymouth*. Washington, D. C.: National Geographic Society.

Grace, C. O., Bruchac, M. M., & Plimoth Plantation, Inc. (2001). *1621: A new look at Thanksgiving*. Washington, D. C.: National Geographic Society.

Gray, R. R. R. (2011). Visualizing pedagogy and power with urban Native youth: Exposing the legacy of the Indian residential school system. *Canadian Journal of Native Education*, 34(1), 9–27.

Green, R. (1975). The Pocahontas perplex: The image of Indian women in American culture. *The Massachusetts Review*, 16(4), 698–714.

Harding, S. (Ed.). (2004). *The feminist standpoint theory reader: Intellectual and political controversies*. New York, NY: Routledge.

Kumashiro, K. (2015). *Against common sense: Teaching and learning toward social justice* (3rd ed.). New York, NY: Routledge.

Levstik, L. S., & Barton, K. C. (2015). *Doing history: Investigating with children in elementary and middle schools* (5th ed.). New York, NY: Routledge.

Loewen, J. W. (1998). Plagues and Pilgrims: The truth about the first Thanksgiving. In B. Bigelow & B. Peterson (Eds.), *Rethinking Columbus: The next 500 years* (pp. 79–82). Milwaukee, WI: Rethinking Schools.

Lomawaima, K. T., & McCarty, T. L. (2006). *"To remain an Indian": Lessons in democracy from a century of Native American education.* New York, NY: Teachers College Press.

Lyons, S. R. (2000). Rhetorical sovereignty: What do American Indians want from writing? *College Composition and Communication,* 51(3), 447–468.

Matias, C., & Liou, D. (2015). Tending to the heart of communities of color. *Urban Education,* 50(5), 601–625.

Miller, J. (2005). Coyote's tale on the old Oregon Trail: Challenging cultural memory through narrative at the Tamástslikt Cultural Institute. *Text and Performance Quarterly,* 25(3), 220–238.

Miranda, D. (2012). *Bad Indians: A tribal memoir.* Berkeley, CA: Heyday.

Moreton-Robinson, A. (2013). Towards an Australian Indigenous Women's standpoint theory: A methodological tool. *Australian Feminist Studies,* 28(78), 331–347.

National Council for the Social Studies (NCSS) (2013). *The college, career, and civic life (C3) Framework for social studies state standards: Guidance for enhancing the rigor of K-12 civics, economics, geography, and history.* Silver Spring, MD: NCSS.

National Museum of the American Indian. (2015). The "Indian problem." Smithsonian NMAI. Retrieved from https://www.youtube.com/watch?v=if-BOZgWZPE.

Oregon Department of Education. (2011). Oregon state content standards. Retrieved from https://www.oregon.gov/ode/educator-resources/standards/socialsciences/Pages/Standards.aspx.

Parker, A. (1916). The social elements of the Indian problem. *American Journal of Sociology,* 22(2), 252–267.

Plymouth 400 Inc. (2015). Chapter 2: "The messenger runner" [video file]. November 12. Retrieved from https://www.youtube.com/watch?v=KBTawl-zTyA.

Reese, D. (2008). Indigenizing children's literature. *Journal of Language and Literacy Education* [Online], 4(2), 59–72. Available: www.coe.uga.edu/jolle/2008_2/indigenizing.pdf.

Richter, D. (2001). *Facing east from Indian country: A Native history of early America.* Cambridge, MA: Harvard University Press.

Rosiek, J. (2003). Emotional scaffolding: An exploration of the teacher knowledge at the intersection of student emotion and the subject matter. *Journal of Teacher Education,* 54(5), 399–412.

Sabzalian, L. (2018). Curricular standpoints and Native feminist theories: Why Native feminist theories should matter to curriculum studies. *Curriculum Inquiry,* 48(3), 359–382.

Seale, D., Slapin, B., & Silverman, C. (Eds.). (1998). *Thanksgiving: A Native perspective.* Berkeley, CA: Oyate.

Sleeter, C. E. (2011). *The academic and social value of ethnic studies: A research review.* National Education Association Research Department.

Solórzano, D. G. (1998). Critical race theory, race and gender microaggressions, and the experience of Chicana and Chicano scholars. *International Journal of Qualitative Studies in Education,* 11(1), 121–136.

Solórzano, D., Ceja, M., & Yosso, T. (2000). Critical race theory, racial microaggressions, and campus racial climate: The experiences of African American college students. *Journal of Negro Education,* 69(1), 60–73.

Sonneborn, L. (1998). *A to Z of Native American women* (Encyclopedia of women). New York: Facts on File.

Sue, D. W., Capodilupo, C. M., Torino, G. C., Bucceri, J. M., Holder, A. M. B., Nadal, K. L., & Esquilin, M. (2007). Racial microaggressions in everyday life: Implications for clinical practice. *American Psychologist*, 62(4), 271–286.

Tallie, T. J. (2014). Failing to ford the river: "Oregon Trail", same-sex marriage rhetoric, and the intersections of anti-blackness and settler colonialism. Decolonization: Indigeneity, Education & Society blog. June 4. Retrieved from https://decolonization. wordpress.com/2014/06/04/failing-to-ford-the-river-oregon-trail-same-sex-marriage-r hetoric-and-the-intersections-of-anti-blackness-and-settler-colonialism/.

Tuck, E. & Gaztambide-Fernández, R. A. (2013). Curriculum, replacement, and settler futurity. *Journal of Curriculum Theorizing*, 29(1), 72–89.

Tuck, E., & Ree, C. (2013). A glossary of haunting. In S. Holman Jones, T. E. Adams, & C. Ellis (Eds.), *Handbook of autoethnography* (639–658). Walnut Creek, CA: Left Coast Press.

UAINE. (2016). United American Indians of New England website. Retrieved from www.uaine.org.

United Nations. (2007). United Nations Declaration of the Rights of Indigenous Peoples. Retrieved from https://www.un.org/esa/socdev/unpfii/documents/DRIPS_en.pdf.

Vaught, S. E. (2011). *Racism, public schooling, and the entrenchment of white wupremacy: A critical race ethnography*. Albany, NY: SUNY Press.

Veracini, L. (2011). Introducing settler colonial studies. *Settler Colonial Studies*, 1, 1–12.

Vizenor, G. (1998). *Fugitive poses: Native American Indian scenes of absence and presence*. Lincoln, NE: University of Nebraska Press.

Vizenor, G., Tuck, E. & Yang, K. W. (2014). Resistance is in the blood. In E. Tuck & K. W. Yang (Eds.), *Youth resistance research and theories of change* (pp. 107–117). New York, NY: Routledge.

Wilson, W. A. C. (2006). Burning down the house: Laura Ingalls Wilder and American Colonialism. In D. T. Jacobs (Ed.), *Unlearning the language of conquest: Scholars expose anti-Indianism in America* (pp. 66–80). Austin, TX: University of Texas Press.

Yosso, T. J., Smith, W. A., Ceja, M., & Solórzano, D. G. (2009). Critical race theory, racial microaggressions, and campus racial climate for Latina/o undergraduates. *Harvard Educational Review*, 79, 659–690.

Zerubavel, E. (1996). Social memories: Steps to a sociology of the past. *Qualitative Sociology*, 19(3), 283–299.

Zinn, H. (1995). *A people's history of the United States: 1492—present*. New York, NY: HarperCollins.

2

HALLOWEEN COSTUMES AND NATIVE IDENTITY

"Let's go now! Let's go now and protest!" yelled one student.

"Yeah!" said another. "Let's make posters and stand out front!"

"I appreciate your enthusiasm," I said. "I'm glad you feel passionate. And I want to go there too ... but how are you going to respond when someone asks why you're there?"

"It's so wrong!" said one student.

"Yeah!!!" echoed the others.

"But what's wrong about it?" I asked. "How are you going to respond when someone says: 'But I am honoring you.' Or 'Quit being so sensitive.' Believe me. I'm half tempted to take you there, but you need to be prepared."

Collective and Critical Literacy

The Native youth in my after-school youth group—a mix of 9th through 12th graders—were responding to a series of photos I had printed out from the Spirit Halloween website. I showed them the costumes for sale—Naughty Navajo, Chief Big Wood, and Pocahottie—along with their descriptions. "Put the wow in pow wow ..." and "Is that an ear of corn in your pocket or are you just glad to see me?" the captions read.

We read the descriptions in small groups. The youth were outraged, but they also laughed goofily and incredulously like teenagers at the images. They were confused and angry, but struggled for the words to express what they were so upset about. And so we began the process of developing "critical race vocabulary" so that students could "name their pain" (Matias & Liou, 2015, p. 615). One of the parents led the youth in a conversation about how the images sexualized women. Noticing how the men were represented, this prompted questions from some on whether men could be sexualized too. We also talked about how regalia differed from "costumes"—one an intimate and important expression of self and identity, the other meant to cover up, escape, or transform one's identity. In response to another critique that feathers in headdresses were earned, not just worn by whomever, one youth responded, "My people don't even wear headdresses." Noticing that the costumes all looked the same—brightly colored feathers, brown suede and buckskin, beaded fringe—one young woman, whose people are from Northern California, stated "And my people don't wear fringe and beads like that. We use shells."

The Native youth's specific, lived experiences disrupted and decentered the dominant representations of Indians from the Spirit website, images many of them found inaccurate and distasteful. This knowledge, learned and lived in Native homes, has historically been characterized through deficit frameworks, deemed "informal" and an impediment to progress that schools must overcome (Lomawaima & McCarty, 2006); yet the youth's knowledge from their families provided the very basis for their critique. That knowledge enabled them to recognize the constructed, false, and harmful nature of such representations and representations.

After searching a bit online, we found Spirit's response in defense of their use of Native costumes.

> "All of these accessories and outfits may only be a simulation of how these noble people lived, however, showing them deference and respect by keeping their memory alive in the traditions of America … is a great thing."

"Lived?!?!" shrieked one student. "This makes us seem like we no longer exist. "Listen to this part!" said one.

> "… don't look at it as disrespectful. Let them in on the knowledge that for a thousand years, before there were cities and highways and the Internet, there was a race of people living amongst the animals and trees."

"Living among the animals and trees?!?!" said another incredulously.

And so we began to write. The youth identified themes: the fact that there are many nations and cultures, not just one; that Natives were depicted in the past, as if extinct; and the portrayal of women as sex objects. They divided into three groups, each tackling a section. They brainstormed, wrote, and revised, and with the help of parents and volunteers, merged their sections into one letter. They were exhausted and proud. The letter read:

Dear Spirit Halloween Store:

> We are so thrilled that you are in the business of bringing Halloween spirit to people in our community. Thank you for sharing so many ways for people to express themselves this holiday.

We believe, however, that you have a few misconceptions about us as Native people and Native culture that we would like to address.

First, there is no one Native culture. There are over 566[1] federally recognized nations in the US, among other Native groups. Each nation has their own beliefs, traditions, languages, and can't be categorized as one group that wears fringe and feathers.

Second, we feel that your costumes exploit not just Native women, but all women. Did you know that Native women are more likely to get sexually assaulted or raped than other women? We believe costumes like this objectify Native women and perpetuate violence toward them. You should help us by not selling costumes that portray our Native women like sex objects.

Finally, when you talk about us in the past tense on your website, we do not feel honored. You make it seem like we no longer exist. We are here, we have always been here, and we will always be here.

It's important to us that you think about what you are teaching to the young children in our community. We do not feel like a "noble race of people" when you continue to sell these costumes. In fact, we feel degraded. We would like to know what you are going to do about our concerns. We trust that you will address this by next Halloween.

Sincerely,

The Oakfield Native Youth Group

We wrapped up for the day and agreed to send the letter off to Spirit Corporate Headquarters and post it on their Facebook page as well as ours. Spirit Halloween Store immediately deleted the letter from their Facebook page and we never heard a response from corporate headquarters. The letter evoked a mixed reaction from the community who followed the program's Facebook page. Some supported our efforts wholeheartedly, asking where they could send a letter of support. A few thanked the youth, one expressing admiration that they were asserting their pride in such a way, rather than being "past-tense caricatures." One community member appreciated the letter, but noted that our framing perpetuated the idea that the clothing instigated violence, an insightful and important critique that uncovered the ways our unit of analysis left contexts of patriarchy and misogyny unexamined. And one Native parent, whose son participated in the program, criticized the letter, calling it a "sad shame" that the youth had to "find fault with everything and make a big deal out of it." This parent said after reading the letter her son no longer wanted to be a part of the program. Though the comments were few, it was clear there wasn't a singular "Native" opinion to this issue. Like any community, there was internal diversity and disagreement.

"She's Kind of Offending Me": When Counterspaces and Classrooms Conflict

The next evening, I received an email from Celeste, one of the students in the youth group. Celeste didn't normally send or answer my emails, so it was unusual to get an email from her. The first words of her email read, "I need help," followed by several paragraphs in an urgent tone explaining what had happened that day. Celeste had felt inspired by our project and decided to propose the topic of cultural appropriation in her art class called "social injustices," but she was met with resistance when she brought her project idea up to her teacher, Sharon. She wrote that when she brought up Native American stereotypes and costumes that her teacher "put it down" and that the stereotypes "don't offend her" so we are overreacting. Speaking of the costumes, Sharon told Celeste: "This is what they really wore, and there's no way anyone could get anything authentic to wear on Halloween ... We are honoring them as they once lived. Cowboys don't get offended when kids dress up like them, why should Native Americans?" Describing how she felt, Celeste wrote:

> I felt so ... flabbergasted in this conversation. I just couldn't find the words to fight back. What can I do to help people understand? I don't want to get anyone in trouble, because I like this teacher ... but I don't want to sweep this under the rug either."

I read the email as my own two children lay in bed. I thought about the various issues they had already faced in schools since preschool, the emotional pain I had felt as a result of these interactions, the discomfort I had felt addressing their teachers, and the concerns I had that speaking up would make their time in school harder. I recognized in Celeste's email similar tropes and resistance I had been met with when raising issues as well—a denial of her concerns, claims that she was overreacting, casually invoking the authority to determine what constitutes an offense, the presumption of disappearance and the use of authenticity. I wanted Celeste to know that this wasn't her fault and that her teacher should know better—that *all* teachers should know better. I wanted her to know too that her concern shouldn't be about protecting her teacher, though the tendency to protect even those who hurt you was all too familiar.

I wrote Celeste back immediately, telling her she could call me if she needed and offering to meet with her. I let her know I could speak to her teacher if that would be helpful, or coach her if she wanted to meet with her teacher again by herself. I told her how proud I was of her for using her voice and trying to take on such important work. It is tough to speak up about these issues and say things in a way others might actually hear them. I attached some links to blogs and infographics for her to look at, like Cherokee scholar Adrienne Keene's blog Native Appropriations (http://nativeappropriations.com/). I let her know that addressing these sorts of issues takes practice and sometimes it is often helpful to see the ways others use their voice so that we can find our own. She thanked me, and said she'd get back to me. I wondered if what I said was enough. I also resented that this is what support for Indigenous students frequently entailed—responding to teachers' ignorance and disrespect, or coaching students to articulate their experiences while in distress.

Celeste left our youth group feeling empowered enough to bring an issue she felt important to the attention to her teacher, only to be shut down and silenced at school. Both the meaningful opportunity to learn and trust in her teacher were foreclosed in that interaction. Celeste's experience might be understood as a "racial microaggression" (Solórzano, Ceja, & Yosso, 2000; Solórzano, 1998; Sue et al., 2007), one of the "brief and commonplace daily verbal, behavioral, or environmental indignities, whether intentional or unintentional, that communicate hostile, derogatory, or negative racial slights and insults toward people of color" (Sue et al., 2007, p. 271). The literature on racial microaggressions is adept at highlighting the "thousand tiny cuts" that students experience in schools, and how these experiences accumulate, leading to "feelings of self-doubt, frustration, as well as isolation" (Solórzano et al., 2000, p. 69). Celeste's experience illustrates why it is no surprise that some Indigenous students don't feel that they belong in school. When a student such as Celeste is confronted with such "stunning, automatic acts of disregard that stem from unconscious white superiority" (Davis, 1989, as cited in Solórzano et al., 2000, p. 60), it is no wonder she would feel flustered, that her perspective wasn't valued, or even that she was inferior. Celeste's teacher used her own frame of reference, one informed by colonial constructs of Indigeneity, to understand and interact with her student. Without explicit attention to critically examining and critiquing these colonial frames of reference, teachers and schools are practically structured to reproduce ignorance about Indigenous peoples and disrespect toward Indigenous students. Racial and colonial microaggressions, though often jarring in the moment, are a familiar feature of Indigenous students' educational experiences, and accumulate as an expected part of school and classroom climates. Consequently, anticipating, interrupting, and responding to such microaggressions becomes an unfortunate, yet necessary, aspect of supporting Indigenous students.

Our efforts to start a Native youth group as an educational counterspace (Solórzano & Yosso, 2002) in the district were in direct response to the feelings of isolation and despair students have felt as a result of moments such as the one Celeste shared. As a group of educators and parents, we wanted a space to affirm Indigenous youths' feelings and experiences, a place to address the "racial battle fatigue" Native students face in schools (Smith, Allen, & Danley, 2007). This group enabled us to form meaningful relationships with students, offer them "micro-affirmations" (Rowe, 2008) to offset and counteract microaggressions, and root our education in an ethic of care (Valenzuela, 1999). It was in such a space that Celeste felt valued and empowered. Celeste's experience, however, also illustrated the limits of such spaces to disrupt the hostile and racial dynamics experienced at school, a place in which she continued to spend the majority of her day.

The next week when our group met, we began with a discussion of the letter and how we felt. My plan was to address the critique posed by one community member which suggested that in our narrow focus on the sexy clothing, we unwittingly overlooked (and perhaps excused) contexts that tolerate, even sanction, sexual violence. The costumes were indeed problematic, but the remedy was not modesty. We needed to connect the costumes to misrepresentations without ignoring or excusing the broader context of misogyny and patriarchy. These were harmful outsider representations for sure, but they were no excuse for *any* woman to be violated. However, the conversation took a different direction. One young man, Donovan, said he spent a lot of time thinking about it, and disagreed with what we did. "What if we're proud? Why *shouldn't* we be able to dress up like Native Americans?" he asked. "That's the problem," said one young woman in response. "You *are* Native, so what you're wearing now is Native. My mom always asks little kids, 'What do you think Natives wear?' They always respond feathers, etc. And then she says, 'I'm Native. What am I wearing?' 'Jeans,' the kids say. 'That's right,' she says. 'We wear jeans. We're Native and we wear jeans.'"

I hoped that I was helping create a space for students to critically reflect on these issues and come to their own conclusions. I thought I was creating that space; however, Donovan's comments and clear ambivalence made me question whether the space felt open to him and his questions a week earlier. As the youth discussed the issue among themselves, I recognized another limit to our counterspace; there wasn't time to thoroughly engage these issues. We didn't have time, for example, to delve into Native feminist literature to ground, complicate, or deepen our discussions. The youth were interested in this issue. Writing the letter was their idea. But they were also interested in beading, weaving, and drumming. They wanted to hike and go to the park and the river. They wanted to play basketball and soccer in the gym. They wanted to eat snacks and watch movies and just hang out. The two hours we had each week on a Monday afternoon after school felt insufficient. In those two hours, it felt as if we had to redress the colonial damage done by schools and society and affirm our students' sense of self and community. Those two hours felt grossly insufficient to enact the type of education we thought Native students needed and deserved. While part of our work was to support Native students emotionally, socially, spiritually, and physically, we also understood Indigenous self-determination as an academic project. Native students need to read Native studies literature, then critically read and write about their experiences in light of that literature. They need time with Native art, poems, stories, science, history, treaties, and laws. They need to read books and reports by Native authors and media, interview Native elders and leaders, learn about Native social, political, and economic development. They need to develop their critical literacy and higher order thinking skills in the context of real problems of practice for their communities. Such a realization placed us in a predicament. We needed that space to be warm, welcoming, and relaxed for them. We didn't want Native youth to stop coming because they felt the Center was just another place to "do school." Yet we knew, from our own lives, and from the reflections of Native college students after taking their first Native studies class, that Native studies supports self-determination. We realized that our counterspace was necessary, but also that equal attention was needed to advocate for sustained academic space in schools for critical ethnic studies and Native studies (Sleeter, 2011).

When the conversation dwindled, Celeste took the opportunity to share her recent experience with the group. She told them how excited she was to propose the project, and then how crushed she felt when her teacher, Sharon, didn't recognize her issue as legitimate; that she felt hurt too when some of her peers didn't see what the big deal was either. She reported that her teacher made the comparison between the Indian costumes and her Irish, German, and French heritage, noting that she "wouldn't be offended by somebody dressing up like a leprechaun" for St. Patrick's Day. Her teacher also suggested that she take up a "more important" topic of social injustice, such as "women's issues." Celeste expressed her disappointment with feeling so empowered, and then let down: "… writing to Spirit and talking about the changes in our community, talking about our past, our present, and our future … I really felt like I needed to become a part of that; that I needed to share with the world that we are here."

Yet despite her hurt and frustration, Celeste made excuses for her teacher. "… I don't want to put down this teacher," she said, "because she's a beautiful person and I'm pretty sure she thinks she's doing right, but I don't really have the guts to tell her that she's kind of offending me." More troubling to me than Celeste excusing her teacher's actions because of her good intentions, was the fact Celeste privileged her teacher's comfort over her own, as well as denied her own courage throughout this experience. Celeste *was* courageous. She had brought the issue to her teacher's attention. She was now processing her hurtful experience in community with her mentors and peers. She was also developing a critique of settler society, while learning of the complexities that arise when that critical lens is directed toward the actions or beliefs of the people she cares about, an intimate and uncomfortable dynamic that often requires profound courage.

The issue at hand was not Celeste's "guts," but her teacher's socialization into dominant cultural discourses which led to her illiteracy regarding Native issues. As a result of this socialization, rather than supporting Celeste in cultivating her critical consciousness—a gesture which would seem more likely to occur in a class titled "social injustice"—her teacher served as a barrier to doing so. She explicitly denied an important issue brought to her by a student, a denial that rest on and reproduced a number of colonial discourses—the belief that "playing Indian" (Green, 1988) honors, rather than appropriates Native culture; a Eurocentric understanding of cultural "authenticity" that holds Native people "to impossible standards of ahistorical cultural purity" (Raibmon, 2005, p. 9); the equivocation of Indigenous peoples with leprechauns and cowboys, an analogy which conflates creatures and professions with identity and erases power relations; and the erasure of Indigenous women through the deployment of a universal white female subject.

Celeste understandably wanted to protect a teacher that she loved, yet responsibility for this missed educational moment and the harm that resulted, fell not on Celeste's shoulders, but on her teacher's. Even so, locating responsibility is slippery given the discursive layers in Sharon's response. Sharon didn't invent the cultural discourses she communicated to Celeste: she didn't invent the narrow notion of cultural authenticity or the practice of "playing Indian"; she didn't invent the categorization of women that naturalized whiteness, erasing and othering Native women. Sharon's knowledge was not just a matter of "stereotypes" or misinformation about Indigenous peoples; instead, her knowledge reflected deeply rooted discourses that naturalized settler superiority, Indigenous erasure, and the economic and social interests that have driven settler representations of Indigenous life. Zeus Leonardo's (2004) critical revision of McIntosh's white privilege framework (1992) is instructive here. In it, he draws specific attention to the macrosocial dimensions of racism, demonstrating how the individual benefits of white privilege are directly linked to broader racial ideologies and policies and how "[p]rivilege is the daily cognate of structural domination" (p. 148). To demonstrate this, he revises McIntosh's list to make visible these macrosocial features of racial oppression:

> Whites have "neighbors ... [who] are neutral or pleasant" (McIntosh, 1992, p. 73) to them *because redlining and other real estate practices, with the help of the Federal Housing Agency, secure the ejection of the black and brown body from white spaces.* Whites can enter a business establishment and expect the "'person in charge' to be white" (McIntosh, 1992, p. 74) *because of a long history of job discrimination.* (p. 148, emphasis added)

Sharon's response might also be understood as a particular stance in relation to dominant discourses. Celeste's teacher Sharon may believe it is acceptable to dress up as Native Americans, for example, *because policies of genocide and dispossession as well as historical narratives of a "vanishing" race create a context in which whites rarely have sustained encounters with contemporary Native Americans.* Or perhaps Sharon thinks dressing as an Indian is a way to "honor" Native people (a statement she repeatedly made), *because the image of Native American as "tragic noble savage" has been used for centuries to naturalize the violence done by whites to Native Americans.*

Sharon's reaction hurt Celeste, but Sharon has also been hurt by dominant narratives pervasive in schools and society that circulate as commonsense (Kumashiro, 2015). In a context that objectifies, romanticizes, demeans, ignores, and relegates Native people to the past, unexamined commonsense is neither excusable nor tolerable, but at least socially understandable. Perhaps it was this very context of socialized ignorance that led James Baldwin (1995) to write a letter to his nephew, pleading him to pity such ignorance, arguing that "these innocent people have no other hope. They are, in effect, still trapped in a history which they do not understand; and until they understand it, they cannot be released from it. They have had to believe for many years, and for innumerable reasons, that black men are inferior to white men" (p. 8). Or perhaps ignorance should not be considered innocence, for as Baldwin also said, "it is not permissible that the authors of devastation should also be innocent. It is the innocence which constitutes the crime" (p. 5).

Celeste's teacher's behavior is inexcusable. Drawing attention to the discursive trajectory of her response is not to excuse ignorance, nor to absolve Sharon of responsibility; rather, it is to suggest that, it is also a logical and consistent response to discursive contexts that make it difficult for individuals to think outside of the erasure and narrow framings of Indigenous life. Said another way, her response is indicative of a settler colonial structure that, as Dorothy Roberts notes, "brilliantly serves its intended purposes" (as cited in Saito, 2014, p. 3). Sharon's response is also a direct result of the cultural knowledge privileged by teacher education programs and educational policy, decisions about the body of knowledge we consider essential for educators. While Sharon must claim responsibility for her actions and ignorance as teacher, resolving the sheer pervasiveness of such moments warrants systemic and systematic change as the whiteness and colonialism underlying Sharon's response was not just individual, but historic, cultural, institutional, and discursive (Castagno, 2014).

Upon hearing Celeste's story, the group offered her support, to which Celeste smiled and offered her gratitude. Storytelling is often a cathartic and healing act (Delgado, 1989) and witnessing the group's support of Celeste provided another justification for counterspaces in which to tell such stories. As the conversation dwindled, one of the interns for the program, a First Nations college student, also spoke up to support her.

> You know, I go back and forth on this issue of cultural appropriation. I sometimes wonder what the big deal is. But I then remember how much racism and sexism there still is. It may not seem like it here in this town. You can walk around here and feel pretty good. But on the reservations, it's still a big issue. Being Native there isn't always a good thing. Native women still get raped. In my home community, they are still raped and often missing … and no one looks for them. And the stereotypes and costumes reinforce that idea, that it's okay to be violent against women.

Her comment lingered in the air for a moment, a sobering reminder of the stakes of such representations. Celeste then thanked the intern and everyone else again for their support and said she would think about how she wanted to move forward.

There were a number of directions Celeste could have taken: addressing a more "important" issue at the direction of her teacher; doing twice the work, as many students often do, pursuing her idea during her own time while also completing a project her teacher found acceptable; or refusing to do the project altogether, an action that could be read simultaneously as failure and resistance. Celeste ultimately picked a new direction for her art project, something she didn't care too much about, in an attempt to get through the experience. Similarly, although the youth group initially planned on following up on their letter, the group ultimately got involved in different projects and lost momentum over winter break. Celeste told me, however, that she was eager for me to meet with her teacher to pursue the issue.

Meeting with Sharon and Missing Moments

When I first met with Celeste's teacher, Sharon, I had to remind her of the incident, a gesture that speaks to the subtlety of microaggressions, as perpetrators of microaggressions are often unaware of the harm that they inflict during interactions (Sue et al., 2007). Reminded of the moment, she remembered that a student (though at first she also couldn't remember who) brought the issue to her attention. At the time, she said she "didn't see what the big deal was." When I gave her some context for the project we did as a youth group, Sharon said she felt bad that she may have offended the student, but that she also wished the student had explained herself better; she wished she could have "tease[d] out what is it that might be so offensive." Sharon was sincere in her concern that she hurt her student, but framing the problem as Celeste's inability to articulate herself obscures the ideological resistance Sharon likely had to Celeste's ideas, resistance that surfaced when she told me the same leprechaun analogy as she did Celeste; resistance that surfaced when she said that she "didn't want to fight every little thing," and that if she were doing a social awareness piece, it would try to get the "heart of things." "Maybe those things do matter," she said, "but do you know what I'm saying, but there are varying degrees of things to get upset about, you know, like women's issues, or whatever issue that is calling to you, you know. I think when you do an art piece, you should really feel passionate about what you're trying to say so that you can convey, you know." When I let Sharon know that the issue was something that Celeste did feel passionate about, and that she tried to express that to her, Sharon expressed remorse again, saying that she misunderstood her and felt badly. Beyond remorse, she asked if we could continue to have frank discussions and if I could offer guidance on how to approach these issues, an effort to turn toward her own discomfort that not all teachers express. In one of those later frank discussions, Sharon reflected back on the moment that transpired between her and Celeste in class: "You know what's so interesting is that I *thought* that I knew ... that's the other thing I would tell you. I *thought* I was good, you know ..."

Following winter break, I also interviewed Celeste and her mom. I asked Celeste why she had not followed through with her idea for the project in her art class. Her response caught me off guard: "I know, and I wanted to ..." she said, but then we had that *other* conversation in group, about how something someone said made me feel that … that it's not as important as women being raped on the reservation. And I'm like, dude, I don't know anything about that. I didn't even know what a reservation really was because I haven't been raised in that setting …

The conversation we had in youth group was supposed to empower her. And from what I remembered, the intern's comment was supposed to show how little acts of violence, like stereotyping, could lead to greater acts of violence. She was trying to connect the symbolic violence that happens here to the physical violence in her own community to Native women. When I told that to Celeste in the interview, she said the comment did make her think that sexual violence is a real issue for Native women, but it also made her feel like what she had to say wasn't as important. I hadn't realized that during our youth group activity that Celeste situated herself and her experiences along a continuum with respect to issues of violence, authenticity, identity, and belonging. What's most disconcerting is that I hadn't picked up on it. Like Celeste's teacher, I thought that I knew what was happening and how my teaching was impacting my students.

In that moment I was reminded how insidious settler colonial discourses are; how they are always at play, even when as teachers we might try to make them visible or resist them. I didn't blatantly minimize Celeste's concerns as her teacher Sharon did when she made the analogy to St. Patrick's Day and leprechauns. I didn't try to dissuade her from her inquiry; in fact, I explicitly offered a context to inspire and support student inquiry into such issues. Yet even as I was conscious of these issues and explicitly tried to create space for these types of conversations that too often get overlooked or trivialized, I didn't track the ways discourses of identity, authenticity, and belonging had affected Celeste. Given Celeste's frustrated attempts to pursue her project, I thought the real issue affecting her would be how her teacher minimized her concerns, so I reached out and offered some informal professional development around these issues. But when Celeste told me the activity I organized and the conversation in our youth group made her feel less authentic, like her experiences as a Native youth weren't as "real" as the ones from the rez, I was disappointed. I didn't pick up on the unintended consequences of my own lesson.

I was making an explicit attempt to critically and constructively support Native students, but during that lesson, I failed to keep in mind that sometimes for students, there is a lot at stake with the lessons we plan, the questions we ask, and the answers we give. Intimately interwoven with these curricular and pedagogical decisions are underlying questions of identity and belonging. I was reminded by my student how settler society discourses can encapsulate and distort even conversations between Indigenous people and make it difficult to hear and support one another. It reminded me how much work lay ahead, how complex these issues are that we face, and most importantly, of Celeste's courage and resilience to negotiate these dynamics while taking care of her teacher, and now me, in the process.

Celeste had a sharp critique throughout the course of this experience. She told me she found it interesting that as a Native student, you "feel like in history class they get it right, but then when you come up with a present day concern, it's dismissed." Reflecting back on the whole affair, she said, "I just finished my assignments for a grade and laughed at the fact that people support freedom of expression until you're expressing something that they don't want to hear." This conversation also made more apparent to me the courage and resilience Celeste showed while negotiating these dynamics, largely without effective adult guidance. Through it all, she retained a compassionate frame of mind, regarding both her teacher and me with generosity and forgiveness. "I mean your intentions were pure," Celeste said to me with respect to her experience in youth group, "but ... in trying to teach me ... a lot of time in teaching one thing, another thing splits through it."

Celeste and I have met frequently since this incident and our meeting that day in the youth group. She is still in my youth group, recently took part in a summer academy for Native students that I taught in, and is an active member of our new Native Youth Center. Despite what I think is a fairly vibrant relationship with Celeste, I had never heard her experience of my lesson and of the things that "split through" it until our interview when I explicitly asked her to recount the events. Her narrative of that experience led me to reflect on all of the moments in teaching and learning that I have likely missed, despite trying to track students' relationship to the content, to their sense of self, to me, to each other, to their future. It led me to consider public and private avenues through which I could offer students an opportunity to share their experiences in our group and learn of the unintended consequences of my own teaching. I believe Celeste was more likely to share her experience because of our ongoing relationship, a relationship that also likely counteracted some of the missed moments and microaggressions that inevitably occur within the messiness and mutually vulnerable experience of teaching and learning.

Though Celeste ultimately never created an art project on cultural appropriation for that particular teacher, she didn't let her idea go. At a Native bridge program at the local university that summer, armed with Native studies literature and a community of Native peers who respected her as an artist, Celeste created a bold visual piece on dehumanizing representations of Native women that she believed represented visual sovereignty. She also declared that summer to the program staff and her peers at graduation that one of her new goals is to create art with a purpose. She hoped to utilize her artistic skills to raise awareness of issues facing Native people and communities.

Celeste's drive and desire led her to create the piece she had originally envisioned. That drive and desire was not just internal, but also nurtured by a supportive community of Native faculty and peers at the summer academy. Unfortunately for her classroom community, because of her experience, Celeste's peers and her teacher at school never got to witness her creativity and resolve. Because Celeste chose to just finish her assignment for a grade because her desires and ideas weren't supported (a reasonable response to her experience), the classroom became a less diverse, dynamic, creative, and critical space as a result. The curriculum that was once possible in that space was foreclosed. Celeste would be okay, however. She had the passion and potential to be a Native artist who would use her talents in disruptive and transformative ways and shed light on these issues; indeed, she already was.

Self-Directed Education Does Not Always Lead to Anticolonial Literacy

I met with Celeste's teacher again the summer before the following school year. Sharon reached out to me because she had a new boyfriend of color that was educating her on some "hard facts" of racism. This had also prompted her to learn about Native peoples' experiences with violence and colonization. She listened to poems by John Trudell and watched Diane Sawyer's special *Hidden America: Children of the Plains* (ABC News, 2011) and learned about the poverty and bleakness on the Pine Ridge reservation. She also watched YouTube videos about Chief Joseph. Sharon felt so strongly about the racism and oppression about which she was learning that at one point during our talk, she began crying. She felt committed to teach her students about the ugly and shameful treatment of Native people by the US government.

Unfortunately, Sharon's self-guided education reinforced damage-based views of Native people (Tuck, 2009). Native people were nearly extinct, and poverty and alcoholism were her frames for understanding contemporary Native life. Moreover, her newfound knowledge on colonization and genocide did little to disrupt the discourses that framed her understanding of cultural appropriation; in fact, her new knowledge may have re-entrenched those discourses. Sharon still couldn't grasp the way wearing Native American costumes—the issue Celeste brought to her attention the previous school year—might be offensive and racist. And her resistance to such an understanding wasn't easily overcome. As I showed Sharon an educational campaign developed by students at Ohio University to draw attention to cultural appropriation[2]—a poster campaign that featured students calling out the mockery of their identities through images and slogans such as "We're a culture not a costume" and "This is not who I am, and this is not okay"—Sharon interrupted me to ask, "Could this ever be an honoring … you know what I mean? When I hear Native Americans like Chief Seattle … there's a part of me that, you know, I wish I could put war paint and breast plates [signaling to her chest] and honor it …" As someone who studies issues of race and colonization and the discomfort, evasion, and fragility (DiAngelo, 2011) of white educators, I shouldn't have been surprised by her response, yet I was caught off guard. I had trouble understanding how upon looking at images of white people dressed up as Indians, a practice that homogenizes and makes a mockery of Indigenous peoples and cultures, she could associate such images with a word like honor. I had trouble understanding how she could look at a poster of a student clearly stating that playing Indian and using his culture as a costume was unacceptable, and still try to justify and salvage those practices by focusing on intentions.

Despite the new understandings of race and oppression unfolding before her, Sharon couldn't relate the concern Celeste brought to her attention to what she understood about Native people. Celeste's concern was in direct competition with her teacher's imagination that was still bounded by colonialist discourses that limited Native Americans to great chiefs, regalia, and war paint. Thus her desire to respect and honor Indigenous people was discursively distorted into a caricature of putting on war paint—a gesture that would not only be silly, but would also be purely symbolic and not require any effective material solidarity with Indigenous struggles for self-determination or sovereignty. Later in the conversation, still not understanding how this issue was offensive to Celeste personally, and Native people more generally, Sharon stated, "Take this for what it is. You can confront me. And it's okay ..." She then repeated to me a version of what she had told Celeste and also told me in our previous interview months earlier, referring again to her Irish heritage: "If somebody dressed as a leprechaun, and I'm just giving you an analogy. For me personally, that wouldn't offend me." Her reliance on the same analogy demonstrated that Celeste—no matter how brilliant, articulate, or careful with her words—would have likely had difficulty convincing her teacher of the issue. Her resistance wasn't necessarily deliberately willful. This was not a matter of Sharon returning home after our conversations, willfully clinging to her logic, then reasserting the same opinion as a testament of her defiance or stubbornness. Instead, the stubbornness was ideological, reinforced by commonsense that she read and watched on her own.

I realized through this process that coaching a teacher to become sensitized to the challenges and tensions that Native students face would first mean unsettling the colonial discourses that she was so deeply embedded and invested in. I naively thought that countering her leprechaun analogy with a quip that Native people, unlike leprechauns, are real, would unsettle her view and cause her to rethink her stance. By making visible her own conflation of mystical creatures and people, I thought she would reflect on her own logic and relate to Celeste's pain. But after meeting with her repeatedly and watching her fall back on the same rebuttal, I could see how enmeshed she was in a discursive context of Indigenous erasure which made visible only some concepts (honoring Native culture or Native pain and suffering, for example), and erased others (the concerns of an Indigenous student, or an understanding of how one's self-expression may be linked to the subjugation of another). Learning to think differently would require more than casual, self-directed education which Sharon attempted. Since dominant and damage-based narratives are so pervasive, teachers need thoughtful guidance to learn to critically read and evaluate Indigenous representations in media and curricula.

The stubbornness of these discourses was further highlighted after an experience Melvina, the Title VI/Indian Education Program Coordinator, and I had after teaching in Sharon's classroom.

Because Sharon had demonstrated an earnest desire to learn more, a tolerance for discomfort, and a clear commitment to these issues (no one was forcing her to talk to me or critically reflect on her own practice), Melvina and I agreed to guest teach in one of Sharon's classes upon her request. As a Native educator in the district, Melvina was used to these requests. Sharon asked that we help her reflect on how to responsibly include and represent Native art, people, and issues in the curriculum, a topic Melvina and I both thought was important, timely, and felt comfortable addressing. However, our comfort with the presentation shifted as Sharon subtly amended her request by asking us to present on "Native culture." Given the coded language she had been using with respect to Indigeneity, evident in her routine use of words like honor, spirituality, and ceremony, we didn't feel that Native culture was the topic that needed to be addressed. Although on the surface such a request might appear inclusive or affirming, to us it felt like another form of Indigenous erasure. We didn't feel like we were being asked to speak in her classroom as subjects, as people with knowledge about particular issues. Rather, we were being asked to speak about the artifacts and products of our culture, the exotic objects that made us Indigenous. In her request for cultural objects, it felt as if she was also asking us to speak as objects, objects of interest and curiosity that would add some flare to the curriculum.

I wasn't entirely averse to giving "cultural presentations." When my son was in first grade, we brought a hand drum to class and he taught his class a Klamath song he had been taught by an elder in our community. "I change you, you change me" went the lyrics. My son had been taught the song with the expectation that he would share it, and so he did. He had been teased a lot that year for his hair, called a girl by many of his classmates, and mistaken as a girl by teachers and aids even three months into the school year. He didn't sing the song in response to that, but somehow sharing the song helped. My son's performance in that context helped him claim some space in that classroom. It also helped fostered a sense of respect among his peers for who he was. In that particular context, his cultural presentation felt meaningful and appropriate. While his performance was cultural, however, the cultural value embodied in his performance for me wasn't necessarily the act of singing or playing of the drum, but the cultural value of responsibility. He learned something with the expectation that he would share it, and he did. For me, he performed the cultural values of respect, responsibility, and reciprocity and just happened to be singing and using a drum to do so.

I could have shared the same song that my son had shared. After all, I was taught the song with the same expectation that I would share it. However, I didn't want to perform for Sharon's class; neither did Melvina. Given my previous experiences with her, I didn't feel that such a performance would be helpful. Being Native was more than the formal, traditional modes of representation I felt she was requesting of us; it also involved contemporary modes of representation informed by a critical consciousness about misrepresentations of Indigenous people in settler society among others aspects. I felt this was what she and her students needed to consider. I was not an artist. I am a critical Indigenous scholar. That is what I had to offer; however, echoing the words of Cherokee author Thomas King's (2012) poem, I don't think we were the Indians she had in mind.

We chose to offer the students a mini-seminar on critical media literacy with a specific focus on Native misrepresentations. For students interested in Native art, we thought it might foster a more respectful engagement with that art by understanding the broader context Native artists operate within. Throughout this presentation, we made a point to position Native artists as pedagogical subjects, not curricular objects. We moved away from a focus on Native artifacts, instead exploring what insights and perspectives Native artists offer to art and society. We also explicitly focused on cultural appropriation, an effort to educate the students as well as Sharon.

We felt good about our presentation, but we knew that comprehensive change would not happen as a result of sporadic class presentations throughout a district. This was one hour on one day in one class of these students' high school career. This was also one class in one school of the 22 schools in the district, and we were speaking to 20 of the 11,000 students in the district. Nevertheless, Melvina appreciated being in classrooms. She wanted to keep a pulse on what was taught in schools, as well as form relationships with students and teachers. Our presentation was limited, but the students and Sharon seemed to enjoy it. Sharon even surprised us at the end of the presentation. She shared about the incident the year prior (omitting Celeste's name), relaying to the students how difficult it was to see the things we can't see, to recognize the stories we've been told and continue to tell without knowing any better, and to confront our own prejudices. Sharon's confession in front of her students about how difficult and personal this work was moved me. Many of us find it difficult to truly challenge our own assumptions privately, yet Sharon had the courage and humility to publicly share that she had struggled with her own stereotypes and had a lot to learn, which was why she invited us to speak to the class.

The next week, however, I got a call from Melvina. Sharon had invited another Native guest speaker to present in her class. The speaker taught students about their drum, sang some songs, and told some stories. Melvina and I joked: *This* was the Indian Sharon had in mind ... This was not, however, a commentary on the other guest speaker; cultural practices aren't inherently stereotypical, but deeply meaningful. We assumed that the guest speaker generously shared a part of who they were with the class. But given our work with Sharon, we saw this request as continuous with her desire for a particular type of Native performance.

I emailed Sharon to learn more about the presentation. "Students loved it," she responded. "The healing vibrations were tremendous and awesome! Great connections are happening surrounding this curriculum. I feel a deep commitment to sharing Native American Culture and Art. I want to be reverent and authentic." Once again, I was confronted with ideological resistance. I felt as if Sharon, the students, Melvina, and I had just created a space of possibilities, an expansion of the narrow ways Indigenous people are framed, but the words in her email felt like they enclosed what we had been working so hard to expand. I read Sharon's email over and over. The words "healing vibrations" and "reverent and authentic" rung in my ears, much like those words "beauty" and "honor" she routinely used.

I probably shouldn't have been surprised. Sharon's response wasn't unusual, but continuous with comments I had heard from other people—the way my son's teacher talked about his beautiful "spirit," the way a former administrator in the district always thanked me for my "wisdom," the way an educator in the area suggested I was part of her "tribe." Sharon's comment gave voice to the context of colonialism that insisted on objectifying and exotifying Indigenous peoples. Sharon had appreciated our presentation, even shared her own story about the long journey we all take toward critical reflection and growth, yet it really felt as if she hadn't heard anything that we had presented. It also felt as if she hadn't internalized any of the conversations we had had over the past year. Those words—beauty, honor, healing vibrations, reverent, authentic—still held sway over how she understood the work we were doing together. Troubling, too, was the patience I had come to see this work demanded, and the feeling that, however slow or incremental the progress, I had to keep at this work because these teachers were teaching our children. Students like Celeste deserved teachers who demonstrated anticolonial literacy, a skill which felt increasingly impossible in a society so illiterate about Indigenous peoples. But even though I felt disheartened, I found solace when thinking about students like Celeste, who, after enduring her teacher's ignorance and arrogance, ultimately pursued her project on her own time and in her own way. Societal ignorance and colonial discourses are stubborn, but students like Celeste remind me that Native survivance is equally enduring, and that Indigenous students are smart, resourceful, and will continue creating spaces for themselves and others, at times, in spite of their teachers.

Notes

1 At the time of writing, the Pamunkey Indian Tribe had yet to be federally recognized as a Native nation by the Office of Federal Acknowledgment within the US Department of Indian Affairs. On July 2, 2015, the Office of the Assistant Secretary for Indian Affairs issued a press release recognizing the Pamunkey Indian Tribe as the 567th federally recognized Native nation in the US. In this same press release, the Department

denied recognition for the Duwamish Tribe in Washington, citing that they failed to meet established criteria. The Duwamish continue to fight for federal recognition, claiming they were once recognized by the Clinton administration, a decision that was overturned when Bush took office (http://www.duwamishtribe.org/).

2 The poster campaign was developed by students in STARS, which stands for Students Teaching About Racism in Society. STARS was founded by Dr. Sheila Williams and Louise Annarino at Ohio University. Their 2013 "We're A Culture Not a Costume" poster campaign can be viewed here: https://www.ohio.edu/orgs/stars/Poster_Campaign.html.

References

ABC News. (2011). *A hidden America: Children of the plains (part 1)*. Retrieved from https://www.youtube.com/watch?v=IJapHc7B8Xs.

Baldwin, J. (1995). *The fire next time* (Modern Library Edition). New York, NY: Modern Library.

Castagno, A. E. (2014). *Educated in whiteness: Good intentions and diversity in schools*. Minneapolis, MN: University of Minnesota Press.

Delgado, R. (1989). Storytelling for oppositionists and others: A plea for narrative. *Michigan Law Review*, 87, 2411–2441.

DiAngelo, R. (2011). White fragility. *International Journal of Critical Pedagogy*, 3(3), 54–70.

Green, R. (1992). The tribe called Wannabee: Playing Indian in America and Europe. *Folklore*, 99(1), 30–55.

King, T. (2012). *Inconvenient Indian: A curious account of Native people in North America*. Minneapolis, MN: University of Minnesota Press.

Kumashiro, K. (2015). *Against common sense: Teaching and learning toward social justice* (3rd ed.). New York, NY: Routledge.

Leonardo, Z. (2004). The color of supremacy: Beyond the discourse of "white Privilege". *Educational Philosophy and Theory*, 36(2), 137–152.

Lomawaima, K. T., & McCarty, T. L. (2006). *"To remain an Indian": Lessons in democracy from a century of Native American education*. New York: Teachers College Press.

Matias, C., & Liou, D. (2015). Tending to the heart of communities of color. *Urban Education*, 50(5), 601–625.

Raibmon, P. (2005). *Authentic Indians: Episodes of encounter from the late-nineteenth-century Northwest coast*. Durham, NC: Duke University Press.

Rowe, M. (2008). Micro-affirmations & micro-inequities. *Journal of the International Ombudsman Association*, 1(1). Retrieved from http://ombud.mit.edu/sites/default/files/documents/micro-affirm-ineq.pdf.

Saito, N. T. (2014). Tales of color and colonialism: Racial realism and settler colonial theory. *Florida A & M University Law Review*, 10(1), 1–107. Retrieved from http://commons.law.famu.edu/famulawreview/vol10/iss1/3.

Sleeter, C. E. (2011). *The academic and social value of ethnic studies: A research review*. National Education Association Research Department.

Solórzano, D. G. (1998). Critical race theory, race and gender microaggressions, and the experience of Chicana and Chicano scholars. *International Journal of Qualitative Studies in Education*, 11(1), 121–136.

Solórzano, D. G., & Yosso, T. J. (2002). Critical race methodology: Counter-storytelling as an analytic framework for education research. *Qualitative Inquiry*, 8, 23–44.

Solórzano, D., Ceja, M., & Yosso, T. (2000). Critical race theory, racial microaggressions, and campus racial climate: The experiences of African American college students. *Journal of Negro Education*, 69(1), 60–73.

Smith, W., Allen, W., & Danley, L. (2007). "Assume the position ... you fit the description": Psychosocial experiences and racial battle fatigue among African American male college students. *American Behavioral Scientist*, 51(4), 551–578.

Sue, D. W., Capodilupo, C. M., Torino, G. C., Bucceri, J. M., Holder, A. M. B., Nadal, K. L., & Esquilin, M. (2007). Racial microaggressions in everyday life: Implications for clinical practice. *American Psychologist*, 62(4), 271–286.

Tuck, E. (2009). Suspending damage: A letter to communities. *Harvard Educational Review*, 79(3), 409–428.

Valenzuela, A. (1999). *Subtractive schooling: U.S.-Mexican youth and the politics of caring*. Albany, NY: State University of New York Press.

3

NATIVE SHEROES AND COMPLEX PERSONHOOD

"I tried to get her to see what Winona LaDuke *actually* wore," said Melvina, the Title VI/Indian Education Program coordinator and one of the few Indigenous educators in the district.

We were in the Native Youth Center closet and Melvina was thumbing through some of the regalia. She lifted up a hanger which held a tan, buckskin dress, and told me:

> When Erin came to get help with her outfit for the wax museum, she originally wanted to wear regalia, something like this buckskin dress ... Winona doesn't wear things like that. Sometimes she wears this nice vest that has some floral embroidery on it, but she doesn't wear regalia like this when she speaks. So we did a Google Search and looked at the images, and I showed her that in each one, she was wearing a button-up shirt and jeans or slacks.

Melvina and I were discussing one of the Native students in the program, Erin, and her upcoming class presentation. Erin was in 5th grade and her teacher, Ms. Carter, had organized a "living wax museum," an auto/biographical activity designed to engage students in research and writing. In the curriculum, students investigate the biography of an influential leader that they admire, researching major life events, important achievements, and contributions that leader has made to society. From this biography, students develop an autobiographical monologue which they present in the culminating activity while outfitted in the attire of their influential leader. At the final presentation, dressed as their leaders, students remain still, like displays in a museum, until participants "bring them to life" by dropping a coin into a can in front of them. As they come to life, students perform their prepared monologue, highlighting for the museum-goer their own notable roles and accomplishments.

I was skeptical about this wax museum activity, given that museums have particularly troubling historic and ongoing relationships with Native peoples and nations. Repatriation of sacred items from museums is intimately linked to sovereignty, and reclaiming the bodies, bones, and baskets of our relatives is real and important work. In such a context of theft, commodification, and voyeurism, figuring out how to support a Native student in emulating a Native leader like Winona LaDuke for this project, without questioning or critiquing the very act of displaying itself, felt problematic. This was a longstanding school-wide project, however, and Melvina and I were asked to "make it better."

I learned about this wax museum activity through a chance meeting I had with Erin's teacher, Ms. Carter, in the hallway at her school. While I was waiting to meet another teacher, we struck up a conversation about the Native Youth Center as it was adjacent to the school, which then led to a discussion on a unit she was teaching about Native Americans. Ms. Carter outlined for me some of the curriculum she had designed and taught so far in her unit. She introduced students to various Native stories and taught them about Yup'ik masks. She then had students create their own creation tales and stories that explain phenomena, making masks to accompany their legends. She told me that class also learned about some of the historical conflicts between Native people in the Plains and the early settlers. As I listened to her unit description, I felt a familiar sense of uneasiness. Native families in this district have clearly stated that they wanted to see more of their lives and cultures reflected in curriculum, and on the surface, Ms. Carter's unit was addressing the gap families had critiqued. Yet I was concerned with how Native content was being included and what students would take away from this unit. I had seen a persistent pattern in the district of erasing contemporary Indigenous life and commodifying Native culture. I also have had the experience of teachers withdrawing from me when I had drawn attention to these dynamics. So when Ms. Carter kindly asked if I had any suggestions for her unit, I was cautious. I didn't want to alienate her, but I did want to be helpful and provide what information I could.

As a result of these interactions, I have found educators appear less threatened and more inclined to critically self-reflect when offered alternative forms of representation to consider, rather than explicit critiques or suggestions. In my work with elementary teachers, I usually make a point to bring contemporary resources as examples or gifts for teachers when possible. Books like *Children of Native America Today* (Dennis & Hirschfelder, 2014) often do indirect cultural and pedagogical work with teachers. By depicting the lives of contemporary Native children, this book not only provides teachers with an opportunity to recognize the diversity of contemporary Native America, but also indirectly invites teachers to reflect on their own curriculum and representations of Native life. The images in this particular book, for example, are intended to intervene into the typical static and stoic portrayals of Native life. While they depict children engaging in traditional activities—dancing in regalia, riding horses, or gathering traditional foods like wild rice or sap—they also depict children in jeans and sneakers, getting piggyback rides or riding in golf carts, and eating ice cream or peanut butter and jelly sandwiches. And in many of the pictures, the children, as children often do, are smiling. In contrast to these diverse, contemporary images, it is my hope the one-dimensional portrayals of Indianness in teachers' curriculum appear a stark oversimplification and demeaning portrayal by comparison.

Decentering my own comments and suggestions, and instead providing educators with resources and representations that juxtapose dominant discourses of Indigeneity with more humanizing portrayals, has been particularly effective in working with educators who embody what DiAngelo (2011) terms "white fragility," "a state in which even a minimum amount of racial stress becomes intolerable, triggering a range of defensive moves" (p. 57). Because disrupting teachers' sense of "racial comfort" (p. 61) can derail their willingness to engage the issues, I have had to intentionally find ways to hold space for teachers' discomfort. This has been challenging given that some educators and administrators in the district seem to want me (as an educational researcher), or Melvina (as the Indian Education director) to support, not challenge, their work. They want us to visit their classes as guest speakers and drum or tell stories, not question the ways their curriculum may be rooted in dehumanization. This dynamic reflects a broader pattern of interactions in which Indigenous people are "praised" for conforming to Eurocentric standards of behavior, but "criticized" when we resist (Furniss, 1999, p. 177).

There are limits to this approach of offering educators more "humanizing" images of Native America. Projects of inclusion, which take up the aim of "humanizing the object into a subject" (Tuck & Yang, 2014, p. 814), are premised on liberal multiculturalism. Such approaches seek to include Indigenous life while simultaneously leaving intact unexamined, dominant "whitestream" (Grande, 2015) curricula. Efforts to humanize Native America might also result in little more than non-Native teachers or children thinking that *they* (Native Americans) are just like *us* (non-Natives), a "we are all the same" logic that Grande rejects because "it not only denies the 'difference' of indigenous cultures and belief systems, but also tacitly reduces indigenous peoples to the status of whites-without-technology" (2015, p. 95).

Any individual intervention, such as the introduction of contemporary Native life through images of smiling children in a book, is of course insufficient in combating not only erasure, but the contemporary consequences of longstanding policies of physical and cultural genocide. Nevertheless, these inclusions, though impartial, are important when we center Native students as subjects in our classrooms. These images contribute positively to Native students' sense of self-worth and dignity and help Native students see themselves positively now and in the future. As Cree singer-songwriter Buffy Sainte-Marie states in the foreword to *Children of Native America Today*,

Indians exist. We are alive and real. We have fun, friends, and a whole lot to contribute to the rest of the world through our reality. Native children, like all children, should also know that there is tremendous good work to be done in which they can share. They have a future. (p. 4)

That teachers and non-Native children learn to see beyond the stereotypes that society inculcates in young children is an indirect, positive consequence.

I wished that when Ms. Carter had asked me for suggestions, I had a book to offer her. However, this visit was unplanned, and so I was unprepared. She seemed eager to discuss her curriculum and get some advice and resources for her unit, which was still in progress, and so I provided a few words of encouragement, and then despite my concerns, decided to pose the fairly benign inquiry I had been asking other teachers.

"What were students learning about Native people today?" I asked her.
"That's a great question," she responded.

It had never occurred to Ms. Carter that her unit might only attend to Native people as existing in the past. For her this wasn't an explicit or intentional orientation, but an inherited and taken-for-granted framing. Unlike other teachers, however, she expressed gratitude for the question as well as an earnest desire to reconsider what she taught.

I also asked about her choice to teach Yup'ik masks. Though she made an effort to teach "Yup'ik" masks as opposed to the more generic "Native American" masks I had seen in a teacher's classroom at a nearby school, she framed mask-making as a fairly abstract and historic cultural practice, detached from contemporary Yup'ik life, culture, and community. Teaching masks devoid of context is problematic, some educators suggesting it is inappropriate for curriculum altogether (Hirschfelder & Beamer, 2000).

"Teaching something as sacred and culturally specific as masks is complex," I offered. "Some might even say inappropriate."
"Yeah, I knew that masks were sacred," she replied. "Some people burn them after they use them," she said, but then she admitted she knew little else.

Like most activities, however, it is not the mask-making itself that is inherently problematic, but rather how mask-making as a curricular activity intersects with the particular historic, social, cultural, political, and discursive contexts within which it is taught. The revitalization of Alutiiq mask-making in Alaska, for example, is gaining momentum. The learning and replication of traditional Alutiiq masks by groups of Alutiiq and Alaska Native children is different, and conceivably appropriate, precisely because of the ways the activity fits within its respective context. As Alutiiq scholar and museum director Sven Haakanson, Jr. (2002) states in the newsletter *Sharing Our Pathways*,

> The carving of masks for dances and storytelling nearly disappeared entirely from practice in the Kodiak Island region. However, this has changed. Over the past ten years, Alutiiq people have rediscovered, relearned and are now recreating traditional masks to be used in dances, given as gifts and to be sold. This spring, the Alutiiq Museum, thanks to support from the Rockefeller Foundation's Partnership Affirming Community Transformation (PACT) grant and a partnership with the Kodiak Island Borough School District, is bringing a traveling mask exhibit and carving workshop to villages on Kodiak. We will spend an entire week working with students and adults, showing them how to care for and use carving tools and how to carve traditional Alutiiq masks. Our goal with this program is not to just exhibit masks, which were historically taken away as curiosity pieces, but to inspire individuals into once again taking up this practice and revitalizing the art of mask making. (n.p.)

These activities felt linked, though they weren't linked by context or purpose. Mask-making as a form of community resurgence and reclamation against historic theft and appropriation is distinct from mask-making as a multicultural activity. Instead, the activities felt linked through exotic desires and cultural extraction. The multicultural activity, though purportedly designed to understand and appreciate Native culture, tacitly seemed to be preparing a new generation of people who, enamored with masks, would desire such "curiosity pieces" for themselves.

As the masks were a backdrop for the children to invent their own "legend," I also inquired into Ms. Carter's approach to teaching Native stories. She responded that she told various Native American legends from different regions in the United States, then students would make their own legends. When I asked her how she helped students understand that some stories are not myths but actual accounts of the world, she offered that she tried to stay away from more foundational stories like creation stories, but said that she had also never really thought about that before.

Significant was the fact that Ms. Carter positioned the stories she taught with respect to particular regions and Indigenous peoples, an explicit intervention into the erasure that occurs when teachers use the generic referent "Native American" legends, a persistent practice I have seen other teachers use in this district. This is the same erasure that occurs when someone quotes "Native American" wisdom, but won't situate the quote with respect to the particular people and place that the saying emerged from. It is the same sleight of hand employed by non-Indigenous artists and storytellers who strive to appear authentic and culturally located through the appropriation of Indigenous signifiers, yet simultaneously refuse to locate the particular people and place to whom their designs and stories belongs (Iseke-Barnes, 2009).[1] Yet despite trying to locate the stories she taught within particular Indigenous nations, Ms. Carter's positioning of Native stories as little more than "legends" or "myths" invalidates Indigenous knowledge and reflects what Mik'maq scholar Marie Battiste (2000) refers to as "cognitive imperialism," "a form of cognitive manipulation used to disclaim other knowledge bases and values" (p. 198).

This approach is commonplace in elementary schools. Growing up in an adjacent district, I remember taking part in such curriculum as an elementary student. We listened to various Native "legends" and other "porquois" stories like Verna Aardema's (1975) *Why Mosquitoes Buzz in People's Ears*, then invented our own stories of how particular phenomena came to be. While I don't remember the legend I created, I remember liking stories like this as a child, and I probably enjoyed creating my own story. As a teacher, I have also come across lessons online that advocate for the approach Ms. Carter took.[2] Yet this approach positions Indigenous accounts of the world as little more than inventive fictions from individuals, rather than longstanding, community-based, place-based, and culturally specific expressions of Indigenous knowledge, values, and worldviews. Of course Native individuals do invent and tell stories, but the bodies of knowledge embedded in particular stories are real and important, and should be respected (which, in some instances, also means they shouldn't be told). Moreover, it can take an individual storyteller decades, even a lifetime, to gain the knowledge needed to properly tell and understand these stories (Archibald, 2008; Iseke-Barnes, 2009).

Because our talk was unplanned, we didn't have enough time to get into all of this. We briefly continued our conversation, during which I learned her unit didn't focus on local Native people and nations because that was covered last year in the Oregon 4th grade content standards (Oregon Department of Education, 2011). I encouraged her, regardless, to continue to think locally and regionally about Native people when possible. The teacher I was supposed to meet arrived, and so I thanked Ms. Carter for her time and let her know I was happy to work with her in the future if she would like. I told her Melvina and I could host her class at the Native Youth Center adjacent to the school. She thanked me for giving her some questions to consider and told me she wished she had talked to me earlier. She appreciated the prompts to consider framing her unit around "here and now" rather than in the "past and over there." She was looking forward to connecting about more resources and we planned on being in touch soon.

Ms. Carter's inclusion of Native curriculum was aligned with both Common Core reading and writing standards, as well as Oregon art standards. In light of current educational discourses regarding academic "achievement," this alignment reminded me that deep consideration must be placed not only on *whether* students are achieving, but on *what* they are achieving. What sorts of knowledge were students gaining if all students—even those traditionally underserved by schools— met or exceeded academic expectations in this unit? What types of values, relationships, and subjectivities was this type of curricular unit producing? The flexibility offered educators in the standards signaled to me the opportunities available for teachers in crafting their curricula, but also the danger and vulnerabilities when Native studies curricula was linked to teacher knowledge, interest, and skills. Ms. Carter's thoughtful reflections during our conversation also reminded me that often times, teachers rely on taken-for-granted curricular framings when they have little opportunity or time to think outside of them. Teachers need time to be in conversation and dialogue about these issues, to be presented alternatives, and to reflect on their own curricular and pedagogical choices in light of them.

The Possibilities of Presence

Ms. Carter reached out to me shortly after our conversation, an action that was naturally welcome, but contrary to my expectations given my experience with other teachers. It was then that she explained that she was organizing a wax museum activity and wanted to offer some present-day Native role models as options for her students during the activity. She wasn't familiar with any contemporary Native leaders, but wanted to take seriously that idea of starting with the present, and asked if I could provide her with any contemporary Native leaders. Though I was disheartened she couldn't name a single contemporary Native leader, I was glad she reached out.

I provided her with a list that included some of the following names along with some informative videos and links for her class:

Winona LaDuke (Anishinaabe)
Susan Shown Harjo (Cheyenne & Hodulgee Muscogee)
Chris Wandolowski (Kiowa)
Al Smith (Klamath)
Shoni Schimmel (Umatilla)
Oren Lyons (Turtle Clan/Haudenosaunee)
Buffie St. Marie (Cree)
John Herrington (Chickasaw)
The Thompson Trio (Lakota lacrosse players)
Supaman (Crow)
A Tribe Called Red (Mohawk, Cayuga and Nipissing Anishnabe)[3]

Ms. Carter later thanked me and told me that she showed her students the list. Erin, one of the Native students in her class, was very excited to learn more about Winona LaDuke. She said she looked forward to bringing her students to the Center so they could learn more about the program. She saw the visit as a great opportunity to connect some of her Native students to the Indian Education program, which she felt was especially important as she thought there were five or six Native students in her class.

I admired Ms. Carter's effort to offer her students contemporary Native role models. She wanted to break out of the pattern of more typical portrayals of Native leaders at the wax museum, leaders she referred to as the "regulars"—Pocahontas, Chief Joseph, or Crazy Horse. There is nothing wrong with studying historic Native leaders and their contributions to their respective nation and society more broadly; in fact, it is important to do so. However, by purposefully offering current Native leaders, Ms. Carter created curricular space for Native people to exist in the present, and for Native students to see themselves in both the present and the future. Historic role models should be studied, yet in an environment where even the teacher couldn't identify a single contemporary Native leader or role model, activities that only reach for the past unwittingly reproduced that very ignorance. Ms. Carter recognized this gap in her understanding and responded professionally by reaching out for assistance—an act I am coming to understand requires more courage than we might reasonably expect. By doing so, she provided Erin the opportunity to learn about and look up to a contemporary Anishinaabe leader.

Though Erin was not Anishinaabe, it was clear that the curricular space Ms. Carter created fostered an opportunity for Erin to see herself in the curriculum, and to nurture a sense of pride in her own Native culture. Erin's enthusiasm about the project was infectious. She talked incessantly about Winona LaDuke, rattling off facts from her life or the impact she has had on the world. Conversations with Erin's teachers also illustrated the way Erin's engagement with her leader opened up space in the classroom for Erin to discuss her own culture. Erin was fairly light-skinned and not always recognized as a Native student by teachers or classmates, despite her commitment to her culture, community, and nation. Ms. Carter knew how important drum group was to Erin because she frequently mentioned her involvement in the Center or the Native summer camps she had been involved in. But, as her student teacher, a white male from the local university noted, these conversations didn't always come up easily among youth, and it seemed to him that Erin wanted to express pride in her culture to her classmates. He explained how her research into Winona LaDuke's life fostered these conversations:

> It gave her an opportunity to talk about her own experiences, too, with her friends. You could tell that it's important to her, but there's not always that avenue to have that conversation, you know, in the middle of something else you're doing.

He believed that it was Erin's focus on Winona LaDuke that "lent itself to that … as they're talking about their people, because that just happens naturally when you have a massive research project. Well my guy did this, did you know that I … [drum, etc.]."

Ms. Carter also witnessed conversations and understandings open up for both Erin and her peers:

It opened up avenues for her to talk about her own heritage and pride. I would overhear her explaining the concept of regalia, the different types of dance ... I mean all those conversations ... It was just nice for them to have someone more modern for the kids to identity with and talk about.

Though the inquiry into Winona LaDuke's life provided Erin with both a role model and the curricular opportunity to express pride in her own culture and community, the act of including contemporary Indigenous life was not without its challenges. Erin's visit to the Center in search of a buckskin dress or other form of regalia to wear as Winona LaDuke illustrated these particular challenges, challenges which were more than incidental. Erin's desire for buckskin is evidence that the "Indian as historic" discourse, what King (2012) has coined the "Dead Indian," is not just a nostalgic desire in non-Indigenous teachers' minds; it can also show up in the minds of Indigenous children. This means teachers need to not only broaden their own understanding of Indigenous identity, but they also need to be prepared to teach a broader understanding to children—sometimes even Indigenous children themselves. This latter work can be complicated, as Erin soon illustrated to us.

The Burden of Authenticity

Erin told us that she needed her outfit to look "Native American-y" to go with her background, a powwow scene that she had created. Initially when Erin approached us, we assumed that she was feeling pressure from her teacher to look "Native American-y." Melvina had routine inquiries at the Center from teachers requesting feathers and chokers, for example, and I had frequent experience with teachers' conceptions of what made something look "Native American," experiences which warranted our initial suspicion. Yet in a later conversation with her teacher, I learned that it was *Erin* who wanted to wear the buckskin dress and who wanted to make sure she looked visibly Native American.

Ms. Carter recalled Erin asking her what to wear, to which she responded, "I bet she wears business clothing." I told Ms. Carter that was what we had told Erin at the Center as well, explaining Melvina's strategy of using a Google image search. I told her Erin told us that it was not "Native American-y enough," and then dared to inquire whether she got that idea from her teacher. "Did you say it wasn't Native American-y enough?" I asked.

"No, that was her ..." she responded. "I said, 'I would imagine a casual business suit, or a business suit. She's an attorney, Erin. I don't think she walks around in Native ... what you're thinking of as Native American ...'"

Ms. Carter was attempting to steer Erin away from a what she viewed as a stereotypical depiction of Winona LaDuke. She told me she saw these same stereotypical representations every year in the ways Pocahontas was portrayed at the wax museum performance—buckskin dress, single feather sticking out of the back of the child's head, and a braid or two. Ms. Carter was trying to thoughtfully guide Erin toward what she considered a more accurate representation of Winona LaDuke, the same careful guidance Melvina had offered when Erin visited the Center by showing actual images of Winona LaDuke.

I wanted to ask Ms. Carter about the nuances in trying to both support Erin's desire to look "Native American-y" while also delicately questioning her idea of what constitutes Native American attire. The markers of Indigeneity that Erin was reaching for, such as the buckskin dress, were not inherently problematic. Buckskin, for example, is a traditional, not stereotypical, form of regalia for some Indigenous peoples and styles of dancing such as Northern or Southern Women's traditional. And yet Erin's reach for buckskin was complex, seemingly driven by the same nostalgia and narrow understanding of authenticity that I have witnessed non-Native educators reach for: the administrator who invites a traditional Native dancer to perform at an assembly for Native Heritage Month (as opposed to a tribal chairwoman in a pants suit). Erin sought markers that didn't necessarily reflect Winona LaDuke's appearance, but a more generic representation of Indianness. I was hoping to discuss these issues with Ms. Carter in more depth, but as we were speaking, the student teacher interjected and his comments threw me off.

> It's like a baseball player ... regardless of whether he's African American or Latino or whatever. When he plays baseball, he wears a baseball uniform. He might wear a poncho or something outside, or sag his britches or whatever else ... or wear a suit, but when he plays ball ... when she's in the courtroom, she wears court attire.[4]

While this white student teacher was trying to support Ms. Carter's remarks, making connections between the professional arenas of law and baseball, his analogy was troubling. The poncho and the saggy pants, markers he associated with Latinx and Black youth, struck me as the same lingering shadows that trailed Indigeneity, and so I thought about whether they were equivalents. The poncho, like the buckskin dress, has deep roots in Indigenous cultures, and importance and cultural meaning within some Indigenous and Latinx communities. Like buckskin, ponchos are not inherently stereotypical, though they get mobilized in tokenizing ways each Cinco de Mayo or Halloween on college campuses around the country as students enact caricatures of Mexican culture. Indeed, this was the marker that the student teacher himself associated with Latinx culture as he connected his hypothetical Latino athlete to the poncho. Sagging britches, on the other hand, do not have as longstanding cultural roots as buckskin dresses or ponchos, but that doesn't mean they don't operate as a form of meaningful cultural expression for Black youth or others who take up that particular style of dress. Sagging pants have been associated with drugs, gang activity, and prison, and there is speculation as to whether they stem from prison culture where inmates are provided ill-fitted clothing. Yet for some youth, sagging pants as a personal statement might serve as a powerful means of counter-culture expression. There are active bans across the country that deplore and try to police the practice, some claiming that the very act creates a pipeline to prison or even death (though society has made it clear that even Black men in more "suitable" attire are not safe in public).

I understood what this student teacher was trying to say. His analogy was intended to support Erin by questioning her immediate reach for mainstream signifiers of Indigeneity. What most struck me, however, was that the casual cultural markers he used appeared reproductive of the narrow notion of cultural representation we were all intentionally trying to disrupt. Ms. Carter then said, "She *did* push [to wear regalia], and I let her." She also told me that she had a wand adorned with a crystal and feather made by a Native woman in Alaska that was displayed on her wall, and that Erin really wanted to hold it during her presentation. "So I let her have that," Ms. Carter said, expressing resignation.

The dynamics Erin, her teachers, and I were navigating were complex. I told Ms. Carter as much, and that we faced similar dilemmas in the program, wanting to support Native students as they try to express themselves in visible ways, but also recognizing that "the desire to be seen is also complicated by the expectations of performing an 'authentic' Indigeneity that burden youth" (Dion & Salamanca, 2014, p. 178). I told her we gave Erin similar advice at the center, questioning her desire for the buckskin dress, and offering a variety of pictures of Winona to highlight how she typically dressed. This was our way of doing our best to support her meaningful desire for visibility, while also gently unsettling her reach for stereotypes. The same discourses that entangle how non-Native teachers make Indigenous people visible in narrow and stereotypical ways can also shape the ways Indigenous students represent their own Indigeneity.

"And then I blew it," she said. "And let her hold it [the wand], but she was so … The night of the event she held it and she had her pose. Man, she was polished."

Visibility in a Context of Erasure

I understood where Ms. Carter was coming from. Perhaps the wand, which had little to do with the actual life of Winona LaDuke, did contribute to the reproduction of a more generic, stereotypical representation of Indigeneity. Perhaps if she hadn't had the wand but instead other critical expressions of Indigeneity on the wall, it wouldn't have been an issue. However, even though Ms. Carter's willingness to be self-critical is important and helpful, I didn't necessarily agree with her that she "blew it." She was caught in the complex space of nurturing a young child's self-esteem and cultural pride, while also questioning whether and how she might be critical of the images and ideas that child brings to the classroom. This complexity was amplified too as Erin, the Native student, was the one reaching for what appeared to be hardened, static portrayals of Indianness, representations that were incongruent with the rich, complex Indigenous life she was actually leading.

We knew Erin as a strong participant in the Center as well as her own nation as a tribal member. We knew Erin to be comfortable in jeans or picking up a shawl and dancing around the drum. We knew her as an active practitioner in her culture, and in the context of the Native Youth Center, she showed little ambivalence about her identity. She knew who she was and where she came from. Yet in the context of her classroom, Erin still reached for symbols that weren't culturally specific or place-based, markers that also weren't accurate depictions of Winona LaDuke for her project. Her own teacher admitted that Erin didn't "look" Native American in the way she had expected, but through engagement with her, she came to see that her understanding was narrow, and that there were important dimensions that couldn't be seen: a political identity (expressed through citizenship in her tribal nation), as well as cultural identity (expressed through participation in her own nation's cultural practices as well as those at the Center). Both teachers also thought the ways such narrow understanding of Indigeneity likely contributed to Erin's disappointment with not being viewed as Native by her peers or other teachers, and perhaps this motivated her to be visibly Native American in her depiction of Winona LaDuke.

Melvina also theorized that perhaps Erin's resistance to the pant suit and desire to be more "Native American-y" had to do with this constant misrecognition, a dynamic she had seen circulate around many Native students with light skin throughout her career in Indigenous education. For a student like Erin whose phenotypical appearance didn't always invite questions about her cultural identity (questions often reserved for those whose name, skin color, or accent, for example, signal them as "exotic" and "Other"), their routine categorization as white may feel like an erasure of their identity. Further, aspects students may feel are important to their identities—their citizenship in a nation, a language spoken, a story they have been told or retell, a connection to land—are not always visible in the ways settler society imagines Indigeneity to be expressed. Melvina had noted that some Native students with lighter skin in the program often experience the quandary of not being "seen" as Native, despite active participation in their communities, nations, and cultures. Some students, grounded in a sense of who they are, are amused by the misnomer when people mistakenly view them as white, especially if they view themselves as fairly "traditional" (having grown up on a reservation, or knowing their language, for example). These students recognized the fallacy in equating Indigeneity with dark skin as it was their light-skinned aunties or grandparents who taught them languages and stories and songs. These confident students fortunately seemed to accurately locate the problem with mainstream society's narrow and inaccurate understandings of Indigeneity, rather than in their appearance. Melvina's own daughter who is an enrolled tribal member with a light complexion is one of these students. She was actively raised in a ceremonial environment, which Melvina believes gives her a deep base of cultural experience and pride to draw from. She knows her songs and the ceremonies, and is deeply embedded in her family and community. She knows who she is, so unlike some of the other students Melvina has worked with, she doesn't feel the need to outwardly reach for certain markers or symbols to be read as Native.

But Melvina noted that other light-skinned Native students feel troubled by others' constant framing of them as white. To counteract what they conceivably view as their erasure, Melvina has seen some of these students occasionally reach for visible ways to mark their Indigeneity, using chokers, big feathered earrings, even Redsk*ns[5] gear—ironically reproducing a parallel form of erasure, despite their attempts to contest it. There is an important element of resistance in those self-representations as students seek to be visible in a context determined to erase them. Yet, in asserting generic, pan-Indian markers of Indigeneity solely for the sake of visibility, students may also be complicit in the erasure of their own tribal specificity. This is also not to suggest that these students *only* viewed and represented themselves in relation to dominant culture and narrow framings, but rather, that students' experiences and connections to family, community, nation, heritage, and culture in part, influence the way they view and represent themselves. For some light-skinned Native students, their perceived erasure is non-threatening, amusing even; for others, it strongly influences the ways they choose to express themselves and assert their Indigeneity.

This routine miscategorization has also been bothersome to some of the students with darker complexions. When Ms. Carter's class visited the center recently, I shared with her class the large US map we have covered with pins, each placed on a students' tribal nation or traditional homelands. We use this as a way to visibly represent the diversity in the program and Native community locally. I had just shown the class the village in Alaska where my grandma was born and moved aside so Melvina could speak. One of the 5th grade students leaned over and whispered in my ear: "I'm not Mexican. I'm Native." I was surprised by her comment as I hadn't met this student before. "Do people often think you're Mexican?" I whispered back. She nodded at me. "I am so happy you are proud to be Native," I told her. She smiled. In the few seconds we whispered as Melvina spoke, there was no time to talk to her about binaries of Indigeneity and authenticity, about Indigenous peoples' experiences in Mexico, about her own desires to be visible as Native, perhaps even her own possible latent prejudice toward Mexicans ... So much was at work in this fleeting moment that I could only offer the young girl a whispered affirmation.

This student, it turns out, was routinely viewed by teachers and others as Latina, a miscategorization that her teachers told me frustrated her. She was not the only one routinely miscategorized. Another Native student came to the center distressed one day when her history teacher made a statement that Native people didn't exist anymore. She suffered quietly in that classroom, wondering if he thought she was Latina, wondering if he knew she was Native, wondering if he would have said that if he had known. She didn't address the issue in class, but processed with Melvina and others at the Center after school that day. For these students, erasure through misidentification, based in narrow notions of what it means to look or not look Native, was a fairly common and disquieting experience.

In navigating settler society's narrow image of Indigeneity, students, such as Erin, may reach for visible markers: the buckskin dress or the feather wand, for example. On the surface it appears Erin as a young Indigenous woman is caught up in a similar dynamic as the non–Native educators who nostalgically tries to recuperate a timeless sense of Indigeneity. Yet just as context shapes the appropriateness of mask-making as a cultural activity, Erin's reach to be visible as a Native person is also different, precisely because of Erin's own particular historical, social, cultural, and political context. Erin's desire to express herself, despite longstanding and (at times forcible) continuing attempts to erase her, her people, and Native people in general, distinguishes her actions from the teacher who glues feathers on a sign, or the administrator who hires a Native dancer. Erin is reaching for *self*-representation to combat her own erasure. For Erin, depicting Winona LaDuke in a pantsuit or business attire, with nothing to visibly mark her as "Indigenous," might have felt as if it were a form of erasure. While comfortable with her Indigeneity at the Center, the context of the classroom and school created an undertow of invisibility and erasure that she contested.

It becomes clear how the context of settler society's normalization of whiteness can stifle a Native student's sense of self and cultural expression. The education of non–Native teachers and students can be tied to this context as some Native students in public schools actively negotiate their identities in a context of erasure and narrow definitions. This invisibility of whiteness and settler society is a feature of settler colonialism and support for Indigenous students must necessarily recognize this unmarked backdrop against which some Indigenous students may try to express themselves. Care must be taken to encourage Indigenous students to interrogate the ways they represent their heritage and pride; but care must also be taken to make visible the ways settler society normalizes particular (white) bodies, rendering them Indigenous only when adorned with beads, buckskin, or feathers. Erin, like all students in that class, must be led to see that there is an unnamed norm against which Indigeneity (or other racial/cultural expressions) must conceivably be distinguished from.

What also distinguishes Erin's dilemma from that of educators who reach for stereotypical representations is that the burden often befalls Indigenous people to distinguish themselves culturally. Whereas the white teacher can feel cathartically clean that they included a Native American unit or invited a Native dancer, the

Indigenous student may negotiate very real and deeply personal dynamics of identity, cultural expression, and belonging. Settler "imperialist nostalgia" (Rosaldo, 1989) as an "innocent" sentiment enables the benevolent recuperation of what was lost, masking complicity in the racial domination. The narrow, static reproduction of Indigeneity can cause an educator to feel good about her multicultural efforts. Yet the Native student who negotiates their identity and problematically reaches for those very markers, even while demonstrating resistance, might be caught up in a problematic web of authenticity that later elicits questions and criticism from their Native peers, even critical self-reflection and regret. Those Indigenous students who are grounded in their own particular lands, languages, cultures, stories, or families may not feel challenged by the deficits in settler society's discourses about Indigeneity, but for some students, they may internalize those very deficit discourses as their own, and reproduce them, even as a means of resistance. What Erin and other light-skinned Native students may be negotiating is not an issue of having the "right" knowledge. Rather, their negotiations point to knowledge of the contextual considerations a teacher may need in order to serve Indigenous students, surfacing the context and terrain of meaning that both teachers and students, Native and non-Native, navigate, which has ties to history and is also lived in the present. At minimum, an educator needs to know enough about these issues in order to recognize that they can be problematic.

When Native Students Wanna Be *Indian* [6]

Educational scholarship notes that children are not blank slates. As Paulo Freire (1970) points out, children are not empty vessels to be filled or containers in which to bank or deposit information. Students bring with them important "funds of knowledge" (Gonzalez, et al., 1995; Gonzalez & Moll, 2002) and "community cultural wealth" (Yosso, 2005). Culturally responsive approaches to teaching based in "difference approaches" and "resource pedagogies" (Paris, 2012) have been important interventions into deficit frameworks. Given the violent relationship Indigenous nations and peoples have had with schools, which were specifically designed to eradicate and domesticate Native children's cultural difference, the idea that teachers should respect cultural difference and the culture a Native student brings to the classroom is important. In response, "culturally responsive teaching" (Gay, 2002) that advocates "using the cultural characteristics, experiences, and perspectives of ethnically diverse students as conduits for teaching them more effectively" (p. 106) make sense. So too do theories of "culturally responsive pedagogy" (Villegas & Lucas, 2002) that instruct teachers to have "an affirming attitude toward students from culturally diverse backgrounds" and to "respect cultural differences" (p. 23).

What are educators to do, however, if a child demonstrates "cultural difference" in ways that do not necessarily reflect their particular cultural worldviews, but more closely reflect dominant discourses of culture and Indigeneity? How will a teacher know if the cultural knowledge and insight a child brings is "culturally inherent," which Leanne Simpson (2013) defines as "ways that reflect the diversity of thought within our broader cosmologies, those very ancient ways that are inherently counter to the influences of colonial hegemony" (p. 279)? Is it even a teacher's place to critique forms of Indigenous self-expression, especially when the educator is non-Native? How would a teacher know if a Native student's culture or cultural representation was counter-hegemonic, or reproduced cultural hegemony? It is precisely because these questions are so hard to answer that I let Ms. Carter know she didn't blow it. We have to be willing to critique ourselves as teachers, to honestly reflect on our practice, even when it is difficult, and then be responsible for the consequences of our pedagogical and curricular choices. Yet the situation we face with how to educate Indigenous students within public schools and in the context of settler colonialism requires much more of us than determining whether a decision was "good" in one instance, or whether we "blew it" in another. As relentless as settler colonialism is to erase Indigenous experience, our teaching must be equally as relentless: to make it visible, to work within it, to disrupt it. There is no endpoint, no right or wrong—just stamina to keep interrogating our teaching in light of its relationship to settler colonial and dominant discourses that are harmful to our students.

Our conversation and collective support for Erin was premised on the dilemma of how we as teachers might productively create space for students to identify with as well as critically reflect on particular cultural expressions and practices. The work of Django Paris and H. Samy Alim (2014) helps illuminate this question, as they unpack a similar dynamic in the context of hip hop culture. Their piece is a "loving critique" that extends Paris's former articulation of "culturally sustaining pedagogy" (CSP), itself an extension of the literature on culturally relevant (Ladson–Billings, 1995) and culturally responsive pedagogy (Gay, 2002). In an earlier articulation of CSP, Paris (2012) urges that we move beyond "relevance or responsiveness" and offers instead the notion of *culturally sustaining*:

> The term *culturally sustaining* requires that our pedagogies be more than responsive of or relevant to the cultural experiences and practices of young people—it requires that they support young people in sustaining the cultural and linguistic competence of their communities while simultaneously offering access to dominant cultural competence. Culturally sustaining pedagogy, then, has as its explicit goal supporting multilingualism and multiculturalism in practice and perspective for students and teachers. That is, culturally sustaining pedagogy seeks to perpetuate and foster—to sustain—linguistic, literate, and cultural pluralism as part of the democratic project of schooling. (p. 95)

Paris and Alim (2014) document how youth enact cultural and linguistic dexterity, fashioning fluid identities and cultural expressions that embody traditions, while also extending them. CSP calls on teachers to recognize the fluidity of youth culture, and commit "to sustaining them in both the traditional *and* evolving ways that are lived and used by young people," addressing "the well-understood fact that what it means to be African American or Latina/o or Navajo is continuing to shift in the ways culture always has" (p. 91). They also propose that a culturally sustaining framework should rid itself of the "White gaze" and ask,

> What would our pedagogies look like if this gaze weren't the dominant one? What would liberating ourselves from this gaze and the educational expectations it forwards mean for our abilities to envision new forms of teaching and learning? What if, indeed, the goal of teaching and learning with youth of color was not ultimately to see how closely students could perform White middle class norms but to explore, honor, extend, and, at times, problematize their heritage and community practices? (p. 86)

It is in this last charge, in asking teachers to problematize youth's heritage and community practices, that they illuminate the practical and complex dilemmas a teacher may face as they try to recognize the "rich and innovative linguistic, literate, and cultural practices" (p. 86) youth bring to the classroom, while also employing the insight and skill to problematize them.

Alim (2011) has termed the important "counterhegemonic forms of youth literacies" that youth bring to the classroom "ill-literacies": the ways a youth's "spoken, rhymed, or written text" exemplifies "linguistic and cultural ingenuity," for example (Paris & Alim, 2014, pp. 92–94). A teacher's recognition of youths' ill-literacies is an important curricular gesture. Allowing a youth to communicate in a freestyle rap, spoken word poem, or engage in a rap battle (improvised linguistic duels), creates space for youth culture and community; yet, these cultural practices and ill-literacies can also problematically revoice "racist, misogynistic, homophobic, and xenophobic discourses" (94). "What happens," they ask, "when ill-literacies get ill? In other words, what happens when, rather than challenging hegemonic ideas and outcomes, the cultural practices of youth of color actually reproduce them, or even create new ones?" (p. 92).

In answer to this complex question, Paris and Alim offer that a critically sustaining pedagogies both affirm students' cultural and linguistic practices, yet also acknowledge that not all aspects of community and heritage practices should be sustained. They argue teachers need a pedagogical stance and critical reflexivity that enables them to create "generative spaces for asset pedagogies to support the practices of youth and communities of color while maintaining a critical lens vis-à-vis these practices" (Paris & Alim, 2014, p. 92). With this critically reflective stance, a teacher might value a youth's spoken word poem in class as a meaningful form of literacy and cultural expression, while simultaneously questioning the way the lyrics reproduce particular systems of oppression, such as homophobia or misogyny (Paris & Alim, 2014).

This acknowledgement of both the "progressive" aspects of youth culture, as well as the need to critique the "oppressive" or "regressive practices" (p. 92) in the reproduction of youth culture is relevant for the ways we were all trying to support Erin, and highlights the tensions in doing so. At the Native Youth Center, we supported Erin's commitment to culture and community. As educators, we were each conscious of Erin's desire to be seen as Native, and understood that such a desire may have been fueled by the ignorance and misrecognition of settler society; yet we were also cautious about what appeared to be tokenizing forms of expression that reproduced static, historic representations of Indianness. A critical stance that asked Erin to dress professionally (which was indeed a more accurate depiction of Winona LaDuke) complicated the idea that Native people were solely cultural or historic, and perhaps an important intervention into those static representations. Yet Erin's continual desire for markers of Indianness was evidence that the business suit, though a more accurate portrayal of her contemporary subject, appeared to Erin a form of erasure. The business suit may have disrupted the stoic Indian, but for Erin, the strategy made her just like everyone else, and didn't satisfy her desire for a sense of distinctiveness; it wasn't "Native American-y" enough. Support for Erin had to creatively contend with the context of erasure and visibility she navigated, especially as a light-skinned Native youth.

Erin was unsatisfied with a pedagogy that merely guided her away from participating in the fetishization of her culture. As such, while troubling the problematic signifiers of Indigenous identity, we also needed to offer her more promising and generative forms of expression. Beyond critiquing the "regressive practices" then, we needed to offer signifiers that preserved the distinctiveness she was craving, but that didn't fall back into historicism. What if we had amplified other signifiers of Indigeneity? Winona LaDuke's values, knowledge, actions, humor, commitment to land and place, use of Ojibwe language, and political actions all conceivably could have been resources for representation. We could have suggested that Erin hold a flag of the White Earth Nation, or a campaign sign from when she ran with Nader as a visible way to mark her distinctiveness. We could have created a replica of the ancient squash that Winona LaDuke helped revitalize, or a made a sign with the word Gete-okosomin (the Anishinaabe word she chose to name the squash meaning "really cool old squash"). Or we could have given Erin a copy of Winona LaDuke's book, *The Militarization of Indian Country*, to hold which featured cover art by Bunky Echo-Hawk depicting a Native person in a gas mask, drawing attention to environmental racism and the biological warfare waged on Indigenous peoples and lands. There were multiple ways we could have supported Erin in negotiating the constraints of settler society's assumptions. Part of what has to be questioned, part of the work that needs to be done, part of why this is a challenge at all is that white, settler society has become deeply normalized. As teachers we have to question the ways our world is often set up by that presumption, and we have to find ways to guide our students in questioning that as well. There is a larger context here—of Indigenous erasure, of constrained visibility as Native people are often only "seen" when embodying the static, stereotypical markers of Indianness—that makes the work of cultural identification fall unfairly on the shoulders of Indigenous students.

What would a teacher need to know to recognize this dynamic and the ways it fits in a larger historical context? What knowledge would a teacher need—about Indigenous identity, sovereignty, self-determination, colonization, representation—to better serve Erin? Even as Native educators, we struggle with how to help students develop comfortable identities that don't reproduce stereotypical representations. Just recently at the Center, a Native student discussed an international trip she would be taking over the summer. As part of the cultural exchange with their host family in the program, each participant is asked to bring gifts to share. Students are instructed that those gifts should reflect the participants' "culture" so that the family and student can engage in an intercultural dialogue. This student was extremely excited to bring a gift and discuss Native culture. She relayed that she was considering making chokers for the host family. As the student relayed the story to Melvina and I, however, I had mixed feelings of pride and concern. I felt proud the student was excited to share about her Native identity and culture. It wasn't long ago that Native people felt shame about their identities, or forced to hide them in order to survive. In this student's family, I knew there were stories of dispossession, shame, and some relatives' denial of their Indigeneity. This student's mother was also the parent who felt identifying her daughter as Native in elementary school led to her placement in a special education class. For this student, this cultural exchange was important, and bone chokers were a way she could express her Native pride. Yet bone chokers per se didn't appear to be a part of this student's particular tribal affiliation. A necklace made from dentalium or pine nuts might have more accurately represented her peoples' place-based cultural practices. Perhaps it was hard to get dentalium or pine nuts, or perhaps the student just hadn't thought about it.

Like buckskin dresses and ponchos, it wasn't that chokers weren't traditional or meaningful, but in this context, it appeared the student was reaching for a generic marker rather than looking for a more "culturally inherent" (Simpson, 2013) gift. And while chokers are central to some forms of specific cultural expression, chokers have also been central to dominant warrior discourses, "warrior images" that Chippewa/Lac de Flambeau scholar Gail Valaskakis (2005) argues are not only prevalent in Westerns, but circulate in media representations today as well. Though Valaskakis was referring to mainstream media's fascination with the image of the Mohawk warrior during the Oka crisis, the depiction of the Native warrior in a bone choker is also a part of the "constructed and contradictory images of Indians" that Valaskakis refers to more generally, images "that are removed from the social meaning of lived experience in Native communities—and appropriated by non-Indians in everything from tourist brochures to the New Age 'White Warrior Society.'" (p. 42).

Melvina and I had had some practice guiding non-Native students and teachers through the conversations surrounding the tensions between appreciation and appropriation. A non-Native person reaching for a bone choker reasonably fits the category of appropriation, or at the very least, begs the question why the bone choker, and what purpose does the choker serve aesthetically, culturally, socially, or politically? But yet when Native students in the program reached for that same choker, a similar tension emerges, though perhaps more nuanced: how might we support these students in expressing cultural pride, while also guiding them in reflecting on expressions that aren't necessarily place-based or deeply rooted? Moreover, who gets to determine what constitutes a place-based or deeply rooted practice or expression? This tension was compounded because our own Indian Education program for many years, including last year, had led students in choker-making workshops. The program's website and brochures were littered with students adorned in chokers. Parents and families seemed to *like* making chokers. Further, the practice of making chokers itself has value, fostering a sense of community, nurturing relationships between children and adults, and instilling patience and a sense of accomplishment among participants. And yet, outside of a meaningful context of story, culture, and place, the choker work-shops seemed to also reinscribe a particularly narrow, warrior-like version of Indigeneity. Thomas King, in his book *The Inconvenient Indian*, reflects on his own cultural expression as a younger man and shivers at the thought of his own self-expression with regards to what he has termed a "Dead Indian."

> I never wore a full feather headdress to protests or marches, but I did sport a four-strand bone choker, a beaded belt buckle, a leather headband, and a fringed leather pouch, and when I look at the photographs from those years, the image of myself as a Dead Indian still sends a tremor up my spine. (2013, pp. 65–66)

In teaching students how to assemble chokers that came in little kits, the program appeared to sanction the sort of Dead Indian that King found so troubling later in life. Intentionally, there were no choker-making workshops this year, but the fact that any curriculum for the program is situated in the complex terrain of Indigenous identity, and that that terrain inevitably includes and competes with historic and hardened images of who Native students may think they should be or look like, is an important one.

Acknowledging Complex Personhood

Students' relationships to Indianness are complicated at times, but it is also foolish to think that they are completely determined by it. To disrupt the deployment of what appears to be hegemonic forms of Indianness unilaterally and without consideration for the various ways Native people use and deploy conceptions of

Indianness is to, in some sense, position Indigenous peoples or students as not knowing who they are or should be. Native identity intersects with the highly fraught terrain of adolescent identity more broadly. It is further complicated when Indigenous families deploy dominant markers of Indianness. Who were we as a program to suggest we knew how students or families should or shouldn't represent themselves as Indigenous peoples, or what a comfortable identity should look like for them? Many Native families came to our program adorned with what could conceivably be dominant markers of Indianness—dreamcatcher tattoos, howling wolf t-shirts, big feather earrings. Some of these forms of expression may be part of these families' own tribal and cultural traditions; others perhaps refashion those dominant markers of Indigeneity to symbolize Native pride; yet others quite possibly are unexamined expressions of the "Dead Indian." Support for these students and families can't mean simply presuming that we, as Indigenous educators, have more accurate or appropriate forms of cultural expression or self-identification.

Native people have a long history of wielding harmful representations to their own advantage, inverting and subverting them, making those images go to work for them or their communities, even profiting from them. Drawing on postcolonial theorist Homi Bhabha, Maureen Trudelle Schwarz (2013) offers the Native American Rights Fund's *Coca Cola* colonialism ad, "Fighting Colonialism at Home," as a form of "mimicry" that "mock[s] the supposed superiority of the colonizer" (p. 8). Plains Cree nation artist Tatakwan inverts and reclaims the word "savage" through creating beaded chokers that are boldly inscribed with the term.[7] Chickasaw metalsmith Kristen Dorsey has created "blood quantum earrings" as a commentary on governmental means of enumerating Indianness. Dorsey's earrings, which feature customizable fractions (1/2, 1/32, 4/4, and so on), are in her words a means to "foster intelligent discussions about issues of race and identity in Native America while creating awareness of how specific historical events are often the triggers of our current perceptions of Native identity."[8] To say that the buckskin dress or choker is entirely problematic not only ignores the significance those items have within particular communities, but also erases all the diverse and creative ways that Native people have been, as Schwarz's (2013) book title suggests, *Fighting Colonialism with Hegemonic Culture*. On one read, the American Indian Movement's (AIM) deployment of hegemonic features of Indianness such as bone chokers and feathers might be considered blatantly stereotypical. They could also be considered a form of what Mireille Rosello offers as a useful stance in relationship to those stereotypes: being a "reluctant witness" toward them; "declining" them by "simultaneously inhabit[ing] them and reus[ing] them in striking and imaginative ways" (as cited in Schwarz, 2013, p. 9). As Schwarz's analysis of the Red Power Movement shows, Native men according to Russell Means "looked ridiculous, all dressed up like Indians." Yet quite possibly, they were also "inhabiting the stereotype of the war-mongering brave—braiding their hair, painting their faces with war paint, adorning themselves with beads and feathers—while reusing these stereotypes in striking and imaginative ways" (p. 16). Of course a Native feminist read would look beyond representation, and call into question the ways AIM, and nation-building and sovereignty movements more broadly, have asked Native women to bracket their concerns for the good of the nation, or worse, reproduced sexism, misogyny, and violence against women within the movements themselves (Maracle, 1996; Mihesuah, 2003; Ramirez, 2007).[9] Nevertheless, Schwarz's claims that Native people have continually taken up the dominant discourse of Indianness in diverse and creative ways to combat colonialism at home remains useful. A pedagogy that supports Native students must simultaneously disrupt narrow and static notions of Indianness, while also leaving room for creativity, inversion, and subversion.

Knowing how much guidance to give students is a challenge. A student might need to work out for herself what it means to be creative and subversive. Yet it also feels important to consider the ways students may very well reflect back on their own cultural expressions, as many of us do as we reflect on our own lives, and feel that "tremor up [their] spine." How would Erin reflect on herself in that buckskin dress? How would that Native student abroad reflect on her gifting of chokers to her host family? I look back at a picture of myself as a 5 year old, dressed as an Indian for the ballet, and wonder what I must have felt. In the image I am standing with my arms folded in a sequined loincloth, a single feather sticking up from my headband, a beaming smile across my face. My non-Native adoptive mother says at the time I was proud; I *wanted* to be the Indian in the ballet. She didn't have the cultural resources or critical awareness to know any better at the time, and so letting me "play Indian" in the ballet was the way she could offer me a chance to show my pride and express myself. Her desire to feed my need to be proud of my identity was an act of love and good intentions. And yet I also know viscerally that tremor to which King refers when I recognize the ways I enacted a caricature: when I visually see the ways deep-seated narratives of race and colonialism can play out in my mother's love for me and my own little 5-year old body. I may have felt pride—indeed, I may have been resisting my own erasure as a Native child adopted into a white family—but that hardly feels now like creativity, inversion, or subversion.

Melvina, Ms. Carter, and I in our various ways were all trying to thoughtfully support Erin and the other students in ways that would nurture pride, while being cautious not to reproduce stereotypes. These students could be more than the Indian in the ballet. I noticed, however, the stubbornness of this discursive territory. Erin had said her teacher wanted her to look "Native American-y"; Ms. Carter said it was Erin who was reaching for those markers. We had some meaningful conversations about what it meant to do this work, conversations that I hoped would continue as a result of our relationship. Yet despite these thoughtful conversations, I was struck by Ms. Carter's display for her unit as I was in the hallway of her school. Glued to each corner of a sign "Legends and Myths" that explained her Native American unit and how it addressed state standards were four little feathers. These four feathers marked the Indianness of the project, a practice I felt we were so consciously trying to reflect on and disrupt. While how to move through this pedagogical and curricular spaces wasn't entirely clear, some practices more clearly supported cultural hegemony than others.

In the end, Melvina and I decided to offer some questions for the high school student to consider regarding her use of chokers: What do chokers mean to you? How are they meaningful to your people? What do you hope to teach through the chokers? We also reminded her of the way our Center engages in cultural exchange, creating friendship necklaces to give elders or as a small way to thank those who participate or volunteer in our program, a practice that emphasizes processes over products. We wanted to create a space for pause and reflection, and provide alternative options. The cultural exchange program's use of gifting was itself a longstanding cultural practice in many Native communities and cultures. Drawing attention to and emphasizing the practice was our way of providing an alternative, offering guidance while not explicitly telling the student what to do.

And in the end, Ms. Carter didn't blow it. In fact, it was only because she offered Erin a contemporary role model to research that she began to see some of the more nuanced and complex aspects of Indigenous education. Her willingness to engage with contemporary Native people provided her a glimpse at a few of the contemporary issues Native students might navigate. Teaching is complicated work and engaging in culturally sustaining pedagogies means recognizing and supporting the "complex personhood" (Gordon, 2008) of our students. As Gordon writes,

> Complex personhood means that all people (albeit in specific forms whose specificity is sometimes everything) remember and forget, are beset by contradiction, and recognize and misrecognize themselves and others. Complex personhood means that people suffer graciously and selfishly too, get stuck in the symptoms of their troubles, and also transform themselves. Complex personhood means that even those called "Other" are never never that. Complex personhood means that the stories people tell about themselves, about their troubles, about their social worlds, and about their society's problems are entangled and weave between what is immediately available as a story and what their imaginations are reaching toward. Complex personhood means that people get tired and some are just plain lazy. Complex personhood means that groups of people will act together, that they will vehemently disagree with and sometimes harm each other, and that they will do both at the same time and expect the rest of us to figure it out for ourselves, intervening and withdrawing as the situation requires. Complex personhood means that even those who haunt our dominant institutions and their systems of value are haunted too by things they sometimes have names for and

sometimes do not. At the very least, complex personhood is about conferring the respect on others that comes from presuming that life and people's lives are simultaneously straightforward and full of enormously subtle meaning. (pp. 4–5)

Drawing on Gordon and the work of Monique Guishard, whose work with youth honored both their critique of global capitalism as well as their desires for new Nikes, Tuck (2009) writes "We can desire to be critically conscious *and* desire the new Jordans, even if those desires are conflicting" (p. 420). Culturally sustaining pedagogy acknowledges and works within and against those both/and spaces that teachers and students navigate.

On the evening of the final presentations for the wax museum Erin presented alongside other Native leaders: a non-Native student portraying a typical rendition of Pocahontas; a Native student in a stereotypical rendition of Crazy Horse; and a Native student in a ballet outfit representing Maria Tallchief (Osage), not only the first renowned Native American ballerina, but America's first prima ballerina. I wondered if the student in the leotard felt any of the pressures that Erin had to look Native American-y. Erin didn't end up wearing the buckskin dress. She also didn't take us up on the suggestion to wear jeans or slacks and a button up shirt either. In the end, she wore a ribbon dress that Melvina had offered her as an alternative, a simple A-line dress adorned with ribbonwork. Melvina said the ribbon dress and ribbonwork were particular to the Great Lakes region (Metcalfe, 2010), close to Winona LaDuke's home on the White Earth reservation. Melvina felt this option gave Erin a sense of visibility she craved, and the pattern of her outfit was connected to LaDuke's homelands. Erin also held the crystal wand for which she had pleaded. In her ribbon dress that evening in the gymnasium, Erin stood tall. She was poised. She was ready. Her eyes stared off into the distance as she stood frozen, but she was not stoic. Rather than emulate a historic hero, she had the opportunity to embody a contemporary Native leader, and when someone dropped a coin in her bucket, she came to life.

Notes

1 See chapter 7: Education on the Border of Sovereignty for another discussion of this bait and switch tactic.
2 A sample lesson, "Porquois Stories: Creating Tales to Tell Why" can be found at the website   ReadWriteThink   (http://www.readwritethink.org/classroom-resources/lesson-plans/pourquoi-stories-creating-tales-324.html).
3 Teachers routinely tell me they do not know much about contemporary Native America. Though I was happy to help this particular teacher, this ongoing statement speaks of the ways ignorance is structured (Calderón, 2009) but also willfully maintained as finding information can be as easy as "liking" a Facebook page or searching for Native media outlets. Indian Country Today Media Network, Indigenous Peoples Issues and Resources, FAIR Media (For Accurate Indigenous Representation), We R Native, News from Native California, or other contemporary media outlets can provide

teachers with news, stories, and links to give a sense of the contemporary issues circulating in Indian Country.

4 I should make clear that Winona LaDuke is not an attorney, despite both teachers' depiction of her as one. She graduated from Harvard with a degree in Native Economic development, received a master's in urban development from MIT, and a second master's in Community Economic Development from Antioch University. She was a former principal, has been an active environmentalist, founded a non-profit dedicated to land recovery, has been a strong proponent of women's rights, was a vice presidential candidate who ran with Nader, authored five books, was inducted into the National Women's Hall of Fame, and was recognized by *Time* magazine as one of America's 50 most promising leaders under 40 … but she was not a lawyer.

5 I follow the lead of the National Congress of American Indians (NCAI) and other organizations and individuals who refuse to spell the racist name and instead use "Redsk★ns" or "R word" (NCAI, 2013, p. 2).

6 I use Indian in this context to refer to what King (2012) refers to as the "Dead Indian" and what Vizenor, Tuck, and Yang (2014) refers to as *indian* as opposed to "Native." Vizenor writes, "The word is forever a problem, and should be printed in italics, because the word has no real referent. Indian is used for everything: language, food, culture, you know, everywhere. The word has no discrete meaning. I used the word 'Native' to describe specific and distinct and unique cultural practices and stories" (p. 112).

   I do this knowing that many in the Native community here, elders especially, still utilize the word Indian as a self-referent and I do not mean disrespect to those self-representations. However, I use the word specifically to conjure up a particular, invented portrayal of Indigenous life that selectively edits and fictionalizes our actual diverse lived realties.

7 Tatakwan's chokers and other art and jewelry can be found at her website (http://www.urbanregalia.com/beadwork/).

8 Kristen Dorsey's earrings can be found at *Beyond Buckskin*, an online boutique featuring Native art, clothing, and jewelry (http://shop.beyondbuckskin.com/product/blood-qua ntum-earrings).

9 Aside from allegations of sexism against AIM leaders, the development of parallel movements such as Women of All Red Nations (WARN) and Indigenous Women's Network demonstrate that Indigenous women's specific concerns, such as forced sterilization or the widespread removal of children from Native families, were not addressed within organizations like AIM. Still, it is important to recognize that some Native women found AIM empowering at the time, despite its problems, and that Indigenous women were active participants in the movement. As Mary Crow Dog reflects on Wounded Knee, "As the siege went on, our women became stronger" (Crow Dog & Erdoes, 1990, p. 137).

References

Aardema, V. (1975). *Why mosquitoes buzz in people's ears: A West African tale*. New York, NY: Dial Books for Young Readers.

Alim, H. (2011). Global Ill-Literacies: Hip Hop cultures, youth identities, and the politics of literacy. *Review of Research in Education*, 35(1), 120–146.

Archibald, J. A. (2008). *Indigenous storywork: Educating the heart, mind, body, and spirit*. Vancouver: UBC Press.

Battiste, M. (2000). *Reclaiming indigenous voice and vision*. Vancouver: UBC Press.

Calderón, D. (2009). Making explicit the jurisprudential foundations of multiculturalism: The continuing challenges of colonial education in US schooling for Indigenous education. In A. Kempf (Ed.), *Breaching the colonial contract: Anti-colonialism in the U.S. and Canada* (pp. 53–77). New York, NY: Springer.

Crow Dog, M., & Erdoes, R. (1990). *Lakota woman.* New York, NY: Grove Weidenfeld.

Dennis, Y., & Hirschfelder, A. B. (2014). *Children of native America today.* Watertown, MA: Charlesbridge Pub.

DiAngelo, R. (2011). White fragility. *International Journal of Critical Pedagogy*, 3(3), 54–70.

Dion, S. D., & Salamanca, A. (2014). inVISIBILITY: Indigenous in the city Indigenous artists, Indigenous youth and the project of survivance. *Decolonization: Indigeneity, Education & Society*, 3(1), 159–188.

Freire, P. (1970). *Pedagogy of the oppressed.* New York, NY: Seabury Press.

Furniss, E. (1999). *The burden of history: Colonialism and the frontier myth in a rural Canadian community.* Vancouver, BC: UBC Press.

Gay, G. (2002). Preparing for culturally responsive teaching. *Journal of Teacher Education*, 53 (2), 106–116.

Gonzalez, N. & Moll, L. C. (2002) Cruzando el puente: Building bridges to funds of knowledge, *Educational Policy*, 16(4), 623–641.

Gonzalez, N., Moll, L. C., Tenery, M. F., Rivera, A., Rendon, P.Gonzales, R. & Amanti, C. (1995) Funds of knowledge for teaching in Latino households, *Urban Education*, 29 (4), 443–470.

Gordon, A. (2008). *Ghostly matters: Haunting and the sociological imagination* (2nd ed.). Minneapolis, MN: University of Minnesota Press.

Grande, S. (2015). *Red pedagogy: Native American social and political thought* (2nd ed.) Lanham, MD: Rowman & Littlefield.

Haakanson, Jr., S. (2002). Alutiiq/Unangax region: Mask carving. *Sharing Our Pathways: A newsletter of the Alaska Rural Systemic Initative*, 7(3). Retrieved from http://ankn.uaf.edu/sop/.

Hirschfelder, A., & Dennis, Y. W. (2000). *Native Americans today: Resources and activities for educators, grades 4–8.* Englewood, CO: Teacher Ideas Press.

Iseke-Barnes, J. (2009). Unsettling fictions: Disrupting popular discourses and trickster tales in books for children. *Journal of the Canadian Association for Curriculum Studies*, 7(1), 24–57.

King, T. (2012). *Inconvenient Indian: A curious account of Native people in North America.* Minneapolis, MN: University of Minnesota Press.

Ladson-Billings, G. (1995). But that's just good teaching! The case for culturally relevant pedagogy. *Theory into Practice: Culturally Relevant Teaching*, 34(3), 159–165.

LaDuke, W., & Cruz, S. A. (2012). *The militarization of Indian country* (American Indian studies series). East Lansing, MI: Michigan State University Press.

Maracle, L. (1996). *I am woman: A native perspective on sociology and feminism.* Vancouver: Press Gang.

Metcalfe, J. (2010). Some history | Ribbon work and ribbon shirts. Beyond Buckskin, March 23. Retrieved from www.beyondbuckskin.com/2010/03/ribbon-work-and-rib bon-shirts.html.

Mihesuah, D. A. (2003). *Indigenous American women: Decolonization, empowerment, activism.* Lincoln, NE: University of Nebraska Press.

National Congress of American Indians. (2013). Ending the legacy of racism in sports & the era of harmful "Indian" sports mascots. Retrieved from www.ncai.org/proud tobe?page=2.

Oregon Department of Education. (2011). Oregon social sciences academic content standards. Retrieved from https://www.ode.state.or.us/teachlearn/subjects/socialscience/sta ndards/oregon-social-sciences-academic-content-standards.pdf.

Paris, D. (2012). Culturally sustaining pedagogy: A needed change in stance, terminology, and practice. *Educational Researcher, 41,* 93–97.

Paris, D., & Alim, H. (2014). What are we seeking to sustain through culturally sustaining pedagogy? A loving critique forward. *Harvard Educational Review, 84*(1), 85–100.

Ramirez, R. (2007). *Native hubs: Culture, community, and belonging in Silicon Valley and beyond.* Durham, NC: Duke University Press.

Rosaldo, R. (1989). Imperialist nostalgia. *Representations, 26,* 107–122.

Schwarz, M. (2013). *Fighting colonialism with hegemonic culture Native American appropriation of Indian stereotypes.* Albany, NY: State University of New York Press.

Simpson, L. B. (2013). Politics based on justice, diplomacy based on love. What Indigenous diplomatic traditions can teach us. *Briarpatch Magazine,* May 1. Retrieved from https://briarpatchmagazine.com/articles/view/politics-based-on-justice-diplomacy-based-on-love.

Tuck, E., & Yang, K. (2014). Unbecoming claims: Pedagogies of refusal in qualitative research. *Qualitative Inquiry, 20*(6), 811–818.

Valaskakis, G. (2005). *Indian country: Essays on contemporary Native culture* (Indigenous Studies). Waterloo, ON: Wilfrid Laurier University Press.

Villegas, A. M., & Lucas, T. (2002). Preparing culturally responsive teachers: Rethinking the curriculum. *Journal of Teacher Education. 53*(1), 20–32.

Vizenor, G., Tuck, E., & Yang, K. W. (2014). Resistance in the blood. In E. Tuck & K. W. Yang (Eds.), *Youth resistance research and theories of change* (pp. 107–117). New York, NY: Routledge.

Yosso, Tara J. (2005). Whose culture has capital? A critical race theory discussion of community cultural wealth. *Race, Ethnicity and Education, 8*(1), 69–91.

PART II

Colonialism in the Culture of Schools

Whereas the previous part focused on the practices of individual teachers in classrooms, the stories in this part broaden the analysis to focus on the structure of curriculum in schools. This wider focus draws attention to the collective socialization of students, and questions the particular types of knowing, being, and doing cultivated by curricular units, schoolwide events, and community service projects.

The first story, "Little Anthropologists," describes a Native American unit taught in a 5th grade classroom. While the survivance story focuses on the curriculum and teaching of two teachers in particular, the structure of the curriculum is broader in scope. At this particular school, a public pedagogical component of this unit in which 5th grade students present their findings to the rest of the kindergarten through fourth grade student body, elevates the scope of curriculum. Further, while this survivance story describes curriculum at one particular school, the Native American unit discussed reflects a more pervasive pattern of positioning Indigenous people as objects of study. This survivance story questions not only the ways these units objectify and commodify Indigenous peoples and cultures, but also the emboldened and colonial ways of knowing these units cultivate in the rest of the student body. Moreover, this survivance story problematizes how cultivating Eurocentric subjectivities imbued with the power to know and define Native people as Other is legitimated through the discourse of multiculturalism. Ultimately, this chapter calls on educators to ground curriculum in a recognition and respect for Native nations by shifting the curricular focus from culture to citizenship and making familiar ways of knowing Indigenous peoples appear strange.

The next story in this part, "Native Heritage Month," focuses on curriculum at the institutional level. For the first time in its history, an elementary school in the district formally acknowledged Native Heritage Month as a school. To do so, the principal invited a Native dancer to perform at a schoolwide assembly. While the performance may have provided a culturally relevant experience for Native students, the performance also invited the broader student population's stereotypical prior knowledge about Indians. Moreover, while the Native dancer thoughtfully mediated his performance to disrupt dominant assumptions, the survivance story questions whether these performances, and particularly without explicit preparation, reproduce, rather than disrupt stereotypes. Situating the survivance story within longstanding conversations about American Indian Day and the value of Indigenous performances for non-Native audiences, the survivance story also explores the question of whether Indigenous students benefit from such performances and wonders how these months might privilege Native students' learning. Taking seriously critiques of the value of heritage months in general, this survivance story explores whether Native Heritage Month can be strategically wielded in service of Native sovereignty.

The final survivance story, "Education on the Border of Sovereignty," moves beyond the classroom and school to consider the possibilities that emerge when teachers, schools, and districts welcome Indigenous knowledges and share power with Indigenous communities. First focusing on a classroom presentation by two Native educators, the story illustrates the ways colonial ideologies are often projected on Indigenous peoples, and how Indigenous peoples refuse such containment—in this case, the educators' refusal to perform or present as Native informants, or their refusal to position Native artists and art as objects of study. The story then broadens the analysis from recognizing Native knowledge in the "community" to recognizing Native nationhood and sovereignty. Focusing on the process of consultation between a classroom, tribal liaison, and Native representatives from several nearby nations—a process institutionalized by the US Forest Service—this story points to the generative aspects of curriculum and pedagogy at the sociopolitical border between schools and Native nations. In particular, it draws attention to Indigenous peoples' refusal to be represented as ecological Indians, and how these refusals, rather than subtractive, offer generative learning regarding respect and recognition of Native sovereignty. The survivance story ends by exploring other types of learning that could occur if Indigenous knowledges, desires, and sovereignty were more seriously invited into the educational process.

4

LITTLE ANTHROPOLOGISTS

As I arrived at Ms. Whitman's classroom, I stopped to examine the coloring sheets taped to the wall. The principal had encouraged me to connect with this teacher because she was doing "great work building on Native American culture" in her school. In her email to me, in which she also cc'd the Director of Elementary Instruction, she attached several images of masks and kachinas.[1] I was disheartened that the principal considered these activities "great work," but I was thankful for the opportunity to learn more about what was happening in the classrooms. Standing outside of the classroom, I read the name and explanation that accompanied each kachina:

> Koyemsi, the Mudhead Clown Kachina, are seen in all Kachina dances. When the other Kachinas are not dancing the Koyemsi play games and act as clowns. Since the Koyemsi is considered very sacred, people never refuse him anything. To do so would bring bad luck.
>
> Soyoko is an ogre woman who often travels with Nata-aska, the black ogre, in the evening after the bean dance, Soyoko visits various houses and asks the boys to hunt game for her (mice and rats). She tells the boys if they do not have some for her within four days she will eat them instead of the game! In the same way Soyoko requires the girls to prepare Piki, a paper thin bread wafer, for her. She likes Piki made from blue, yellow, or pink cornmeal.
>
> It is believed that Hahai-i Wu-uti is the mother of all Kachinas. She appears in many ceremonies and is the main actor in the water serpent ceremony.[2]

I wondered how Ms. Whitman had helped students make sense of these descriptions. What had she taught students about Katsinam who Hopi people consider sacred beings? What context did she provide to prevent words like sacred, ogre woman, or water serpent ceremony from being interpreted by students as superstition or foolishness? More importantly, was this even a matter of providing cultural context? Hopi religion is intentionally private, its details protected from outsiders, but also from young Hopi children. Should students even have been learning about Hopi Katsinam at all?

Though endorsed by the principal as exceptional, this appeared to be the familiar practice of taking Native culture out of context and emphasizing exotic and beautiful objects over the place-based, cultural practices of which those items (or beings) are a part. With a focus on Katsinam, however, the stakes were higher as the sacred was made into a spectacle. Adjacent to the images of the kachinas were student drawings intended to replicate tithu, or Hopi dolls given to young girls.[3] Instead of replicating actual tithu, however, these dolls were customized, created specifically to help students. A photo of two students accompanied a statement above the artwork:

> School kachinas help students with many things. There are kachinas to help students who forget to be respectful. My brother needs a visit from that kachina.

Below the sign were drawings of the students' invented kachinas: Artenwa (who helps students with art); Bookery (who helps students read); Geowa (who helps students with geometry); and so on. On the surface, the creative drawings and loopy, child-like handwriting from young children explaining how their imitation Katsinam would help them read better or improve their geometry felt endearing; but when read against the cultural, religious, and spiritual contexts within which those Katsinam have meaning, the activity felt inappropriate, even sacrilegious. It would hardly seem appropriate to invite children to canonize their own Catholic saints as a multicultural art activity—St. Broccolis, an homage to the saint of healthy eating and proponent of green, leafy vegetables; or St. Assistus, a tribute to the patron saint of homework questions, for example.[4] As Old Elk and Stoklas (2001) clarify, "The Hopi Katsina religion is a system of beliefs, guaranteed by the U.S. Constitution, equal to the Jewish faith, Lutheran, Mormon, Roman Catholic faiths, etc." (p. 17). Unfortunately, Native spiritual and religious practices are not often afforded the same respect and regard. The analogy to other faiths also has its limits according to Pearlstone (2000):

> Unlike a Christian symbol like the Cross, orthodox Pueblo people do not see katsinam as public property. In contrast to the selling of Christianity, Pueblo members believe that outsiders *show respect by not knowing about their rituals*. Even for the most liberal Hopi it must be unsettling to keep seeing "katsinam" in contexts completely removed from their culture of origin. (p. 820, emphasis added)

A book about teaching Native American content that I had recently bought to support teachers in the district emphasized the inappropriateness of including kachinas in the curriculum by providing a list of "NO-NOs" for teachers, one of which was directly relevant:

> NO-NO 4!! No kachinas, sandpaintings or pipes! These are also part of religious ceremonials, sacred objects meant to be used by special people in an honored way. Yes, we do note that some kachinas are sold as dolls, but we prefer that you not even attempt to address any sacred subjects. Sandpaintings are not permanent works of art like oil paintings; they are used only for healing and then destroyed. Pipes should not even be displayed—there are simply too many rules to follow to respect the customs. (Hirschfelder & Beamer, 2000, pp. xvi)

Parameters like this can be useful for teachers, especially "to help [educators] not make glaring errors" (Hirschfelder & Beamer, 2000, p. xvi). But providing teachers with lists of content to avoid doesn't necessarily explain or intervene into the persistent and troubling dynamic of routinely framing Native people and cultures as objects of study and inquiry. Nor does such a list address the distinctions and tensions that underlie Eurocentric and Indigenous (in this case Hopi) cultural paradigms, such as divergent conceptions of property, ownership, rights, and knowledge (Spencer, 2001). Hopi knowledge, for example, "is consistently and purposely segmented, compartmentalized, and shared on a 'need-to-know' rather than 'right-to-know' basis" with particular specialized knowledge, skills, or ceremonies protected even "from other Hopi whose nonmembership in a particular group excludes them from access to the knowledge" (Spencer, 2001, pp. 171–172). This stands in contrast to Euro-American understandings that knowledge is collective and shared freely, for example, evident in values such as "freedom of the press, free speech, and academic freedom" (Spencer, 2001, p. 171). Though a liberal multiculturalist perspective might advocate for the inclusion of Native content and "culture" as a means to foster respect for cultural diversity, another perspective of this curriculum might claim that "'the greatest respect that can be paid to [Hopi] culture is not to know'" (Pearlstone, 2001, p. 40).[5] In this instance, respect might be shown through an intentional effort to *not* include Katsinam in the curriculum, to refuse to teach about Katsinam altogether.[6]

All of this was on my mind before I had even met Ms. Whitman. Telling her that her work made a spectacle of the sacred was not how I wanted to introduce myself, and so when Ms. Whitman greeted me at the door, smiling, I greeted her back and thanked her for having me. It was the principal's idea to connect us, not hers, but Ms. Whitman seemed happy to discuss her curriculum with me and led me into her classroom.

"Careful," she said as we maneuvered around desks that were covered with cardboard and papier-mâché totem poles, an activity not addressed in the list of

NO-NOs. The totem poles were propped up on tables around the room, waiting to dry so the students could paint them. These would be gifts for the students' families and part of the "Native American Christmas" theme she was having that year, she explained. She then guided me around the room to view what she referred to as Native dwellings, stored in various nooks and crannies of the classroom: a tipi, a wigwam, a longhouse. One in particular, what appeared to be an expertly built wikiup, caught my eye.

Mounted on a clay base, the wikiup was carefully constructed with thin twigs woven around several thicker twig posts and topped with cedar branchlets. The wikiup was a stark contrast to the construction paper tipi it sat next to which appeared to be hastily thrown together. The construction paper was crumpled, forcibly twisted around three twigs, and held together with heaps of masking tape. To remedy the sloppy construction, some care was put into the base of the tipi which was adorned with drawings of little fires, yet it was hard looking at the tipi to see how this activity fostered respect or understanding. I commented on the remarkable wikiup and Ms. Whitman told me it was made by Elizabeth, a Native student in her class. I thought about the possible value of this activity for her in particular.

The professional development book I had bought didn't prohibit dwellings, but actually included a lesson on Navajo hogans, a traditional form of housing that are still used by Diné people today. The lesson was careful to preface that "Native Americans, like any other people, live in apartment buildings, eat pizza, bowl, shop at the mall, dance at clubs, go on picnics, get their hair styled, play video games, skateboard, serve on the PTA, and listen to rap music" (Hirschfelder & Beamer, 2000, p. 53), a preface likely intended to intervene into exotic or historic stereotypes of Native life. Yet it remained hard for me to see how recreating traditional housing would intervene into dominant notions of Indianness, let alone foster solidarity with Indigenous peoples. I tended to be quick to dismiss activities like this, but the care Elizabeth took in crafting her wikiup challenged my instinct to dismiss the activity outright. As I imagined the young girl and her family working together, I could see the activity's value for Native students like her. My son would someday be a 5th grader, and while I had always imagined we would build something snarky together like a two story house, I could see value in him learning how ciqlluat, or barabaras as they are called in Russian, are made and how they are not just ancient dwellings, but still fondly remembered by elders, even used today for social or ceremonial gatherings and a source of Alutiiq pride (Steffian & Laktonen Counceller, 2015). I realized my caution or concern didn't lie in the activity itself; rather, I didn't trust the community context in which the activity would take place. I thought about the intersections between curricula, intended audience, and classroom community.

As Ms. Whitman led me around the room, I craned my neck to peer at the masks the students created which loomed overhead, their vibrant colors and hollow eyes looking down at me as they dangled from the ceiling, swaying slightly from the breeze flowing out of a nearby vent. I recognized them from a coloring book teachers commonly used for their Native American units. Another passage from the professional development book I purchased came to mind:

> NO-NO 1!! No using masks. Do not make them, wear them, or display them. Masking, a feature of many Native religious traditions throughout North America, is used in a large number of contemporary ceremonies ... They are sacred; many are seen as living and must be fed ... Indian children never wear sacred masks. You can foster respect for these and other sacred objects by making them off-limits in the classroom. (Hirschfelder & Beamer, 2000, pp. xv–xvi)

The Grand Council of the Haudenosaunee's (1995) felt strongly enough about the misuse of masks that they developed official policies about such matters:

> All wooden and corn husk masks of the Haudenosaunee are sacred, regardless of size or age. By their very nature, masks are empowered the moment they are made. The image of the mask is sacred and is only to be used for its intended purpose. Masks do not have to be put through any ceremony or have tobacco attached to them in order to become useful or powerful. Masks should not be made unless they are to be used by members of the medicine society, according to established tradition. (np)

The Haudenosaunee "False Face" mask that dangled from the ceiling was presented in the coloring book as "well-researched," "accurately rendered," and "authentic" (Gaspas, 2002). The author was unaware of or ignored altogether any conversations or controversy regarding their reproduction. Similar mask projects involving Zia Pueblo traditions were also on display.

Given what I know about Haudenosaunee and Zia traditions, I found these displays deeply problematic and distracting. Yet, as with the wikiup, I was drawn again into thinking about context. Alutiiq mask-making has been encouraged as a cultural activity for Native youth in Alaska, and I believe the mask my cousin made at her elementary school in the village of Chignik *did* foster appreciation and respect for Alutiiq arts and culture. In contrast to the context of Chignik, however, Elizabeth or most other Native students in this district were often the only, or one of a few, Native students in their class. The low density (NCES, 2012) of Native students in the class functioned as a kind of hidden curriculum by creating an undertow of caricature and appropriation. In this context, it was hard to see how children would take away anything from these activities aside from the idea that Native people were historic, superstitious, exotic objects. It was even harder to see how Native students in this context could construct themselves as dignified human subjects given such blatant cultural commodification and objectification.

The Native American Unit as Salvage Ethnography

"Our Tribe is the Kickapoo" ... Giggle, Giggle, Smirk

The art activities were part of a broader unit in which students researched Native American tribes and wrote reports. I returned the following week to observe the student presentations and sat in the back as the students who researched the Crow nation presented. A student opened by saying:

> Our tribe is the Crow. They live on a reservation where they can make their own rules.

That the students opened by speaking in the present tense and acknowledging that Native people "make their own rules" surprised me, even had me hopeful—a sense of hope I desperately needed as I glanced around the room at the masks, dwellings, and totem poles. Most reports and curricula on Native Americans that I had observed in the district so far were situated in the past, a focus that many Native families in the district have expressed felt hurtful. The group went on to talk about Crow children, who "go to school just like us," and to discuss Barney Old Coyote, a famous Crow veteran in WWII. They didn't highlight his prominence as a code talker and the service and role of the code talkers in WWII (which I think the students would have found fascinating),[7] but their report did focus a bit on contemporary Native people and alluded to sovereignty by offering that they "make their own rules." This focus, however, was not shared by the reports that followed which covered nations such as the Blackfoot, Cherokee, Nez Perce, Apache, Dakota, Iroquois, Cheyenne, and Kickapoo (which students responded to with giggles and smirks, a reaction that was ignored by the teacher). Rather, the reports were primarily historic and ethnographic:

> *Cherokee:* They used to live in grass houses with hay beds ... They wore this [putting a paper band around his head] because they didn't have bandanas back then ... They used bows and arrows for fishing, hunting, and protection ... They played lacrosse.
> *Iroquois:* They used to play lacrosse. They used clubs. They lived in longhouses.
> *Kickapoo:* The men were hunters, the women raised the children ... They used bows and arrows for fishing, hunting, and protection.

One exception was the Hopi group who stated specifically, "the Hopi are citizens of the Hopi nation and the US." This attention to Hopi citizenship and nationhood was important, though the students did not elaborate. Any details about tribal government and citizenship, past or present, were ignored as the group followed the brief political acknowledgement with a few historic statements about adobes, bows and arrows, and breechcloths.

For the most part, student presentations were awkward and perpetuated the notion of tribal people as only existing in the past. Students talked about bows and arrows, clubs and spears, tipi and wigwams as they giggled nervously. They told legends. They demonstrated games Native people "used to play." Missing from the reports was the importance, complexity, or contemporary relevance of these traditions as students performed what appeared to them as quirky and puzzling practices of historic, simplistic, and backwards peoples.

I smiled wryly to myself, imagining one of my Native friends witnessing these reports. *This* was what students were learning about their people in school. *This* was the knowledge being produced out of this activity. *This* was what would inform their "schemas" about Indigenous people and would later become the "prior knowledge" they would draw from in middle and high school.

I also wondered how Elizabeth was experiencing all of this. Multicultural education is often promoted as a way for students to see themselves in the curriculum, the curriculum functioning as a "mirror" to reflect back their experiences (Bishop, 1990). While Ms. Whitman believed her curriculum was doing something positive for Native students, I actually *feared* that Elizabeth would see herself in these stories. As Laguna Pueblo scholar Leslie Marmon Silko (1996) notes, it is through stories that "we hear who we are" (p. 30). I feared she would identify with the curricular distortions and caricatures that exotified Indigenous life, oversimplified Indigenous technologies and histories, and ignored contemporary Indigenous realities. As Bishop (1990) cautions, "When children cannot find themselves reflected in the books they read, or when the images they see are distorted, negative, or laughable, they learn a powerful lesson about how they are devalued in the society of which they are a part" (p. 2). This classroom context with its appropriated masks and invented kachina dolls made such concerns feel warranted. This was coupled with racist literature like *Sign of the Beaver* that the teacher used, a text that is widely recognized as problematic for its use of perpetuation of Native stereotypes and derogatory language (Lambert & Lambert, 2014; Reese, 2007; Slapin & Seale, 2003), though also still widely circulated. In their review, describing a scene where the Native boy refuses to free a fox caught in an iron trap, claiming the fox will gnaw its own foot off, Slapin and Seale (2003) ask "How could a child think anything except that the speaker of such words really is a savage at heart?" (p. 160) Ms. Whitman's curriculum left me with similar impressions and questions. From this unit, how could students think anything except that the Native people were extinct and exotic?

It is clear that not all students internalize such distortions. Plains Cree scholar Emma LaRocque (2010) reflects on how distant and incongruent "the Indian" she learned about in school was from "the consummate humanity" of her family (p. 36). I hoped that Elizabeth would also feel dissonance with the caricatures presented to her as official knowledge in the curriculum. I hoped too that the "unsung humanity" and "vilification of Native peoples" might prompt her, like LaRocque, to a "place of engaged research and discourse" (p. 36). I knew Native students were capable of this. I had witnessed such resistance in young children. And yet I couldn't keep thinking of the pressures these sorts of curricula placed on Native students in public schools.

The Indian as National Curriculum

Thinking through the problems with this particular unit, it would be easy to assign blame to this individual teacher; yet the issue with this unit is cultural, not individual. And the cultural issue at hand is *not* how to more accurately or respectfully include Native "culture" in the curricula, but rather, how to disrupt the widespread cultural phenomenon of positioning Native people as exotic curricular objects of study. The issue at hand is a question of how to upset the longstanding cultural phenomenon of searching for an authentic Indigenous essence located in the past, or how to interrupt dominant cultural understandings of Indigeneity that are so pervasive in teacher thinking (Higgins, Madden, & Korteweg, 2013).

Native American units like Ms. Whitman's aren't unique to this particular school or even this school district. The sheer scope of this kind of miseducation almost elicits a sense of vertigo. In this particular district, the Native American unit has become a staple, the normative template for including Native content, rather than the exception. Mr. Smith, the teacher next door to Ms. Whitman, organizes a similar unit each year. He has been teaching for 13 years and in his sixth year implementing the Native American unit at this particular school, a unit he was taught by his mentor teacher. The students' reports from Mr. Smith's class were strikingly similar to those from Ms. Whitman's classroom: the Ojibwe "shaved their heads in a mohawk form" and "painted their faces and arms for occasions"; the Apache "smothered themselves in fat"; the "Navajo people sang songs to scare away evil spirits"; and many, like the Iroquois, used bows and arrows. The impact of Mr. Smith's reports, however, was more far-reaching. As a form of public pedagogy rooted in the value of having an authentic audience, his students showcased their Native dwellings and presentations, not just to their class, but to the rest of the kindergarten through 4th grade students in the school. With a student population of roughly 400 students, this means that each year, for the past six years, 300 students have listened to the 5th graders they admire talk about tipi, wigwams, or wikiups. Each year, 300 students have listened to accounts of a historic people, receiving an implicit message that Native people are no longer here. Each year, 300 students have likely anticipated the chance to create their own Native villages in the 5th grade.

The scope of this type of miseducation becomes overwhelming as I think of this unit being reproduced in various ways in thousands of classrooms around the country. This type of Native American unit is the predominate template for teaching about Native Americans in two nearby school districts, a pattern I have learned is pervasive in other districts, and one I know to be used nation-wide. While approaches to this type of unit vary, there are a variety of pre-packaged units available to teachers. A "best seller" and one of the most frequently downloaded Native American Unit on the popular site Teachers Pay Teachers has been purchased and positively rated by over 2,000 teachers. One activity in the unit asks each student to choose an Indian name. "My name is Fearless Bulldog. I chose this name because I am not afraid of anything," states the example which accompanies a dark skinned, construction paper Indian with a bare chest, body paint, and feathered headdress. In another activity, a teacher suggestion accompanying the totem pole activity states, "beat a drum as students present their writing."

Focusing on units like this overlooks the growing demographic of elementary educators committed to critical elementary social studies teaching (Agarwal-Rangnath, 2013; Picower, 2012; 2017; Shear et al., 2018), yet the more than 2,000 teacher reviews of this unit, each of which gave it four out of four stars, also demonstrates widespread and uncritical acceptance of such curricula. "What an awesome resource! We started today by creating our Native American names," comments Catherine L. "The totem poles were a huge hit!" notes Blair. R. "It looks respectful and authentic. Thanks!" said Kristin K. "I believe that it honors the culture of Native Americans respectfully, as well as provides a rich history and plenty of information," comments Casey W. The endorsement of this unit by so many teachers reflects the pervasive, taken-for-granted fram-ing of Native people as historic objects of study, and the curricular endorse-ment of replicating Native arts and crafts. Even more daunting is the knowledge that administrators in schools often sanction these types of units as good, multicultural curriculum.

To be fair, not all teachers have their students choose Indian names or play drums. Not all teachers make masks and kachinas like Ms. Whitman, or sand-paintings like Mr. Smith. Not all teachers use racist literature like *Sign of the Beaver*. Yet it remains important to recognize that even when these Native American units appear to be "factual" and "research" oriented, they can reflect and reproduce deep-seated colonial discourses that participate in a larger curri-cular project of erasure and objectification.

The curriculum in Ms. Whitman and Mr. Smith's class was ripe with the "unsung humanity" (LaRocque, 2010) of Indigenous peoples as well as missed opportunities. I couldn't help but think of the various pedagogical roads not taken. Framing lacrosse as a historic game Iroquois people "used to play," for example, erased the current importance of the sport to Haudenosaunee and other Native people today. The group covering Iroquois could have researched and shared about the Thompson Trio, two Onondaga brothers and their cousin, who have dominated the sport recently, bringing pride to both their Onondaga nation and Indigenous peoples today (ESPN, 2014). While no teacher is expected to be aware of or make every connection between their curricula and contemporary life in Native America, framing the unit as solely historic made any of those important connections nearly pedagogically impossible.

The occasional nod in the reports to important historical leaders, such as Chief Joseph or Geronimo, was the most accurate and meaningful reporting in the presentations. The study of historic leaders *is* important; these men were not stereotypes or caricatures, but real leaders invested in the continuity of their people. Yet Chief Joseph and Geronimo weren't the only important Nez Perce or Apache leaders to inquire about. Students could have inquired into Apache leader Jeff Houser's strong objections to the use of "Geronimo" as a military code name (Indian Country Today, 2011), or San Carlos Apache Chairman Terry Rambler's advocacy to protect Oak Flat, a sacred Apache site, against encroachment from the mining company Resolution Copper (Allen, 2015). Instead of a reporting historic ethnographies, students could learn from Native leaders' current efforts to protect their people, nations, and homelands. Rather than replicating crafts or investigating historic heroes, students could survey contemporary leaders and take action within the important battles they are fighting today for their lands, communities, and nations.

But these opportunities to engage contemporary issues and Native leadership were missed. Native leadership, like Native life, was relegated to history, and aside from the Crow and Hopi group's brief mention that they can "make their own rules" or that "the Hopi are citizens of the Hopi nation and the US," most conversations in the present tense were constrained by a desire to understand "Indianness," not actual Indigenous peoples. Even when the curricula purportedly focused on a particular nation, such as the Hopi nation, the activities (e.g., making kachinas) or student comments (e.g., "They dress up in costumes and do a dance for rain"), reveal the ways "Hopiness" (Pearlstone, 2011)[8] shaped the curricula and students' understanding, a focus that never seemed to translate into recognition, respect, or learning to stand in solidarity with actual Hopi people. Moreover, as Pearlstone (2001) observes of the commodification and sale of art and artifacts based on Katsina imagery, "those who benefit from the sale of these items are not Hopi" (p. 115).

While the Native student in this classroom may have appreciated the chance to create a wikiup, a similar conclusion could be drawn from the commodification of culture in this unit: in general, those who benefit from this Native American unit are not Native.

It was hard to be critical of these 10- and 11-year olds who were doing their best to fulfill their teacher's expectations. And while this curriculum felt inappropriate, even profane, this teacher's unit is an expected byproduct of settler society's widespread exotification and fascination with Native culture; teachers are practically conditioned to teach in such ways. It was also unsurprising that the principal considered this unit "great work." This teacher's curriculum and the principal's endorsement of it were shaped by both misinformation and nostalgia that is pervasive in schools and settler society generally. This kind of a Native

American unit is commonplace in public schools and as such, is an indication that the problem is less about individual knowledge deficits, and more properly thought of as deficits in broader narratives that circulate about Indigenous peoples in society. These narratives shaped the school's curriculum, which in turn reinforced the pervasiveness of the narratives themselves. All of this happened with few, if any, interactions actual with Native people. It was hard to imagine an entry point into this self-perpetuating and self-congratulating system of misrepresentation.

I thought about the unit as a whole: the crafts, the racist and fictitious literature, the research reports, and what I might say to this teacher. She didn't ask for my help, nor did she assume she needed it; rather, she was being held up in the school as an exemplar of Native cultural inclusion. To me, however, the course of study appeared problematic to the point of caricature. It seemed ludicrous that reading a few stereotypical books, learning about the historic Indian, and replicating a few crafts could appear to educators as a relevant and meaningful effort to understand Native peoples. This was not a feeling of condemnation as much as a feeling of absurdity and distance. It is strange to have earnest and intelligent people look right past the Indigenous people around them and see only historical and stereotypical images. Yet the strangeness of this project—the focus on exotic cultural difference, on authenticity, on classification and documentation—felt "uncanny" and "oddly familiar" (Kaomea, 2005, p. 26). It was upon finding *The North American Indian*, a seminal collection of photo volumes by Edward Curtis, as a sanctioned resource on the school library webpage for this curriculum, that the strange sense of familiarity began to make sense.

"Rescue Artists"

Funded by JP Morgan and with the support of President Theodore Roosevelt, *The North American Indian* was a 40-year project at the turn of the 20th century in which Edward Curtis "trek[ed] through the entire American West with wagons and cameras to document 'The Vanishing Race' of Native American Tribes" (The Curtis Collection, 2014). Curtis aimed to document "the old time Indian, his dress, his ceremonies, his life and manners" (Curtis, as cited in Paakspuu, 2007, p. 290) as he was convinced that Native people would soon vanish, inevitably suffering the fate of progress. Photography was a fitting means for this epic project as the "fixed form and static realism of images contributes to notions of the 'other' that are difficult to refute or challenge once established as a visual record" (Martin, 2013, p. 5).[9]

Curtis' photographs of "old time" Indians—Native men in headdresses, or unmarried Hopi women's traditional "butterfly" whorl hairstyles—are often lauded for their aesthetics. Many, including Indigenous people, have collected his portraits for those very qualities,[10] and collectors have paid more than a million dollars for a complete set of his photographs. Yet critical readings of Curtis's work demonstrate that his photographs are not neutral reflections of reality, but instead cultural and colonial constructions (Vizenor, 2009). Curtis routinely altered the subjects of his portraits, removing any traces of Western culture from his pictures—parasols, suspenders, wagons, etc.—so that Native people appeared "untouched" by civilization. Covering his subjects in blankets was a "familiar Curtis trick throughout *The North American Indian* and often served to hide clothing that appeared too modern and threatened to break the nostalgic feel he worked so hard to create" (Gonzales-Day, 2018, np). Curtis paid Native people for their time as he staged and manipulated their images, using "not only 'phony' costumes, additions, and poses ... but indeed, in some cases actual phony Navajo" (James Faris, as cited in Vizenor, 2009, p. 202). As King (2005) points out,

> Curtis was looking for the literary Indian, the dying Indian, the literary construct. And to make sure that he would find what he wanted to find, he took along boxes of "Indian" paraphernalia—wigs, blankets, painted backdrops, clothing—in case he ran into Indians who did not look as the Indian was supposed to look. (p. 34)

The opening photo in the volume *The North American Indian*, titled "The Vanishing Race—Navaho" (1904), most directly illustrates Curtis' ideological filter. Focusing directly on a line of horses traveling away from the camera into the darkness, an Indian atop each one, Curtis describes this photo as intending to portray "that the Indians as a race, already shorn in their tribal strength and stripped of their primitive dress, are passing into the darkness of an unknown future" (n.p.). However, like each of Curtis' photos, this moment was carefully constructed to match his theories of Native disappearance and his ideologies of culture and authenticity.

Curtis' editorializing of Indigenous life was pervasive. He photographed Hopi women in a photograph "Grinding Meal" (1907) who wouldn't typically wear their ceremonial dress as they performed daily activities and labor (Paakspuu, 2007). He portrayed Geronimo (1905) as "frail and immobile," despite the fact that he would march in President Roosevelt's inaugural parade the next day (Gonzales-Day, 2018), or drive a Locomobile Model C while wearing a suit and top hat several months later (P. C. Smith, 2009). And his photo *Oglala War Party* (1907), in which Curtis describes "a group of Sioux warriors as they appeared in the days of intertribal warfare, carefully making their way down a hillside in the vicinity of the enemy's camp" (n.p.) not only misrepresented a "war party" (who wouldn't likely go into battle with eagle staffs), but also misrepresented who the enemy was at the time, "a time when natives were starving on reservations," and not engaged in "intertribal warfare" as much as oppression and colonization inflicted by the US government (Vizenor, 2009, p. 205). As Vizenor continues, "He paid natives to pose as warriors at a time when their rights were denied, and their treaties were scorned and evaded by federal agents and the military" (p. 205).

While Edward Curtis had a profound influence on the public's social imaginary regarding Native Americans, his colonial gaze was a byproduct of social discourses and anthropological practices of his day. The Western gaze used to document and know the exotic Other has deep-seated, historical roots in colonial projects. These projects began with travelers' tales and amateur ethnographers, but were eventually refined and carried out in anthropological practices premised on the notion of science for the public good. Native cultural difference was systematically documented, classified, and preserved. The purported focus of these projects was Native peoples, but critical reads make clear the central and dominant role of Western subjects in shaping these projects (Said, 1978). While perhaps not obvious at first glance, there is a long history of this sort of erasure of Indigenous life stemming from the field of anthropology that uses the ethnographic gaze to narrate Indigenous and Other peoples' lives. When this history is recognized, the ways the curriculum today resonates with those earlier practices comes into focus.

Curtis, like early anthropologists and ethnographers in the 19th century, was in a frenzy to document, detail, record, categorize, classify, and understand Indigenous peoples—to *know* them—before they vanished. This practice is commonly known as "salvage ethnography," a frenzied practice of scientific, ethnographic documentation driven by an "urgency of collection for the sake of preserving data whose extinction was feared" (Gruber, 1970, p. 1290). Yet not just *any* Native person was studied; rather, much attention was paid to what Standing Rock Sioux scholar Vine Deloria Jr. (1969) has termed the "real" or "mythical, super-Indian" (pp. 81–82). As Lenape scholar Joanne Barker (2011) notes,

> In the mad rush to preserve and catalogue Native cultural artifacts and human remains in the late nineteenth and early twentieth centuries, some archaeologists and anthropologists seemed to care less about how Natives were living than what they remembered or were willing to recount of their ancestors' traditions … Those Natives considered especially worthy of study were those considered to be less assimilated (the infamous "last of" narratives dominating the popular media and sciences of every kind). (p. 20)

The anthropologist, as arbiter of authentic cultural difference, selectively edited Indigenous peoples' experiences through a narrow filter and desire "for a pure subject, for pure difference" (Simpson, 2011, p. 207). As Mohawk scholar Audra Simpson (2011) writes, "[t]hese desires, like the raw materials that fuel capitalism, also removed and ignored, and engaged, and selected for the difference that mattered" (pp. 207–208). The difference that mattered was "the timeless, the pure, the past-perfect, the thing (the people and their culture) that in its purity needed to be saved, to be recorded for the consumptive pleasure of (settler) science, memory, and a hopeful, shared (now liberal) future" (p. 208).

Reading students' project against the grain of anthropological practices of the 19th and 20th century draws attention to the "endurance of categories that emerged in moments of colonial contact, many of which still reign supreme" (Simpson 2007, p. 69). These inherited categories shaped official knowledges about Native people in schools. Students also imposed concerns and curiosities that weren't necessarily relevant to those whom they studied. Like earlier anthropologists, the students paid little attention to the concerns and issues facing those they documented. Moreover, like Curtis' body of work, or the ethnographies of that era, students selectively edited out features of Indigenous life they found unnecessary, undesirable, and unreportable, projecting upon Indigenous peoples' their own desires, priorities, and understandings of culture and Indigeneity. In this extractive and selective process, as Winnebago scholar Rayna Green (1988) notes, "Indians become 'data' which only non-Indian scholars can interpret" (p. 37).

This editorializing came into focus when comparing the resources offered students and the content of their reports. Both classes engaged primarily in a self-directed, constructivist research process. Students in Ms. Whitman's class had access to the tribal nations' websites, for example, but chose to ignore contemporary leaders or issues that were prominently featured and instead report primarily historic and ethnographic information. The few references to contemporary life or tribal governance came from "Native American Facts for Kids" which had links to information on various tribes (Native Languages of the Americas, 2015b). Even this site was selectively used. In response to the question "Can you help me find a good Native American arts and crafts project for my class?," the website replies:

> Please avoid projects that mimic Native American religious objects like kachinas or spirit masks. These objects are sacred to many Native Americans, and making inaccurate imitations out of toilet paper tubes and papier-mâché is offensive to them. (Native Languages of the Americas, 2015a)

The most striking comparison was the direct correspondence between the students' reports and the headings Curtis used to document Hopi people—language, location, dress, dwellings, and religion and ceremonies. These headings filtered the varied information students had access to, packaging the information into concise ethnographic statements: The Hopi lived in adobe houses; they used bows and arrows; they wore breech cloth; they ate baked beans, cornbread, and hominy; they used kachinas to teach lessons to children.

Mr. Smith provided his class more contemporary information than Ms. Whitman, bringing the ideological filter of the content into sharper focus. Students in Mr. Smith's class used a Scholastic resource entitled *TrueFlix* which included short videos and magazines about various Native nations, including Apache, Comanche, Inuit, Iroquois, Pueblo, and Sioux peoples. The student magazines provided a much more robust resource for students to examine a variety of contemporary and historic issues. The Apache magazine, for example, included a section on how the American thirst for gold led to encroachment and conflict on Apache lands. And in a magazine on Pueblo people, one section explicitly states, "Whites stole their land and even dragged their children to schools to make them learn American ways" (Cunningham & Benoit, 2011, p. 40). The magazines and videos also acknowledge contemporary Indigenous presence, though this was limited to a few pages at the end of the magazine or a statement at the end of each video.[11] Like many curricular materials, the magazines are imperfect, rooted in Eurocentric perspectives and focusing predominately on history; moreover, the high quality graphics and professional appearance, much like the *National Geographic*, gives the illusion of truth while simultaneously obscuring the source's ideological filter.[12] Nevertheless, the magazines included more than the usual ethnographic fare, making the students' selective editing more apparent.

The groups who reported on the Apache, for example, said nothing of Apache governance, despite a section in the book titled "Controlling Their Own Future," which stated "Apache reservations are similar to small nations" and Apache people "have their own governments, business, police, and schools" (Friedman & Benoit, 2011, p. 42). The student reports also said nothing of land grabs, the Gold Rush, or conflict with settlers described in the magazines; in fact, there was not a single reference to Indigenous–settler relations. Like Curtis' photos, any traces of "civilization" were removed. Despite access to a range of information, only the ethnographic accounts of food, tools, houses, and clothing made the reports: "They used spears or hooks to catch fish"; "The men did the hunting while the women did the farming and gathering"; "The Apache men wore leather war shirts and breechcloths and the women wore buckskin dresses"; "The Apache hunted buffalo, deer, antelope, and small game. The Apache would smother themselves in animal fat to take there [*sic*] sent [*sic*] away"; "This might seem a little sad but here are some of the foods that they ate. They ate rabbit, deer, and other animals in the area."

Reading these Native American reports and units in light of colonial discourses, it appears the students were being trained as little anthropologists, asked by their teachers to detail the strange and curious practices of exotic Others. Listening to the students' reports, it was as if I could see the pith helmets on their heads and the diaries in hand as they shared all that they discovered about historic, authentic Native life. Students were being socialized toward Native people in particular ways, and ethnographic ways of knowing were being cultivated and refined. Like early ethnographies, these students approached Native life from the anthropological concept of the "ethnographic present," an idealized (and fictionalized) understanding of "pre-contact" life. Like earlier ethnographies, these reports were also justified through the greater public good, this time with multicultural enrichment as key goal and public benefit.

Curtis' volumes of photographs and the students' Native American reports were strikingly similar. Both projects involved staging and editorializing, each ignoring, overlooking, or erasing particular aspects of Native life, while making others visible and points of study. Both projects extracted Native life from the varying political, legal, colonial, economic, or racial contexts of the day, emphasizing instead only Native cultural and spiritual differences. Both were profoundly ideological, though portrayed as truthful, factual, even scientific, whether through the pretense of photography or formal "research reports." Both were also highly marketable, Curtis' photographs sold to collectors and turned into exhibits or coffee table books; the students' projects marketed as diversity activities in a multicultural economy.

Like Curtis, the teachers' curricula positioned their students as "rescue artists" who salvaged and documented Indigenous cultural difference (Vizenor, 2009, p. 202). The particular ways of seeing and knowing cultivated in these units, based on "denial and fantasy" (hooks, 1992, p. 28), was neither neutral, nor natural, but profoundly cultural and colonial.

Surfacing Colonial Discourses

> We have a history of people putting Maori under a microscope in the same way a scientist looks at an insect. The ones doing the looking are giving themselves the power to define. (Merata Mita, as cited in L. T. Smith, 2012, p, 61)

The deeply rooted colonial discourses and investments made in-service professional development around these units challenging. Given the broad acceptance of units such as this in the district, Melvina, the Title VI Coordinator, and I had tried to support teachers in rethinking their curriculum. As outsiders to the schools and classrooms and with little institutional capacity to make curricular changes within the district, we reached for short sayings or aphorisms to help unsettle the deeply entrenched logics that insisted on framing Indigenous peoples as historic and as always living elsewhere, whether that meant on reservations or living in the Plains.[13] By suggesting that educators "start with *place*," for example, we intended to direct educators to Indigenous peoples of Oregon and the Northwest. "Starting with the *present*" was an intervention into teachers' historic focus, one endorsed by state content standards that heavily emphasize the study of Native people pre-1900 (Shear et al., 2015).

Yet we realized more was needed to disrupt the power dynamics reproduced by these lessons. Our purpose wasn't to prevent teachers from teaching Native history, another form of Indigenous erasure; after all, understanding history is crucial to ensuring that we learn from and do not repeat past mistakes. Our experiences also taught us that deeply rooted colonial discourses can distort attention paid to contemporary Native people. This was evident not only in the coded language people in this district have used to discuss Native people (words like honor, spirit, authentic, etc.), but also in the acceptance by even our critical colleagues of projects like Jimmy Nelson's "Before They Pass Away" (2014). Nearly a century after Edward Curtis, Nelson's project *nearly replicates* Curtis' style and mission as he embarked on a project to document "some of the most fantastic indigenous cultures left on the planet today."[14] Like Curtis, Nelson's project was fueled by and feeds into Eurocentric desires for exotic and authentic culture, evident in the 1.2 million views of his TED talk, or his widely purchased art prints, coffee table book, or upcoming film contract.

What became clear was that our aphorisms—starting with place and the present—were helpful and necessary, but weren't sufficient in disrupting the ways the civ-sav discourse (LaRocque, 2010) bled through students' historical focus, nor the ways these units reinforced students' positional authority (Said, 1978) to know and narrate Native Others.

The Civ-Sav Dichotomy

The students' reports were not only historically focused, but they were also shallow accounts of that history: "They lived in adobes"; "They used bow and arrows." It's not that people *didn't* live in adobes, or *didn't* use bow and arrows, but the flattened and reductive nature of the reports left little room for recognition of adobe earthen houses as a brilliant adaptation to the landscape, or bows and arrows as a formidable and sophisticated hunting technology. Yuchi/Muscogee Creek scholar Daniel Wildcat (2009) has termed this respect for Indigenous knowledge and ingenuity, *indigenuity*, an acknowledgement "Earth-based local indigenous deep spatial knowledge" (p. 48). These reports not only overlooked the fact that Native people *still* utilize spatial knowledge and Indigenous technologies today—in their homelands, communities, and cities—but the reports also miscast place-based, creative, and highly sophisticated knowledge systems as primitive. The references to adobes, bows, and arrows weren't represented as *knowledge*, but functioned to primitivize Indigenous people. Such oversight and oversimplification of Indigenous technologies appeared premised on beliefs that traditions are outdated and should be outgrown, and that change is both inevitable and inherently progressive, beliefs Quechua scholar Sandy Grande (2015) has identified as part of the "deep structures of colonialist consciousness" (p. 96).

Teaching students about "original technologies" can be an effective educational approach to "repatriate" Indigenous technologies, an intervention into the ways the term "technology" itself has been coopted by Western assumptions as a Western practice (Bang et al., 2013). Bang and colleagues are careful to caution, though, that "this must be done in ways that do not reify narratives in which Indigenous technologies are positioned as less sophisticated and Western technologies as advanced" (p. 717).[15] The students giving the reports, however, consistently positioned Indigenous technologies as less sophisticated and less progressive than those used today.

On the surface, the shallow nature of the students' accounts might have been forgiven as the oversimplified reporting typical of 5th graders, or perhaps explained and justified as the nerves of 10-year olds who were asked to present in front of their peers; but this was not just a matter of oversimplified reporting about Indigenous life. Instead, these reports reflected one of the *sophisticated* ways the continuum of savagery and civilization surfaces and is rehearsed, reproduced, and maintained by settler society. Plains Cree scholar Emma LaRocque (2010) has termed this continuum the civ-sav dichotomy which positions Indigenous people as primitive, savage, and uncivilized, a groundwork necessary to justify "civilization" and the dispossession of Indigenous lands. In the "great chain of being" that is vertically oriented (Winfield, 2007), primitive societies are viewed as earlier stages of more advanced forms of being human. This continuum casts Indigenous peoples as both uncivilized and as awaiting civilization, presuming "that which exists on the 'other' side of the frontier is an object waiting to be transformed" (Rose, 1996, p. 7).

The students' reports and the unit as a whole never explicitly state that Indigenous cultures were lesser forms of humanity that haven't quite reached the apex of human development, but in a sense, it was implicit in the orientation of the unit. Teachers used language that framed Indigenous peoples as "nomadic" and "primitive" societies, language that has long been used to divest and dispossess Indigenous peoples of their rightful claims to land. Students minimized complex Indigenous knowledge systems by framing them as simple and antiquated. Rather than merely a historic discourse used by early settlers, the civ-sav dichotomy continues to "find voice" in the curricula (Kaomea, 2005, p. 34). The students' reports were continual with longstanding colonial discourses that have dehumanized Indigenous peoples by legitimizing prior conquest and violence, undermining Indigenous sovereignty, and shaping how students view Indigenous peoples today (Kaomea, 2005, p. 29). Even educators who claim to engage in more respectful efforts to study Indigenous knowledge systems would need to recognize and be responsible for the asymmetrical "looking relations" (hooks, 1992) that characterized these units.

Knowers of Native Life

The act of representing Indigenous life—regardless of how accurate or respectful the content—reproduced the "positional authority" (Said, 1978) of these students to be *knowers* of Native life. Pointing out that educators focus too narrowly on Native people in the past leads to curricular interventions that focus on Native people *today*. Cautioning educators that these units partake in commodifying, exoticizing, or misrepresenting Native life leads to suggestions that educators offer more *accurate* representations of Native people, culture, and practices. While these interventions might appear positive, witnessing the reports led me to question the curricular project of asking students to report on Indigenous life at all, a dilemma captured in a story told by Paul Chaat Smith (2009):

> A few years ago I had the chance to visit a number of museums, interpretive centers, and heritage centers in the Canadian province of Saskatchewan. I was

fortunate enough to get a backstage tour of the redesigned Natural History Museum in the capital city, Regina. The staff had completely rethought and redesigned the wing of the museum dealing with Indians. They consulted with Native people and hired Indians to paint and construct exhibits; I was especially impressed with a beautiful display of a modern canvas sweat lodge. Another had Indians in a tipi with a dog sled out front, and next to that there were Indians in a cabin with a snowmobile out front. In these exhibits we managed not to be extinct.

I left the tour with nothing but respect for the efforts of a staff that obviously had thought long and hard about how to represent Indian culture. At the same time, for me the nagging question remained: *Why are we in this museum at all?* (p. 24, emphasis added)

A similar question could be asked of the curriculum: *Why did Indigenous peoples remain objects of study at all?* The problem with these units was not solely that the representation of Indigenous life that had to be transformed, but the very dynamic of knower/known had to be challenged. There is an inherent superiority and hubris cultivated in students by training them to represent Native life at all. Starting with the "here and now" as an aphorism to orient curriculum is an important intervention; yet by itself would do little to disrupt the ways the curriculum continued to privilege the Western gaze, center settler subjectivities, and arm students with the desire and skills to know the Other as a legitimate form of multiculturalism.

As inheritors of the ethnographic project, teachers and students appeared driven by the same sentimental longing, or "imperialist nostalgia" (Rosaldo, 1989), that compelled earlier anthropologists. This sentiment serves "as a mask of innocence to cover their involvement with processes of domination" (Rosaldo, 1989, p. 120) and "makes racial domination appear innocent and pure" (p. 107).[16] The "innocent yearning" (p. 108) for diverse, multicultural activities masks the ways whiteness and Eurocentrism permeate the curricula, including the ways Eurocentrism informs the very desire to study a multicultural Other as an historic and exotic object.

The systematic study of Native people using ethnographic description is a fine-tuned curricular machine in this school and district, indeed nationwide. It has become unquestioned curricular commonsense and lauded as multicultural curriculum that exposes students to diverse peoples and cultures. Yet arming students as little anthropologists whose lives "will be richer, more pleasurable" if they "accept diversity," might also be thought of as a form of "consumer cannibalism" that positions students to "eat the other" (hooks, 1992, p. 31). As hooks (1992) argues,

the commodification of difference promotes paradigms of consumption wherein whatever difference the Other inhabits is eradicated, via exchange, by a consumer cannibalism that not only displaces the Other but denies the significance of that Other's history through a process of decontextualization. (p. 31)

While hooks' metaphor of cannibalism stems from cinema critique, this same model of "racial pluralism" that is rooted in "a model of change that still leaves a white supremacist capitalist patriarchy intact, though no longer based on coercive domination of [Indigenous] people" (p. 31) permeates this curricular approach. These units were not based on "mutual looking"; they were rooted in a desire for "contact with the Other even as one wishes boundaries to remain intact" (p. 29). The Native Other was cast as a multicultural object of study to be known, used "to enhance the white palate … to be eaten, consumed, and forgotten" (p. 39).

While our initial work with teachers aimed to transform what was known or said about Native people in curricula, it became clear that the deeper issue was that students were being trained, like earlier anthropologists, *to know and say something of the Native Other at all*. These units cast Native people as objects of curiosity, and the students as anthropological subjects who were empowered from these dominant and dehumanizing ways of looking at Indigenous peoples. Our aphorisms were not enough to disrupt this longstanding, deeply habituated colonial pattern of viewing Indigenous peoples. We needed to teach students different ways of looking and knowing.

Ground Curriculum in a Recognition and Respect for Native Nations

In 1969, Vine Deloria Jr. denounced the field of anthropology as a whole, particularly in relation to Native peoples:

> The fundamental thesis of the anthropologist is that people are objects for observation, people are then considered objects for experimentation, for manipulation, and for eventual extinction. The anthropologist thus furnishes the justification for treating Indian people like so many chessmen available for anyone to play with.
>
> The massive volume of useless knowledge produced by anthropologists attempting to capture real Indians in a network of theories has contributed substantially to the invisibility of Indian people today. After all, who can conceive of a food-gathering, berry-picking, semi-nomadic, fire-worshiping, high-plains and-mountain-dwelling, horse-riding, canoe-toting, bead-using, pottery-making, ribbon-coveting, wickiup-sheltered people who began *flourishing* when Alfred Frump mentioned them in 1803 in his great work on Indians entitled *Our Feathered Friends* as real?
>
> Not even Indians can relate themselves to this type of creature who, to anthropologists, is the "real" Indian. Indian people begin to feel that they are merely shadows of a mythical super-Indian. Many anthros spare no expense to reinforce this sense of inadequacy in order to further support their influence over Indian people. (pp. 81–82)

Deloria's piercing critique links anthropologists' ethnographic methods to power and Indigenous dispossession, a critique echoed in various ways by other Native scholars (L. T. Smith, 2012; Medicine & Jacobs, 2001; Trask, 1999; Ramirez, 2007; Simpson, 2007; 2011). While these critiques and conversations have influenced the field of anthropology with respect to issues of power, purpose, voice, representation, and ethics, these conversations have yet to make their way into this school district where framing Indigenous peoples as "objects for observation" continues to be accepted and commonplace.

The implication to abandon these widely embraced (and often conveniently prepackaged) units might seem overwhelming, yet a vast array of perspectives and materials are available to interrogate, challenge, and transform the taken-for-granted anthropological project. What would happen if the Native Other—the mythical super-Indian—was no longer an object of the students' gaze? What new insights, experiences, values, or relations would emerge if educators refused ethnography as a mode of knowing Indigenous peoples and "*object[ed] to* the very process of objectification/subjection" (Tuck & Yang, 2014, p. 814)?

The information and scholarship to employ refusal as a stance is there. What we need are educators willing to divest from this longstanding colonial investments and patterns of looking. We need educators committed to new looking relations (hooks, 1992). What if the educators involved focused on the *political* rights of Native peoples and nations, instead of Native cultures, cultivating an appreciation for Native nationhood and governance, much the way students are already taught to respect local, state, and federal governments? Or what if educators guided students through an inquiry on what they know (or do not know) about Indigenous peoples, a focus that subjects *the production of knowledge and ignorance* (and not Indigenous peoples themselves), to sustained inquiry and critique?[17] In both instances, educators could move students away from curricula premised on a desire to consume Indigenous cultural difference, and toward curricula premised on respect for Indigenous sovereignty and a commitment to interrupt colonial dynamics.

Move from Culture to Citizenship

Indigenous identities are often included in racial or multicultural frameworks as "people of color," but Indigenous identities are not only cultural; they are also political. Given the tone of caricature that often underlies curriculum in schools, educators might more productively frame Indigeneity through discourses of citizenship (Calderón, 2009; Lyons, 2000; Tuck & Yang, 2012; Sabzalian & Shear, 2018; St. Denis, 2011).[18] As Lyons (2000) observes, Indigenous sovereignty has been eroded through *rhetorical imperialism*, the subtle degradation of Indigenous sovereignty through language in which Indigenous sovereignty has shifted "From 'sovereign' to 'ward,' from 'nation' to 'tribe,' and from 'treaty' to 'agreement'" (p. 453). Educators can intervene into rhetorical imperialism by referring to

Indigenous peoples, not as members of cultural "communities," but as citizens and descendants of sovereign Native nations. Educators can use language—sovereign, nation, treaty, citizenship—to foster respect for Indigenous sovereignty and nationhood by reframing curricula to recognize Indigenous citizenships instead of Indigenous cultures.

This discursive shift better aligns with concerns typically expressed by actual Native nations. As Simpson (2007) observes in her ethnography of Mohawk citizenship within her own nation,

> The people that I work with and belong to do care deeply about ceremony and tradition, but hinged those concerns to nationhood, citizenship, rights, justice, proper ways of being in the world, the best way to be in relation to one another, political recognition, invigorating the Mohawk language—they did not talk about the usual anthropological fare that dominated the prodigious amount of research upon them. (p. 68)

Rather than impose research upon Indigenous peoples, teachers can ground curriculum in a recognition and respect for the political status and rights of Native nations, and align curriculum to issues and concerns Native nations currently face. Such a grounding would necessarily shift the curricular resources and activities that would be considered appropriate or supportive.

Taking seriously Hopi nationhood, for example, would cast the Hopi nation's website, rather than Edward Curtis' photos, as an appropriate and authoritative classroom resource. With a focus on Native citizenship, nationhood, and governance, for example, a guided scavenger hunt through the Hopi nation's website would yield knowledge that the Hopi nation has a chairman, a tribal council, its own constitution, and creates and follows its own particular laws. This knowledge directly intervenes into colonial discourses and cultural commodification by invoking Hopi people as active subjects with political and civic identities.

Centering Hopi governance doesn't preclude student learning about Hopi culture; students might even come across information on Katsina Friends. However, Hopi culture—at least as it appears on the Hopi nation website—is situated within a context of tribal sovereignty, Hopi customary law and tradition, and Indigenous rights. Instead of learning the meaning of Hopi spiritual and religious practices, for example, students would learn of the very real political and social contexts and practices that threaten Hopi culture, like the recent auction of Katsina Friends in Paris without Hopi permission or authorization. Moreover, Hopi people would be positioned as active subjects and agents to learn *from*, not *about*. Students could learn from the leadership and advocacy of Hopi Chairman Herman G. Honanie (The Hopi Tribe, 2013; 2015), for example, or the allied advocacy of Robert G. Breunig (2013), the non-Native Director of the Museum of Northern Arizona in Flagstaff. In so doing, student learning and identity development would not be framed in relation to an ability to consume cultural difference. Instead, reframing this unit within citizenship and civics education would help students recognize Indigenous citizenship and nationhood, as well as develop more robust conceptions of democratic citizenship that take seriously constructs like recognition, respect, and responsibility for Indigenous sovereignty.[19]

Make Familiar Ways of Knowing Appear Strange

The vast supply of books on Native stereotypes—*American Indians: Stereotypes and Realities* (Mihesuah, 1996), *Everything You Know about Indians is Wrong* (P. C. Smith, 2009), *Do All Indians Live in Tipis?* (National Museum of the American Indian, 2007), *Everything You Wanted to Know about Indians But Were Afraid to Ask* (Treuer, 2012), and *"All the Real Indians Died Off" and 20 Other Myths about Native Americans* (Dunbar-Ortiz & Gilio-Whitaker, 2016)—attests to widespread ignorance about Indigenous peoples, ignorance that likely stems from socialization in mainstream public schools and society. It is this base of stereotypical representations and dominant discourses that comprise knowledge of Indigenous peoples that could guide curriculum inquiry.

Instead of a unit focused on the Native Other, teachers could guide students through an inquiry into how schools, media, and society frame and produce knowledge about Indigenous peoples and issues. The very mechanism of Othering would become the unit of analysis. Students could learn, too, of Native efforts to write back and examine how Native people use diverse media such as blogs, photographs, videos, literature, and podcasts to tell stories on their own terms.

Following an approach laid out by Lenape/Potawatomi scholar Susan Dion (2008; 2012), students could first explore their own biographies in relation to knowledge about Native people and life, an intentional curricular approach designed to disrupt what she has termed a "perfect stranger." This positioning, Dion (2012) argues, "allows teachers and actually all Canadians to be off the hook when it comes to thinking about Aboriginal issues, thinking about Aboriginal people, or the relationship between Aboriginal and non-Aboriginal people" because it allows teachers to place Native people and "their" concerns outside of themselves (np). To counteract the "perfect stranger," which is "informed simultaneously by what teachers know, what they do not know, and what they refuse to know" (2008, p. 179), Dion invites her students to "identify and collect 'cultural artifacts' … that are reflective of their relationship with Aboriginal people or Aboriginal knowledge" (p. 182). These artifacts form a "file of (un) certainties" that are situated alongside contemporary works from Native peoples—artists, scholars, storytellers, among others. This juxtaposition—a "stereoscopic" positioning of Native and newcomer (Valaskakis, 2005) knowledge—creates dissonance, inviting "students to interrogate their own and each other's understanding and expectations of Aboriginal people and Aboriginal knowledge" (2008, p. 180). More than merely a critique of this knowledge as something "out there," students could intimately investigate the ways their own relationship to Indigenous peoples, and knowledge and representations about Indigenous peoples, has been shaped, not just by media, but by their families, home, school, community, state, region, or nation. This intentional approach to surfacing and revisiting students' biographies is a way to "radically reconfigure the relationship between the past and present ... challenging the existing modes of inheritance of our views of our selves, others and our environment with new patterns and forms of presentation, representation and association" (Simon, 1992, as cited in Dion, 2008, p. 181). Through a sustained look at their experiences and memories, students "begin to recognize their investments in relationships structured by particular ways of knowing Aboriginal people" (p. 181), and come to understand the ways particular forms of knowing are embedded with assumptions, techniques, investments, and consequences. This honest and guided introspection, Dion (2008) argues, enables "remembrance" to become a "source of radical renewal" (p. 180).

While this frame appears to center non-Indigenous students' subjectivities (a subtle form of erasure discussed in other chapters), Indigenous students also benefit from interrogating and developing critiques of dominant ways of knowing Native people. They also benefit when their familial and cultural knowledges are affirmed within curriculum. Moreover, Native students in particular could benefit from examining the various ways Native artists have decentered, recast, or appropriated dominant discourses. Edward Curtis' photos, for example, could be placed alongside Native artists like Will Wilson (Diné/Bilagáana) who reinvent and speak back to his work.[20] Students could watch "Smiling Indians," a short film by the 1491s dedicated to Curtis, that reverses the gaze and reasserts a more complex (and smiling!) portrait of Native America to counteract stoicism, or view photos from Matika Wilbur's Project 562, a photo project that captures the diversity and dignity of Native America today. The point, however, would not be to merely provide more humanizing portrayals of Native America, but to help students question and critique the various tools of dehumanization.[21]

Teachers could then move the unit beyond reflection and critique to facilitating change and social action by providing pathways for students to challenge such knowledge constructions (Agarwal-Rangnath, 2013). Using the critical, reflective, and respectful knowledge base developed in the unit, students could examine the inventory of books available to them in their school libraries. They could develop critiques of such materials, and provide evidence of their inquiry to a school librarian, principal, or school board. Students could also take part in broader campaigns such as We Need Diverse Books or Step Up Scholastic. Examining their textbooks for bias, students could rewrite sections from a critical lens, or write letters to those who adopt curriculum, such as a curriculum committee or school board. Students could even write the publishers of such books, making clear the biases within texts, and the consequences of such misrepresentation. The possibilities are numerous, but in each case, the focus of the unit is the site of knowledge production, not Indigenous peoples. Subjecting such knowledge to examination and critique enables students to develop their multicultural identities in ways that aren't dependent on the dehumanization of Indigenous peoples. Instead, these activities place Indigenous and non-Indigenous students as co-conspirators in an effort to humanize curriculum and pedagogy. In this relationship, non-Native students aren't tacitly positioned as consumers of Indigenous life and culture, but rather work alongside their Indigenous peers to challenge and create knowledge that affords everyone dignity and respect.

Rather than the self-congratulating system of multicultural lessons designed to "know" Native Others to benefit non-Native subjectivities, refusing to objectify Native peoples offers students opportunities to interrogate their relationship with knowledge and ignorance of Native life, and commit to learning to know and be in ways that are mutually beneficial and in service of Indigenous self-determination and sovereignty. For hooks (1992), the "mutual recognition of racism, its impact both on those who are dominated and those who dominate is the only standpoint that makes possible an encounter between races that is not based on denial and fantasy" (p. 28). It is uncomfortable to think that one's way of looking and knowing is rooted in colonial histories and relations, but discomfort can be generative (Boler, 1999; Boler & Zembylas, 2003). Once Native American units are seen as an extension of "White North America's propaganda machine" (LaRocque, 2010, p. 35), I am hopeful teachers will reach for more humanizing, respectful, and mutual ways of looking and knowing. I don't believe that educators really want to teach their students to be cannibals.

Notes

1 I use the term "kachina" to refer to the commodified (Pearlstone 2001) and "flattened" representations of Hopi religious worldviews (Whiteley, 2003) or when the literature uses this spelling. In contrast, I use Katsina or Katsinam (plural) to refer to Hopi supernatural beings (Pearlstone, 2011), and capitalize Katsina/Katsinam following the Hopi Tribe (2015). I make no claims that I understand Hopi religion or Katsinam which are not only private, but complex, layered, and to be understood within the context of Hopi life (Pearlstone, 2001). I claim responsibility for any mistakes or misrepresentations. My aim in this article is not to document Hopi religious practices, but the context of cultural commodification and appropriation.

2 The kachina images and explanations came from the books *Kachina Doll Coloring Book* and *Kachina Doll Coloring Book 2* published by Donna Greenlee (1972; 1973).

3 As Pearlstone (2001) notes, "Tithu are Hopi-made representations of the Hopi supernaturals, cottonwood root carvings that were and are given at certain rituals by the katsinam, the supernaturals who visit the Hopi mesas for six months of the year, to infants, young girls, brides, and adult women. Hopis refer to these carvings as tithu, or dolls, never as katsinam or *katsina* carvings" (p. 579). When made by non-Pueblo people, Pearlstone (2001) argues these are not referred to as "*tithu*; Hopis generally refer to these items as 'imitation Katsinam'" (Pearlstone, 2001, p. 47).

4 Hopi/Miwok poet Wendy Rose's poem *Builder Kachina* is perhaps a counterexample (Rose, 1980). Rose states, "The identities and roles of the Kachina Holy People are traditionally somewhat flexible; this is one that is not part of the Hopi tradition, but is part of my imagination" (as cited in Warrior, 1992, p. 14).

5 There is no singular Hopi perspective about who is authorized to replicate or represent Katsinam or Katsina imagery, but instead a range of opinions on the issue (Pearlstone, 2001). "A common theme, however, is the requirement for *respect*—respect for the Katsina as a sacred symbol, because for the Hopi, there is no bifurcation of sacred and secular" (Spencer, 2001, p. 177). Spencer (2001) places understandings of Katsinam within

> the reciprocal relationship shared by Hopi people and the Katsinam, the covenant for mutual obligation forged at the beginning of time to maintain life and balance in the universe. To not understand and respect this arrangement, most Hopi believe, may threaten the covenant, and life itself. When Katsina dolls and other forms of Katsina imagery in the public domain are viewed from this position, Hopi outrage at appropriation of these sacred symbols becomes easier to understand. Protection of the Katsina images goes well beyond cultural pride or Hopi nationalism; the Hopi must protect the Katsinam from exploitation in order to protect the ancient trust (p. 177).

6 In the current climate of cultural appropriation and exploitation, respect might also mean education regarding the significance Hopi Katsinam. This context has contributed to Hopi efforts to partner with museums "to educate viewers about the covenant for reciprocity. The goal is to have non-Hopi see the Katsina 'dolls' not as toys or decorations or simply colorful, whimsical figurines, but as cultural property of the Hopi people" (Spencer, 2001, p. 177).

7 The National Museum of the American Indian (NMAI) Education Office provides in-depth lessons and materials that investigate "American Indian Code Talkers, the servicemen who used their traditional tribal languages to transmit secret messages for the United States military during World War I and World War II." The lessons, which are geared toward grades 6–12 but can be adapted to engage younger students, can be found at the NMAI website (http://nmai.si.edu/education/codetalkers/html/lessons.html).

8 "Hopiness," states Pearlstone, "is such a powerful marketing factor that the whole process today can proceed without either the creator, seller, or buyer being Hopi. An imitation doll can be made in the Philippines, marketed in Florida, and bought by someone in Vermont from a store or a mail-order catalog" (2011, p. 602).

9 Edward Curtis was not only a photographer, but also an ethnologist, a profession whose aim is to delineate and compare differences across various races and cultures (much like a cynologist is tasked with systematically studying various breeds of canines, their characteristics, origins, and differences).

10 Native peoples' interpretations and relationships with Curtis' body of work are often more complex, ambiguous, and deeply personal than the ways his work "seized the Euroamerican imagination" (Martin, 2013, p. 10). As reflections of both "memory and loss" the photos were ironic as they enable some Native people connections to their homelands and peoples: "If not for colonialism, the theft of land, extermination of culture and language, and the genocide of a people, the need or use for Curtis' photographs may not have the same importance. Yet without them, the loss would be 'incalculable' as Horse Capture observes" (p. 10).

11 When I asked Mr. Smith how he addressed contemporary Native life, he said, "I don't really need to talk about it. It's embedded in each of the videos on the website. There's always a 90 second or so bit at the end that says, Native people are still here, and live in cities or on the reservations." I reviewed the videos, which were each approximately one-minute long. The last 10 seconds of each video included a short statement about contemporary Native life, such as "Today about 57,000 Apache live in the Southwest and across the United States. Their way of life has changed, but they are proud of their culture and history"; or "Today, about 80,000 Iroquois live in North America. They take pride in their history as the People of the Longhouse."

12 For example, on the first page of each magazine students are told that "**Everything you are about to read in this magazine is true _except_** for one of the sentences on this page." This is meant to peak their interest as they are prompted to read the magazine and figure out "which one is true?"; however, presenting the magazine in such a way disguises the discourses underlying words like nomadic, for example, or the ideological filter that led to a heavy emphasis on Native history rather than contemporary life (e. g., the first 37 pages in the Apache magazine consign Apache life to the past, leaving 5 pages to address contemporary Apache life at the end of the magazine).

13 Writing from the Northwest, the Plains is geographically elsewhere. If I wrote from the Dakotas, Nebraska, Kansas, Oklahoma, or any other places within the Great Plains region, this reference would not apply physically. However, I also use the Plains to signify an ideological framing of Indianness underwritten by Plains culture (e.g., horses, headdresses, etc.) that pervades dominant discourses of Indigeneity (Green, 1988).

14 Nelson (2014) claims his work "is intended to be a controversial catalyst for further discussion as to the authenticity of these fragile disappearing cultures," yet there is little invitation to critically interrogate the work. Instead, like Curtis, Nelson selectively edited Indigenous life for its aesthetic beauty, sense of authenticity and culture, and timelessness, and reeks of colonialism. Nelson's photos were intended "to put these [Indigenous] people on a pedestal in a way they've never been seen before" (para 4), yet he ignores this is the _usual_ colonial framing. Moreover, in the last part of his talk, he refers to the audience as a collective tribe: "and we have this global digital fireplace, don't we, but I want to share you with the world, because you are also a tribe. You are the TED tribe, yeah?" (para. 20). His work not only reproduces the vanishing Indian discourse, but also undermines sovereignty. That his talk is so widely circulated and his material available for purchase illustrate the desire, audience, and market for that work as well.

15 The context of their work—an afterschool program for Indigenous youth—shifts the educational dynamics and possibilities. The assumptions and sociocultural dynamics within a learning community of Indigenous students learning about "original technologies" is markedly different than a community of predominately non-Indigenous students learning the same. For example, as Bang and colleagues (2013) note, "for these designers, fire technology is not associated with historicized images and narratives of Indians. Rather, these designers view fire technology as a lived, heterogeneous technological practice infused with cultural origins and meaning" (p. 718). Nevertheless, it remains useful for teachers to reconsider the ways a more robust and complex understanding of "original technologies"—which they define as "technologies that Indigenous people have used from time immemorial and are embedded in our stories, traditions, and histories" (p. 716)—can disrupt discourses of primitivization based on linear notions of progress.

16 Rosaldo (1989) states at length:

> Imperialist nostalgia thus revolves around a paradox: a person kills somebody and then mourns his or her victim. In more attenuated form, someone deliberately alters a form of life and then regrets that things have not remained as they were prior to his or her intervention. At one more remove, people destroy their environment and then worship nature. In any of its versions, imperialist nostalgia uses a pose of "innocent yearning" both to capture people's imaginations and to conceal its complicity with often brutal domination. (p. 108)

17 Because in-service teachers have so little time to substantially engage Indigenous studies literature, aphorisms have still been helpful for my professional development work with practicing teachers. In a recent in-service teacher training, I expanded Melvina and my earlier aphorisms to also include: focus on Native _perspectives_, recognize the

political rights and status of Native nations, and acknowledge the ways *power* has shaped both historical and present relations.

18 This is not to say that Indigenous identities *aren't* racialized, cultural, or that sharp lines delineate politics and culture. As Chickasaw scholar Amanda Cobb (2005) with respect to Indigenous governance, "Government and culture are not separate ideas; each is manifested in and reflective of the other" (p. 123). However, given the narrow ways "culture" has been taken up in curriculum and pedagogy (Hermes, 2005), I am arguing here that curricula that draws from political framings of Indigeneity (rather than narrow framings of "culture"), will more likely support Indigenous sovereignty and self-determination by centering issues of politics, nationhood, and governance. While some argue that this legal/political understanding of sovereignty foregrounds Western constructions of nationhood and recognition (Alfred, 1999; Coulthard, 2014), Indigenous sovereignty rooted in legal and political discourses has and continues to be an effective form of advocacy for Native rights (Barker, 2005; Deloria, 1998; Wilkins, 1997).

19 Recently in Klamath Falls, for example, police seized dozens of cultural items thought to be headed for sale on the black market (Sherwood, 2015). The unit of study would *not* be the cultural items that were culturally significant or ceremonial, but rather the context that created a market for such items to be dug out of the ground while water levels were low. Students could critically interrogate that context, situate themselves within it, and take up projects that disrupted those extractive practices through making them visible or acting in solidarity with Native nations trying to reclaim significant items.

20 See Martin (2013) for decolonizing readings of Curtis's work; Onondaga artist Jeff Thomas (available at The CCCA Canadian Art Database); or the work of Cree artist Jane Ash Poitras.

21 Countless resources are available for such a purpose. Students could explore primary documents such as ethnological charts of various "races" of Indigenous peoples, or perhaps detailed images of cranial measurements. Placed alongside categorizations of canines and other animals, these forms of knowing would no longer appear neutral, and might give students new eyes to see the posters that adorn their classrooms typifying "Indians of the Plains" and "Indians of the Eastern Woodlands" as contemporary curricular forms of ethnology. Students could watch excerpts from the 1986 Australian film *BabaKiueria* (Featherstone, 1986) that satirizes relations between Aboriginal and settler Australians, or the film *Qallunaat! Why White People Are Funny* (Sandiford et al., 2006), an Inuit commentary on white culture. They could fill out the *Basic Skills Caucasian Americans Workbook* (Slapin & Esposito, 1994) which satirizes the study of Native Americans by turning the gaze on white culture.

References

Agarwal-Rangnath, R. (2013). *Social studies, literacy, and social justice in the common core classroom: A teachers' guide.* New York, NY: Teachers College Press.

Alfred, G. (1999). *Peace, power, righteousness: An indigenous manifesto.* Don Mills, ON: Oxford University Press.

Allen, L. (2015). Repeal the deal: The San Carlos Apache tribe and supporters take on corporate backroom politics in a fight for the sacred lands of Oak Flats. *Tucson Weekly.* July 2. Retrieved from www.tucsonweekly.com/tucson/repeal-the-deal/Content?oid=5389209.

Babcock, B. (2001). Preface: Five hundred years of tourism. In Z. Pearlstone (Ed.), *Katsina: Commodified and appropriated images of Hopi supernaturals* (pp. 9–12). Los Angeles, CA: UCLA Fowler Museum of Cultural History.

Bang, M., Marin, A., Faber, L., & Suzukovich, E. S. (2013). Repatriating Indigenous technologies in an urban Indian community. *Urban Education*, 48(5), 705–733.

Barker, J. (2005). *Sovereignty matters: Locations of contestation and possibility in indigenous struggles for self-determination*. Lincoln, NE: University of Nebraska Press.

Barker, J. (2011). *Native acts: Law, Recognition, and cultural authenticity*. Durham, NC: Duke University Press.

Bishop, R. S. (1990). Mirrors, windows, and sliding glass doors. *Perspectives*, 1(3), ix–xi.

Boler, M. (1999). *Feeling power: Emotions and education*. Hoboken, NJ: Taylor & Francis.

Boler, M., & Zemblyas, M. (2003). Discomforting truths: The emotional terrain of understanding difference. In P. Trifonas (Ed.), *Pedagogies of difference: Rethinking education for social change*. New York, NY: RoutledgeFalmer.

Breunig, R. (2013). The sale of the "friends": One director's perspective. *Museum Anthropology*, 36(2), 102–103.

Calderón, D. (2009). Making explicit the jurisprudential foundations of multiculturalism: The continuing challenges of colonial education in US schooling for Indigenous education. In A. Kempf (Ed.), *Breaching the colonial contract: Anti-colonialism in the U. S. and Canada* (pp. 53–77). New York, NY: Springer.

Cobb, A. (2005). Understanding tribal sovereignty: Definitions, conceptualizations, and interpretations. *American Studies*, 46(3/4), 115–132.

Coulthard, G. (2014). *Red skin, white masks: Rejecting the colonial politics of recognition*. Minneapolis, MN: University of Minnesota Press.

Cunningham, K. & Benoit, P. (2011). *The Pueblo: A True Book*. Children's Press; A division of Scholastic.

Deloria, V. (1969). *Custer died for your sins: An Indian manifesto*. New York, NY: Macmillan.

Deloria, V., (1998). Intellectual self-determination and sovereignty: Looking at the windmills in our minds. *Wicazo Sa Review*, 13(1), 25–31.

Dion, S. D. (2008). *Braiding histories: Learning from Aboriginal peoples' experiences and perspectives*. Vancouver, BC: UBC Press.

Dion, S. D. (2012). Introducing and disrupting the perfect stranger [Video file]. July. Retrieved from http://vimeo.com/59543958.

Dunbar-Ortiz, R., & Gilio-Whitaker, Di. (2016). *"All the real Indians died off": And 20 other myths about Native Americans*. Boston, MA: Beacon Press.

ESPN 2. (2014). Spirit of the game—Thompson trio, Onondaga lacrosse. [Video file]. May 25. Retrieved from https://www.youtube.com/watch?v=g2CmZbuVMtE.

Featherstone, D. (1986). *Babakiueria*. Sydney: ABC with assistance from Babakiueria Film Commission.

Friedman, M., & Benoit, P. (2011). *The Apache: A true book*. New York, NY: Scholastic.

Gaspas, D. (2002). *Native American masks coloring book*. Mineola, NY: Dover Publications, Inc.

Gonzales-Day, K. (2018). *Mosa—Mohave. Visualizing the "vanishing race": The photograavures of Edward S. Curtis*. March 16. Retrieved from http://scalar.library.oregonstate.edu/works/performingarchive/visualizing-the-vanishing-race-5.

Grand Council of the Haudenosaunee. (1995). Retrieved from www.nativetech.org/corn husk/maskpoli.html.

Grande, S. (2015). *Red pedagogy: Native American social and political thought* (2nd ed.) Lanham, MD: Rowman & Littlefield.

Green, R. (1988). The tribe called Wannabee: Playing Indian in America and Europe. *Folklore*, 99(1), 30–55.

Greenlee, D. (1972). *Kachina doll coloring book*. Scottsdale, AZ: Fun Pub.

Greenlee, D. (1973). *Kachina doll coloring book 2*. Scottsdale, AZ: Fun Pub.

Gruber, J. (1970). Ethnographic salvage and the shaping of anthropology. *American Anthropologist*, 72(6), 1289–1299.

Hermes, M. (2005). "Ma'iingan is just a misspelling of the word wolf": A case for teaching culture through language. *Anthropology & Education Quarterly*, 36(1), 43–56.

Higgins, M., Madden, B., & Korteweg, L. (2013). Witnessing (halted) deconstruction: White teachers''perfect stranger' position within urban Indigenous education. *Race, ethnicity, and education*, 18(2), 251–276.

Hirschfelder, A., & Beamer, Y. W. (2000). *Native Americans today: Resources and activities for educators, grades 4–8*. Englewood, CO: Teacher Ideas Press.

hooks, b. (1992). *Black looks: Race and representation*. Boston, MA: South End Press.

Indian Country Today. (2011, May 5). Indian country responds to Geronimo, bin Laden connection. *Indian Country Today*. Retrieved from https://newsmaven.io/indiancoun trytoday/archive/indian-country-responds-to-geronimo-bin-laden-connec tion-Q8f8fQXQXuYKGYKGkWhoZxQKQK6IYIYxw/.

Kaomea, J. (2005). Indigenous studies in the elementary curriculum: A cautionary Hawaiian example. *Anthropology Education Quarterly*, 36(1), 24–42.

King, T. (2005). *The truth about stories: A native narrative* (Indigenous Americas; v. 1). Minneapolis, MN: University of Minnesota Press.

Lambert, V. & Lambert, M. (2014). Teach our children well: On addressing negative stereotypes in schools. *American Indian Quarterly*, 38(4), 524–540.

LaRocque, E. (2010). *When the other is me: Native resistance discourse, 1850–1990*. Winnipeg: University of Manitoba Press.

Lyons, S. R. (2000). Rhetorical sovereignty: What do American Indians want from writing? *College Composition and Communication*, 51(3), 447–468.

Martin, K. J. (2013). Native footprints: Photographs and stories written on the land. *Decolonization: Indigeneity, Education & Society*, 2(2), 1–24.

Medicine, B., & Jacobs, S. E. (2001). *Learning to be an anthropologist and remaining "Native": Selected writings*. Urbana, IL: University of Illinois Press.

Mihesuah, D. (1996). *American Indians: Stereotypes & realities*. Atlanta, GA: Clarity Press.

National Center for Education Statistics. (2012). *National Indian Education Study 2011 (NCES 2012–2466)*. Institute of Education Sciences, U. S. Department of Education, Washington, D. C.

National Museum of the American Indian. (2007). *Do all Indians live in tipis? Questions and answers from the National Museum of the American Indian*. New York, NY: HarperCollins Publishers, Inc., in association with the National Museum of the American Indian, Smithsonian Institution.

Native Languages of the Americas. (2015a). American Indian FAQs for Kids: Information on Native Americans. Retrieved from www.native-languages.org/kidfaq.htm.

Native Languages of the Americas. (2015b). Native American facts for kids: Resources on American Indians for children and teachers. Retrieved from www.native-languages.org/kids.htm.

Nelson, J. (2014). Gorgeous portratis of the world's vanishing people. TEDGlobal 2014. Retreived from https://www.ted.com/talks/jimmy_nelson_gorgeous_portraits_of_the_world_s_vanishing_people?language=en.

Old Elk, A., & Stoklas, J. (2001). *After the rain: Using the rain*. Phoenix, AZ: Heard Museum.

Paakspuu, K. (2007). Photographic encounters of the western frontier. In D. Macedo & S. Steinberg (Eds.), *Media literacy: A reader* (pp. 288–298). New York, NY: Peter Lang.

Pearlstone, Z. (2000). Mail-order 'Katsinam' and the issue of authenticity. *Journal of the Southwest*, 42(4), 801–832.

Pearlstone, Z. (2001). The contemporary Katsina. In Z. Pearlstone (Ed.), *Katsina: Commodified and appropriated images of Hopi supernaturals* (pp. 38–127). Los Angeles, CA: UCLA Fowler Museum of Cultural History.

Picower, B. (2012). Using their words: Six elements of social justice curriculum design for the elementary classroom. *International Journal of Multicultural Education*, 14(1), 1–17.

Ramirez, R. (2007). *Native hubs: Culture, community, and belonging in Silicon Valley and beyond*. Durham, NC: Duke University Press.

Reese, D. (2007). The word "squaw" in SIGN OF THE BEAVER. [Web log post]. Retrieved from http://americanindiansinchildrensliterature.blogspot.com/2007/10/word-squaw-in-sign-of-beaver.html.

Rosaldo, R. (1989). Imperialist nostalgia. *Representations*, 26, 107–122.

Rose, D. B. (1996). Land rights and deep colonising: The erasure of women. *Aboriginal Law Bulletin*, 3(85), 6–13.

Rose, W. (1980). *Lost copper; Poems*. Banning, CA: Malki Museum Press.

Sabzalian, L., & Shear, S. (2018). Confronting colonial blindness in civics education: Recognizing colonization, self-determination, and sovereignty as core knowledge for elementary social studies teacher education. In S. Shear, C. M. Tschida, E. Bellows, L. B. Buchanan, & E. E. Saylor (Eds.), *(Re)Imagining elementary social studies: A controversial issues reader* (pp. 153–176). Charlotte, NC: Information Age Press.

Said, E. (1978). *Orientalism*. New York, NY: Pantheon Books.

Sandiford, M., Nungak, Z., Martin, K., Beachwalker Films, National Film Board of Canada, CTV Television Network, & Aboriginal Peoples Television Network. (2006). *Qallunaat!: Why white people are funny*. Canada: ONF/NFB.

Shear, S. B., Knowles, R. T, Soden, G. J., & Castro, A. J. (2015). Manifesting destiny: Re/presentations of Indigenous peoples in K-12 U. S. history standards. *Theory & Research in Social Education*, 43(1), 68–101.

Shear, S., Sabzalian, L., & Buchanan, L. (2018). Teaching Indigenous sovereignty in elementary civics education. *Social Studies and the Young Learner*, 31(1), 12–18.

Sherwood, C. (2015, Feb 24). Oregon police seize Native American relics headed for black market. *Reuters*. Retrieved from www.reuters.com/article/us-usa-crime-oregon-i dUSKUSKBNBN0LTLT03K20150225. 5.

Silko, L. (1996). *Yellow woman and a beauty of the spirit : Essays on Native American life today*. New York, NY: Simon & Schuster.

Simpson, A. (2007). On ethnographic refusal: Indigeneity, "voice," and colonial citizenship. *Junctures*, 9, 67–80.

Simpson, A. (2011). Settlement's secret. *Cultural Anthropology*, 26(2), 205–217.

Slapin, B., & Esposito, A. (1994). *Basic skills Caucasian Americans workbook* (2nd ed.). Berkeley, CA: Oyate.

Slapin, B., & Seale, D. (2003). *Through Indian eyes: The Native experience in books for children*. Berkeley, CA: Oyate.

Smith, L. T. (2012). *Decolonizing methodologies: Research and indigenous peoples* (2nd ed.). London: Zed Books.

Smith, P. C.. (2009). *Everything you know about Indians is wrong* (Indigenous Americas). Minneapolis, MN: University of Minnesota Press.

Spencer, V. (2001). Intellectual and cultural property rights and appropriation of Hopi Culture. In Z. Pearlstone (Ed.), *Katsina: Commodified and appropriated images of Hopi supernaturals* (pp. 170–177). Los Angeles, CA: UCLA Fowler Museum of Cultural History.

St. Denis, V. (2011). Silencing Aboriginal curricular content and perspectives through multiculturalism: "There are other children here". *Review of Education, Pedagogy, and Cultural Studies*, 33(4), 306–317.

Steffian, A. F., & Laktonen Counceller, A. G. (2015). *Alutiiq traditions: An introduction to the Native culture of the Kodiak archipelago.* Kodiak, AK: Alutiiq Museum and Archaeological Repository.

The Curtis Collection. (2014). Curtis Collection reference materials. Retrieved from www.curtis-collection.com/curtis/curtisinfo.asp.

The Hopi Tribe. (2013). Press release: The Hopi tribe opposes auction of sacred objects in France, April 4, 2013. *Museum Anthropology*, 36(2), 102.

The Hopi Tribe. (2015). Media fact sheet: Hope Tribe demands return of sacred objects being sold illegally in Paris auction. Retrieved from www.hopi-nsn.gov/wp-content/up loads/2015/05/HOPHOPI-PARPAR ISIS-AUCAUCTIOTION-SALSALE-FACFACT-SHESHEETET1.1.pdf.

Trask, H. (1999). *From a native daughter: Colonialism and sovereignty in Hawai'i* (Revised ed.). Honolulu: University of Hawai'i Press.

Treuer, A. (2012). *Everything you wanted to know about Indians but were afraid to ask.* Saint Paul, MN: Borealis Books.

Tuck, E., & Yang, K. W. (2012). Decolonization is not a metaphor. *Decolonization: Indigeneity, Education and Society*, 1, 1–40.

Tuck, E., & Yang, K. W. (2014). Unbecoming claims: Pedagogies of refusal in qualitative research. *Qualitative Inquiry*, 20(6), 811–818.

U. S. Department of Education, National Center for Education Statistics, Schools and Staffing Survey (SASS), "Public School Teacher Data File," 1987–88 through 2011–2012; "Private School Teacher Data File," 1987–1988 through 2011–2012; and "Charter School Teacher Data File," 1999–2000.

Valaskakis, G. (2005). *Indian country: Essays on contemporary Native culture* (Indigenous Studies). Waterloo, ON: Wilfrid Laurier University Press.

Vizenor, G. (2009). *Native liberty: Natural reason and cultural survivance.* Lincoln, NE: University of Nebraska Press.

Warrior, R. A. (1992). Intellectual sovereignty and the struggle for an American Indian future. *Wicazo Sa Review*, 8(1), 1–20.

Whiteley, P. (2003). Do "language rights" serve Indigenous interests? Some Hopi and other queries. *American Anthropologist*, 105(4), 712–722.

Wildcat, D. (2009). *Red alert!: Saving the planet with indigenous knowledge.* Golden, CO: Fulcrum.

Wilkins, D. E. (1997). *American Indian sovereignty and the U. S. Supreme Court: The masking of justice.* Austin, TX: University of Texas Press.

Winfield, A. (2007). *Eugenics and education in America: Institutionalized racism and the implications of history, ideology, and memory.* New York, NY: Peter Lang.

5

NATIVE HERITAGE MONTH

As the First Americans, Native Americans have helped shape the future of the United States through every turn of our history. Today, young American Indians and Alaska Natives embrace open-ended possibility and are determining their own destinies. During National Native American Heritage Month, we pledge to maintain the meaningful partnerships we have with tribal nations, and we renew our commitment to our nation-to-nation relationships as we seek to give all our children the future they deserve.

President Barack Obama (The White House, 2016)

A Season Rife with Stereotypes

"Why did they have to make Native Heritage Month in November?" groaned Melvina, the Title VI/Indian Education Coordinator for the Oakfield school district. Melvina had worked in the field of Indigenous education for years. She saw some value to the month, but felt the timing of the month was problematic. "Spring would be a more appropriate time," she said. "In November we're competing with Columbus Day, Halloween, and Thanksgiving ..."

National Native American Heritage Month[1] wasn't always in November. Its roots can be traced to the early 1900s when Seneca scholar and advocate Dr. Arthur C. Parker advocated for American Indian Day to be on June 22nd "since then nature has brought the year to perfection and it is the moon of the first fruits" (as cited in Hertzberg, 1971, p. 83). Parker, along with other Native advocates, such as Reverend Red Fox James (Blackfoot) and Reverend Sherman Coolidge (Arapaho), sought to set aside a day each year to recognize the "First Americans." Dolores Calderón (2014) would likely critique the positioning of

Indigenous peoples as the "First Americans" as a "settler grammar" that merges Indigenous peoples "into narratives of immigration and settler nationalism, thereby erasing a central tenet of Indigeneity—that Indigenous peoples originate from particular places in North America" (p. 321). Indigenous peoples were not "First Americans," but numerous prior nations who have lived in what is now known as the United States of America since time immemorial. Nevertheless, Parker envisioned this day as an opportunity to raise awareness about Native people and issues, and to educate the "Anglo-Agglomerated race" (Porter, 2001). He saw it as a chance for "Indians to be seen and treated as 'American people in America'" (Porter, 2001, p. 106), and part of a broader movement toward respecting Native people as citizens and "Americans."

While Parker had support, not all Native people agreed with his efforts. One of the most vocal opponents was Carlos Montezuma (Apache) who questioned the movement, and criticized it as a little more than a parade for whites and part of a broader agenda for assimilation. In 1916, Montezuma wrote in the first issue of his publication, *Wassaja*, that American Indian Day was "a farce and worst kind of a fad. It will not help the Indians, but the Indians will be used as tools for interested parties. To the Indian it is a laughing mockery because he does not enjoy freedom, but is a ward and is handicapped by the Indian Bureau" (as cited in Hertzberg, 1971, p. 142).[2]

American Indian Day eventually took hold, first adopted by the Boy Scouts (a connection that ironically reinforced Indigenous erasure through the organization's ritual of "playing Indian"),[3] and later by several states. American Indian Day was later developed into Native American Awareness week in October by President Ford, and ultimately recognized as National American Indian Heritage Month by President Bush in November 1990, solidifying the connections between Native Heritage Month and Thanksgiving that Melvina found so troubling.[4] Melvina remained hopeful she could provide educational opportunities during the month, but also shared Montezuma's concerns that the month might result in tokenism—a token performance or display case—while doing little to improve the actual lives of Native students she was working so hard to serve.

There were valid reasons for Melvina's concern. Fall was a time when stereotypes of Native Americans frequently circulated in the media as well as school curriculum. Columbus Day and Halloween preceded the month, and the month encompassed Thanksgiving and its attendant curriculum. As Weatherford (1991) argues, fall is when "Indian Season opens throughout the nation's schools" (n.p.). Melvina was tuned into the harmful stereotypes and damage that circulate this season. She witnessed young children innocently rehearse rhymes about Columbus sailing the ocean blue; she saw the ways teachers' renditions of the first Thanksgiving positioned Native people as colonization's "helping hand." She had comforted Native students in her program who witnessed their peers dressing as Indians for Halloween. And each fall, the ongoing debate regarding the appropriateness of Native mascots impacted some of her students, a debate animated through the competitive jeers of R★dskins fans or the hostile arguments deployed by those defending their rights to "honor" Native people through Indian mascots or costumes. In a season ripe with myths, caricatures, and hostility, it is hard to imagine how any respectful recognition of Indigenous people and culture could take place.

One could claim that this is an ideal time to promote Native studies and foster students' critical literacy, but in this district, the month had typically been ignored, and when recognized, involved a display case, bulletin board, or replicating caricatures in the form of arts and crafts activities as a means to "honor" Native culture.

Is There Even Value to Heritage Months?

Melvina was not alone in questioning the values, limits, and possibilities of heritage months. Montezuma questioned the value of American Indian Day as an effective approach to cultural pluralism in the early 1900s. Since then, scholars have debated the possibilities and pitfalls of liberal multiculturalist approaches to curriculum generally (Castagno, 2009; Ladson-Billings & Tate, 1995; Nieto & Bode, 2008; Sleeter & Bernal, 2004), and heritage months and weeks in particular (Menkart, 2008; Woodson, 1933). "What is often presented as multicultural education," Dixson and Rousseau (2006) note, "has generally been a superficial 'celebration of difference' through 'foods and festivals' activities rather than an examination of how 'difference' serves to disadvantage some and advantage others" (p. 41). These forms of "boutique multiculturalism" in which students "admire or appreciate" benign and superficial cultural difference (Fish, 1997) or "tourist" approaches (Derman-Sparks & the A.B.C. Task Force, 1989) that allow children to "'visit' non-White cultures and then 'go home' to the daily classroom, which reflects only the dominant culture" (p. 5), leave Eurocentric foundations of curricula unexamined, and thus, unchallenged. Cultural difference, in this approach, is domesticated into what Lomawaima and McCarty (2006) term the "safety zone," a paradigm of "safe" and "dangerous" expression of culture. Native cultural expression that dominant society finds non-threatening, even beneficial, to American ideals and identities (songs, arts, and crafts, for example) are allowed, while language, religious expression, or other forms of cultural difference that threaten American ideals are deemed dangerous and restricted.

Curricula regarding heritage months in particular can reproduce stereotypes rather than challenge them, and trivialize communities by failing to acknowledge structural inequities embedded in schools (Menkart, 2008). It was this claim that led Gilbert de la O, a former proponent of Cinco de Mayo celebrations in schools, to stop speaking or performing at such events until structural issues were seriously addressed. He was fed up with pattern of "hear[ing] Mexican music, see [ing] people eat Mexican food, and hear[ing] speeches about 'celebrating diversity'" without corresponding efforts "to increase the hiring and promotions of Chicanos/Latinos." He refused to perform for any more Cinco de Mayo celebrations until "Chicanos/Latinos" had "parity" with their peers, represented as equally in "board rooms" as they were in "cloak rooms" (as cited in Menkart, 2008, p. 374). Heritage month also routinely precipitate a question many communities of color are familiar with: "When is White History Month?" Despite these limits, debates, and critiques, there were Native families in the district who felt that some form of celebration was better than the outright invisibility they often experienced, and so cautiously looked forward to the month.

Native American Heritage month has usually been overlooked in this district, though for the past two years, one of the 22 schools has asked the Title VI program to create a display case. When efforts have been made, they were usually the result of an individual teacher or principal's passion or will, rather than collaborative and comprehensive approaches by schools or the district. Melvina, for her part, answered the phone, which rang more often in November with teachers asking for help. She wished teachers reached out year round, but she also appreciated the phone calls because it gave her a sense of what was being taught in the classrooms. "Some teachers don't like you to know what was going on in their classrooms. They want to do their own thing. They don't want us to challenge what they are doing because they don't want to feel bad about it." The teachers who called were at least reaching out for help, she said, and that was a starting point.

Making the Most of the Month: A Fact a Day

Melvina, through her experience as a Title VI coordinator in several school districts over the years, felt that the lack of background knowledge teachers and administrators had about Native peoples and nations might be one of the reasons schools were hesitant to take more comprehensive approaches during the month. In her former position as a Title VI coordinator on the Oregon coast, she sought to address this ignorance by coordinating with the principals at each school in the district to read "a fact a day" about contemporary Native people and nations during morning announcements. This was a small activity, inadequate to transform the core of teaching and learning within each school; however, as a part-time coordinator responsible for serving Native students, it was her way, despite her limited FTE, to provide some sort of educational intervention within each school. Reading the facts, she hoped, might educate teachers, raise awareness of gaps in their knowledge, and provided talking points for morning meetings or curricula.

Melvina had hoped to implement the same practice here. With 22 schools in the district, this was a much bigger feat. At a local grant meeting, a team of Native educators took that task on, drafting a fact a day for the schools to use during the month. The Director of Elementary Education was on this committee and committed to sending out the list of facts along with a comprehensive list of resources on the tribal nations in Oregon, contemporary Native media outlets, and resources for Native pedagogy and curriculum. Despite all of this information being sent out weeks before the heritage month began, there seemed to be little shift in the curriculum for the month, and hard to know which schools took this task on and how. As I sat in an elementary classroom on the first day of Native Heritage Month, I listened intently, waiting for the first fact to be read over the announcement, wondering what the teachers and students would do after it was read. The first fact, adapted from the book *Do All Indians Live in Tipis?* (National Museum of the American Indian, 2007, p. 2), would have stated:

> Many people want to know what the correct word is to refer to Native people … Should I say American Indian, Indian, Native American, Native, or Indigenous? All of those terms are acceptable, however many Native people generally prefer to be called by their tribal affiliation, when possible— Aleut, Navajo, Klamath, or Siletz for example.[5] The term "Indian" originated with Christopher Columbus. He thought that he had reached the East Indies when he landed in America and therefore named the inhabitants Indians. But this term for such a diverse group of people erases the fact that most Native communities have distinct languages, religious beliefs, ceremonies, and social and political systems. Even though people say words like Native American or American Indian to show similarities among them, it's important to remember each Native group in the US has its own unique and diverse culture and government. (p. 2)

The facts we drafted for the month were inevitably insufficient, but so too was the reality and pressure we felt to prioritize and consolidate a comprehensive, accurate, and contemporary portrait of Native America into 60-second sound bites. We still hoped they would spark conversations. But as I sat there grading spelling tests, I heard the usual welcome, then students were asked to stand and recite the Pledge of Allegiance, followed by the Peace Pledge that students recited each Monday. I didn't hear any of the facts our team had worked so hard on.

As I left the school, I checked in with the principal. I was curious why she hadn't read the facts. She told me that she hadn't had a chance to read them yet but would shortly. She made a point to say to me, however, that these heritage months feel "like tokenism," and that we should be respecting and learning about diverse peoples and cultures throughout the year. It was impossible for me to read the actual intent behind her words, but her comment felt a bit like a deflection. There was merit, of course, to her concern surrounding tokenism,[6] and yet her tone and the knowledge we had sent the facts along with other resources for the month weeks earlier left me with the impression that had I not inquired, the materials we sent would likely have been ignored.

Later that afternoon I received an email from the principal inquiring about a company that provided Native educational assemblies. The company was in the area, had a recent cancellation, and was offering a discount for their assembly. The principal wondered if I had heard of the company, and whether or not it would be a good fit for Native Heritage Month. Her email about the assembly struck me as ironic given her previous comment about tokenism; however, like Melvina, I appreciated the opportunity to learn what curriculum was being considered.

The advertisement for the company framed the assembly as a "culturally diverse program" in which "students will learn about the beauty and symbolism of Native American music, dance, regalia, and storytelling. The performance will include insight into the history of Native American life. It will empower, educate and entertain your students about Native American traditions" [personal communication]. I hadn't heard of the company and so perused the website. It was created by an Indigenous performer who hoped that sharing his music, dance, and storytelling would foster communication among all people. The company was Native-owned and operated, and discussed the diversity of Native American cultures, situating each dancer as a citizen of a different nation. This is a common protocol among Indigenous peoples, but contrasts mainstream curricula that usually collapses diverse Native peoples and nations into a single, cultural group. The dancers were also dressed in beautiful and intricate regalia, which I knew teachers and children would admire. The hopes the founder and other artists expressed on the company website felt similar to Parker's desires for American Indian Day.

Despite the thoughtful aims of the company, I felt apprehensive and struggled with how to respond to the principal's inquiry. Perhaps if the school were predominately Native, or the assembly held in the Indian Education program, I wouldn't have felt such trepidation. It was the context and audience of the performance that prompted my anxieties. I was also hesitant to criticize the first and only effort this school had ever taken for Native Heritage Month, especially since there were Native students at the school. Yet I was concerned with how the performers' regalia, adorned with beautiful bustles and roaches, or their painted faces, would intersect with what kids already "knew" about Indians. Beyond reproducing stereotypes, I was concerned with whether that knowledge would distort how non-Native students perceived their Native peers. This is not, of course, to reduce the significance or beauty of regalia to a stereotype or cliché. Regalia is an important spiritual, material, and cultural aspect of Indigeneity for some people, yet it is only one of many ways of embodying tradition. For some, even three-piece suits could be seen as traditional.[7] And beyond the outward cultural expression of regalia, Indigenous cultures are embodied in relationships to land, stories, languages, values, families, communities, and nations among other relations. Because representations were few, and because students aren't afforded a diverse and broad range of understandings and representations of Indigenous peoples, this performance as a representation seemed to carry a great deal of weight.

I wrote the principal back, thanking her for her consideration and also offering my misgivings. I cautioned her that if she went through with the assembly, pre-teaching and then follow up by the teachers would be necessary, connecting this performance to the contemporary lives of the Native people of Oregon today, and situating the performer and performance as one expression of the many ways to be Indigenous. I also offered to help provide information about the Native people and nations in Oregon, as well as other contemporary Native role models to use in follow-up activities. The principal thanked me for my opinion, shared that my comments were helpful, and then shortly after booked the assembly and invited me to attend. Later that day, she shared our list of facts and resources out with staff in her school to educate and foster awareness, and committed to reading some of the facts during the morning announcements as well.

Melvina, it turns out, would *not* have endorsed the assembly. She also wondered why the principal hadn't contacted her about the dancer. If the principal had asked her, she would have suggested something entirely different, either reserving time at the Center to support Native students, or coordinating Native students in the program to visit classrooms or hold their own assembly. Melvina recognized the limits of a month like Native Heritage Month, but also thought months like this could be explicitly used to create spaces and opportunities for students in the Indian Education program to embody and express their heritage and pride. I wished that instead of replying I would have forwarded the email to Melvina, especially after witnessing students' reactions to the assembly.

"An Indian is Coming!"

On the day of the assembly I went to the school.

> "I'm the Indian Chief," said one 2nd grade student to another in the hallway.
> "No, I am. I'm going to get you with my spear!" said the other lunging forward.

I watched the boys lunge back and forth at each other, play fighting like "Indian Chiefs." The teacher had come out and greeted me amidst their play fighting, ignoring their stereotypical battle. I wondered why she hadn't addressed it. Perhaps she was busy getting students together in line. I thought about what I should say to the boys.

> "Most Chiefs don't have spears," I finally said. "They are more like Barack Obama, the President."

The boys just looked at me. One smiled at me. "Whose mom are you?" the other one asked.

The children were standing in the hallway in preparation for the assembly the principal had arranged for Native Heritage Month. She had moved forward with contracting the performer, despite my apprehensions.[8]

"Are you here to watch the Indian guy dance?" one student asked me as we waited.

"Is that what's going to happen today?" I asked.

I stood in line with a group of second grade students, waiting to go watch the "Indian guy" dance. I thought about the Native students who might feel a sense of pride at this event. I also thought about those that didn't dance or attend pow wows. I thought about the non-Native students and teachers and what they would take away from this assembly I also thought about the principal's comment that she wanted to do more than "token" activities.

"Am I Indian?" asked one student as we waited in line, pointing at his light skin.

"I'm not sure," I said. "You can't tell if someone is Native by looking at their skin."

Another student passionately tugged at my shirt. "I'm part Native American" she exclaimed. "And he's part Native American too!" pointing to a boy next to me.

It was nice to see that a few of the Native students in the class felt proud to openly identify this way. Native students made up only 3% of the school popula-tion. It was important for them to have opportunities to feel pride and see them-selves represented in the curriculum. The idea of the assembly, like the founder of the company had hoped, appeared to be prompting a sense of pride in these stu-dents. It was also interesting to see a 7-year old had already internalized the word "part." I wondered if she had gotten this from her family. A response taught to one of the Native students I worked with by his grandmother rang in my head: "Which 'part' specifically? Your arm? From your elbow to your wrist maybe?"

Already, the students' diverse reactions to the assembly—ranging from non-Native students' caricaturizing of Native people to Native students' expressions of interest and pride—sat in tension with each other. This assembly already invited different reactions from different students. It reminded me of Stephanie Fryberg's (2004) work on Native mascots. Fryberg, a citizen of the Tulalip tribes, found that not only do Native mascots decrease Native students' self-esteem, but they actually *increased* white students' self-esteem. The gentleman coming to dance was no mascot and the Native students seemed to be excited about the assembly. Yet Fryberg's research felt relevant as I had witnessed the ways the mere idea of a Native performer prompted non-Native students to play Indian (Green, 1988; Deloria, 1998) in the hallway—a "characteristically American kind of domination in which the exercise of power was hidden, denied, qualified, or mourned" (Deloria, 1998, p. 187). I couldn't confirm that the non-Native students felt superior in this case, but it was apparent that the same content or curriculum could invite different reactions or experiences by students, and that some of those reactions embodied subtle rehearsals of erasure and domination.

As we walked down the hall toward the gym, I noticed other curriculum teachers had used that month. One hallway was lined with artistic renditions of the raven in Gerald McDermott's *How Raven Stole the Sun*, a book depicting a traditional Northwest tale of a raven by non-Native author Gerald McDermott, which has received reviews ranging from laudable to outright cultural appropriation.[9] In the main hall to the gym, we passed by a series of cutout Mayflower ships, part of a larger unit on Pilgrims that the second grade teachers were implementing. Native Americans were surely included in that unit, though the emphasis on the Mayflower hinted at the dominant perspective from which the unit was framed. Intentionally or unintentionally, this was part of the curricular backdrop for these students during Native Heritage Month and I wondered what else teachers were doing for November.

We arrived at the gym and took our spots on the floor. Four hundred students did their best to sit still in rows, their bodies wriggling as they fidgeted in anticipation and chattered excitedly, waiting for the special guest to arrive. As I kneeled down, several students exclaimed, "An Indian is coming! An Indian is coming!" From what I had witnessed so far, it didn't appear that teachers had prepared their students for the assembly, which felt like it was about to be a spectacle.

"I Didn't Come Here on a Horse": Native Performance or Spectacle?

Native performers and artists have long negotiated issues of audience, mediating cultural expression so as to be legible to both those from within and outside of their cultural frameworks and communities. Indigenous storytellers, for example, engage in complex negotiations, often working "at two levels" in their storytelling as they simultaneously try to reach Native and non-Native listeners (Cruikshank, 1997). Those with limited exposure to Indigenous narratives, however, often miss the nuances and subtleties, despite their yearning for an authentic experience. Despite the "social agency" of the storytellers, "translation" of the stories often relies on the listeners' cultural schema, enabling "some listeners [to] hear levels of humor or pathos opaque to others" (p. 59). Native writers engage in similar negotiations and mediations, some explicitly privileging Native cultural frameworks, while others create multi-layered pieces that aim to engage diverse audiences. In either case, Native authors often position the Native reader as the "the insider, privileged and empowered. The *métropole* [in this case, the non-Native audience] is pushed to the periphery, made liminal, at best littoral, in the same way that a non-Native town may exist on the border of a reservation" (Weaver, 2001, p. 41). Just as an audience member depending on his frame of reference may miss particular meanings in a Native storyteller's performance, a reader's assumptions can also shape interpretations of a book, leading the same piece of Native fiction to be read as stereotypical by a non-Native reader, while simultaneously being deeply meaningful to a Native reader: "... what may be read as derivative Romanticism within a white context may also have stronger and more complex reverberations within relevant Indian cultures" (Murray, as cited in Weaver, 2001, p. 41). It is apparent, then, that Indigenous performers, storytellers, and authors engage in dynamic and creative negotiations as they represent Indigenous life; those representations can be read simultaneously as stereotypical and deeply meaningful, and can simultaneously reproduce and disrupt dominant discourses.

I recognized that the Native students had already expressed some pride in anticipation of the performance, and so I was hopeful they would get something positive out of the upcoming performance. I also recognized that the performer might have the tools to effectively communicate within this context, working his performance at "two levels." I didn't assume this, however, as I have seen Native people sell caricatures of their own community for economic benefit with little self-consciousness. And of course, I couldn't help but read this type of performance as a continuation of Native performances at world fairs, where Native people were literally put on display as spectacles of "primitivism" that contrasted Eurocentric displays of "civilization" and "progress" (Raibmon, 2005). Even in those displays, though, Native people often asserted their own ideas and purposes—whether to make money or travel to new places. And so I sat there with the students, feeling both trepidation and curiosity. I was hopeful the performer would be witty and surprising, as Native performances often are, but I also feared he would be read as a caricature and the performance a spectacle. For those few moments as we waited for him to come out, the climate felt ripe with voyeurism.

The principal introduced Mr. Barry, who entered the gym dressed in traditional regalia, as a Native American fancy dancer. The room was noisy as children oohed and awed, some student nearby me commenting that they loved his "costume." It was mistaken, but understandable, that a student would use the term "costume," a common misnomer, as opposed to the proper term, regalia. Many people don't see regalia within the context of Native communities to learn accurate terms and protocols. I couldn't hear the other side conversations that were taking place, but the murmurs as the dancer entered felt like general excitement.

When Mr. Barry came out, he introduced himself, his tribal affiliation, and his Indian name and its meaning. As I listened to him share his name, a contemporary practice within many Indigenous communities (though one that varies considerably between Indigenous communities), I also wondered if some of the non-Native kids would want "Indian names" like those who requested them at last year's powwow. It felt like each time we created a meaningful event for Native students and families, an unintended consequence was that Native students and families faced even more exposure to stereotypes and racial microaggressions from the broader community. I scanned the room looking for the two Native second graders whom I walked in with earlier. They appeared engaged, attentively watching Mr. Barry. Despite my apprehensions, I was hopeful that this assembly would affirm them in some way. Mr. Barry then shared three things that he said were important for the students to know:

> I don't wear this outfit every day.
> I don't live in a tipi or in the mountains.
> I didn't come here on a horse. I drive a Honda.
> I get asked those three questions every time.

Mr. Barry chuckled, clearly engaging the kids on his own terms, sharing not only who he was, but anticipating how he thought he might be perceived. He exuded what Du Bois (1961) has referred to as "double consciousness" (p. 16), an agility that develops as a result of consistently navigating other peoples' perceptions. Mr. Barry was, as many Native performers do, "oust[ing] the inventions" of the Indian "with humor," and creating "an active sense of presence" (Vizenor, 1999, vii). He was a contemporary Native man, but aware that this could seem like a contradiction to students who may have little to no interaction with actual Native people, their only references to Native life coming from history books or pop culture. He prefaced his performance with these statements because he anticipated that he would be interpreted through a colonial lens.

Mr. Barry continued, sharing a bit about his porcupine roach and golden eagle feathers. He sang a few songs and then explained the warrior dance he would perform. Students marveled at the dance, many of them fidgeting around on the floor as children do, soaking it all in. Mr. Barry then invited groups of students up to dance with him. I watched as the two Native students' hands jutted in the air when he asked for volunteers, followed by their disappointed faces when they didn't get called on. Twenty students or so were chosen by their teachers, and lined up in front of their peers, mirroring Mr. Barry's various dance steps as their peers clapped along and giggled. At the time I wondered why the teacher didn't call on the Native students. I also thought of the tensions inherent if she had. I remember the pressures of being asked to speak for all Native people, or even all people of color, when I was a student. But this felt different. Their intensely raised hands indicated that these Native students *wanted* to participate. In a later interview I learned that one of the Native boys waving his hand frantically in the air was called on at the previous assembly, and so his teacher though it might not have been fair for him to be called on again. Her explanation made sense. I also thought about how rare these opportunities were for Native youth and whether, given the circumstances, she should have called on them anyway.

A second group of students was called up. Kids raised their hands frantically, desperate to be called on and dance on stage. Again, the Native students wildly waved their hands in the air. Those called on ran up to the front of the gym and, side by side, wriggled their bodies. Some moved to the rhythm, many of them were off beat, but they were all smiling and laughing as they tried to mirror Mr. Barry's steps and motions. In the last few minutes of the assembly, the students chanted that their teachers go up on stage. I remember as a kid loving to see my teachers do things, wanting them to make fools of themselves. Mr. Barry called the teachers up and I watched as he led the teachers through a variety of moves—some traditional dance moves, but others thrown in like "the sprinkler" and "the Cabbage Patch." Mr. Barry could have been mocking the teachers, teasing them with their own desires; he could also have just been having fun. There was laughter and joy in the room, but it was also hard to know what purpose this assembly was serving. Heritage celebrations don't always communicate what organizers hope or intend. Upon attending a Hispanic Heritage assembly in Washington DC, a student was asked "what she had learned about Latinos" from the assembly. "Well, they are good at dancing," she replied (Menkart, 2008, p. 374). I wondered if students would take away a similar conclusion from this performance.

Performances aren't inherently problematic or stereotypical, yet this assembly seemed to reach for a Native performer as a curricular *product* rather than view performance as a cultural and educational *process* (Pepper et al. 2014). The school could have, as Melvina suggested, invited Native students to perform songs and dances they have been learning in the Title VI program. While inviting such a performance would appear to contain the same complexities, contradictions, and voyeurism that surrounded the performer at the assembly, not to mention function as an add-on approach to curriculum for the month, enlisting Native students in such a performance would have at least given them an opportunity to embody cultural revitalization, decolonization, and critical pedagogy (Jacob, 2013; Topkok & Green, 2016).

In his work with Iñupiaq and other youth, for example, Asiqłuq (Sean Topkok) illustrates how Iñupiaq cultural values are embodied through traditional stories, drumming, and dance. Asiqłuq began a group, the Pavva Iñupiaq dancers, to nurture Iñupiaq well-being through dance, exemplifying how dancing and drumming, when rooted in Indigenous knowledge, values, and traditions, "can provide a meaningful educational approach for transmitting cultural knowledge, wellness, and identity to youth and future generations" (Topkok & Green, 2016, p. 185). While the group has performed at various Alaska Native cultural and non-Native events, the central purpose of the group is for those involved to embody and enhance Iñupiaq well-being and to pass Iñupiaq knowledge on to future generations. Some in the audience may be inspired to join the effort at learning Iñupiaq cultural values and practices, however, his work shows how the intended audience for such cultural revitalization are not the onlookers, but those who perform as a process of learning and sustaining Iñupiaq knowledge and traditions.

Similarly, in her book *Yakama Rising*, Yakama scholar Michelle Jacob examines the Wapato Indian Club, a club that teaches Native youth on the Yakama reservation Yakama songs and dances, as a site of cultural revitalization and decolonization. Jacob opens the book with a beautiful portrayal of Native youth from the club dancing to commemorate the 100th anniversary of Washington

State. In their performance, youth not only embody the beauty and grace of a traditional Yakama Welcome Dance, but also cultural values and responsibilities. As Jacob states, the children are "expected to embody these values, as they learn and carry on the teachings of their elders. As such, the children's bodies become a site for critical pedagogy" (2013, p. 45). From her read of the Wapato Indian Club, Jacob calls on educators "to remember the potential and contribution of recognizing young people's leadership and the importance of the body as a liberatory tool for critical awareness, leadership development, and decolonizing praxis" (pp. 45–46). Through their participation in the club, students learned to embody respect, healing, inclusivity, self-awareness, unity, listening, and responsibility, embodying a Yakama decolonizing praxis (Jacob, 2013). Jacob also recognized the conflicting and contradictory ways the youth's Welcome Dance performance could read by non-Indigenous audience members:

> Perhaps it is a fitting irony that Indian children danced to commemorate Washington's one-hundredth anniversary. Perhaps the dance reminded state officials of their obligation to our people. After all, the officials worked for a bureaucracy that existed as a result of the genocide and destruction of Indian peoples. Perhaps the display of dancing children and the presence of so many Indian bodies reminded officials that they were on Yakama homeland. Or, perhaps the audience simply saw, in amazement, that even after over one hundred years of the violence of colonization, settlement, war, and reservation policies, Yakama children could take center stage at an official event and steal the show. (p. 5)

For Jacob, it wasn't the audience's reading, but the process and practice of embodiment that made such a performance decolonizing.

The assembly didn't likely remind students or teachers of their obligation to Indigenous people; nor did it likely remind everyone they were on Indigenous land. As curriculum, it more likely functioned as entertainment, one in which Mr. Barry "stole the show." What distinguishes the Pavva Iñupiaq Dancers and the Wapato Indian Club from the school assembly, however, was an emphasis on decolonizing *processes* as opposed to *products*. In Alaska and in Yakama, Native students embodied practices and processes of cultural revitalization and critical pedagogy through dance; and rather than a day-of-product, their performances were part of a larger process that supported Indigenous well-being, cultural revitalization, and empowerment throughout the year.

Between Erasure and Caricature

I walked out of the gym with the two Native second graders who chattered to each other about the dancer, giving me the impression they enjoyed the performance. Yet I remained concerned with what the rest of the school took away. The assembly provided a curricular moment of visibility for contemporary Native people, perhaps the reason why that one Native student seemed so eager to identify herself to me as Native; but the assembly also invited blatant misrepresentations by that student's peers earlier in the hallway. The war whoops and talk about chiefs and spears stemmed from societal curriculum (Cortés, 1979) about Indians, learned in these students' homes, communities, prior schooling, reinforced by media that included Indigenous peoples in particular ways, a pattern one First Nations elder identified as the 4Ds: Native people are included when they are drumming, drinking, dancing, or dead (McCue, 2014). This societal curriculum surfaced hostile fictions that became part of the educational climate for Native students. It was hard to see how such an environment could be supportive of Native students when what circulated around them were disrespectful caricatures.

Mr. Barry clearly performed at "two levels" during his performance, but I wasn't sure students had picked up on the nuances of his performance. And because the school did little to surface and intervene into the misconceptions students brought with them regarding Indians, it was hard to see how the assembly could have done anything other than reify dominant narratives. It wasn't necessarily that children shouldn't have had fun or giggled, or that they needed to be overly reverent toward the performer (a more nuanced type of colonial relationship), but the context hadn't set up students to engage in resistant readings of his performance. Instead, the assembly reproduced a familiar pattern of positioning Native people between the poles of erasure and caricature.

This spectrum of erasure and hyper-visibility left little room for nuanced, contemporary understandings and expressions of Indigenous identities and life. This spectrum also felt largely invisible to many of the educators with whom I have worked with in the district, often white women. This tension between erasure and caricature is a persistent feature of efforts to include content about Indigenous people and cultures in K-12 curriculum. This is not a necessary or inevitable tension. There is a great deal more about which students could be educated. Schools could focus on Native sovereignty and tribal governance, focus on any number of contemporary issues that Native communities and nations face today, focus on the insights and perspectives Indigenous peoples bring to issues such as language, literature, or environmentalism, or critically interrogate stereotypes Native people constantly contend with as a means of developing critical literacy. These possibilities, however, remain invisible to most of the professionals in K-12 educational systems I have worked with. This ignorance creates an impossible situation when events like Native American Heritage Month force some degree of attention to Indigenous lives and culture. Even knowledgeable advocates working within the school system are constrained by the limits of what teachers and administrators find legible, and so schools revert to hosting events like dance performances without any accompanying critique, historicizing, or humanizing of contemporary Indigenous life. It is inclusion of a sort, but without interrogating the Eurocentric basis of such a gesture, such forms of inclusion operate more practically as "enclosures" (Richardson, 2011), containing the possibilities of Indigenous knowledges and cultures (Hermes, 2005) and foreclosing systemic change.

The Indian in some of those second graders' imaginations, the Indian in the tokenizing curriculum I had witnessed in the school district generally, and even the Indian that the students and staff watched perform, each exemplified King's (2013) "Dead Indian," "the stereotypes and clichés that North America has conjured up" (p. 53). King contends that "America no longer *sees* Indians"; instead, "What it sees are war bonnets, beaded shirts, fringed deerskin dresses, loincloths, headbands, feathered lances, tomahawks, moccasins, face paint, and bone chokers" (p. 54). This is the Indian that America *wants* to see; the Indian that educators *want* to include. Mr. Barry, of course, is clearly a "Live Indian," making part or all of his living doing something that he enjoys and is good at, something that connects him to his heritage and culture, and for which, as he shared in the assembly, he feels immense pride. However, Mr. Barry's enactment as a Live Indian didn't contradict him being read as a Dead Indian by educators, several of whom later told me that his performance gave them goosebumps, or nearly brought them to tears. Rather, King's category of the Dead Indian helps theorize how Mr. Barry can perform in a way that is personally meaningful, while also being perceived as an exotic object to be consumed and enjoyed. More globally, King's categories help theorize why the principal, when thinking of how to foster awareness of Native people and cultures, chose to bring in Mr. Barry as a cultural performer, rather than entertain other curricular possibilities.

As I left the assembly, surrounded by the contradictory readings that likely took place in the gym, the principal, who was speaking with another parent, stopped me in the hall.

"Wasn't that wonderful?!?!" she exclaimed. "What did you think?!"

From Poetics to Politics of Native Performance

I couldn't help but wish that the principal hadn't asked that question. Her question led me to believe that we had very different experiences of the assembly. Her question asked me to validate her efforts. As she stood there proudly next to a parent, her cheeks flush from dancing, I struggled with how to respond in that moment. I feared an honest response might come off as pointedly critical and unsupportive. I didn't want to endorse the performance, but was also worried that any critical suggestions might cause her discomfort and foreclose future efforts. This was, after all, the first time the school had ever formally acknowledged Native Heritage Month.[10] And so I smiled, shifting my eyes to avoid contact with her beaded choker which featured a wolf pendant, and thought for a second about what to say. Luckily, a stream of students and teachers poured out of the other exit from the gym and in between us, and I was off the hook to affirm her efforts.

While I read the principal's efforts for Native Heritage Month as a sign of intended support, I had other experiences which indicated to me that she needed to develop critical literacy with respect to Native representations in curriculum. This was the same principal who had endorsed masks and cardboard totem poles as "great" curriculum. In another conversation with me, she had also fondly recalled making spirit rain masks as a second grader, indicating to me that her conception of Indigenous people was wrapped up in understandings of Indianness underpin by "the romantic, mythical Other" (Dion, 2008). This feeling was heightened when Melvina showed me that the video of teachers and administrators dancing at the assembly was being proudly and widely shared throughout the district. The assembly was a hit among educators and administrators, but what sorts of knowledge and relationships was it fostering between them and the Indigenous students and families in the district? I wasn't sure ...

This terrain of Indianness that surfaced during the month often appears invisible to educators I work with, many of whom seem unaware that Native people are *"always already* 'Indian,'" already enclosed by images of "CHIEF BRAVE MEDICINE MAN WARRIOR PRINCESS SQU[*]W FRY BREAD MAKER PAPOOSE CARRIER" (Barker & Teaiwa, 2005, p. 111). Yet this navigation of ignorance and misrepresentation of Indigenous life is now a central feature of contemporary Indigenous life in a post-apocalyptic[11] world colonized by European settlers. It is an appreciation of this feature of contemporary Indigenous life by educators, perhaps more than any particular piece of information, that is needed in mainstream schools. This knowledge of the ways Indigenous peoples are often concealed or caricaturized in mainstream narratives is a central component of teacher practical knowledge needed to better serve Native students and teach Native-themed curriculum. Familiar ways of knowing Indigenous peoples must become strange, uncomfortable, and intolerable. This knowledge would enable teachers to begin detecting bias in the curriculum often taught about Native peoples, whether that bias manifests in Eurocentric accounts of explorers, the commodification of Native culture, or silence around contemporary issues. This knowledge would reframe the struggles of many Indigenous students and families—transforming the discourse from a focus on personal deficits to an understanding that Indigenous students are often the ones strained to work around the deficits of others (including the deficits of their teachers or administrators). This understanding would first require an acknowledgement of such deficits on the part of many teachers, administrators, and institutions, something that both people and institutions have historically been resistant to doing. These deficits, however, are real, as are the consequences of denying them, which result in the deficits being projected onto Indigenous children and their families.

What should be circulated, rather than caricaturizing narratives, is an awareness of the ways those caricatures operate to silence the real, diverse, and contemporary lives, issues, and aims of Native peoples and nations. What should be normalized, rather than hegemonic representations of the Dead Indian, is a self-consciousness on the part of educators as to the stakes of such problematic and pervasive misrepresentations. This self-consciousness shouldn't paralyze efforts to include Indigenous studies content, but serve as a critical basis from which educators mediate and evaluate their own efforts.

The principal's question to me is reflective of the need for *everyone* in schools—administrators, educators, Native and non-Native students—to be educated about a critique of settler society and develop critical literacy with respect to Indigenous studies curriculum; to develop an anticolonial literacy. This is not the work of Indigenous scholars, educators, or parents alone. If the principal had this sort of critical anticolonial literacy, she likely would have asked me a different question. If she had this sort of critical anticolonial literacy, she would have focused not only on the "poetics" of the performance (attending only to the specific elements within the performance, such as the dancer or storytelling), but also read the "politics" of the performance, a reading of the assembly that attends to particular configurations of power and knowledge, one that reads the performance in light of the broader sociopolitical, cultural, and historical contexts (Lidchi, 1997).

Attempting to extract the poetic without attending to the politics of such performances can be deeply problematic. It was this sort of "politics" of exhibiting that led Indigenous peoples to call for a boycott of a museum exhibit in Canada, *The Spirit Sings*, sponsored by Shell Oil. While the exhibit aimed "to highlight the 'richness, diversity, and complexity' of Canada's Native cultures at the moment of contact" among other intentions (Lidchi, 1997, p. 202), Indigenous political critiques read the exhibit in light of a broader context of power, knowledge, and unresolved land claims. As Chief Bernard Ominayak noted, "The irony of using a display of North American Indian artifacts to attract people to the Winter Olympics being organized by interests who are still actively seeking to destroy Indian people seems painfully obvious" (as cited in Lidchi, 1997, p. 203).

It was reading beyond the poetics to a politics of performance that led Gilbert de la O to refuse performing for Cinco de Mayo; it was reading this politics of performance that led Carlos Montezuma to question the value of Indians being paraded around on display for whites, while remaining wards to the BIA. Similarly, a political reading of the assembly would question the broader contexts of how and when Native people are invited into curricula and educational processes. The performer was not an object in a museum,[12] but a political reading would question the ways Indigenous peoples are included into curricula—as historical subjects, multicultural objects of study, or contemporary performances—and how such inclusions likely reproduce colonial discourses.

In his reading of the "Spirit Sings" museum exhibit sponsored by Shell Oil, Peter Kulchyski (1997) notes, "The question is whether this exhibit—which follows what seems too [sic] commonly be done in museum practice—celebrated dead culture at the expense of living Aboriginal culture, and thereby contributed to the process of cultural destruction" (p. 615). The same question applies here: did curriculum for Native Heritage Month celebrate dead culture at the expense of living Native culture?

From Dead Indians to Legal Indians and Native Sovereignty

> … while North America loves the Dead Indian and ignores the Live Indian, North America *hates* the legal Indian. Savagely. (King, 2013, p. 69)

To say that heritage months could potentially be reclaimed as sites of resistance, sites of empowerment for Native youth, and sites of learning non-Native students is to claim a site that is already marginalized. Perhaps reviving the potential that the originators of heritage months hoped for is futile, particularly as they function as an "add on" approaches to education within educational systems that Dolores Calderón (2009) so bluntly (and accurately) diagnoses as the "functionary arm of colonialism" (p. 53). Indeed, attempting to restore the potential of Native Heritage Month within such colonial systems can feel futile, and lead to further marginalization if curriculum, pedagogy, and policy for the rest of the year remain unexamined. Yet if refashioned, Native Heritage Months could provide sustained curricular space dedicated to teaching about Indigenous self-determination and tribal sovereignty. To do so, it seems important to understand why educators often refrain from doing so—ignorance or arrogance, or both?

What seems to be lacking is not the will to represent Indigenous peoples, but an unwillingness to abandon hegemonic curricula rooted in narrow, Eurocentric understandings of "culture" and "authenticity." As King (2013) notes, "all North America can see is the Dead Indian. All North America dreams about is the Dead Indian. There's a good reason, of course. The Dead Indian is what North America wants to be" (p. 73). Occasionally this desire to see, even be, the Dead Indian surfaces in clearly observable ways. Another principal who hosted the same assembly for Native Heritage Month at another elementary school in the district expressed such a desire when commenting on how embarrassed she was at her students' initial reactions to the dancer: "I was mortified when the assembly started, because he started dancing and there was tittering and I was mortified because it was like oh my gosh … I mean I look at that, and feel like I'm this White Anglo Saxon Protestant and have no cultural heritage. Nothing rich like Native Americans … I don't have any rich heritage, and I look at that and think, oh I wish." Such colonial logics influence how educators conceptualize curriculum. Not only did this administrator normalize her own whiteness as acultural, she also coveted the performer's cultural difference—a "desire to *become without becoming [Indian]*" (Tuck & Yang, 2012, p. 14). Such ways of conceptualizing Indigeneity directly influence the types of activities and curriculum educators consider for events like Native Heritage Months.

The ways Indigenous peoples are included in curriculum is not just "misinformation," but an investment in particular ways of knowing. The "ignorance" produced about Indigenous peoples in schools is also not "a simple omission or gap but is, in many cases, an active production" (Tuana, 2004, p. 195). As Tuana (2006) notes elsewhere, "not knowing is sustained and sometimes even constructed" (p. 3). Knowledge and ignorance are both guided by what Tuana (2006) refers to as "configurations of interest" (p. 4). There is a collective benefit to settlers, for example, to knowing Indigenous peoples only as Dead Indians. Whether such benefits manifest as feelings of "innocence" (Tuck & Yang, 2012) or as the "framing of Whites as the new natives" (Calderón, 2011, p. 112) so they feel entitled to Indigenous lands, ignorance can be productive. The inclusion of Indigenous performances as Native Heritage Month curriculum similarly benefits educators; they can feel good about their multicultural efforts to include Native people in the curriculum. Their racialized emotional responses—evident in their goosebumps and tears from the performances—provide affective returns on their diversity and multicultural investments. They also benefit from the appearance of inclusion, while masking the subtle relations of domination they sustain. This narrow focus on Dead Indians produces its own particular "gaps" or "blind-spots" as well, what Calderón (2009) refers to as *colonial blindness*. The routine desire by educators to see Dead Indians as curriculum helps them avoid the inevitable discomfort if serious consideration were given to other dimensions of Indigeneity, such as land, colonization, or the responsibility to uphold treaty rights. In contrast to the goosebumps and tears from Native performances, or the feeling that the curriculum is rich and diverse, it doesn't necessarily feel as good to know land has been illegally usurped, that Indigenous rights have been and continue to be denied, or that the US government is complicit in the historic and present-day assaults on Native peoples, lands, and nations. It doesn't feel good to know one has benefited from and continues to be complicit in dispossession. The curricular focus on Dead Indians is driven by such tacit desires—for innocence (Tuck & Yang, 2012), for superficial efforts at multiculturalism that leave Eurocentrism intact, or for comfort. Perhaps this is why curricular activities for Native Heritage Month more often involve invitations to Native dancers to perform, rather than invitations to tribal chairwomen who might remind students and teachers of their tenuous claims to place.

Educators often avoid focusing on Live Indians as well, perhaps because they're viewed as boring, perhaps because they're not even seen as "Indian" at all without their "cultural debris" (King, 2013, p. 53). Live Indians, as Mr. Barry demonstrated, might challenge their own relegation to discourses of backwardness, timelessness, and authenticity. Avoided at almost all costs are Legal Indians who assert and uphold claims to land, place, and rights that unsettle dominant narratives of entitlement and rightful ownership. By keeping quiet about other important dimensions of Indigeneity, the multicultural assembly becomes a microcosm of a broader pattern of negating and eroding sovereignty. However, this framing, which limits meaningful curricular opportunities and democratic education for everyone, could be made visible and disrupted. Doing so requires not only critical anticolonial literacy to interrogate Native representations, but an exploration of other, more generative frames for including Native studies content. What if Native Heritage Month focused on supporting Native students as

Live Indians, by providing opportunities for Native youth in the district to embody decolonizing and critical pedagogies? Or what if the orientation for Native Heritage Month was Legal Indians, and focused not on Native cultures, but on Native nationhood, governance, and sovereignty, the "bedrock," Mvskoke Creek scholar Tsianina Lomawaima (2000) argues, "upon which any and every discussion of Indian reality today must be built" (p. 3)? Writing within this particular context, my focus here is on Legal Indians so that Native Heritage Month might be a curricular site to teach about tribal sovereignty.

There is enough anecdotal evidence by now—from my own schooling experience, from my experiences working with Native youth and families, from society's ongoing fascination with Dead Indians—that curriculum in mainstream public schools that focuses on Native "culture" has done little except reproduce static and stoic portrayals of historic Indians. While the teachers and principals may have felt emotionally moved by the assembly, I doubt the performance fostered substantive engagement with Native studies curriculum in the classroom, inquiries into Native student success in the school or district, or even respect for Native students or people more broadly. There is also a wealth of scholarship that theorizes the limits of such narrow notions of "culture" (Erickson, 2010; Grande, 2015; Gutiérrez & Rogoff, 2003; Hermes, 2005; Ladson-Billings, 2014; Kulchyski, 1997; Paris & Alim, 2014). In particular, some have also critiqued the ways that multiculturalist discourses function to erase Indigenous distinctiveness and undermine sovereignty, insisting that Indigenous peoples are not "people of color," but citizens and descendants[13] of sovereign nations (Calderón, 2009; Tuck & Yang, 2012; St. Denis, 2011). These scholars "reject multiculturalism as an instrument of colonialism" (St. Denis, 2011, p. 311).

Given the pervasiveness of Indigenous erasure in public schools—through cultural caricatures, curricular silences, or liberal multiculturalism—a more generative curricular response in such contexts could be to forsake culture as a lens through which to understand and teach about Indigenous peoples. In its place, curriculum could explicitly make visible other dimensions of Indigeneity, such as Native nationhood and sovereignty. Instead of focusing on cultural distinctiveness, schools could inquire into the political distinctiveness of Indigenous peoples as the original peoples of this land, who hold not only moral, but also also legal and political claims to territory in the US. This focus on political nationhood and sovereignty is already embedded into curriculum in various ways. When teachers ask a city council member, mayor, or congressman to visit a classroom, for example, they don't ask them to sing a song, dance, or tell a story, but ask about their roles and responsibilities as government officials. Problematically, however, this same sense of respect for Indigenous governments and leaders has yet to be widely applied in K-12 curriculum.

As a result of the advocacy of Indigenous educators and allies, these shifts have already occurred in states like Montana, which passed the Indian Education for All initiative, or Washington, which passed the Since Time Immemorial (STI)

Tribal Sovereignty Curriculum. For example, elementary outcomes for the STI curriculum state that "By the time Washington State students leave school, they will":

1. understand that over 500 independent tribal nations exist within the United States today, and that they deal with the United States, as well as each other, on a government-to-government basis;
2. define tribal sovereignty as "a way that tribes govern themselves in order to keep and support their cultural ways of life";
3. understand that tribal sovereignty predates treaty times;
4. explain how the treaties that tribal nations entered into with the United States government limited their sovereignty; and
5. identify the names and locations of tribes in their area. (Office of Superintendent of Public Instruction: The Indian Education Office, n.d.)

These are *elementary school* standards, an important intervention for *young* citizens so that they do not need to unlearn colonial framings of Indigenous peoples at an older age.

Educators oriented toward learning about Indigenous political difference, rather than cultural difference, would engage in different sorts of curricular questions and activities. They would more productively focus on Indigenous nationhood, treaties, citizenship, and rights (Sabzalian & Shear, 2018; Shear, Sabzalian, & Buchanan, 2018).

A review of the Yakama Nation Museum's "Fun Facts" designed to educate students before visiting the museum illustrates such an orientation. Students are asked the following:

1. Do you know what year the Yakama Nation Treaty was signed and who was the main signer?
2. Do you know how many tribes and bands signed the Yakama treaty?
3. Do we have a flag?
4. Who the current executive chairman of the Yakama Nation?
5. Are there two branches of government for the Yakama Nation?
6. How many elected positions are there?
7. What is the formal name of this nation?
8. When do the Yakama elections occur and who can vote? (Yakama Nation Museum, n.d.)

Notice that the questions do not ask about Yakama culture or spirituality; they ask students to know something of the Yakama treaty, nation, and system of governance.

The information needed to begin this shift is there. In nearly every Presidential proclamation and resolution for Native Heritage Day, Week, or Month, Presidents have acknowledged the unique political, government-to-government relationship between the federal government and tribal nations (Bureau of Indian Affairs, 2017; Library of Congress, 2015). Yet while these proclamations recognize Native nationhood, sovereignty, and the nation-to-nation relationship between the US and Native nations, schools reproduce drastically different discursive understandings of Indigenous peoples. This outwardly acknowledged nation-to-nation relationship by the federal government is actively "unlearned" (Calderón, 2011) in schools where Indigenous peoples are cultural subjects in a multicultural mosaic. But just as schools can become sites for unlearning, they can be sites for learning as well.

For Carter G. Woodson in his advocacy for Negro History Week, *history* was a site for critical engagement, but for Indigenous peoples, often rendered historic, a grounding in *sovereignty* might be a more suitable base from which students and staff could then critically respect and recognize Native American nations, people, and their contributions in respectful rather than tokenistic ways. Sovereignty predates Indigenous encounters with settler society. It is, as many Native people have continually asserted, *inherent*. As the Confederated Tribes of Warm Springs' "Declaration of Sovereignty" (1992) states,

> Our people have exercised inherent sovereignty, as nations, on the Columbia Plateau for thousands of years, since time immemorial. Our Sovereignty is permeated by the spiritual and the sacred, which are, and always have been, inseparable parts of our lives, for the Creator leads us in all aspects of our existence. (para. 1)

As Lyons (2000) states, "Sovereignty as I generally use and understand the term, denotes the right of a people to conduct its own affairs, in its own place, in its own way" (p. 450). Lyons contends sovereignty is more robust than how it is conventionally understood, "more than arguments for tax-exempt status or the right to build and operate casinos ... nothing less than our attempt to survive and flourish as a people" (p. 449). Grande (2015) also reminds us that sovereignty is not only political, but also an intellectual, pedagogical, and spiritual project, as well as a "restorative process" (p. 74). Native peoples have long been discussing the principle of sovereignty, and for many Native peoples, sovereignty is more than merely a legal or political project (Alfred, 1999; Alfred & Corntassel, 2005; Grande, 2015; Raheja, 2010; Warrior, 1992). Yet the legal and political basis for tribal sovereignty nevertheless offers more potential for public schools to generate respect for Native nations than the current cultural framings that undergird most curricula.[14]

Students in public schools should be learning about the treaties in their area. They should examine current events and issues affecting nearby Native nations, and spend time in class learning about and supporting such issues. They should study Native nations' flags and systems of government. An orientation toward sovereignty would shift curriculum. Rather than drawing stylized salmon modeled after Northwest Coast style formlines (a common activity in the district), students could instead learn about how current land and water use policies affect Indigenous peoples' relationship to salmon as a cultural and physical lifeway. A political orientation doesn't preclude learning about culture, but subsumes culture as an important element of Indigenous peoples' ability to thrive as peoples and nations.

Native Heritage Month is framed here as a placeholder and launch pad for these activities because of the curricular silences around Indigenous peoples *as* nations, but more broadly, this type of knowledge—about land, treaty rights, sovereignty, trust relationships and responsibilities—should be seen as *central* to democratic citizenship education and educating an informed citizenry. Imagine if a public school took this month as a chance to "honor" Native nations, not by inviting dancers or replicating cultural crafts, but by investing in tribal nations, by instilling a sense of responsibility toward tribal nations and their citizens, by educating youth in a comprehensive understanding of sovereignty. The youth educated in public schools may be the next generation of lawyers, natural resource managers, educators, social workers, or any another profession that might be crucial in upholding sovereignty (whether it's through an understanding of Indian law, upholding important fishing, hunting, and gathering rights, educating Native youth, or recognizing the impact generations of child removal have had on a nations' sovereignty). They will also be the next generation of voters whose ballots support or undermine sovereignty; the next generation of policy makers whose decisions impact Native nations.

Nearly 100 years ago, Carlos Montezuma was concerned American Indian Day would be "a farce and worst kind of a fad." What good would it do for Indigenous peoples to parade around for whites? "It will not help the Indians," he said, "but the Indians will be used as tools for interested parties." The dynamic which concerned Montezuma holds true today. Indigenous students reap little benefit from the ways Native Heritage Month is typically framed, a focus on Dead Indians at the expense of numerous other curricular possibilities. Heritage months are compromised curricular spaces, an appendage to the colonial body of schools; yet if Native Heritage Months in public schools were taken seriously as an opportunity to disrupt antiquated notions of authenticity and culture and a chance to begin substantially engagement with the actual lives and political realities of Indigenous peoples, then I would sincerely look forward to next November.

Notes

1 This month was formerly termed National American Indian Heritage Month. For the sake of brevity and to be inclusive of both Native American and Alaska Native peoples, I will use "Native Heritage Month" throughout the article unless otherwise noted in the literature.

2 Parker believed American Indian Day would actually intervene into and disrupt the "show Indian" that accompanied Buffalo Bill's Wild West show (Porter, 2001), but he also expressed hesitation with the way his colleague Red Fox James was eliciting support, riding on horseback from town to town, a an approach he was worried "would not

lend anything to the dignity which the original intention sought" (as cited in Porter, 2001, p. 120). Montezuma's admonition ran deeper than a critique of "American Indian Day," however, illustrating tensions at the time between the Society of American Indians (SAI) that Parker was involved in, the Bureau of Indian Affairs (BIA), and "radicals" such as Montezuma who didn't have faith in SAI and their tactics of "meeting and discussing" (Hertzberg, 1971) or the BIA. I highlight these examples specifically to illustrate the complex negotiations happening in the early 1900s among Indigenous people about how best to serve Indigenous peoples, and illuminate tensions that still exist among "pan-Indian" approaches, as well as working with/in colonial institutions such as the BIA (or public schools).

3 See Green (1988) and Deloria (1998) for more on this history concept of "playing Indian."

4 In his December 1989 observation of National American Indian Heritage Week, President George H.W. Bush commented on Thanksgiving, noting "The settlers at Plymouth Colony were able to reap that harvest largely because of the help they received from neighboring Indians" (Bush, 1989, para 1). Since this address, Native Heritage Month has been observed in November, reinforcing the problematic connection between Pilgrims and Indians that Melvina did not want the month to be associated with. Proclamations by US Presidents can be found at *The American Presidency Project* website (http://www.presidency.ucsb.edu/index.php) or Bureau of Indian Affairs (https://www.bia.gov/as-ia/opa/national-native-american-heritage-month) and are an excellent way to examine how colonial ideologies permeate public policies, as well as how presidents continue to acknowledge the government-to-government relationship between the US and Native nations. The State of Oregon observes Native American Heritage Month in November, Tribal Governments Day in February, and American Indian Week in May.

5 In our first edition of the fact a day, we did not discuss how Indigenous peoples often have terms in their own languages for themselves—Unangax̂ instead of Aleut, or Diné instead of Navajo for example.

6 The *Teaching Tolerance* website by the Southern Poverty Law Center provides a variety of articles that speak to this fear of tokenism. "Native Cultures Should be Taught Year Round," "Heritage Months: Hard to Handle?", "Mining the Jewel of Black History Month," and "Five Things Not to Do During Black History Month" are all thoughtful reflections on how to make the most of these curricular space holders for heritage month, while also integrating content throughout the year. These and other reflections can be found at the *Teaching Tolerance* website (http://www.tolerance.org/).

7 The three-piece suit is in reference to an article I read recently by Frank Hopper (Tlingit, Kagwaantaan clan) who discusses assimilation and resistance to it. In the end, he states: "For me the three-piece suit now represents the three qualities that will keep our culture alive no matter how much assimilation damages it. These qualities are: love for our people, respect for our traditions, and courage to fight for what's right" (Hopper, 2015, para. 13).

8 I later found out the principal had emailed the coordinator and me welcoming us to prepare a PowerPoint of images or pictures to show the students a few minutes beforehand. I am not sure how we missed this email and opportunity. Of course, a "few minutes" of speech or pictures isn't necessarily what I had in mind when I cautioned about pre- and post-teaching, but the principal did hear my suggestion and tried to accommodate part of it. I felt badly I somehow missed the message. In retrospect, however, I also realize this was another example of the burden of the pre-teaching being placed on our program staff and volunteers rather than being integrated into the teachers' responsibilities in their own classrooms, or even the principal herself. Since we did not present anything, there were no lessons to accompany the assembly.

9 See Judy Iseke-Barnes' (2009) article "Unsettling Fictions: Disrupting Popular Discourses and Trickster Tales in Books for Children" for an analysis of the ways McDermott's book appropriates Indigenous stories while simultaneously endorsing its own authenticity. This

colonial maneuver is also discussed in Chapter 6. This book has been used previously by the local Title VI program, though has recently being taken out of circulation in program activities in light of these critiques.

10 This principal has since left the school. There have been no events or programming for Native Heritage Month since.

11 See Cutcha Risling Baldy's (Hoopa Valley Tribe, Karuk, Yurok) article (2013) "On telling Native people to 'get over it," or why I teach about the Walking Dead in my Native Studies classes…" for a connection between Native people and post-apocalyptic times.

12 I struggle with ways to explore the limits of such a performance without reducing the awareness, purposes, and intentions of the performer. Scholars like Cruikshank show the dangers in analyzing performance as solely a representation. Drawing on Frank Myers who "suggests that public performances of indigenous culture should be understood as tangible forms of social action rather than as texts or representations standing outside the real activity of participants," Cruikshank highlights that "such analyses…erase the ways indigenous peoples confer meaning on circumstances that confront them, having the effect of a double erasure of agency—first by the colonial forces, then by postcolonial analyses" (p. 56). Yet I am also looking for a way to talk about how non-Indigenous audiences often overlook these forms of social action and consume such performances.

13 Though not all Indigenous people are citizens/members of tribal nations (and not all tribal nations recognized as such), I still read Indigenous descendancy as a political rather than solely racial identity. I do so because colonialism, not racism alone, shapes the context of whether or not a person is recognized as a tribal citizen (or whether or not a tribal nation is federally recognized).

14 As Chickasaw scholar Amanda Cobb (2005) states, "Government and culture are not separate ideas; each is manifested in and reflective of the other" (p. 123). Nevertheless, for the purpose of this discussion, I am making this distinction to draw attention to the legal and political dimensions as understood in the context of tribal-federal relationships.

References

Alfred, G. (1999). *Peace, power, righteousness: An indigenous manifesto.* Don Mills, ON: Oxford University Press.

Alfred, T., & Corntassel, J. (2005). Being Indigenous: Resurgences against contemporary colonialism. *Government and Opposition*, 40(4), 597–614.

Baldy, C. R. (2013). On telling Native people to just "get over it" or why I teach about the Walking Dead in my Native Studies classes. Sometimes Writer-Blogger Cutcha Risling Baldy, Dec 11 [weblog]. Retrieved from: www.cutcharislingbaldy.com/blog/on-telling-native-people-to-just-get-over-it-or-why-i-teach-about-the-walking-dead-in-my-native-studies-classes-spoiler-alert.

Barker, J., & Teaiwa, T. (2005). Native InFormation. In I. Hernández-Avila. (Ed.), *Reading Native American women: Critical/creative representations* (pp. 107–128). Lanham, MD: Altamira Press.

Bureau of Indian Affairs. (2017). National Native American Heritage Month Celebration. Retrieved from www.bia.gov/as-ia/opa/national-native-american-heritage-month.

Bush, G. (1989). Proclamation 6080 - National American Indian Heritage Week, 1989: By the President of the United States of America. A proclamation. December 5. Retrieved from www.bia.gov/as-ia/opa/national-native-american-heritage-month.

Byrd, J. A. (2011). *The transit of empire: Indigenous critiques of colonialism.* Minneapolis, MN: University of Minnesota Press.

Calderón, D. (2009). Making explicit the jurisprudential foundations of multiculturalism: The continuing challenges of colonial education in US schooling for Indigenous education. In A. Kempf (Ed.), *Breaching the colonial contract: Anti-colonialism in the U.S. and Canada* (pp. 53–77). New York, NY: Springer.

Calderón, D. (2011). Locating the foundations of epistemologies of ignorance in normative multicultural education. In N. Jaramillo & E. Malewski (Eds.), *Epistemologies of ignorance in education* (pp. 105–127). Charlotte, NC: Information Age Press.

Calderón, D. (2014). Uncovering settler grammars in curriculum. *Educational Studies: Journal of the American Educational Studies Association*, 50(4), 313–338.

Castagno, A. E. (2009). Making sense of multicultural education: A synthesis of the various typologies found in the literature. *Multicultural Perspectives*, 11(1), 43–48.

Cobb, A. (2005). Understanding tribal sovereignty: Definitions, conceptualizations, and interpretations. *American Studies, 46*(3/4), 115–132.

Confederated Tribes of Warm Springs. (1992). Declaration of sovereignty. June 25. Retrieved from https://warmsprings-nsn.gov/treaty-documents/declaration-of-sovereignty/.

Cortés, C. E. (1979). The societal curriculum and the school curriculum: Allies or antagonists? *Educational Leadership*, 36(7), 475–479.

Cruikshank, J. (1997). Negotiating with narrative: Establishing cultural identity at the Yukon International Storytelling Festival. *American Anthropologist*, 99(1), 56–69.

Deloria, P. (1998). *Playing Indian*. New Haven, CT: Yale University Press.

Derman-Sparks, L., & the A.B.C. Task Force. (1989). *Anti-bias curriculum: Tools for empowering young children*. Washington, DC: National Association for the Education of Young Children.

Dion, S. D. (2008). *Braiding histories: Learning from Aboriginal peoples' experiences and perspectives*. Vancouver, BC: UBC Press.

Dixson, A., & Rousseau, C. K. (2006). *Critical race theory in education: All God's children got a song*. New York, NY: Routledge.

Du Bois, W. (1961). *The souls of Black folk*. New York, NY: Fawcett Publications.

Erickson, E. (2010). Culture in society and in educational practices. In J. A. Banks & C. A. McGee Banks (Eds.), *Handbook of research on multicultural education* (7th ed.) (pp. 33–52). San Francisco, CA: Jossey-Bass.

Fish, S. (1997). Boutique multiculturalism: Or, why liberals are incapable of thinking about hate speech. *Critical Inquiry*, 23(2), 378–395.

Fryberg, St. (2004). American Indian social representations: Do they honor or constrain American Indian identities? Conference presentation, 50 Years after Brown vs. Board of Education: Social Psychological Perspectives on the Problems of Racism and Discrimination. University of Kansas, May 13–14, 2004. Retrieved from www.indianmascots.com/ex_15_-_fryberg_brown_v.pdf.

Grande, S. (2004). *Red pedagogy: Native American social and political thought*. Lanham, MD: Rowman & Littlefield.

Grande, S. (2015). *Red pedagogy: Native American social and political thought* (2nd ed.) Lanham, MD: Rowman & Littlefield.

Green, R. (1988). The tribe called Wannabee: Playing Indian in America and Europe. *Folklore*, 99(1), 30–55.

Gutiérrez, K. D., & Rogoff, B. (2003). Cultural ways of learning: Individual traits or repertoires of practice. *Educational Researcher*, 32(5), 19–25.

Hermes, M. (2005). "Ma'iingan is just a misspelling of the word wolf": A case for teaching culture through language. *Anthropology & Education Quarterly*, 36(1), 43–56.

Hertzberg, H. (1971). *The search for an American Indian identity: Modern Pan-Indian movements*. New York: Syracuse University Press.

Hopper, F. (2015). Assimilate this! The Alaska Native Brotherhood and the three-piece suit of courage. *Indian Country Media Today Network.* February 26. Retrieved from http://indiancountrytodaymedianetwork.com/2015/02/26/assimilate-alaska-native-b rotherhood-and-three-piece-suit-courage-159362.

Iseke-Barnes, J. (2009). Unsettling fictions: Disrupting popular discourses and trickster tales in books for children. *Journal of the Canadian Association for Curriculum Studies,* 7(1), 24–57.

Jacob, M. (2013). *Yakama rising: Indigenous cultural revitalization, activism, and healing.* Tucson, AZ: University of Arizona Press.

King, T. (2013). *The inconvenient Indian: A curious account of native people in North America.* Minneapolis, MN: University of Minnesota Press.

Kulchyski, P. (1997). From appropriation to subversion: Aboriginal cultural production in an age of postmodernism. *American Indian Quarterly,* 21(4), 605–620.

Ladson-Billings, G., & Tate, W. F. (1995). Toward a critical race theory of education. *Teachers College Record,* 97, 47–68.

Ladson-Billings, G. (2014). Culturally relevant pedagogy 2.0: A.k.a. the Remix. *Harvard Educational Review,* 84(1), 74–135.

Library of Congress. (2015). National American Indian Heritage Month. July 31. Retrieved from www.loc.gov/law/help/commemorative-observations/american-indian.php.

Lidchi, H. (1997). The poetics and politics of exhibiting other cultures. In S. Hall. (Ed.), *Representation: Cultural representations and signifying practices* (pp. 151–208). London: Sage.

Lomawaima, K. T. (1994). *They called it prairie light: The story of Chilocco Indian School.* Lincoln, NE: University of Nebraska Press.

Lomawaima, K. T. (2000). Tribal sovereigns: Reframing research in American Indian education. *Harvard Educational Review,* 70(1), 1–21.

Lomawaima, K. T., & McCarty, T. L. (2006). *"To remain an Indian": Lessons in democracy from a century of Native American education.* New York, NY: Teachers College Press.

Lyons, S. R. (2000). Rhetorical sovereignty: What do American Indians want from writing? *College Composition and Communication,* 51(3), 447–468.

McCue, D. (2014). What it takes for Aboriginal people to make the news. *CBC News,* January 29. Retrieved from www.cbc.ca/news/indigenous/what-it-takes-for-aborigina l-people-to-make-the-news-1.2514466.

Menkart, D. (2008). Heritage months and celebrations: Some considerations. In E. Lee, D. Menkart, M. Okazawa-Rey (Eds.), *Beyond heroes and holidays: A practical guide to K-12 anti-racist, multicultural education and staff development* (pp. 374–376). Washington, DC: Teaching for Change.

National Museum of the American Indian. (2007). *Do all Indians live in tipis: Questions and answers from the National Museum of the American Indian.* New York, NY: Collins, in association with the National Museum of the American Indian, Smithsonian Institution.

Nieto, S., & Bode, P. (2008). *Affirming diversity: The Sociopolitical context of multicultural education* (5th ed.). Boston, MA: Allyn & Bacon.

Office of Superintendent of Public Instruction: The Indian Education Office. (n.d.). K-12 outcomes. Retrieved from www.indian-ed.org/about-sti/k-12-outcomes/.

Paris, D., & Alim, H. (2014). What are we seeking to sustain through culturally sustaining pedagogy? A loving critique forward. *Harvard Educational Review,* 84(1), 85–137.

Pepper, F., Oregon Department of Education, Fuller, J., & Butterfield, R. (2014). *Indians in Oregon today: Oregon middle school—high school curriculum.* Salem, OR: Oregon Dept. of Education, Division of Special Student Services, Federal Programs.

Porter, J. (2001). *To be Indian: The life of Iroquois-Seneca Arthur Caswell Parker*. Norman, OK: University of Oklahoma Press.

Raheja, M. (2010). *Reservation reelism: Redfacing, visual sovereignty, and representations of Native Americans in film*. Lincoln, NE: University of Nebraska Press.

Raibmon, P. (2005). *Authentic Indians: Episodes of encounter from the late-nineteenth- century Northwest coast*. Durham, NC: Duke University Press.

Richardson, T. (2011). Navigating the problem of inclusion as enclosure in Native culture-based education: Theorizing shadow curriculum. *Curriculum Inquiry*, 41(3), 332–349.

Sabzalian, L. (2016). Native feminisms in motion. *English Journal*, 106(1), 23–30.

Sabzalian, L., & Shear, S. (2018). Confronting colonial blindness in civics education: Recognizing colonization, self-determination, and sovereignty as core knowledge for elementary social studies teacher education. In S. Shear, C. M. Tschida, E. Bellows, L. B. Buchanan, & E. E. Saylor (Eds.), *(Re)Imagining Elementary Social Studies: A Controversial Issues Reader* (153–176). Charlotte, NC: Information Age Press.

Shear, S., Sabzalian, L., & Buchanan, L. (2018). Teaching Indigenous sovereignty in elementary civics education. *Social Studies and the Young Learner*, 31(1), 12–18.

Sleeter, C. E., & Bernal, D. D. (2004). Critical pedagogy, critical race theory, and antiracist education: Implications for multicultural education. In J. A. Banks & C. A. McGee Banks (Eds.), *Handbook of research on multicultural education* (2nd ed.) (pp. 240–258). San Francisco, CA: Jossey-Bass.

St. Denis, V. (2011). Silencing Aboriginal curricular content and perspectives through multiculturalism: "There are other children here". *Review of Education, Pedagogy, and Cultural Studies*, 33(4), 306–317.

The White House. (2016). National Native American Heritage Month, 2016: By the President of the United States of America. A proclamation. October 31. Retrieved from www.bia.gov/as-ia/opa/national-native-american-heritage-month.

Topkok, S. A., & Green, C. (2016). Following the pathways of the ancestors: Well-being through Iñupiaq dance. In F. Deer & T. Falkenberg (Eds.), *Indigenous perspectives on education for well-being in Canada* (pp. 173–186). Winnipeg, MB: ESWB Press. Retrievable from www.ESWB-Press.org.

Tuana, N. (2004). Coming to understand: Orgasm and the epistemology of ignorance. *Hypatia*, 19(1), 194–232.

Tuana, N. (2006). The speculum of ignorance: The women's health movement and epistemologies of ignorance. *Hypatia: A Journal of Feminist Philosophy*, 21(3), 1–19.

Tuck, E., & Yang, K. W. (2012). Decolonization is not a metaphor. *Decolonization: Indigeneity, Education and Society*, 1, 1–40.

Vizenor, G. R. (1999). *Manifest manners: Narratives on postindian survivance*. Lincoln, NE: University of Nebraska Press.

Warrior, R. A. (1992). Intellectual sovereignty and the struggle for an American Indian future. *Wicazo Sa Review*, 8(1), 1–20.

Weatherford, J. (1991). Indian season in American schools. *Social Studies*, 82(5), 172–175.

Weaver, J. (2001). *Other words: American Indian literature, law, and culture*. Norman, OK: University of Oklahoma Press.

Woodson, C. G. (1933). The mis-education of the Negro. Retrieved from https://books.google.com/books?id=zF6J8Zge4XgC&printsec=frontcover&source =gbs_ge_summary_r&cad=0#v=onepage&q&f=false.

Yakama Nation Museum. (n.d.). Fun facts. Retrieved from www.yakamamuseum.com/museum-exhibits-activities.phpwww.yakamamuseum.com/museum-exhibits-activities.php.

6

EDUCATION ON THE BORDER OF SOVEREIGNTY

Encoded Language

An elder at one of the local Longhouses once told me about a non-Native educator in the district who routinely treats him with an absurd amount of reverence and deference. "I'm an elder," he said. "Not a king." He was a person who has earned and was deserving of respect, but he was certainly not the caricature that this educator thought she was interacting with. I had a similar feeling as I left the grocery store one afternoon and ran into Sharon, the high school art teacher I had been working with in the story in Chapter 2. "Fancy meeting you here!" she said. "It's like we're on the same journey." Her tone and how she looked at me had a particular inflection to it. There was nothing inherently wrong with what she said to me, and if this were an isolated incident, I probably wouldn't have thought twice about it. However, because in our previous interactions she has told me that we are on a "sacred journey" together, or that she "honors" my "wisdom"—encoded language that I'm not sure she would say if I weren't Native—I remember feeling like I occasionally do with her: like I'm this tiny person inside, peeking out of the eyeholes of the mystical mask she projects onto me. She didn't treat me with the same absurd amount of reverence given to that elder, but the pattern was the same: projecting colonial ideologies onto Indigenous bodies.

Sharon and I had been conversing together for about a year as a result of a cultural conflict in her classroom.[1] To her credit, she kept requesting to meet with me and talk, an active gesture that was entirely voluntary and demonstrated a sincere desire to learn more and reflect on her own work incorporating Indigenous studies content into her teaching. There were other teachers in the district who avoided me or Melvina, the Title VI coordinator, altogether. I had been feeling lately that Sharon saw a little more of me each time we talked, but in that brief interaction, her encoded language reminded me of the work still to do. It reminded me too that the goal of this work can't only be to make Indigenous peoples more visible—we needed to also make visible the colonial ways of understanding Indigenous peoples that erased us in the first place.

Sharon thanked me for visiting her class that day and for the great conversation with her students. Melvina and I had spent an hour and half earlier that day in Sharon and her partner teacher Kelly's class. Their course, "Native American Art and Culture," stemmed from a yearly opportunity at the arts-based charter school in which teachers have the opportunity to develop a month-long course based on their interests. Sharon wanted to design a class that focused on local Native art and culture, and her partner teacher wanted to organize the term around a service project. The two teamed up and reached out to a local ranger station, hoping there would be some sort of service project that the class could undertake. The forest rangers responded that a mural at their bunkhouse might be an ideal opportunity for a student project, and so the course was organized around this culminating activity.

Neither Melvina or I were artists, but Sharon asked us to visit the class and talk about responsibility and Native American art and culture. Although Sharon's request subtly morphed into a request that we present on "Native culture," we stayed grounded in our initial intention to support students in critically reading and appreciating Native art and artists. That day, we talked about Native artists, and then accompanied the class to the Longhouse on campus to see a Native art show that was on display and speak with a local Native artist. Students seemed engaged during our presentation and the field trip, asking thoughtful questions, even openly, but respectfully, questioning or challenging each other. We hadn't gotten through even half of the activities we had prepared for her class, and so Sharon and her teacher invited us to come back the next day to finish.

Sharon and I chatted for a few more minutes in the parking lot. Sharon told me the class had been working on the mural project, but was waiting for the tribal liaison to get back to them about the designs. The tribal liaison worked with four tribal representatives who would need to approve the mural design before students painted, a much lengthier process than either of the teachers had anticipated, and what Sharon described as a lot of back and forth that was slowing the project down. I hadn't yet seen any of the proposed designs, and asked Sharon if she could forward those to me. I also made a note to reach out to the tribal liaison.

Sharon then thanked me again, and let me know that Melvina and I helped her and the class reflect on the course content in ways she hadn't considered. Her comments tempered the fact that although Sharon wasn't quite seeing all of me, she was kind and enthusiastic and willing to learn. Still, I was struck by Sharon's encoded language, especially after the lengthy discussion and activities we had done earlier that day to disrupt the "single story" (Adichie, 2009) of Indigeneity she was so committed to.

Earlier that Day: Disrupting the Single Story

Aside from the mural idea and Sharon's vague request to come present on Native art and culture, Melvina and I didn't know much about the class before presenting, but we agreed to present because Melvina wanted to be more involved in the schools. In her role as Title VI coordinator, she was explicitly responsible for supporting Native students, yet Native students were spread out across 22 schools in the district and spent the majority of their day with their teachers. She saw Native students only a few hours at most at the Native Youth Center after school, and this was only those who came. Because of this, Melvina wanted to learn more about how teachers were supporting Native students and the Native-related content they were teaching. Her hope was to develop mini-presentations that she could present in classes throughout the district to provide Native students with accurate and meaningful content and to teach all students to think critically about Native issues. This was also her way of indirectly educating teachers on cultural sensitivity. While teachers often make requests of Melvina, especially in November, their requests, like Sharon's, typically ask her to focus on Native culture. But Melvina wanted to present something different, something more critical and subversive.

Melvina and I had already presented in Sharon's class that year. Although Sharon asked us to present on Native American cultures, we chose instead to speak with the students about stereotypes and misrepresentation of Indigenous peoples. We chose to speak, not about Native cultures, but about the cultural contexts Native people navigate that routinely objectifies and commodifies their culture. We took a similar approach in this presentation: we used the presentation as a way to surface and disrupt the taken-for-granted framings of Native art that focuses on objects, artifacts, and other material aspects of Native culture.

Our goal was to highlight how dominant discourses and assumptions about authenticity (Raibmon, 2005) narrow the diverse range of Indigenous identities and cultural and artistic expressions that exist. We did this in a variety of ways. We talked about hegemony, using an activity developed by Vanessa Andreotti (2011). We asked students to picture an ear of corn. When all but two pictured a yellow corncob, we discussed how our mental images, despite our differences and sense of individuality, could be so remarkably similar. After linking our socialization via our families, geographical region, the media, local economy, available markets, and broader influences such as industrialization and globalization to our mental images, we did the same activity, asking students to create a mental image of a Native American.

Nearly every student said their mental image resembled one of the photos we had up on the projector—black and white images of Sitting Bull, Chief Joseph, and Lucille, a Dakota woman, all images taken from Edward Curtis' photo collection *The North American Indian*. [2] It shouldn't have surprised me, though the enduring power of Curtis' work felt ironic as we stood there in front of the students. "I was thinking of something more contemporary," exclaimed one student. Anticipating some students might picture contemporary Native people, we had prepared another slide that included a picture of a grass dancer and a women's traditional dancer at a pow wow.[3] "Exactly," he said upon seeing the image. Another student said he was picturing someone native to South America. When asked to describe what he saw, the student said his image was similar to the pow wow pictures, but the dress was more specific to South America and included brightly colored feathered headdresses. "You didn't say contemporary Native American," said another student, though he seemed to state this more thoughtfully than defensively. "I guess I just assumed that," he commented. After everyone else had spoken, Celeste, one of the members of our Native youth group, looked at both of us and said matter-of-factly: "I thought of you." The students laughed and Melvina responded, "No matter how many times I have stood in front of students asking them what a Native American looks like or dresses like, they never think of me."

Whether Celeste's understanding came from her home or her involvement in the Native Youth Center, her comment illustrated the value of counterspaces (Solórzano & Yosso, 2002) where different stories are lived and told. Celeste's schema of Native Americans included ordinary folks such as Melvina or myself, and her comment resisted and ruptured hegemonic constructions of Indianness, resembling Ojibwe scholar Scott Lyon's (2000) reminder about dominant discourses: "the dominant stance achieved by the Americans must continue to be seen as merely that—dominant, not omnipotent—which is far from saying all things are said and done" (p. 453). Celeste's knowledge, whether facetious or said in earnest, displaced what seemed to be universal, taken-for-granted commonsense.

This commonsense characterization of Indigenous peoples has a long history. As Paige Raibmon (2005) notes in her book *Authentic Indians*: "Anthropologists, government officials, missionaries, reformers, boosters, settlers, and tourists were diverse, their aims and goals often contradictory" (p. 6). Yet, she continues, "[w]hether they used definitions of Indianness in the context of policy, religion, amusement, or science, colonizers shared an understanding of authenticity. They were collaborators in a binary framework that defined Indian authenticity in relation to its antithesis: inauthenticity" (pp. 6–7). At the heart of this framework, Raibmon continued,

> was the distinction between Indian and White. Indians, by extension, were traditional, uncivilized, cultural, impoverished, feminine, static, part of nature and of the past. Whites, on the other hand, were modern, civilized, political, prosperous, masculine, dynamic, part of society and of the future. (p. 7)

This static understanding of authenticity used to characterize Indigenous peoples in the 1800s persists over two hundred years later, and as we showed students, is even embedded into Google's search algorithm. In contrast to the diverse representation of contemporary people that come up when you search for "African American" and "Asian American" in Google, and in contrast to the banners across the top that prompt you to refine your search by "African American history" or "Asian American history," Indigenous peoples are always/already historic. As we showed students, a Google search for "Native American" results in mostly historic images of Native people in headdresses or with painted faces, and the banner across the top prompts the researcher to learn more about "Native Americans Today." That the world's most widely used search engine rests on a historic framing underpin by a colonial binary of authenticity makes the consistency of students' mental images of Indigenous peoples—perhaps even the teacher's request for a "cultural presentation"—understandable.

Though our purpose was to counter the single story of Indigenous peoples, we were careful to convey to students that the Native people in these images were not themselves stereotypes, but actual people whose purposes and contexts are often ignored. The two dancers, for example, were engaged in meaningful cultural practices on their own terms and should be read as such. The frequently circulated image we used of Chief Joseph (born Hin-mah-too-yah-lat-kekt), the revered leader of the Wallowa band of Nez Perce (also known as Nimi'ipuu), should be read in a similar way. In this iconic image, taken by Edward Curtis during Chief Joseph's visit to Washington in 1903, Chief Joseph sits alone, staring beyond the camera, adorned in traditional Nez Perce attire that included furs, necklaces, and a full headdress. Those who purchase and display this image in museums, homes, or classrooms likely do so for the image's aesthetics or the sense of nostalgia it evokes. However, Chief Joseph was not a passive victim, nor was he a stereotype; he had, in fact, just finished actively wielding his power for his people. The photo was taken the day after his speech to the Washington State Historical Society in which he expressed one desire: *to return to his homelands in the Wallowa Valley.* "I like the white people," Chief Joseph said,

> ... but they have driven me out of my home ... [T]he government has broken its promises ... They are big liars ... I fought for my land and lost it at that time. They have told me time and again for the last few years that I might go back, but I have not had an opportunity. I am going to keep on asking the government to go back to my old home. Colville is not my home. (as cited in Stein, 2013, n.p.)

Showing the dancers and a Chief in regalia was a way to surface dominant cultural expectations of Indigeneity, however, we also wanted to disrupt easy, sanitized readings of Indigenous cultural expression. The people in those images were actors, not objects. Our purpose was not to deride cultural expression, nor to deny the important curricular focus on Native history. Instead, we wanted to surface the discursive frames that only made visible particular expressions of Indigeneity, and erased others, including Melvina and I, from view.

Art *of* Natives ... or Produced *by* Natives?

Predictably, the collective assumptions that have defined commonsense under-standings of Indigenous authenticity also define the cultural, sociopolitical, and eco-nomic contexts within which Native artists imagine, create, and sell their artwork. The art market, primarily driven by non-Indigenous curators, museum directors, and buyers, has been historically characterized by a "single story" (Adichie, 2009) of what constitutes Native art. According to this story, Northwest coast style form lines, basketry, or totem poles are acceptable and desirable Indigenous artistic practices. Erased from view are other diverse modes of Indigenous creative expression and praxis. Native aesthetics are decontextualized, removed from the political sites of Native artistic creation, production, and sale. This myopic emphasis on Indigenous material culture often ignores "the artistic praxis of artists and communities engaged in *material struggle for decolonization*" (Martineau & Ritskes, 2014, p. II).

Such views of Native art are "safe" (Lomawaima & McCarty, 2006). They are the same views that guide curriculum units in which students recreate kachinas or totem poles with little attention to issues of cultural appropriation, the past and present theft of such sacred beings/items, or the ongoing Indi-genous demands for repatriation. These same views framed this course on Native American art and culture in which the teachers' primary desire was for students to learn about and reproduce a "Native" mural with little attention to the sociopolitical context of their curriculum. We wanted to make this socio-cultural and sociopolitical realm visible as "Indigenous art is inherently political" (Martineau & Ritskes, 2014, p. I).

To highlight the politics of Indigenous art and to make visible contexts that Native artists navigated, we drew from artists who were actively engaged in dis-rupting and decentering the single story of Native art and culture, artists who were both speaking back and, in various ways, speaking beyond colonial dis-courses that sought to ignore, encapsulate, or distort their creative praxes. Many of these artists—such as Bunky Echo-Hawk (Yakama/Pawnee), Gail Tremblay (Onondaga/Mi'kmaq), Fritz Scholder (Luiseño) Wendy Red Star (Apsáalooke/ Crow), Dwayne Wilcox (Oglala Lakota), or Natalie Ball (Modoc/Klamath)— queer assumptions about Native art, and use Indigenous knowledge, tools, and aesthetics to disrupt, not only the narrow frames of Native art, but also the con-texts of colonialism Indigenous peoples navigate today. Students could learn from these artists. Echo-Hawk's series *Weapons of Mass Media*, for example, could invite students to explore how artists can "use mass media against itself":

> Mass media has long been a weapon of mass destruction for Native American people. It was used early on in American history to garner widespread public support for, and to justify the violent occupation of this land and policies encouraging the extermination of Native American people and culture. Cur-rently, it is used to romanticize the culture, promote negative stereotypes, and

maintain the fallacy that Native Americans are a people of the past ... In this series, I use mass media as a vehicle; the images are all recognizable as American cultural icons and convey a message that is both palatable and subtly challenging ... In this way, I am using the mass media against itself. (Echo-Hawk, 2005, n.p.)

Echo-Hawk "appropriates American cultural institutions, like the Star Wars movies and news-talk celebrity Larry King" (Barnd, 2008, p. 203), and Indigenizes them, dressing Shrek and Donkey in full regalia, Yoda in a headdress, and placing Sitting Bull across from Larry King in the television studio.

Echo-Hawk's series *Gas Masks as Medicine* also provides important links between Indigenous culture and politics by explicitly addresses the dumping of toxic waste on Indigenous lands. His bold use of color and his juxtaposition of traditional regalia with toxic gas masks deploys the gas mask as "a formidable image [that] conjures up memories of past wars," inviting the viewer to wonder about the ways Indigenous peoples are still at war today, "bridg[ing] the gaps between wars, the present, and the future" (Echo-Hawk, 2014, n.p.).

We wanted students to learn, too, that there were numerous ways to decenter and refashion dominant discourses, such as Gail Tremblay's basketry, which quietly displaces notions of authenticity and traditionalism by combining "the traditional" (the strawberry stitch, a technique learned from her family's longstanding tradition of weaving baskets and gathering strawberries), and "the contemporary" (strips of film, a more contemporary medium that has long misrepresented Indigenous peoples). If a teacher's conception of "Native art" in general, and basketry in particular, were limited to "traditional" materials such as sweet grass, bear grass, or cedar, for example, one might miss the beauty and subtle critiques embodied in Tremblay's baskets, which often used strips of film from old Westerns featuring Cowboys and Indians. As Tremblay notes of her work:

> I enjoyed the notion of recycling film and gaining control over a medium that had historically been used by both Hollywood and documentary filmmakers to stereotype American Indians. I relished the irony of making film take on traditional fancy stitch basket patterns. (as cited in Fowler, 2007, p. 75)

Tremblay's art challenges hegemonic constructions of Indigeneity and authenticity. Moreover, by wielding that creative force into baskets like "Strawberry and Chocolate" (Tremblay, 2000), a basket whose title derives from *Fresa y Chocolate*, a Cuban film about homophobia and gay rights, Tremblay's work challenges other forms of oppression, such as heteronormativity (Fowler, 2007), that impact Indigenous as well as other communities.

By foregrounding artists like Echo-Hawk or Tremblay, our hope was to engage in the sort of subversive critical curricular work Melvina had desired—an approach which she hoped would prompt both students and teachers to reflect on their own assumptions. Our curriculum also tried to serve dual purposes. While we wanted to raise the awareness of non-Native students about their own cultural expectations, we also wanted to provide Native students in the class with meaningful models for how to engage, contest, work creatively within, or even refuse the terms of this dilemma. Native artists have long used their creativity to engage in survivance, resurgence, and decolonization (Dion & Salamanca, 2014; Martineau & Ritskes, 2014; Pedri-Spade, 2014), and we wanted to offer Native students examples and experiences of these decolonial struggles. Our presentation was also influenced by an essential question posed by a renowned Navajo artist in the community: "What is Native art? Is it the art *of* Natives? Or is it art produced *by* Natives?" Native artists have long been wrestling with this idea,[4] and so we decided to make this dilemma explicit for the students.

To surface latent assumptions, we showed students' fictionalized portrayals of individual artists, and in each portrayal, adjusted their physical features (adjusting their phenotypical appearance to be lighter or darker) and their Indigenous identity (enrolled member, descendant, non-Indigenous). We also adjusted their artistic medium, which ranged from making Native American hand drums to creating water color portraits of German Shepherds. "Is this Native American art?" we asked after we showed each image. The classroom discussion and dynamics were exciting and tense. Some students were adamant that non-Natives making hand drums was more "Native" than an enrolled citizen of a tribal nation making watercolor paintings of German Shepherds. Others weren't so sure. In response to the image of Billy, an enrolled tribal citizen who painted dogs for a living, several students were adamant that his work wasn't "Native art."

"It's not really Native art," said one.
"Definitely not," replied said another.
"I guess that dog looks sort of …" expressed one student, his words trailing off.

He appeared to be trying to find words to express how something might look "Native." Another student chimed in with the question, "What makes Native American art then?"

Our goal wasn't necessarily to define Native art—neither of us were artists, nor had we ever studied art history. Instead, our goal was to unsettle dominant assumptions that constricted possibilities for Indigenous artists, assumptions that were made visible to students when the fictionalized characters challenged their preconceived ideas.

"It's just hard to think about," said one student. "In Greece, they had all of these beautiful statues, but then they were destroyed. The Romans wanted to recreate some of those statues, so they did, but they were still considered Greek art."

"Well, and I don't know how to say this," said another student. "We studied art from Europe, and it was their being European that made the art European."

Our conversation amplified tensions that the binaries of authenticity create for Native artists, a "powerful Catch-22 for Aboriginal people" which holds them to "impossible standards of ahistorical cultural purity" (Raibmon, 2005, p. 9). While change and innovation are expected of dominant culture, Indigenous peoples face the unique dilemma of their art no longer being seen as traditional, or even Indigenous, if they "deviated from their prescribed cultural set" (p. 9). While not often visible to members of the dominant culture, even as they purchase Native art, Native artists understand and artfully negotiate the social, cultural, and political expectations that often require that they produce *as* Natives in order to market and sell their art.

In her examination of Alutiiq mask making as a form of cultural remembrance in Alaska, for example, Nadia Jackinsky-Horrell's (2007) interviews with Alaska Native artists illustrate the ways the non-Native art market constrains the artistic choices of Alaska Native artists and forces Native artists to creatively negotiate these dynamics in their work:

> Not only does the non-Native art market establish the marketing of Native art, it influences the style and materials that Native artists use. Without the market, some artists expressed that they would not make art in the same form. Although there are examples of historical masks without eyeholes for example, Sven [Haakanson] mentioned that, "people don't want to buy masks that don't have eyes." As a result, he discussed possibly reworking one of his masks without eyes so that it might sell. Coral discussed how some mask forms she "made because they sold, not because (she) felt anything for them." She added, "people think that primitive sells. If you stick a feather in it, it sells." Doug echoed her comments describing that feathers make his masks sell better, "but it makes the price (in constructing the masks) go up." Mask makers from other areas of Alaska such as Inupiaq sculptor Susie Bevins-Erickson, face similar tensions relating to the materials that they use, "When I began to incorporate plastic and metal in my sculpture, the gallery sales dropped because the collectors like the traditional materials" ... These market driven choices demonstrate that the artists' sellable work responds to the non-Native buyer. (pp. 78–79)

Though Alaska Native artists negotiate colonial contexts, these tensions and constraints do not overly determine the artists' production. Native artists continue to exert their own purposes and meanings into their art, despite whether or not these meanings are apparent to those who purchase them. Alutiiq artist Jerry Laktonen's piece "Joe Hazelwood" (1999) uses the traditional formlines of Alutiiq masks, but by invoking Joe Hazelwood, the Captain of the Exxon Valdez tanker which ran aground in Prince William Sound, Laktonen politicizes the mask and "provides an Alutiiq perspective to an event which completely transformed life for many Alutiiq people" (p. 81). Furthermore, even as Alaska Native artists thoughtfully negotiate the politicized terrain of Indigenous art, they also refuse particular concessions or performances: Jerry refused to tie a mask he made to a pick-up to transport it; Doug refused to make traditional whaler's masks once he learned about the mask's spiritual connections; and Coral refuses to wear a kuspuk to sell her art (Jackinsky-Horrell, 2007). As Mary Mitchell, former executive director of the Inuit Art Foundation notes, "people are buying not the 'art' but an outdated and static image of Inuit life"; nevertheless, Inuit artists still "exert ownership over their art."[5] This cultural practice of living within and against a politicized context is just part of the terrain of artistry that Indigenous peoples thoughtfully navigate, yet many people, including the teachers we were working with, remain unaware of this creative contested landscape.

Our purpose in highlighting this context did not negate the importance of providing Native students in the program the opportunity to learn from what some might refer to as "traditional" artists. Indeed, the Native Youth Center intentionally hosted art classes taught by master carvers and basket makers. As educators, we valued these cultural practices, the teachings within them, their aesthetics, and the intergenerational sharing of knowledge and community-building these practices foster. But in this context specifically, we aimed to blur the myopic vision that could only see particular forms as "Native," and bring into sight the range of Indigenous artistic expression that colonial narratives ignored. We wanted to surface the impossible standards Indigenous artists navigate, and raise questions about who benefits from these notions of cultural authenticity.

We Can't Tell You What to Do

To illustrate the stakes of the questions—What is Native art?—we explained the Indian Arts and Crafts Act of 1990 and 2010 (US Department of the Interior, 2018), legislation that neither the students nor teachers had heard of. This Act makes it illegal "to offer or display for sale, or sell any art or craft product in a manner that falsely suggests it is Indian produced, an Indian product, or the product of a particular Indian or Indian Tribe or Indian arts and crafts organization." Falsely marketing art as "Indian produced" or an "Indian product" is punishable with a fine up to $250,000 or a five-year prison term, or both. Given these potential consequences, the question of authenticity, who legally counts as Indian, became a live and pertinent question.

"Does this change what counts as Native American art?" we asked. "Does it matter, then, if someone learns from a tribal member how to make drums? Does he have a right to sell them as such?"

"Well it depends on if he's saying he is Native American, or if the drum is Native American," said one.

This question was directly relevant to our community where, at a local community market, a non-Native gentleman makes and sells Native-themed hand drums. This pattern of non-Native artists appropriating Native art, however, is widespread. In this community, this particular artist makes no overt claim of being Indigenous, yet in light of the Indian Arts and Crafts Act, his art should likely not have been sold in a local store which specialized in "Traditional and Contemporary Native American Art." And while he doesn't claim an Indigenous identity, his work is laden with Northwest Coast references that function to authenticate his work—the repeated referent to "Northwest Coast Style" on his webpage, his use of NW coast style formlines and designs, or his use of stories like "Salmon Boy" or "How Raven Stole the Sun." Yet departing from protocols often found within Indigenous communities, this artist's work isn't situated within any specific place or community, an abstract positioning which absolves him from being responsible to anyone in particular.

Metís scholar Judy Iseke-Barnes (2009) takes up this particular trope in her critical reading of Gerald McDermott's book *Raven: A Trickster Tale from the Northwest*. In it, she carefully makes visible the rhetorical strategies McDermott uses to simultaneously authenticate his "trickster tale," yet avoid "identify[ing] the origins of the story [or] the people from whom this story is taken" (p. 36). With respect to his subtitle "A Trickster Tale from the Northwest," Iseke-Barnes states,

> McDermott tries to sell two ideas at the same time; locating a point of common interest for the audience, hence the comedic and simple idea of Raven as trickster, but at the same time validating this work in a culturally appropriate foundation. In these ways the book attempts to present the story as belonging to everyone in the cultural location of the Pacific Northwest rather than from the Indigenous peoples from whom it came. By marketing the book as geographically and culturally located within all culture of the Pacific Northwest it justifies the use of this story without acknowledging from whom it came and simultaneously obscures and rejects that this is an appropriation. (p. 38)

This non-Native artist's positioning of his own work accomplishes a similar sleight of hand. While his t-shirts and serigraphs depict iconic formlines, characters, and trickster tales that authenticate his work, it is the artist who deploys the clever trick of framing his work as Northwest coast style while simultaneously refusing to locate himself or his work specifically within a particular land, community, or Native nation. He acknowledges being influenced by Indigenous peoples of the Northwest, trips to British Columbia, museums, and designs he found in books, but primarily describes himself as a "self-taught artist." Further complicating matters is his deployment of copyright over his images, a defensive legal move which prevents others from using or profiting off of *his* designs while obscuring the detail that those designs were likely rooted in the intellectual property of Indigenous peoples.

One student wondered aloud how he was able to get around the requirements of the Indian Arts and Craft Act, and why he or other non-Native artists weren't facing consequences of the law. Melvina and I didn't have a clear answer why this particular artist hasn't been held accountable, only that his work wasn't explicitly marketed as "Native American-made." Instead, like other non-Native artists, he justified his work through deceptive language like Native American "Style," Native American "Themed," or Native American "Inspired." This led us into a discussion of cultural appropriation. To talk about this, we drew from the work of Cherokee scholar Adrienne Keene and Turtle Mountain Chippewa designer Dr. Jessica Metcalfe. We also used a definition and framework by Susan Scafidi who defines cultural appropriation as "Taking intellectual property, traditional knowledge, cultural expressions, or artifacts from someone else's culture without permission" (Baker, 2012). We shared with students Scafidi's three-part framework—Source, Significance (aka Sacredness), and Similarity—to guide those who wanted to be thoughtful to not appropriate, but were unclear what that meant in everyday practice:

> Has the source community either tacitly or directly invited you to share this particular bit of its culture, and does the community as a whole have a history of harmful exploitation? What's the cultural significance of the item—is it just an everyday object or image, or is it a religious artifact that requires greater respect? And how similar is the appropriated element to the original—a literal knockoff, or just a nod to a color scheme or silhouette? (as cited in Baker, 2012)

Students scoffed at overt examples of cultural appropriation—that people would wear headdresses, or that Coachella would consciously ban "war bonnets" yet still rent out tipis at their music festival for $2,000–$3,000. But students were more deliberative about nuanced examples like dreamcatchers, feathers, or Native designs.

We were struck as teachers by the challenges in artfully facilitating this conversation. We didn't want to dictate universally what was appropriate or off-limits to students as the issue of cultural appropriation is complex, not to mention there is not a singular "Native" perspective. However, we also didn't want to lapse into a relativist stance that justified or excused appropriation. To negotiate this tension, we asked students a central question to consider: who benefits from the creation and sale of these Native-inspired items? We then highlighted several Native artists and platforms such as Nooksack/Chinese/French/Scottish artist Louie Gong's organization Eighth Generation and his educational and entrepreneurial initiative "Inspired Natives," and Turtle Mountain Chippewa scholar and artist Jessica Metcalfe's online boutique "Beyond Buckskin." Supporting Native artists was our effort to foreground Native artistry and artists in the discussion. One student, however, was particularly distressed about the blurred lines between appreciation and appropriation.

"Just tell me what to do!" she blurted out.

Though this student seemed visibly upset, we couldn't tell her what to do. Our task that day, especially as guest teachers, was not to delineate what a critical consciousness entailed. Moreover, the uncertainty she was wrestling with was likely disruptive and productive. The pedagogical border we were working was ethical. Our task was to raise awareness of these issues, to provoke space for thoughtful engagement and critical reflection, and to situate students within a complex matrix of relationships and responsibilities with the hope that this approach would translate into respectful and responsible actions. In this presentation, our work was to help this young student wrestle with uncertainty, not tell her what to do, an act of closure and comfort that might foreclose critical thinking and the messiness of living with responsibility.

I found out later, however, that the students and teachers actually *were* being told what they could and could not do in their mural negotiations with the tribal liaison and tribal representatives. Rather than presenting new information with the *hope* that teachers and students would engage in respectful representational practices, the students and teachers were learning about respect through *actual* limits that structured what that representation could and could not entail. Our educational practice as educators was based on an ethical curricular and pedagogical border; the tribal liaison and tribal representatives' practice, however, was based on the sociopolitical borders between the school and sovereign Native nations.

Curriculum and Pedagogy at the Border of Sovereignty

Due to Native nations' ancestral ties with the forest, the US Forest Service, as a federal entity, maintains a government-to-government relationship with four Native nations in the area, a relationship facilitated by a tribal liaison (US Forest Service, 2015). Through an ongoing process of consultation with these nations, the US Forest Service developed a "tribal engagement roadmap" to facilitate meaningful and respectful partnerships. As a result of their roadmap, the US Forest Service has attempted to "institutionalize Trust responsibilities and Tribal engagement within Forest Service [Research and Development]" (US Forest Service, 2015, p. 14).

Chief Justice John Marshall first established the federal trust obligation in *Cherokee Nation v. Georgia* (1831) where Marshall established tribal nations as "domestic dependent nations" and set the precedent for the "doctrine of federal trust responsibility." While Marshall's legal decisions have been key in dispossessing Indigenous peoples and eroding tribal sovereignty, the federal trust responsibility remains "one of the most important doctrines in federal Indian law" (NCAI, 2015, p. 21). As the National Congress of American Indians' (NCAI) report *Tribal Nations and the United States: An Introduction* continues, this federal trust responsibility:

> derives from the treaties between tribes and the US government and from traditional European legal theory. It is the obligation of the federal government—all branches and agencies—to protect tribal self-governance, tribal lands, assets, resources, and treaty rights, and to carry out the directions of federal statutes and court cases. The Supreme Court [in *Seminole Nation v. United States*, 1942] has defined this trust responsibility as a "moral obligation of the highest responsibility and trust." (p. 21)

Because this was a relationship structured into the Forest Service protocols, and because the proposed mural design involved Native artistic elements, the tribal liaison told the teachers they would need to run the design by the tribal representatives for approval.

It was only after our presentation, months after the mural was finished, that Melvina and I were able to see the images that the class had initially proposed for their mural in the bunkhouse. Describing the process, Sharon explained that before the term had started, she looked up different symbols from local tribes that she found in books and on the Internet and presented them to the students as potential design options. The students worked with her suggestions and conducted their own research, developing a few sample designs for the murals. The teachers then sent the designs that the class had worked on to the tribal liaison, who in turn forwarded them to representatives of the Native nations in partnership with the Forest Service. This prompted what one teacher described as "flurry of emails," and through this consultation process, the Native representatives required that the class make adjustments to their originally proposed designs.

It was fairly easy to see why they made such a request. The first image initially proposed depicted two shirtless boys sitting in a canoe on a river lined with cattails, dressed only in loincloths, peering out into the water at a salmon below. Another proposed design depicted an eagle, mid-air, its talons spread trying to catch a salmon, the whole scene set against a skyline of majestic white mountains. From the adjacent mountains, the head of a Native person branched out, bodiless, adorned with long hair and a few feathers. In a third proposed image, a soaring eagle flew alongside the head of a long-haired Native man, both hovering against a scenic mountain backdrop and above a salmon adorned with NW coastal inspired designs. In the last image, a NW coast stylized salmon sat just below the surface, a predatory eagle soaring above with outspread talons eager to pluck it from the water below. Each image was rife with Native signifiers, what Vizenor (2008) has termed "simulations," constructed images of Indians that did not reflect "real" Native presence, but instead reflected colonial constructions. Of course salmon, long hair, formlines, and canoes are *real*, and have *real* significance to Native peoples; however, these images were not real, but simulations of Indianness.

Had we learned earlier of the designs, we would have agreed with one of the Native representatives who noted that they were "stereotypical" referents. It was because they were viewed as stereotypical that students were asked during the consultation process to revise the original designs that they proposed. The final mural design, approved by the representatives, was ultimately stripped of the stereotypes and empty signifiers that the students and teacher had used intentionally to honor Indigenous peoples and aesthetics. What was left after the process of consultation was what one teacher disappointingly referred to as "a bland nature scene." "The hard part of the process," said Kelly, the other teacher involved in the project, "was that we wanted it to honor Native American people, but we didn't want it to just be a 'bland nature scene.'"

While Kelly may have felt that her curriculum didn't honor Native people in the ways she intended, the interactions and experiences that took place on the border between the school and the Native nations led to curriculum that was profoundly generative of actions that honored and respected Native people. Through the process of consultation, students and teachers experienced respect and responsibility in action. They did so, not by paying homage to some timeless notion of Indigeneity, but through actual interactions with Indigenous peoples and nations. This process, and not the Native-themed mural as a curricular product, was pedagogical. Importantly, they also learned this, not through a process of raising awareness, but through the tribal nations' practices of refusal (A. Simpson, 2007).

Refusal, as a theory and method, is generative, an analytic that can make, through its focus, particular structures and sets of relations visible. The presentation from Melvina and I, for example, was premised on various refusals. We refused the particular performances expected of us as Indigenous guest speakers. We also refused and reframed the terms of the invitation to discuss "Native art and culture." Rather than discuss Native art, culture, and artists as objects of analysis, we instead rhetorically positioned Native peoples as subjects in relation to their own art, defined in their own aesthetic and political terms. Our patterns of interaction with Sharon demonstrated various refusals as well: requests from her part, and refusals from ours. Sharon wanted suggestions for "Native music" for her class; we gave her A Tribe Called Red, a First Nations electronic group that blends hip-hop, reggae, and other musical genres.[6] She asked for "Native art"; we offered her Dwayne Wilcox,[7] Fritz Scholder,[8] Wendy Red Star,[9] and Natalie Ball.[10] She wanted the spiritual feeling and reverence she felt when she saw Chief Seathl; we told her instead about Ted Perry, the screenwriter who fabricated Chief Seathl's speech. Sharon's requests were continually rooted in desires to learn *about* Native people, but we continued to reflect back ways that she could learn *from* Native people. She asked for cultural objects (flute music or NW coast style designs); we gave her pedagogical subjects (contemporary musicians and artists who spoke against their objectification). Positioning Native artists as subjects was our sincere way of engaging what Lyons (2000) terms "rhetorical sovereignty," "allow[ing] Indians to have some say about the nature of their textual representations" (p. 458).

Yet the Native nations, in partnership with the Forest Service, exerted a different kind of sovereign authority and engaged in a different practice of refusal. Because the Forest Service had institutionalized trust responsibility into the department through liaisons, the tribal nations were given the authority to determine how they wanted to be represented on their homelands. They were allowed to delineate the terms of engagement, the context they wanted to be represented in, and refuse the representational practices they disagreed with. This was not a practice premised on raising awareness or developing a critical consciousness, a theory of change that undergirded our presentations in Sharon's class. Instead, it was premised on a fair and just redistribution of power and authority. The sociopolitical border between the schools and Native nations required and compelled (rather than pleaded and implored) recognition, respect, and responsibility. That border enabled the nations to set actual limits on what the teachers could and couldn't do, and guided the teachers through a process of what respectful and disrespectful representation entailed. Refusals, as Tuck and Yang (2014) argue, are not just a no; they can be generative. While whittling the mural away to a "bland nature scene" may have felt like a reductive or subtractive experience for students and teachers, it was profoundly generative: relationships were fostered between the Native nations and the students and teachers in the school, and this process broadened students and teachers' understanding of and respect for sovereignty. The education on that border was a much more valuable and lived experience of sovereignty, recognition, and respect than the hypothetical scenarios we used in class that invited students to theorize their actions in ethical ways. Students didn't get to honor Native people by drawing what they wanted, but they learned about honoring Native people by honoring the treaties. Importantly, this practice of respect and responsibility wasn't dependent on the choice, consciousness, or commitment of an individual Forest Service employee; it was structured to be so, an institutional commitment to respect and responsibility.

After the month-long class had ended, Sharon and I talked about that process of framing and designing the mural, encountering limits, and working with the tribal liaisons only to find what they had proposed wasn't acceptable. In speaking of the requirement and process of getting tribal approval, she said, "... of course I *wanted* to get the approval of the tribal leaders, but I don't think I thought through the mural design. I recognized later that it had potential to offend." I was drawn to Sharon's use of the word recognized. Some definitions of the term are rooted in a cognitive process: recognition happens when a person identifies or recalls prior information, perhaps prompted by a social cue. Recognition, however, is more than a cognitive process. Recognition is also a sociopolitical relationship. This meaning is important because Sharon didn't just recognize the mural designs were offensive because of some internal realization she had; rather, she had this moment of realization precisely because of her external engagement with a Native nation due to a relational and sociopolitical principle of recognition. Sharon's learning (her recognition that the mural was offensive) was the result of the Forest Service's explicit and institutionalized recognition of Indigenous sovereignty.

Indigenous studies scholars critique the politics of recognition, in part because such approaches can grant too much power to settler institutions to validate Indigeneity and Indigenous nationhood (Coulthard, 2014). Critical of the emancipatory promise and goals of pursuing recognition, some advocate for pursuing resurgence, an internally oriented rather than externally focused, process of reclaiming and revitalizing Indigenous lifeways and futures (Alfred, 1999; Coulthard, 2014; L. Simpson, 2011; 2014). While these scholars rightfully center Indigenous self- and collective recognition (L. Simpson, 2015), and while their advocacy for resurgence as collective action and movements that aren't reliant on settler nation-states is important, this focus doesn't elide the responsibility of settler governments and institutions to recognize Indigenous sovereignty and nationhood. Indigenous nations shouldn't need to pursue or demand recognition; but settler nation-states and institutions should never-theless recognize their political sovereignty. For this class, the border was edu-cational, compelling the school and students to recognize Indigenous nations' sovereignty.

Like the other teacher, Sharon had initially lamented the final design which was stripped of many of her original ideas, but she also said she was thankful for the tribal liaisons and the process she went through, despite how uncomfortable it was.

> I think it is better though. I learned a lot doing the murals because a lot of things we wanted to create didn't get included. It was good for me to recognize that my idea of what I wanted didn't even matter ... Now I don't think I would, you know ... trying to do a Native American art project and we're not Native American. It just made me think about it ...

Sharon attributed this realization to both our presentation on Native art as well as the negotiations with the tribal liaison and representatives. But given the ways our relationship and interactions have consistently been marked by an under-current of exoticism and caricature, her newfound reflections seemed to stem less from our presentation which relied on raising awareness, and more directly from the consultations during the mural-making process, a process which structured respect into the experience, and fostered awareness as a result.

I wondered what a school district that was premised on that same structural commitment and respect for sovereignty might look like. What if schools and school districts took seriously the notion of trust responsibility for its Native stu-dents and institutionalized that trust responsibility? What if schools recognized and partnered with nearby Native nations? What might those processes and partnerships teach students about sovereignty? What proved educational for the students and teachers was not necessarily an awareness of the sovereignty and the potential borders and limits it might set, but an *encounter* with that border, and an *experience* of those limits. How might other such encounters and experiences be integrated into public schools and classrooms to generate curricular opportunities for students to understand, recognize, and respect tribal sovereignty?

Toward a Democratic Education that Takes Seriously Tribal Sovereignty

Indigenous education is already a "trust responsibility," one of the many "promises which were given in exchange for land" (Deyhle & Swisher, 1997, p. 114) through more than 400 treaty negotiations with Native nations; yet it is a rare occurrence in this district to hear mainstream educators frame their work as such. Instead, Indigenous education is often displaced from the central processes and practices of schooling, referred to instead as something that happens in tribal schools, on reservations, or in public schools with large populations of Native students. If educators *do* talk about Indigenous education, it is usually because they are talking about what the Indian Education program does, not what they do daily in their classrooms. As a result, Native students have long been subjected to assimilative and inadequate forms of public schooling.

Choctaw scholar Mike Charleston (1994) has termed these types of schooling *pseudo* Native education ("education that strives to assimilate Native people into the mainstream American society" (p. 43), and *quasi*-Native education ("education that sincerely attempts to make American education more culturally relevant and supportive of Native students and Native communities," but reflects a "band-aid" approach that is "woefully insufficient to meet the needs of Native students" (p. 27). To address this longstanding problem, in 1994, Charleston wrote a paper, "Toward True Native Education: A Treaty of 1992," a draft of the Indian Nations at Risk Task Force report. In it, he drew attention to the "secret war" the United States has waged against Native nations and tribal peoples, a war "in the new battlefield of the public school" in which "the odds are overwhelmingly against lonely and isolated Native students fighting for the survival of their Native cultures, languages, and tribal identities" (p. 24). "Wars are stopped by treaties" Charleston argued; "let's make a treaty to end this war between our societies" (p. 18).

Charleston's proposed Treaty of 1992 was an assertion of Native sovereignty, a refusal to accept the premise of The Act of March 3, 1871, which officially ended treaty-making between the US government and Native nations. His aim was to unite Native nations in a National Native alliance, vested with the power and authority of tribal governments, to provide "collective support for Native education in accordance with the wishes of the participating tribes" and "to reestablish *true* Native education systems for our people and lead the way for the reform of mainstream American education" (p. 51). Charleston felt that institutionalizing *quasi*-education in public schools would provide an improvement and more choices for Native students and families, however, the "essential elements of *true* Native education are equally valid for mainstream American education" (p. 43).

Charleston's vision of a *true* Native education is a comprehensive theory of education comprised of ambitious goals and essential elements which included the tribal community, local school governance structures, education philosophy, plans, programs, and budgets, funding and resources, people, quality curricula, materials, facilities, and equipment, and information, research, evaluation, and communication (p. 34). Significant in his theorization, and most relevant to the course on Native American art and culture, is his reminder that education is a "trust responsibility" which he embeds into proposed "tribal education codes" that would enable tribes to "exercise their jurisdiction over the education of their members in public schools" (p. 43). Much like the ways engagement with the tribal liaison and tribal representatives compelled a respectful relationship and representation, Charleston's tribal education codes are diplomatic protocols designed to compel respect, responsibility, and responsiveness toward Native students:

> Tribal education codes are necessary to establish the legal framework to incorporate all the essential elements and resources into a systemic regional approach to Native education that compels all schools to be responsive to the academic and the cultural needs of Native students. The codes must be developed locally, make sense in the region and maintain and respect local diversity in Native cultures and languages. (Charleston, 1994, p. 43)

Similar to the "tribal engagement roadmap" offered by the US Forest Service, these tribal education codes are intended to institutionalize trust relationships and responsibilities into the partnerships between schools and Native nations. Lyons (2000), commenting on Charleston's notion of "true" Native education notes, "What true Native education calls for in the final analysis is nothing less than the formal institutionalization of rhetorical sovereignty" (p. 464). As David Beaulieu (Minnesota Chippewa) (2008) has noted, "We need to reconsider ways in which tribal governments can represent the interests of their students in state public schools" (p. 60).

Due to the ongoing advocacy of Native educators and allies, there are already pathways for institutionalizing trust responsibility in public schools. Title VI/Indian education programs, for example, require Native parent consultation and involvement.[11] While this provides an avenue for parent input into Indian Education programs, this doesn't give families much say or insight into what is happening in classrooms or public schools. Most recently, under the recent authorization of the Every Student Succeeds Act (ESSA) (2015), local educational agencies (LEAs) are now required under section 8538 of Title VI/Indian Education to

> consult with appropriate officials from Indian tribes or tribal organizations approved by the tribes located in the area served by the local educational

agency prior to the affected local educational agency's submission of a required plan or application for a covered program under this Act or for a program under title VI of this Act. (p. S. 1117—316–317)

While affected local educational agencies include LEAs with a population of 50% or more American Indian/Alaska Native students, they also include LEAs who have received a Title VI grant that exceeded $40,000. Sharon's classroom and school are situated within such an LEA.

The story of the negotiations between the classroom, tribal liaison, and Native representatives illustrates some of the promising outcomes of tribal consultation. Moreover, this process disrupted typical assumptions about how meaningful learning takes place, for example, as a result of the intentional and planned curriculum by teachers. While we learned later that the teachers did seek out contemporary Native voices and perspectives via guest speakers, and provided students a diverse and vast array of literature and videos from Native perspectives to provide accurate historical and contemporary information to students, the learning about recognition and sovereignty wasn't intentional.[12] The teachers' intentional learning targets for the course included: "identify 5 tribes of Oregon," "greet others in Chinuk Wawa," "create drawings/sketches that reflect synthesis of local Native American values and artistic expression" and "collaborate with peers to produce a Native American-inspired mural." It was actually through the denial of several learning objectives that teachers and students learned a great deal. Students were not allowed to combine stereotypical, pan-Indian representations to honor Native people; they weren't even ultimately allowed to represent Native people at all. But as a result of the consultation process, new relations, understandings, and ways of being developed that weren't dependent on colonial logics of domination and possession (Moreton-Robinson, 2016).

This small example points toward other pedagogical and curricular opportunities that might exist at this border, opportunities for new relationships and understandings to emerge if schools institutionalized respect and recognition of Native sovereignty. This learning took place as a result of meeting obligatory minimum requirements for tribal consultation. Imagine if schools entrusted nearby tribal nations to engage in legitimate partnerships with schools on "*Indigenous* terms" (Lomawaima & McCarty, 2014, p. 9), partnerships that weren't reactive, but that enabled Indigenous peoples to help determine educational aspirations and priorities from the ground up. For Indigenous peoples, this points toward the *true* Native education that Charleston theorized, which would "include the specific aspirations of tribes and Native communities for their populations" and "reflect the ambition and full participation of Native people and tribes" (1994, p. 31). However, for Charleston, widespread public education about sovereignty is also needed to end the "siege" against Indigenous peoples. Public schools should also teach "all present and future generations of American citizens" about Native sovereignty, treaty rights, the dual citizenship of Native citizens, the government-to-government relationship Native nations have with the federal government, and how to relate to Native nations. This sort of curriculum is essential for meaningful co-existence between Native peoples, nations, and the United States government and its citizens (p. 29).

Lifting up tribal consultation as an educational intervention is not without its own set of challenges and complications. Determining the specific tribal nation/s with whom schools and districts should consult can be a complicated process as present-day tribal nation borders are narrower than tribal nations' traditional territories. Indigenous homelands can also overlap, meaning schools and districts would need to consult with various tribal nations that may have different educational aspirations or priorities. Moreover, the process of federal recognition itself is grounded in colonizing discourses and institutions that overlook the inherent and continual sovereignty of those who refuse to pursue or have been denied federal recognition. Tribal nations must, for example, meet seven specific criteria for acknowledgement, a rigorous process regulated by the Office of Federal Acknowledgement within the Office of the Assistant Secretary—Indian Affairs of the Department of the Interior. This process—which requires nations to undertake intensive genealogical, political, and bureaucratic labor—has denied more nations recognition than it has officially recognized. Such a process, for example, requires Native nations to prove their continual existence as a "distinct community" despite longstanding attempts to fracture the linguistic, cultural, and political distinctiveness of such communities through assimilative federal policies. The Chinook Nation in Washington state, who aren't federally recognized, yet have existed as a people and nation in their aboriginal territory near the mouth of the Columbia River since time immemorial (Chinook Nation, 2018), are just as deserving of consultation by schools near their territory as are the other 29 federally recognized nations within the state of Washington. Finally, consultation with Native nations shouldn't come at the expense of urban Indigenous communities, who are often left out of such processes. This erasure has been redressed by requirements that Indian Education programs establish parent committees, yet it still leaves unaddressed districts without Indian Education programs.

Advocacy for schools to recognize and consult with nearby Native nations and urban Indigenous communities, then, must be seen as an important, yet complex, intervention. What if Native nations and communities have different aspirations that the district or school? What if Native nations don't agree on what should be taught? The tensions, uncertainty, and possibilities that might surface if schools took seriously tribal sovereignty are unforeseen, but we should struggle for such processes anyway. Public schools have yet to live up to the espoused values of democracy, yet continue to struggle toward such a vision anyway. These same schools should struggle toward a democratic vision that takes seriously tribal sovereignty. As this consultation process demonstrated, tribal sovereignty provided an important framework for such learning. Moreover, the tribal nations' refusals and the limits that emerged through this process were more than just a "no" (Tuck & Yang, 2014); they moved student learning beyond information *about* sovereignty, to an experiential process that deepened respect for Indigenous peoples.

Notes

1 See the Chapter 2: "Halloween Costumes and Native Identity" for an account of this incident.

2 Photos of his collection can be found at the Northwestern University Digital Library Collection (http://curtis.library.northwestern.edu/).

3 Our use of these images in no way implies that dancing or regalia are stereotypical; rather, we were drawing attention to the dominant discourse that "cultural debris" (King, 2012) is what signals Indigeneity.

4 As Native artist Robert Hart stated at the "Indian Art in a Changing Society" conference in 1962, "It is almost impossible to define [Native American Art]; there are two things involved: is it traditional Indian arts and crafts, or is it arts and crafts designed and produced by an Indian?" (as cited in Crouteau, 2008, p. 236).

5 For another example of the complex terrain Indigenous artists navigate, see the essay "Inuit Art is Inuit Art," parts 1 and 2, in *Inuit Art Quarterly* (1997) which describes how museums and markets constrain and shape the production of Inuit art, but also how Inuit artists enact agency and defy these constraints by persistently trying to make the art "their own."

6 One of their albums can be listened to and downloaded here for free at their website (http://atribecalledred.com/).

7 Dwayne Wilcox is an Oglala Lakota artist who uses ledger paper, a traditional medium, "to convey, in the most contemporary way, a living culture through humor, dance, or vices of the modern times" (http://www.doghatstudio.com/).

8 Fritz Scholder is an enrolled member of the Luiseño tribe, though "he often said he was not Indian…His revolutionary paintings broke away from stereotypical roles and forever changed the concept of 'Indian artist'" (http://fritzscholder.com/index.php).

9 Wendy Red Star was raised on the Apsáalooke (Crow) reservation in Montana. She uses various media—photography, painting, fibers—to "explore the intersections of Native American ideologies and colonialist structures, both historically and in contemporary society" (http://www.wendyredstar.com/).

10 Natalie Ball is a Chiloquin-based artist who identifies as Klamath and Modoc, as well as a descendant of African slaves and English soldiers. These identities all influence her artwork, which vary in medium, including installation and performance art, painted quilts, and sculptures among others (https://nataliemball.com/home.html).

11 This was the result of the Indian Education Act (1972) and its later reauthorization under the Elementary and Secondary Education Act (2001). At a national level, the US Department of Education has attempted to consult with Native leaders via the White House Initiative on American Indian and Alaska Native Education (WHIAIANE) in which they conducted listening sessions and a final report (US Department of Education, 2015). Under Executive Order 96–30 established in 1996, Oregon has been engaged in government-to-government consultations since 1996, which include education clusters (Oregon Department of Education, 2017). Indian Educator Advisor April Campbell has also worked with tribal nations in Oregon to develop a new Tribal Communication and Consultation Policy which will be released in Spring 2017 (ODE, 2017).

12 The teachers did make an explicit effort to include historically accurate and contemporary content from Native perspectives, and undoubtedly students learned something important from this curriculum. Students read excerpts from *First Oregonians*, a book that addresses historic and contemporary accounts of Oregon's nine tribal nations based in tribal voices and perspectives with over half of the chapters written by tribal members. They read excerpts from *The People Are Dancing Again* about the Confederated Tribes of the Siletz Indians, visited their tribal website, and watched *Skookum Tillicum: The Strong People of Siletz*, a short YouTube documentary on the nation from a tribal perspective. They learned about the importance and revitalization of Chinuk Wawa, a language that has long

connected diverse Native peoples together, by examining dictionaries, listening to language recordings, and inviting a Siletz tribal member to come in and teach the class some words in the language. They also watched a video and read a eulogy that commemorated a contemporary Klamath Hero, Alfred "Al" Leo Smith, an instrumental advocate for Native religious freedom who recently passed away.

References

Adichie, C. (2009). The danger of a single story. TedGlobal [Video file]. July. Retrieved from www.ted.com/talks/chimamanda_adichie_the_danger_of_a_single_story?language=en.

Alfred, G. (1999). *Peace, power, righteousness: An indigenous manifesto.* Don Mills, ON: Oxford University Press.

Andreotti, V. (2011). *Actionable postcolonial theory in education* (Postcolonial studies in education). New York, NY: Palgrave Macmillan.

Baker, K. J. M. (2012). A much-needed primer on cultural appropriation. *Jezebel,* November 13. Retrieved from https://jezebel.com/5959698/a-much-needed-primer-on-cultural-appropriation.

Barnd, N. (2008). *Inhabiting Indianness: US colonialism and Indigenous geographies.* (Unpublished dissertation.) Retrieved from https://escholarship.org/uc/item/7gc357ch.

Beaulieu, D. (2006). A survey and assessment of culturally based education programs for Native American students in the United States. *Journal of American Indian Education,* 45(2), 50–61.

Charleston, M. G. (1994). Toward true Native education: A treaty of 1992. Final report of the Indian Nations at Risk Task Force. *Journal of American Indian Education,* 33(2), 7–56.

Chinook Nation. (2018). www.chinooknation.org.

Coulthard, G. (2014). *Red skin, white masks: Rejecting the colonial politics of recognition.* Minneapolis, MN: University of Minnesota Press.

Crouteau, S. A. (2008). *"But it doesn't look Indian": Objects, archetypes and objectified others in Native American art, culture and identity.* (Unpublished doctoral dissertation.) University of California, Los Angeles.

Deyhle, D., & Swisher, K. (1997). Research in American Indian and Alaska Native education: From assimilation to self-determination. *Review of Research in Education,* 22, 113–194.

Dion, S. D., & Salamanca, A. (2014). inVISIBILITY: Indigenous in the city Indigenous artists, Indigenous youth and the project of survivance. *Decolonization: Indigeneity, Education & Society,* 3(1), 159–188.

Echo-Hawk, B. (2014). About my gas mask paintings … [Web log post]. March 14. Retrieved from http://bunkyechohawk.com/gas-mask-paintings/#more-537.

Every Student Succeeds Act. (2015). Retrieved from www.gpo.gov/fdsys/pkg/BILLS-114s1177enr/pdf/BILLS-114s1177enr.pdf.

Fowler, C. (2007). Hybridity as a strategy for self-determination in contemporary American Indian art. *Social Justice,* 34(1), 63–79.

Iseke-Barnes, J. (2009). Unsettling fictions: Disrupting popular discourses and trickster tales in books for children. *Journal of the Canadian Association for Curriculum Studies,* 7(1), 24–57.

Jackinsky-Horrell, N. (2007). Masks as a means of cultural remembrance: Kodiak Archipelago Alutiiq mask making. Unpublished master's thesis, University of Washington.

King, T. (2012). *Inconvenient Indian: A curious account of Native people in North America.* Minneapolis, MN: University of Minnesota Press.

Lomawaima, K. T., & McCarty, T. L. (2006). *"To remain an Indian": Lessons in democracy from a century of Native American education.* New York: Teachers College Press.

Lomawaima, K. T., & McCarty, T. L. (2014). Introduction to the special issue examining and applying safety zone theory: Current policies, practices, and experiences. *Journal of American Indian Education*, 53(3), 1–10.

Lyons, S. R. (2000). Rhetorical sovereignty: What do American Indians want from writing? *College Composition and Communication*, 51(3), 447–468.

Martineau, J. & Ritskes, E. (2014). Fugitive indigeneity: Reclaiming the terrain of decolonial struggle through Indigenous art. *Decolonization: Indigeneity, Education & Society*, 3(1), I–XII.

Moreton-Robinson, A. (2016). *Critical indigenous studies: Engagements in first world locations*. Tucson, AZ: The University of Arizona Press.

National Congress of American Indians. (2015). *Tribal Nations and the United States: An Introduction*. Washington, D.C. Retrieved from www.ncai.org/about-tribes.

Oregon Department of Education. (2017). American Indian/Alaska Native education. Retrieved from www.oregon.gov/ode/students-and-family/equity/NativeAmericanEducation/Pages/default.aspx.

Pedri-Spade, C. (2014). Nametoo: Evidence that he/she is/was present. *Decolonization: Indigeneity, Education & Society*, 3(1), 73–100.

Raibmon, P. (2005). *Authentic Indians: Episodes of encounter from the late-nineteenth-century Northwest coast*. Durham, NC: Duke University Press.

Simpson, A. (2007). On ethnographic refusal: Indigeneity, "voice," and colonial citizenship. *Junctures*, 9, 67–80.

Simpson, L. B. (2011). *Dancing on our turtle's back: Stories of Nishnaabeg re-creation, resurgence and a new emergence*. Winnipeg: Arbeiter Ring Pub.

Simpson, L. B. (2014). Land as pedagogy: Nishnaabeg intelligence and rebellious transformation. *Decolonization: Indigeneity, Education & Society*, 3(3), 1–25.

Simpson, L. B. (2015). The place where we all live and work together: A gendered analysis of "sovereignty." In S. N. Teves, A. Smith, & M. H. Raheja (Eds.), *Native Studies Keywords*, 18–24. Tucson, AZ: The University of Arizona Press.

Solórzano, D. G., & Yosso, T. J. (2002). Critical race methodology: Counter-storytelling as an analytic framework for education research. *Qualitative Inquiry*, 8, 23–44.

Stein, A. J. (2013). Chief Joseph watches a University of Washington football game and gives a speech in Seattle on November 20, 1903. In *HistoryLink*. January. Retrieved from www.historylink.org/index.cfm?DisplayPage=output.cfm&&file_id=10286.

Tremblay, G. (2000). Strawberry and chocolate. [Basket]. Retrieved from www.nmai.si.edu/searchcollections/item.aspx?irn=273177.

Tuck, E., & Yang, K. W. (2014). R-words: Refusing research. In D. Paris & M. T. Winn (Eds.), *Humanizing research: Decolonizing qualitative inquiry with youth and communities* (pp. 223–248). Thousand Oaks, CA: Sage.

US Department of the Interior. (2018). The Indian Arts and Crafts Act of 1990. Retrieved from www.doi.gov/iacb/act.

US Forest Service. (2015). Forest Service Research and Development: Tribal Engagement Roadmap. Washington, DC: United States Department of Agriculture. Retrieved from www.fs.fed.us/research/tribal-engagement/roadmap.phpwwwfs.fed.us/research/tribal-engagement/roadmap.php.

Vizenor, G. (Ed.). (2008). *Survivance: Narratives of Native presence*. Lincoln, NE: University of Nebraska Press.

CONCLUSION

Interventions for Urban Indigenous Education

This is what we know about our stories. They go to work on your mind and make you think about your life. Maybe you've not been acting right. Maybe you've been stingy. Maybe you've been chasing after women. Maybe you've been trying to act like a Whiteman. People don't *like* it! So someone goes hunting for you—maybe your grandmother, your grandfather, your uncle. It doesn't matter. Anyone can do it.

So someone stalks you and tells a story about what happened long ago. It doesn't matter if other people are around—you're going to know he's aiming that story at you. All of a sudden it *hits* you! It's like an arrow, they say. Sometimes it just bounces off—it's too soft and you don't think about anything. But when it's strong it goes in *deep* and starts working on your mind right away. No one says anything to you, only that story is all, but now you know that people have been watching you and talking about you. They don't like how you've been acting. So you have to think about your life.

(Nick Thompson, as cited in Basso, 1984, pp. 41–42)

Nick Thompson used a hunting metaphor to describe a Western Apache theory of storytelling to anthropologist Keith Basso. When an individual isn't acting right, he said, someone stalks them with a story, an act that may cause that person "anguish" by thrusting that person into "periods of intense critical self-examination" (Basso, 1984, p. 43). Historical tales are valuable. They "make you think hard about your life," and often, if a story goes to work on someone, the individual emerges more "determined to 'live right'" (p. 43). Importantly, this Apache conception of storytelling is not only the work of individuals, but also an integral feature of the Apache landscape. "Mountains and arroyos step in symbolically for grandmothers and uncles," and "[j]ust as the latter have 'stalked' delinquent individuals in the past, so too particular locations continue to 'stalk' them in the present" (p. 43). Places are pedagogical. As Basso observes of this

Apache worldview, "surveillance is essential, because 'living right' requires constant care and attention, and there is always a possibility that old stories and their initial impact, like old arrows and their wounds, will fade and disappear" (p. 43).

While Thompson was referencing historical Apache stories, I would like to respectfully draw from this hunting metaphor and offer this book as a practice of research that has stalked the mainstream educational practices in public schools that continue to underserve Indigenous students and undermine Indigenous self-determination and sovereignty. As Castagno and Brayboy (2008) note in their comprehensive literature review of culturally responsive schooling for Indigenous youth, despite a wealth of scholarship and case studies available to make education more meaningful, engaging, and supportive of Indigenous students, "educators and policy makers have not taken the suggestions seriously and have continued schooling in a 'business as usual' fashion" (p. 981). In response, these stories were told as an intervention into the normalizing logics of Eurocentric educational practices (Moreton-Robinson, 2016). They were written to "go to work" on the subtle ways colonialism surfaces in "a nice field" like education (Ladson-Billings, 1998). As a collective, these stories support evidence that colonization continues to structure (though not overdetermine) Native students' experiences in public schools (Brayboy & Castagno, 2009; Castagno & Brayboy, 2008; Goodyear-Kaʻōpua, 2013; Martinez, 2010). They make visible the marginalization of Indigenous education and Indigenous students in public schools and the persistent disregard for Indigenous studies scholarship, highlighting the ways that schools play a role in "perpetuating and refreshing colonial relationships among people, practices, and land" (Patel, 2016, p. 12). Visibility, however, relies on a theory of change designed to raise awareness, an approach some critical race scholars argue has done little to challenge structural racism and stratification (Vaught & Castagno, 2008). Consequently, these stories are not just designed to raise teachers' awareness; they also designed to place teachers in relationship with institutions and practices that reproduce erasure, as well as the impossible subject positions of working within and against such structures.

Some stories stalked the particularly stubborn educational practices I have seen educators use that explicitly harm Indigenous students and tokenize Indigenous education—curriculum that privileges Eurocentric histories or relegates Indigenous peoples to the past, Native American units which caricaturize and commodify Native culture, the token inclusion of Native guest speakers, or the disregard for Indigenous students' knowledge and perspectives. More globally this book stalks the commonsense assumption that colonization is a historic event, and that Indigenous education is someone else's responsibility. Drawing from Indigenous theories of storytelling, my aim was to tell stories in such a way that "the story became a teacher" (Ellen White, 1993, as cited in Archibald, 2008, p. 138). These stories aren't intended to tell educators *what* to think or feel; rather I wrote them with the goal of *"giving them the space to think and feel"* (as cited in Archibald, 2008, p. 134, emphasis added). "A good story," notes Lorna Mathias (1992), "can reach into your heart, mind and soul, and really make you think hard about your relationship to the world" (as cited in Archibald, 2008, p. 140). I hope these stories invite teachers to think hard about their relationships to place, to Indigenous students and families, to settler colonialism, to self-determination and sovereignty. I hope they invite teachers to think hard about their relationship to teaching and the history of schooling. I hope they provide teachers an opportunity to reflect and wonder: "Could I have been overlooking something all along?" (Delgado, 1989, p. 2440).

As colonialism is constantly "shape shifting" (Corntassel, 2012), there is no discrete set of knowledge, no one conceptual frame, no single book or research study, that can account for its varied mechanisms. Educators need to become practiced at recognizing how colonialism surfaces. This is not something that can easily be distilled into a workshop, a single course, or even a teacher preparation program (though a central argument of this book is that Native studies must become requisite teacher knowledge, and so, should be required coursework within teacher education programs and, dare I say, K-12 curriculum). Drawing from the Apache theory of surveillance and theories of haunting (Basso, 1984; Morrill, Tuck, & the Super Futures Haunt Qollective, 2016), these stories infuse the persistent threat of colonialism and Indigenous erasure into the landscapes of schools, reminding educators that the architecture, curriculum, pedagogy, and policy of schooling is embedded with Eurocentrism, racism, and settler colonialism. Teachers must learn to anticipate and critically read these landscapes.

Like other forms of critical forms of narrative research (Chang & Rosiek, 2003; Dibble & Rosiek, 2002; Sconiers & Rosiek, 2000), these survivance stories sought to illuminate the sociocultural and political contexts of teacher knowledge. However, in a slight divergence from aims to develop more "culturally responsive" approaches to teaching (Chang & Rosiek, 2003; Sconiers & Rosiek, 2000), these stories are intended to cultivate teachers' "sensibilities" (Wilson, 2006) to detect colonialism and anti-Indianism (Cook-Lynn, 2001) in practice. More than awareness, this is a practice of cultivating teachers' *anticolonial literacy*, the ability to critically read and counter Eurocentric and colonizing educational discourses and practices. These stories purposefully did not attend to Indigenous students' culture and how to better support their cultural difference in the classroom. I am indebted to the rigorous and robust base of research conducted by Indigenous and allied scholars on culturally responsive/culture-based education,[1] and I find this work extremely valuable in Indigenous contexts. However, I have grown weary of teachers' narrow use of "culture" (Hermes, 2005a; 2005b) and am skeptical that increasing educators' understanding of culture will be sufficient to intervene into settler colonial contexts of mainstream public schools, at least those in which this research took place. Indeed, as some of these chapters demonstrated, colonial understandings of culture mediated the ways educators tried to support Indigenous students as "Other," reproducing settler colonial relational dynamics. Thus, these survivance stories aimed specifically to make visible the ways *colonialism* (not culture) mediates students' educational experiences and teachers' professional knowledge landscapes (Clandinin & Connelly, 1995).

While a substantial portion of this book was critical, I also sought to illuminate the types of knowledge and practices that might help educators support Native students and support the aims of self-determination and sovereignty. As hooks (1992) offers, "There is power in looking … Not only will I stare. I want my look to change reality" (pp. 115–116). Like hooks, my looking has been "a way to know the present and invent the future" (hooks, 1992, p. 131). These stories have been my attempt to critically look at educational policy and practice as it is lived in one particular district, looking not only for the ways that settler colonialism surfaced, but also for moments or curricular and pedagogical pathways that were overlooked, missed, or made impossible because of the discursive frames from which educators or schools operated. By reading into the stories theories and tools from Native Studies scholarship, literature, and my own experiences, I centered Indigenous knowledges and analytics. These analytics and knowledge should be essential to theorizing and enacting more responsible practices of integrating Native studies, serving Native students, and furthering Indigenous aims of self-determination and sovereignty. My aim was to sensitize educators to the nuanced dynamics that Native students, families, and educators artfully negotiate, offering a contrapuntal reading (Said, 2012) of education, a practice of reading and writing back (Smith, 2012) that reflected not only experiences of colonialism within schools, but also desire, hope, and possibility.

Together, these chapters demonstrate that despite our supposed progress beyond the eras of physical and cultural genocide, schools and institutions are clearly still engaged in more veiled forms of erasure, and that some of these erasures are encoded in (and even endorsed as) educational practices within schools. It is also clear that Native students, families, and educators are often knowledgeable about these dynamics, and engage in practices of "resistance to Western cultural assimilation" (Lee, 2011, p. 289). In short, as much as this book bears witness to colonialism, it is also a testament to Native survivance. Educators must learn to critically read the ways coloniality surfaces; they must also learn to read for survivance.

While most instances of Indigenous erasure described in this book were not intentional in any obvious ways, *they were also not incidental.* Indigenous erasure is central to the structure of settler colonialism. It is not incidental, for example, that most mainstream educators have little knowledge of Indigenous life (Dion, 2008), cannot name the Native nations in their state, and have little knowledge of Native community events in their area. Both society and schools are often structured to produce such ignorance (Calderón, 2011). As Lee (2011) notes, teachers' "misperceptions largely stem from a lack of direct experience with Native communities and families and from misunderstandings about the nature of the political relationship that Native Nations hold with the federal government" (p. 278). But teachers can work against this, and being Native is not a prerequisite for doing so.

Because settler colonialism is a structure, and surfaces and circulates in commonsense and everyday ways, efforts to further anticolonial and Indigenous education require, as Maori scholar Linda Tuhiwai Smith (2008) argues, "multiple layers of struggles across multiple sites" (p. 117). In considering how to challenge whiteness in schools, Castagno (2014) argues that approaches must be "systemic and systematic." Similarly, contesting colonialism must entail equivalent and complementary systemic and systematic efforts.

Although I sincerely believe that stories and storytelling are, as Peter Cole offers, "a way of experiencing the world rather than imposing decontextualized denotative 'truth' claims" (as cited in Million, 2014, p. 37), I also recognize that in the current context of educational reform, providing direct recommendations—even if they risk being decontextualized—can be useful. Some of these recommendations are difficult and disheartening to write, as many of my suggestions were proposed by Indigenous scholars decades earlier; *some were proposed nearly a century ago.* That Native people should be seen as "'real time' beings" in schools and curriculum is agonizing to repeat nearly 30 years after Creek educator Floy Pepper did in 1990 (Pepper, 1990). To recommend that more honest and accurate histories be taught in schools is painful to write, as my recommendation nearly replicates the argument Seneca scholar Arthur C. Parker made in 1916 (Parker, 1916).

I situate my recommendations within this longstanding stream of Indigenous scholars who have made similar recommendations as a performative gesture, an invitation for educators to question why these insights and recommendations have been ignored for so long. This pattern of erasure is part of the problem. I also hope that by situating the practical knowledge, insights, theories, and conceptual tools *within* the context of stories, educators will reflect on and revisit their own practices in light of these insights, a process that hopefully sensitizes educators to hear these recommendations more clearly today.

What follows are recommendations geared toward individuals, institutions, educational policy, and educational research. These are recommendations for teachers, teacher education programs, educational policies, and research practices to better support Indigenous students and to support educational self-determination and sovereignty. Within each domain, I draw attention to concrete and conceptual knowledge, and well as relational practices that will support such efforts.

Developing Teachers' Concrete Knowledge

While I do not wish to individualize the scope of the problem (i.e., this is an issue for individual teachers to address), I do believe developing a more robust conception of teacher knowledge that includes Indigenous studies is nevertheless imperative. Said differently, teachers' professional knowledge landscapes (Clandinin & Connelly, 1995) should be accountable to Indigenous peoples given their formation on Indigenous lands.

Survivance stories point to a variety of practical information and concrete knowledge that teachers could have drawn upon to more effectively engage Indigenous education in this district. While I am not delineating *the* knowledge base (as I believe no such discrete knowledge base exists), I will outline various forms of knowledge from these stories that would have helped educators better support Indigenous education. This includes an awareness of resources in the school, district, and community to support Indigenous education, basic knowledge of Native studies concepts and the history of Indigenous education, and the ability to detect bias in curriculum.

All teachers should be aware of (and consciously seek out) resources in the district and community to support Native students and families specifically, as well as to support their efforts to teach Indigenous studies. In the territory where I am writing, there are two longhouses that actively support a vibrant Native community through weekly potlucks, community events, seminars, guest speakers, memorials, Waashat services, sjima and stick game tournaments, and a summer bridge program for Native high school youth, among other activities. There are also two other Indian Education programs in adjacent districts (relevant to support families as they move between districts), a Native listserv and calendar that detail important community events, and a program Facebook page that communicates relevant events and opportunities for students and families. Educators aware of these resources can help families connect to academic, cultural, and social opportunities. Moreover, educators aware of the vibrant Native community would be hard pressed to continue teaching antiquated myths premised on Native disappearance. Recreating longhouses as elementary curriculum with no attention to their contemporary use in the community would likely feel strange to educators who knew of the active Longhouse communities in the area.

The stories in this book also point to a general knowledge base in Native studies that educators need to support Native students and teach Native studies. This base must minimally include a recognition of the diversity and contemporary presence of Indigenous peoples, accurate historical information to ground curriculum, and a working knowledge base of Native citizenship, nationhood, and sovereignty. With this knowledge of Native diversity, for example, teachers should no longer feel comfortable teaching about Pilgrims and generic "Indians." The term Indian—now coded into the landscape of curriculum as a construction of whiteness—should trigger in educators an uneasy feeling. Like Kanaka Maoli scholar Julie Kaomea's (2005) experience of Hawaiian Studies curriculum that purported to "foster appreciation for the Native people of Hawai'i," yet degraded Hawaiian life, my hope is that educators similarly experience "'odd'—'queer'—'wrong'—'strange'—'fishy'" feelings (p. 26) when they encounter generic Indians in curriculum. Though Indian may be an appropriate self-referent for Indigenous peoples, generic Indians as curriculum should be seen as colonial construction and an erasure.

Teachers also need basic information about history that is accurate. *One hundred years ago*, Seneca scholar Arthur C. Parker (1916) wrote:

> No race of men has been more unjustly misrepresented by popular historians than the American Indian. Branded as an ignorant savage, treacherous, cruel,

and immoral in his inmost nature, the Indian has received little justice from the
ordinary historian whose writings influence the minds of school children ...
The Indians have a right to know that their name as a people is not hidden
forever from its place among the nations of the earth. They have a right to
ask that the false statements and the prejudice that obstructs historic justice
be cast aside. They have a right to ask that their children know the history
of their fathers and to know that the sins and savagery of their race were
no worse than those of other races called great for bravery and conquest.
(pp. 261–262)

In the 1930s, Luther Standing Bear (Oglala Sioux) wrote, "No longer should
the Indian be dehumanized in order to make material for lurid and cheap fiction to embellish street-stands ... Rather, a fair and correct history of the
native American should be incorporated in the curriculum of the public
school" (as cited in Lyons, 2000, p. 465). Native people have long been saying
history should be more accurate and honest. I draw from this scholarship a
century earlier to highlight the resistance (whether explicit or tacit) toward
critically revising the historical myths that educators often teach as facts. The
material needed to critically engage these histories is there, much of it written
by Native people trying to re-right and rewrite (Smith, 2012) historical
wrongs. Without such histories, Native students learn that Native peoples were
colonization's "helping hand," undermining Indigenous resistance and perspectives embedded in Native counterstories.

Teachers also need to understand and explicitly disrupt stereotypes in curriculum. Native studies curriculum is not the reproduction of stereotypes: Native
people are not generic bodies made Indian when the familiar set of cultural
markers are added, and Native content does not mean gluing feathers to a sign, or
inviting students to make masks, kachinas, tipis, or totem poles. Teachers need
knowledge, skills, and practice to detect bias, racism, and anti-Indianism (Cook-
Lynn, 2001) in the curriculum. Bias surfaces in numerous ways—invisibility, stereotypes, imbalance/selectivity, unreality, fragmentation/isolation, linguistic bias,
or shiny/cosmetic bias (Sadker, 2009). And while racism is institutional and
structural (Leonardo, 2004) and should not be reduced to interpersonal exchanges
between individuals, it is also locatable in student-teacher interactions. It was clear
that the curriculum reinforced particularly harmful "ways of knowing" that
weren't explicitly racist, but reflective of more "deep structures" (Grande, 2015)
of colonialism. Nevertheless, there were multiple instances where teachers failed
to detect or interrupt bias or racism.

Some of this racism reflects what Robertson (2015) has termed "legitimized racism."
That educators are still allowed to use *Sign of the Beaver* despite its routine use of the
word squ★w and despite widespread critiques (Lambert & Lambert, 2014; Reese, 2007;
Slapin & Seale, 2003) is unacceptable. Subjecting students to degrading language such as
squ★w and the "Tonto talk" in *Sign of the Beaver* positions Native students at risk of

internalizing those demeaning and dehumanizing representations. If Native students are conscious of the overt and latent prejudice in either curricular material or their peers' comments, they are faced with myriad decisions including quietly withstanding the hostility or choosing to address the bias, a choice Zeik made that was fortunately met with no resistance, but a choice other families have made and were met with resistance and feelings of marginalization and retaliation as a result.[2]

Teachers must also recognize the reproduction of essentialized and one-dimensional caricaturizations of Indigenous peoples. Talking about Indigenous peoples as "circular thinkers" who may like to "gather in circles" rather than stand in lines is a form of racism. More subtly, the relentless tokenization of Native culture through the guise of appreciating diverse cultures demonstrates this legitimized racism and anti-Indianism. Though only several stories addressed the practice of tokenizing Indigenous life, it was pervasive throughout the district: Thanksgiving murals featuring Indians prominently displayed on the walls, worksheets for November with little Indians adorned in feathers, or huge mural displays in schools titled "*What's Your Spirit Animal?*" that depicted Native "totems." These are but a few of the ways racism was reproduced and legitimized in schools. As these stories have shown, these are not problematic solely because they are degrading stereotypes and caricatures, but also because they socialize students in particular ways toward Indigenous people. Beyond the consequence of dehumanizing representations, these practices reinforce particular sorts of "looking relations" (hooks, 1992) and investments. As Leonardo (2004) argues,

> There is the other half of domination that needs our attention: white invest-
> ment. To the extent that racial supremacy is taught to white students, it is
> pedagogical. Insofar as it is pedagogical, there is the possibility of critically
> reflecting on its flows in order to disrupt them. The hidden curriculum of
> whiteness saturates everyday school life and one of the first steps to articulating
> its features is coming to terms with its specific modes of discourse. (p. 144)

Such representations are not just stereotypes, but are investments that can be linked to the dispossession of Indigenous lands and the erosion of tribal sovereignty (Corntassel & Witmer, 2008). Speaking in the context of Hawaiian sovereignty, Kanaka Maoli scholar Lisa Kahaleole Hall (2005) writes, "making Hawaiian-ness seem ridiculous, kitsch functions to undermine sovereignty struggles in a very fundamental way" (p. 409). She continues, "A culture without dignity cannot be conceived of as having sovereign rights, and the repeated marketing of kitsch Hawaiian-ness leads to non-Hawaiians' misunderstanding and degradation of Hawaiian culture and history" (p. 409).

Finally, educators need basic information about Native citizenship, nationhood, and sovereignty. As I have argued here and elsewhere (Sabzalian & Shear, 2018), mainstream curriculum and pedagogy will more productively serve Indigenous peoples by framing Indigenous peoples and nations through the political lens of citizenship, nationhood, and sovereignty (rather than a cultural lens of multiculturalism). Identifying as Cherokee or Haida, for example, is not just a word choice, and not just a cultural identity; it is also a way to privilege one nationality over the other, placing the US identity as a secondary status (Turner, 2006). This entails understanding that Native students have cultural, racial, *and political* identities, and that Native nations aren't just cultural communities: "Native Americans are nations of people within a nation" (Brayboy & Morgan, 1998, p. 348). Like the federal government and the states within it, Native nations are sovereign entities, despite their "domestic dependent" status and their location as nations within the geopolitical confines of the US (Grande, 2015).[3] Native students need to learn about their rights, treaties, systems of governance, and roles and responsibilities as citizens in order to uphold those rights, roles, and responsibilities.

A vast base of scholarship attests to the ways discourses of multiculturalism undermine Indigenous sovereignty (Lomawaima, 1995; Calderón, 2009; Cook-Lynn, 2001; Tuck & Yang, 2012; St. Denis, 2011). As Cook-Lynn (2001) argues, "the age of diversity" has been "the most recent weapon used against us in education," one which denies Indigenous peoples as "citizens of Indian nations" (p. 152). Cook-Lynn considers this framing a form of anti-Indianism. This book contributes to this scholarship by arguing that curriculum, instead of framing Indigenous peoples through the anthropological lens of culture, should include the study of Native citizenship and nationhood within the political realm of *civics education*. Again, the information needed to address Native citizenship, nationhood, and sovereignty is there.[4] I recognize that Native nations are not "impervious to reinforcing the violence of normativities" (Brandzel, 2016, p. 9). Native feminist scholars in particular have courageously drawn attention to the ways colonialism has "silenced Native peoples about the status of their women and about the intersections of power and domination that have also shaped Native nations and gender relations" (Goeman & Denetdale, 2009, p. 10; see also Barker, 2005; Denetdale, 2006). While citizenship and nationhood can be limiting frameworks, they nevertheless remain important conceptual interventions into the widespread ignorance about Native sovereignty. Teachers should have knowledge to teach about Native citizenship and nations, that Native people are often dual citizens, and even why some Indigenous peoples adamantly tried to refuse the "gift" of US citizenship (Bruyneel, 2007)

Developing Teachers' Conceptual knowledge

The previous disucssion of the nuances of Native citizenship underscores a more conceptual knowledge base teachers need to inform their practice. For example, the idea that Indigenous people are not artifacts of the past but contemporary peoples is a concrete understanding that can lead to more constructive efforts to support Native students and teach Native content. However, as the story "The Wax Museum" demonstrated, providing space for Native people to be "real time beings" (Pepper, 1990, np) is not without complications.

This Indigenous present is personally and politically complicated. It doesn't lend itself to a simple or easy pan-Indigenous prescription. Not all Native people are alike. The assumption that they are leads to stereotypes, but the alternative is not a single correct view of Indigeneity or Indigenous peoples. Instead, teachers need to recognize differences among Indigenous nations in their region, as well as the differences between individual Indigenous peoples (Montana Office of Public Instruction, 2012). This orientation toward recognizing and affirming difference would lend itself to an appreciation of the diversity of even those local experiences that are marked by geographic locations (urban, rural, etc.) or political experiences (being terminated or confederated, etc.), among other dynamics.

I don't presume that this section will delineate *the* conceptual knowledge base educators need in order to more responsibly serve Native students and teach Native curriculum. Nevertheless, I have identified several conceptual themes that merit conversation and more sustained focus by educators. As my discussion will show, conceptual knowledge will lead to more concrete and practical knowledge, an iterative process of learning as knowledge is disrupted, deepened, or expanded, a process that generates new possibilities for teacher practices and commitments. For example, as teachers understand the ways discourses of authenticity or culture serve to frame Indigenous peoples in the past or as objects of study, this conceptual knowledge base will provide grounds for new concrete knowledge and teacher practices.

Conceptual knowledge takes time for teachers to develop, as it will likely involve an excavation of deeply rooted assumptions some teachers have about Native students and issues. Below I will offer a discussion of several of these concepts, and where relevant, I offer practical examples of the knowledge and practices this might generate.

Recognize the ongoing marginalization and erasure of Indigenous peoples

Perhaps the most important concept teachers need is a recognition of the marginalization and erasure of Indigenous life. Educational contexts have long been inhospitable to Indigenous peoples (Stewart-Harawira, 2013), and no time soon will the marginalization of Indigenous students in schools be ended. As a result, teachers must lean in to the understanding that the erasure of Indigenous life is built into the institutions in which they work. These programs do not need non-Native teachers who are fascinated with Native culture (a dynamic that circulates broadly in settler society, but has also trailed the Indian Education program in particular); rather, they need educators who are aware of the ways Indian Education programs and Native communities more generally have been marginalized, and who offer their support and skills to assist the program- or community-designed goals. These programs need educators who recognize that active efforts have been made on behalf of the federal government to erase Indigenous presence, to dispossess Native people both physically and ideologically (Calderón, 2014), and that even slight acts of erasure or the negation of Indigenous presence are contemporary iterations of this history. Educators must be made aware, not only of the violent history of extermination, dispossession, and assimilation, but also of the ways these erasures continue to structure encounters (and non-encounters; Veracini, 2011) between settler society and Indigenous peoples. With knowledge of the erasure and marginalization of Native life, an educator might see that any curriculum, pedagogy, or program necessarily works within and against that context, and will thus work to make these practices and process of erasure visible to administrators or other educators. In so doing, they work to amplify and make visible the issues, concerns, and needs of Native programs, communities, or even nations, in order to hold schools and districts accountable.

Move beyond individuality to a relational understanding of subjectivity

The education of Indigenous peoples has been explicitly framed throughout history as a mode of (often violent) assimilation. In light of this history, educators should move beyond viewing themselves solely as individuals (a privileged position and practice of whiteness), and instead understand they act as educators within that stream of institutional history that informs patterns of interactions and experiences today. This means that educators must not only develop a "sociocultural consciousness" that recognizes the ways society is stratified or that schools often reproduce that stratification (Villegas & Lucas, 2002); teachers must also develop a relational awareness of their subject positions as educators within assimilative institutions. Non-Indigenous educators can enhance their effectiveness with Native students by developing a relational awareness of their positionality and learning about the "history, culture, and current circumstances of their students" (Hermes, 2005a). As Lyons (2000) prompts, teachers should "think carefully about their positions, locations, and alignments: the differences and connections between sovereignty and solidarity" (467).

For example, the literature on culturally responsive education calls on educators to have affirming views of diverse students (Villegas & Lucas, 2002), an important intervention into deficit framings of students by positioning students' cultural knowledge, values, and practices as valid, and positioning education as an important site for sustaining the rich cultural and linguistic diversity students bring (Paris, 2012). Yet educators must also recognize the widespread and longstanding fascination non-Indigenous peoples have had and continue to have with Native culture (Green, 1988; Deloria, 1998) so that such affirmations do not get coopted by practices of whiteness and lapse into appropriations. The teacher Sharon's negation of Celeste's concern, described in Chapter 2 is continual with a social pattern of white women denying the concerns and issues specific to Native women (Moreton-Robinson, 2000). But her fascination with Native culture illustrates another extractive relationship that non-Indigenous peoples have with Indigenous communities and cultures.

Complicate conceptions of culture

"Culture" as it was used in practice by educators often referred to cultural products rather than cultural processes (Pepper et al. 2014), and anthropological categories that mirrored Edward Curtis's framework (dwellings, weapons, dress, food, etc.). This abstraction and extraction of Native culture perpetuate the idea that "Native Americans are people of the past or creatures of fantasy," a belief which supports "continued aggression against Native peoples" (Hirschfelder, Molin, & Wakim, 1999, p. 76).

Throughout this book, when I did attend to Native culture, I tried to offer glimpses of Native culture as constant and continual, rooted and mobile (Castagno & Brayboy, 2008). In the story "Education on Border of Sovereignty," Melvina and I shared the work of Native artists who use traditional ways to make sense of current issues. We were careful to emphasize that traditions aren't static, but dynamic. In "Little Anthropologists," I shared how Indigenous cultural rights are intimately connected to political struggles for sovereignty. Moreover, I also shared that when my son taught his classmates a song, the cultural values he embodied were as much the act of sharing and teaching as they were the song itself.

Additionally, I tried to recast institutional practices as also cultural, rather than a set of values and practices specific to Native or other nonwhite people. I did this by highlighting the "cultural work" of Eurocentric curriculum and teaching. Implementing a Native American unit that commodifies Katsina Friends, totem poles, masks, and Native technologies and frames them as cultural crafts to be imitated, for example, not only encompasses stereotypes and bias, but reflects a deep-seated, settler colonial cultural practice of dehumanizing Indigenous peoples (LaRocque, 2010) and reinforcing dialectics of Indigenous absence and presence (Calderón, 2014b). The Native American unit as a whole might be viewed as an extension of a longstanding American cultural project that Yup'ik scholar Shari Huhndorf (2001) has termed "going Native." Going Native in this instance does not describe an anthropologist's attempt to understand a culture more objectively by "going Native" (immersing himself in the language, values, and customs of those he studies, for example). Rather, this curriculum "goes Native" as a whole through its continual erasure, rewriting Native peoples as part of US history and engaging in activities that nostalgically recuperate the life that was "lost." As Huhndorf (2001) states, "European Americans rewrote [their] history in a self-justifying manner by redefining Native Americans as part of their own past." This rewrite enabled European America to "go native" "by claiming Indianness as part of its own collective identity" (p. 15). This cultural pattern not only masks colonial violence, but by reproducing Indians as part of the past, and Indianness as a part of "Americanness," it also reinforces "the racial hierarchies it claims to destabilize" (p. 3). These "tourist approaches" (Derman-Sparks & the A.B.C. Task Force, 1989) to multicultural education allow children to "'visit' non-White cultures and then 'go home' to the daily class-room, which reflects only the dominant culture" (p. 5). This is a cultural practice of commodifying and then consuming cultural difference (hooks, 1992) and leaving Eurocentric foundations of curricula unexamined. In this cultural pattern and prac-tice, Natives remain historic, marginal, and Other, while non-Native subjectivities and identities are supposedly enriched, a practice legitimized by liberal multiculturalist discourses that ignore the power and politics of difference.

Educators would benefit from more nuanced theories of culture, including the-ories that politicize the context of cultural inclusion, such as Lomawaima and McCarty's (2006) theory of "the safety zone." Informed by such theories, educators might recognize the pattern of inviting Native students to drum or make dream-catchers, yet resisting Native desires to wear regalia to graduation, are continual with a history of domesticating "dangerous" forms of Indigenous cultural differ-ence. Even Indian Education program language, when taken up uncritically, posi-tions culture as a "unique" need designed to help educators *meet the same challenging State student academic achievement standards as all other students are expected to meet*" (20 U.S. C. § 6102(b), emphasis added). Thus, Native students' cultures are framed as a means to attain dominant cultural knowledge. Recent reauthorization of Indian Education under the Every Student Succeeds Act (ESSA) (2015) contests this safety zone by infusing two new amendments of purpose:

> (2) to ensure that Indian students gain knowledge and understanding of Native communities, languages, tribal histories, traditions, and cultures; and (3) to ensure that teachers, principals, other school leaders, and other staff who serve Indian students have the ability to provide culturally appropriate and effective instruction and supports to such students. (20 U.S. C. § 6102(b))

Whereas the prior purpose to help students meet state standards is retained, this amended purpose leans toward an additive, even restorative, theory of schooling—Native students should *gain* knowledge of their languages, histories, traditions and cultures. Moreover, this amended purpose places responsibilities on educators and administrators to enact this approach. It remains an open question whether this new purpose will be absorbed into the safety zone, and culture and tribal histories interpreted and recast by educators and curriculum in innocuous ways. But there is an opening here, a moment of "interest convergence" (Bell, 1980) for educators versed in the politics of culture and assimilative schooling, to use this legal language in service of Native self-determination and sovereignty.

Learn from rather than about Indigenous peoples

"To speak of Indigeneity," states Mohawk scholar Audra Simpson (2007), "is to speak of colonialism and anthropology, as these are means through which Indi-genous people have been known and sometimes are still known" (p. 67). The educational contexts I witnessed were structured to "know" Indigenous peoples in particular ways, which I connected to longstanding ways of knowing the Indigenous other. In "Little Anthropologists," I described how the Native American unit the teachers developed framed Native people as historic objects of study. This positioning not only denies Native peoples the chance to be "real time beings" (Pepper, 1990) discussed in the previous section, but reaffirms Eurocentric viewpoints as natural, normal, and central. It reproduces the "positional authority" (Said, 1978) of students to "know" the Native Other. It became clear to me throughout working with teachers in this district that the aphorisms Melvina and I used to guide educators—start with contemporary Indigenous peoples, or begin with local Indigenous nations and communities—were useful interventions into the ways curriculum often framed Indigenous peoples as historic or as typically living elsewhere, but the sayings also did little to disrupt the ways schools were structured to know Native peoples as objects of study.

In several stories, I provided examples of our attempts to move the study of Indigenous peoples from curricular objects to pedagogical subjects, hoping that such a positioning would invite educators to learn *from* rather than learn *about* Native peoples. In other examples, I offered conceptual frameworks for curriculum, such as sovereignty, that steered the lens away from learning *about* Native peoples. Instead of studying Native people, I argued that studying the current issues Indigenous peoples and nations are facing, such as Apache resistance against encroachment on their territory, or the Hopi nation's advocacy to repatriate their sacred Katsina Friends, might be more generative approach. In another example, I drew on the work of Dion (2008) to suggest that students could study the biography of their relationship to Indigenous peoples, an attempt to disrupt the "perfect stranger" subjectivity many teachers (and likely the students they teach) presume. These interventions were intended to disrupt curriculum that authorized students to know and narrate Native Others and Otherness.

Understand that Indigenous identities are complex

Educators should also recognize the complexity of Indigenous identities. I take seriously Quechua scholar Sandy Grande's (2015) caution that the "current obsession with questions of identity and authenticity obscures the sociopolitical and material conditions of American Indian communities," and "suggests to the non-Indian world that the primary struggle of American Indians is the problem of forging a 'comfortable modern identity,'" displacing the "real sites of struggle (sovereignty and self-determination)" and "the real sources of oppression—colonialism and global capitalism" (p. 138). Moreover, as Corntassel (2003) argues, "The question of 'who is indigenous?' is best answered by indigenous communities themselves" (p. 75). Nevertheless, educators should recognize that Indigenous peoples use diverse justifications to assert their identities, including self-identification, legal, biological, or cultural frameworks (Garroutte, 2003),[5] or by foregrounding land, relationships, and responsibilities (Grande, San Pedro, & Windchief, 2015). The point here is not to define Indigeneity, as the question of Indigeneity is complex and taken up by numerous scholars (Doerfler, 2015; Forte, 2013; Garroutte, 2003; Grande, San Pedro, & Windchief, 2015; Lawrence, 2004; Lyons, 2010; Sturm, 2002), but educators should understand that the question "who is Indigenous" is complex, that the stakes of that question are high for Native individuals and tribal nations, and that the question itself is underwritten by power (Forte, 2013).

Indigeneity is much more complex than the invitation to check a box on an enrollment form suggests. Native identity claims are made within a long and violent history of physical and cultural genocide and erasure. These claims are often a testament to tribal nations' and Native communities' longstanding efforts at restoration, renewal, and resurgence (Curry-Stevens, Cross-Hemmer, & Coalition of Communities of Color, 2011). For some families, the invitation to fill out a form for Indian Education may be welcome and seen as a way to connect them to community; for others, it may be a burden, inviting histories of resistance or resentment, of authenticity, or of the social, personal, cultural, or emotional costs of such questions. Educators must have a basic understanding of Indigenous identity: the diverse ways Native people claim their identities; what it means to be a citizen or descendant; and how Indigenous identity is both racial and political. They should be familiar with what it means for a tribal nation to be federally recognized or unrecognized; understand the ways blood quantum can legitimize or delegitimize Indigeneity, and be aware of how those discourses circulate among Indigenous peoples. Educators should also appreciate the complex bureaucracy, time, and money it can take people to establish or maintain their citizenship (e.g., for some families, especially those who are highly mobile, maintaining enrollment cards and records can be challenging and the cost of original documents needed in order to reapply for one's tribal membership ID prohibitive).

At a classroom level, educators should recognize that Native students negotiate and develop their identities against a backdrop of whiteness and dominant discourses of Indianness. As the survivance stories illustrate, Indigenous students' sense of their identities varies widely and can also change across contexts. Even when students are enrolled in their nation or feel confident in their cultural knowledge and identities, for example, they often must negotiate discourses of authenticity, or navigate the ignorance of peers, their teachers, or curriculum, as did Erin and Zeik. As the story "Halloween Costumes and Native Identity" illustrates, even Indigenous educators like myself can miss moments when Native students struggle with discourses of authenticity. Assertions of identity can also be complex. When a student exclaims "I'm part Native American!" this can be seen as both a statement of pride, and simultaneously an expression of a colonial metric of Indigeneity. When educators tune into these dynamics, they will also learn to listen for the survivance stories of Indigenous families and communities that contest these metrics—"Which 'part' specifically? Your arm? From your elbow to your wrist maybe?" one student was taught to respond by his grandmother to the statement of being "part" Native.

At a broader level, educators should examine how definitions of Indigeneity are linked to resource allotment. Indian Education program enrollment criteria, for example, include students who are enrolled tribal citizens or the children or grandchildren of enrolled members. But what are educators' responsibilities toward Native students from unrecognized nations? And how do educators explain to Native students who were eligible for Indian Education programs through their grandparents' status as enrolled tribal citizens, that the program will not consider their future children eligible for the program? Educators must see this waning pattern of trust responsibility as connected to the settler colonial method of Indigenous erasure.

The conceptual knowledge about Indigenous identity can help orient educators to the ways schools, curriculum, and pedagogies intersect with these identity dynamics in complex and unexpected ways. These are not necessarily issues for educators to resolve; they are dynamics to be read so that educators can support Indigenous students and families as they navigate, resist, and contest them.

Recognize and nurture Native survivance

Native people have, as Tuck (2009) adeptly noted, been framed through lenses of pathology and "damage," so much so that at times we have occasionally come to see our own experiences through these pathologies and "damage-centered" lenses. Educators attuned to stories and acts of Native survivance, however, locate Native assertions of "presence" within constraining discourses as more than resistance, more than survival, and definitely more than pathology. This perspective helps educators avoid blaming students for whatever predicament they may be in, and avoid viewing them solely as victims of such circumstances. Seeing Indigenous students through "desire-based" frameworks can support educators in acknowledging pain or oppression, while also seeing the courage and wisdom in their lives (Tuck, 2009).

I tried to model how to tune into Native stories and acts of survivance. In the story "The Wax Museum," for example, Erin's reach for buckskin to look more "Native American-y" was not simply the ignorant reach of a child for stereotypical representation of Indianness, nor was it the mere social reproduction of those discourses. Rather, through a lens of survivance, I wrote about how Erin's actions reflected the purposeful refusal of a young child to be erased by being made to look like everyone else. The markers Erin reached for—the buckskin and the crystal wand—may have been shaped in part by dominant discourses of Indigeneity, yet her reach to assert a distinct difference was also a nuanced, albeit complicated, form of youth resistance. Similarly, Celeste's proposal in her social (in)justice art class to address cultural appropriation was also a form of survivance. So too were the ways she processed with her peers, the care and consideration she offered her teacher despite being shut down, and her commitment to that project (that she eventually completed on her own time). Zeik, the 2nd grader who raised his hand in response to the ways Native people were represented in a book used by his teacher, and who drew himself as a brown-skinned Pilgrim, was also enacting survivance as he created social and discursive space within in the curriculum. Each of these small acts reflects Native students' survivance as they lived in creative contradiction with assumptions embedded in dominant culture and their teachers' practices.

Recognize and affirm sovereignty and self-determination

While sovereignty is *inherent* as well as *political* (Lomawaima, 2008), (and a concrete form of teacher knowledge I argued earlier that educators should be versed in), educators should also have a conceptual knowledge base around sovereignty. Sovereignty as a principle is too vast and complex to discuss in one paragraph, and a definition and project that is not without disagreement; nevertheless, Native studies scholars and communities continue to contest, define, and wield the concept in service of Indigenous peoples and Indigenous futures (Barker, 2005; Teves, Smith, & Raheja, 2015).[6] And while I argued earlier that educators should understand and teach about the rights and principles of political sovereignty, "rhetorical sovereignty" (Lyons, 2000) can also be a meaningful guiding principle for practice. Lyons offers rhetorical sovereignty as "the inherent right and ability of *peoples* to determine their own communicative needs and desires in the pursuit of self-determination" (p. 462). Students like Celeste want to pursue questions and projects that are meaningful to them.

Supporting those desires can contribute to what Lyons (2000) terms, the "American Indian publics." We tried to support this form of "public literate action" (Wells, as cited in Lyons, 2000, p. 465) in our own small way in the youth group with the letter we wrote to Spirit Halloween store. But teachers should create spaces for this sort of public literacy and action within the school day. Native youth, when supported, have effectively wielded public literacy in service of sovereignty and self-determination. Recent campaigns such as *More than that* by Native youth at Todd County High School, Earth Guardians and Rising Youth for a Sustainable Earth, or *Rezpect Our Water* DC all exemplify the power of Native youth to engage in collective, public action.[7] Whether making videos, writing letters to the President, and running 2,000 miles from Standing Rock to Washington, these activities demonstrate possibilities Native youth could generate, possibilities that are too often stifled in public schools and classrooms. However, just as schools can be sites of reproduction of dominant discourses, they can also be sites of survivance and self-determination. With educators equipped to hear and support Indigenous students' "communicative needs," schools can become strategic sites to develop public intellectuals. Again, being Native isn't necessarily a prerequisite for this work. The teacher at Todd County High School who supported Native youth in creating the video "More than that" as a response to Diane Sawyer's 20/20 special Hidden America: Children of The Plains which pathologized Indigenous peoples, wasn't Native; she listened and followed the lead of Native students at her school who wanted to speak back to Sawyer's damage-based lens (Tuck & Yang, 2014b).

Citing two recent public victories for Native rights—a Supreme Court decision to uphold Native hunting and fishing rights on ceded lands, and federal trademark trial to appeal the Washington Redsk*ns trademark—Lyons (2000) argues,

> These victories were won by Native people who learned how to fight battles in both court and the culture-at-large, who knew how to read and write the legal system, interrogate and challenge cultural semiotics, generate public opinion, form publics, and create solidarity with others ... Shouldn't the teaching of (American Indian) rhetoric be geared toward these kinds of outcomes? (p. 466)

Educators versed in the concept of rhetorical sovereignty would be more inclined to support such critical knowledge and skills with their students, and better positioned to support them in using their knowledge and skills to support Indigenous publics.

Finally, sovereignty, beyond a curricular framework to further respect for Indigenous nations, and beyond a rhetorical framework to support Indigenous aims and aspirations *is always what is at stake with Indigenous education*. This is not the work of tribally controlled schools alone. Teachers in urban and suburban public schools are also educating the next generation of Native leaders who can strengthen their nations. Whether they eventually return home, or engage in assisting their nations from afar, Indigenous education is always, in a sense, a project of Native sovereignty, self-determination, and "nation-building" (Brayboy et al., 2012).

Beyond Teacher Knowledge: A Relational Practice of Care, Commitment, Courage, and Connectedness

Teachers versed in the types of concrete informational and conceptual knowledge previously discussed are likelier to responsibly and generatively support Indigenous students and teach Native studies. However, this study and my own experiences tell me that information and concepts alone won't enable teachers to equitably and ethically support Indigenous students; they will be necessary, but insufficient, resources. Such knowledge is inadequate as the ways in which colonial violence and erasure manifest in schools is constantly changing, constantly "shape-shifting" (Corntassel, 2012). No one piece of knowledge or conceptual frame provides sufficient guidance for navigating these dynamics. As Tsianina Lomawaima (1995) states,

> The search for a single teaching method or learning style that best serves or typifies a racially, linguistically, ethnically, or economically defined subgroup of U.S. society is like the search for the Holy Grail. It risks becoming a sacred calling that consumes resources in the search for an illusory panacea for complex social and educational ills. (p. 342)

Because of this, there is no recipe for when one particular piece of knowledge or a particular concept will be relevant. This work takes place in a context of uncertainty, and with high stakes. There are institutional forces at work that counter the interests of these students. Making decisions in this shifting and always uncertain terrain will ultimately be based not on deduction from prior principles, but on judgments made in motion, influenced by affect, values, and imperfect estimations of possible consequences, and always with an ongoing responsibility for our decisions. This will require teachers to be involved in a way that is not just conceptual. This kind of teaching, in other words, is ultimately a form of relational practice, as much about ethics and politics as epistemology. In what follows, I offer that beyond the suggested forms of knowledge I surveyed, teachers will also need to develop a relational practice of care, commitment, courage, and connectedness.

Care

Caring has been asserted as an important relational orientation in the literature on culturally responsive schooling for Indigenous youth (Castagno & Brayboy, 2008; Demmert & Towner, 2003; Deyhle & Swisher, 1997; Powers, 2006). In their examination of Native youth who stay in school and succeed, Deyhle and Swisher (1997) draw on a wealth of research to state that "caring teachers are critical to their success" (p. 167). "We know," they later state, "that caring teachers make a difference in the decisions students make to persist or leave school before graduation" (p. 182).

One prominent theory of education comes from feminist educational theorist Nel Noddings (1984) who theorized teaching as a relational practice of care. Rather than an "aesthetical" form of caring, which she offers as "caring about things and ideas" (p. 21), Noddings argues that teachers should strive for a relational and reciprocal "ethics of care" in which teachers are attentive and receptive to students' lives and needs. Ethical care, Noddings (2002) states, "is always aimed at establishing, restoring or enhancing the kind of relation in which we respond freely because we want to" (pp. 13–14).

Noddings' theory of care provided an important intervention into "the proclaimed universalism and narrow rationalism of androcentric ethical and educational theories" at the time (Thompson, 1998, p. 528), but scholars have also critiqued the inattention to race and whiteness within such theories (Rolón-Dow, 2005; Thompson, 1998). Angela Valenzuela (1999), for example, draws from "Noddings' (1988) concept of authentic caring" (p. 61), but situates caring theory within the racialized and political landscape of schooling for immigrant and US-born Mexican youth. As Valenzuela argues,

> The overt request [that youth "care about school" in order to be cared for] overlies a covert demand that students embrace a curriculum that either dismisses or derogates their ethnicity and that they respond caringly to school officials who often hold their culture and community in contempt. (pp. 24–25)

Thus, Valenzuela's theory of care, *educación*, draws attention to the subtractive and assimilative contexts of schooling in which caring relationships are forged or foreclosed.

Others, like Thompson (1998), have drawn explicit attention to whiteness within dominant theories of care, arguing that they remain "colorblind" when they "proclaim a commitment to diversity," but "fail to acknowledge and address the whiteness of their political and cultural assumptions" (p. 525). By theorizing "caring as if it were synonymous with the home or the private sphere," these theories ignore the fact that the home "has not been the protected site for African American women that it has been for White, middle-class women" (p. 532). Thompson's examples—that even safe and loving homes haven't protected African Americans from racism and poverty, from "the effects of low wages ... the burning of crosses on the front yard, invasion from lynch mobs, sexual harassment on the job, or joblessness due to racism" (p. 532)—ring true for Native families who, despite providing loving homes for their children, haven't necessarily protected them from the theft of their homelands, languages, or traditions, or from the blatant and subtle racism/colonialism they experience in society or schools.

Caring as a relational practice, then, can be undermined without critique of underlying power dynamics. "Caring," for example, was a driving force of assimilative schooling practices. "Caring" educators and policy makers were convinced their methods were less violent than warfare or policies of Indian removal. As Jacobs (2009) notes, citing anthropologist Ann Laura Stoler, "'the politics of compassion was not an oppositional assault on empire, but a fundamental element of it'; the 'production of harnessing of sentiment' comprised a key 'technology of the colonial state'" (pp. 25–26). Teachers must recognize the limits of "false empathy" (Delgado, 1996), and realize that "despite teachers' good intentions, love and caring can be racist, limiting, and oppressive" (Bartolomé, 2008, p. 3).

Teachers must develop a "critical care praxis" (Rolón-Dow, 2005), or "critical position of care" (MacGill, 2016, p. 242) in which they recognize their "ethic of care is not neutral, but is located within race, class and gender structures and is expressed through either nuclear or community models of care" (p. 239). For Rolón-Dow (2005), this means developing a practice of critical caring that is "grounded in a historical and political understanding of the circumstances and conditions faced by minority communities," "seeks to expose how racialized beliefs inform ideological standpoints," and "translates race-conscious historical and ideological understandings and insights from counternarratives into authentic relationships, pedagogical practices, and institutional structures that benefit Latino/a students" (p. 104). For Thompson (1998) this means countering the colorblindness in care theories and developing specifically antiracist curriculum and practices of care. This is important because "African American students cannot trust teachers who (wittingly or unwittingly) lie to them about racism, ignore Black achievements, gloss over slavery and segregation, or confine the study of Black history and culture to Black History Month" (p. 540).

Similarly, Indigenous students need teachers who care for them by working to "ensure that Indigenous students are successful in school while developing *as Indigenous peoples*" (Goulet & Goulet, 2014, p. 5), that help Indigenous students pursue their personal and communal educational aspirations (e.g., rhetorical sovereignty), and that are committed to disrupting colonization, in all of its forms. Among other things, this critical practice of caring requires commitment and courage.

Commitment and courage

Dealing with dynamics of power requires commitment and courage. When schools are structured in ways to ignore, erase, or demean Indigenous students' lives, educators need courage to speak back to those institutions. Melvina embodied this courage and commitment as she navigated bureaucratic and ideological roadblocks to serving Native students. Courage and commitment manifest in subtler ways as well. Equally as significant as speaking up is the courage educators demonstrate through critical self-reflection and vulnerability. That vulnerability can be personal, demonstrated through a willingness to look at oneself critically, and in light of traits, values, or histories one might not want to see. This sort of courage entails turning toward one's ignorance, for example, a practice some educators avoided. Ms. Carter, the 5th grade teacher who designed the wax museum project, turned toward her ignorance by recognizing gaps in her own knowledge and reaching out for help. This was not only evident in her admitted ignorance of any contemporary Native leaders, but also in her thoughtful reflections on the ways her curriculum had positioned Native people in the past, or entailed the study of cultural objects outside of their cultural contexts.

Native students, families, and educators routinely demonstrate courage and commitment by showing up in institutions that often deny and degrade their existence. Educators must recognize this, and embody equivalent practices of courage and commitment in order to advocate for and stand in solidarity with the students and communities they are there to serve. Importantly, forming relationships and connections with Native students and families is an effective way to continually reflect on and renew one's commitments.

Connectedness

The concepts of care and courage are not solely personal. Courage, for example, is not just a self-conscious practice of a teacher replacing bad ideas with good ones, leaving an enlightened teacher in tact as the moral authority; it also requires the courageous practice of relinquishing authority. Beyond these personal commitments, teachers and schools need to foster connections with Indigenous peoples, communities, and nations, placing themselves within a matrix of relationships and responsibilities.

This connectedness can be inter/personal as teachers foster relationships with Native students and parents. Ms. Carter worked to foster connections to the programs, evident in her commitment to bringing her class to the Center, the only teacher in her school that has made that effort so far. Sharon and her partner teacher Kelly also worked to create connections between their course and the Native community by inviting Native people to their class and giving them the authority to speak on issues important to them. However, the story "Education on the Border of Sovereignty" also demonstrates what a broader commitment to connection entails.

Because the US Forest Service had institutionalized a tribal liaison as a structural commitment to ensuring its "trust responsibility" to Native nations and lands, Sharon and Kelly's class were required to negotiate with the tribal liaison and representatives regarding the representation of Indigenous life in the mural. This also involved a practice of relinquishing pedagogical, epistemic, and representational authority. Though restrictive in the sense that the range of potential mural designs was limited, I argued that this connection to the tribal liaison and representative was actually generative of respect and new learning. While Sharon's individual practices of self-reflection (despite the stubbornness of discourses) might be thought of as courageous (i.e., her admitting to her students she had a lot to learn), I suggested that Sharon's ability to reflect on her actions came not from internal cognitive processes, but from a formalized and structured connection to the tribal liaison and Native nations premised on the recognition of tribal sovereignty. Fortunately, new tribal consultation requirements under ESSA (2015) will support Native nations' partnerships with districts. This process of partnership and consultation will support tribal authority and control (Charleston, 1994; Executive Office of the President, 2014) as a necessary intervention into Indigenous education.

What Institutions Can Do to Support Indigenous Education

While the previous section addressed issues of teacher knowledge to better support Indigenous education, the professional development to support such knowledge must be institutionalized. What follows are concrete, conceptual, and relational recommendations for districts and schools, teacher education programs, state level educational policy, and research.

Districts and schools

Districts should apply for and support Indian Education programs systematically by circulating information about such programs to all administrators, teachers, and office staff, orienting each new employee to the program's location, purpose, and services. Districts should have administrators (e.g., the Director of Elementary Education) who can provide basic training to administrators and teachers to detect and eliminate stereotypes from curricula that create hostile climates for students. They should also acquire and disseminate culturally relevant materials for school and teacher use. Beyond this practical knowledge, districts should utilize equity analyses to evaluate educational policies and practices. Districts might even begin to evaluate such policies and practices through an anticolonial/self-determination/sovereignty lens, reflecting on how such practices support or undermine Native sovereignty. Districts should also intentionally recruit and support the hiring of Native teachers, a recommendation echoed in much of the literature (Beulieu & Figueira, 2006). Moreover, districts and schools should support ongoing professional development for teachers regarding Indigenous education. To do this, districts could develop teacher learning communities (Cochran-Smith & Lytle, 1999; Grossman, Wineburg, & Woolworth, 2001) and support site leaders at schools that could work with teachers within their building on localized professional development. As an example, I recently worked with a dedicated group of 4th grade teachers who, after training on how to detect colonial bias in curriculum, met over the summer to revise and map out 4th grade curriculum for the year. These teachers then worked specifically with the grade level teams at their respective schools to train and support the other teachers in their building on implementing the revised curriculum. This process was possible because the district's Equity Director received a grant to support these teacher leaders to educate themselves and then undertake the labor to revise the curriculum. Districts can find ways to support this train the trainer model so that Indigenous studies literacy becomes a shared knowledge base.

Beyond knowledge, districts can facilitate relationships between schools and Indian Education programs. They should also assume collective responsibility for the support of Indian Education and education of Native students. This might mean providing administrative, financial, or personnel support. Some districts, recognizing the limited funds of Indian Education programs, offset costs by providing FTE to support additional personnel. It is not enough to be "in relationship" with programs; it must also mean being responsible for providing sufficient support. Districts and schools should also foster relationships with families and Native parent committees, as well as provide various venues—public and private, informal and formal—for Native students and families to share their experiences within schools. Finally, districts should develop formal relationships with nearby Native nations. Premised on a recognition of and respect for tribal sovereignty, districts should develop tribal-district partnerships that can assist the district's support of those nations' tribal members, and the implementation of more responsible Native content. This could be implemented through a tribal advisory board, the establishment of "tribal education codes" (Charleston, 1994), a memorandum of understanding, or by following the US Forest Service's example, through institutionalizing trust responsibility through a tribal liaison.

Teacher education programs

Teacher education programs can support Indigenous education in a variety of ways. Beyond providing preservice teachers with the concrete knowledge to support Native students articulated earlier, all future teachers should have knowledge of the history of schooling within a context of genocide and colonialism. This knowledge is foundational for understanding the ways schools continue to be structured as systems that erase, marginalize, or assimilate Native students. As Lee (2011) argues,

> For teaching about Native peoples, teacher education should support critical inquiry into the scholarship, multimedia representations, and historical positioning of Native peoples. Teachers must be prepared with inclusive and accurate portrayals of who Native people are today and their unique cultural and political sovereignty over their lands in addition to their distinct political relationships with the United States. (p. 277)

Teacher education programs should provide a range of opportunities for preservice teachers to develop conceptual knowledge. Just as most college and universities require "diversity" or "multicultural" courses, teacher education programs should require that each and every teacher take an Indigenous studies course. Indigenous studies as a discipline has provides substantial conceptual tools to critique colonialism and recognize and affirm Native survivance. Such courses could provide educators with conceptual tools to understand and enact theories of culture, identity, knowledge, land, language, and community that further, rather than undermine, Native survivance, self-determination, and sovereignty. This is in addition to foundational knowledge these programs should provide educators regarding critical theories of race, whiteness, and other structures and discourses of oppression. Following the work of Dion (2007; 2008), teacher education programs can also help educators develop critical self-awareness of their subjectivities in relation to Indigenous peoples and to discourses and practices of colonialism, disrupting the "perfect stranger" positioning that enables educators to continually disregard Indigenous peoples and issues. As I have argued in this book, counterstorytelling, critical narrative research, and case study approaches can be effective in developing teacher knowledge (Atwood & López, 2014; Chang & Rosiek, 2003; Clandinin & Connelly, 1995; Connelly & Clandinin, 1999; Connelly, Clandinin, & He, 1997; Dibble & Rosiek, 2002; Rosiek & Atkinson, 2007; Sconiers & Rosiek, 2000; Shulman, 1986; Shulman, 2004; Solórzano & Delgado Bernal, 2001; Solórzano & Yosso, 2002). Critical case studies and counterstories provide context-rich narratives to examine experiences shaped by macrosocial discourses, and material through which student teachers can begin to appreciate the discursive dynamics Native students, communities, and service providers navigate in the education process. Finally, teacher education programs should promote the hiring of Indigenous professors. To support the development of preservice teachers, teacher education programs must have professors with the capacity to address issues of colonization and survivance in education. Though arguably all professors within the program should be versed in Indigenous studies, there are already educators versed in the politics of Indigenous knowledge, issues, and representation. Policies and practices should be developed to promote the hiring of Indigenous teacher educators who might already be versed in such knowledge, or are implementing research agendas that engage Indigenous studies and support Indigenous peoples.

Beyond building knowledge, teacher education programs should develop relationships with Native programs and Native nations, providing a model for educators as they transition into their work. This might include developing relationships with Indian Education programs/Native-serving schools so that students gain practical experience in these settings. This might also include tribal-teacher education programs which support the recruitment and licensure of Native students, and support Native communities' needs for highly qualified Native teachers. Created in partnership with Oregon's nine federally recognized tribal nations, the University of Oregon provides a model for such collaboration through the Sapsik'wałá Teacher Education Program which aims to prepare Native teachers who are committed to teaching in Native-serving schools upon graduation. Following the work of projects such as the Harvard Project on American Indian Economic Development and the recent publication *Universities and Indian Country* (Norman & Kalt, 2015), teacher education programs could also design action-research courses aimed to further tribal sovereignty, nation-building, and self-determination through developing partnerships between students and tribal communities. Such partnerships would gear student coursework and projects to directly address tribal nations' needs and goals, while also developing teacher practical knowledge.

Educational policy

There are a variety of ways educational policy can support statewide efforts and school districts. Educational policy can support the development of concrete information regarding local Native nations, and support the circulation of such materials. Conceptually, educational policy as it relates to supporting Indigenous students should not only consider issues of equity, access, and social justice, but should also support Native students' unique aims of self-determination and sovereignty. The Oregon Department of Education, for example, drafts documents that advocate for Native students' rights to wear regalia at graduation ceremonies. Policy should also be written to support the development of curriculum that supports tribal sovereignty. Further, following the lead of states like Washington, Montana, and New Mexico, states should develop policies to mandate Native studies curriculum statewide. Oregon recently passed Senate Bill

13: Tribal History/Shared History, which funds, mandates, and supports the development of curriculum on tribal history, governance, and sovereignty to all students in K-12 public schools in Oregon. These initiatives should be the norm, not exceptions.

As a relational practice, states should engage in meaningful consultation with Native nations. Through Executive Order 96–30, the State of Oregon formalized these state/tribal government-to-government partnerships, and later, created "clusters" to focus on specific areas of policy. Oregon's government-to-government education cluster, for example, "focuses on areas of partnership that expand along the education spectrum from early childhood to college" (Oregon Department of Education, 2014, p. 2). Beyond consultation, states can institutionalize tribal liaisons, advisors, Indian Education directors, or other such positions, to support districts in implementing Indigenous education.

Research

Research can support Indigenous education in a variety of ways. Providing descriptive statistics on Native graduation, achievement, discipline, and attendance rates, for example, can support states, districts, and institutions in being accountable for Indigenous students' success. Such research should explicitly attend to the erasures embedded in demographic data collection and reporting processes that often erase Native students through categories such as "Hispanic/Latino," "two or to more races," or "multiracial." Although these categories were designed to more effectively capture the racial and ethnic diversity of students, they often times recast Native students as students of color (erasing their Indigeneity and reframing them as multicultural settlers). Surveys should also be designed and developed to better understand what teachers know and don't know about Indigenous students' lives and Indigenous education in order to guide professional development.

Following the call from Castagno and Brayboy (2008; see also Brayboy & Castagno, 2009), research should conceptually continue to explore the intersections of education and colonization, and foreground Native knowledge, theories, and experiences. As Lee (2011) argues,

> For Indigenous peoples, research on teacher education must take a stronger stance to address the marginalization of Native peoples in curriculum, content, and pedagogy in order to ignite SCR education on behalf of Native peoples. This type of research agenda allows for reclamation of what it means to be Native. It includes authentic representations of Native peoples and acknowledgement of their contemporary lived experiences. It also contributes to the dearth of academic knowledge in teacher education regarding SCR education for and about Native peoples. (p. 288)

Research is also needed that looks at how teachers engage the colonial contexts of schools in a constructive fashion and with attention to complexity. This research could support teachers working in schools through the development of teacher-research collaboratives (see Sconiers & Rosiek, 2000), while also providing meaningful content for preservice and in-service professional development.

Relationally, and as articulated by a vast body of scholarship in Indigenous research methodologies (Brayboy, 2005; Chilisa, 2012; Hart, 2010; Kovach, 2009; Rigney, 1999; Smith, 2012; Steinhauer, 2002; Weber-Pillwax, 2001; Wilson, 2008), research should not solely be geared to learn *about* Native students' lives and communities, but should be actively committed to improving them. This means teacher education research must be "of use" (Fine & Barreras, 2001) and "be relevant and address problems of the community" (Brayboy, 2005, p. 440). To know what is of use to communities, educational researchers must utilize methodologies that respect the lives, needs, and aspirations of Indigenous communities, and adapt research agendas accordingly. Indigenous studies scholars provide critical approaches for theorizing research that attends to the colonizing histories and ongoing extractive practices of researchers and institutions (Simpson, 2007; Tuck, 2009; Tuck & Yang, 2014a; 2014b). Teacher education programs should consider the ways their faculty research agendas can directly support school districts in implementing more effective forms of Indigenous education in their own backyard, as well as provide direct support for Indigenous education programs already engaging in that work. Research is also needed that supports Native teachers' and community efforts at survivance, recognizing the ways that survivance is often improvisational, using the resources at hand to support Native students and families despite, at times, dire circumstances.

Maintaining Hope Despite Hardship

In keeping with this observation, and in recognition that critical narrative educational research that attends to colonization and survivance is an important, yet insufficient educational intervention, I conclude this book with a final survivance story. This story resonates with a quote by critical pedagogue Paolo Freire:

> If education could do all or if it could do nothing, there would be no reason to speak about its limits. We speak about them, precisely because, in not beign able to do everything, education can do something. As educators ... it behooves us to see what we can do so that we can competetently realize our goals. (as cited in Brayboy & McCarty, 2010, p. 197)

It resonates, too, with words Kanaka Maoli scholar Emalani Case (2017) delivered to a graduating class of seniors at Kanu o ka 'Āina, a Hawaiian focused public charter school on Hawai'i island. She was disheartened in her Pacific Studies university class when a student of hers "had lost her ability to dream good dreams, to have hope, to be radical, to fight even if and when she may lose just because it's the right thing to do." This student felt that "car[ing] so much about something she could not change was a waste of time, a waste of energy." Emalani

Case felt disheartened, but reflected upon her visit with the senior class at Kanu o ka 'Āina who were "bold and brave dreamers":

> Yes, it does indeed take a lot of effort to care about something you may not be able to change: to stop sea levels from rising, to prevent destruction and desecration, to end genocide. But these haumāna were willing to care anyway: to care for the potential, for the possibility, for the chance of huli-hia. (n.p.)

Reflecting on the courage of these Hawaiian students, and sharing a story of the Hawaiian prophet Kapihe, who dared to voice an unpopular prophecy for which he was criticized—"What is up shall come down. What is below shall rise."—Case told the students:

> In other words, there is always the possibility of change, even when you think you are helpless, even when you think your people are doomed, even when you think that your efforts and energies are wasted on dreams. His words teach us to dream anyway.

Case left the graduating class with a charge: "take up the task to maintain hope" (n.p.). This story, too, represents a community effort to maintain hope and attempt "to see what we could do" to address the violence against Indigenous women. Our efforts, as this story will show, did not stop physical assaults on Indigenous women; and yet, they were also not useless. This story of our effort addresses the impossible positions we are put in as educators, positions we must face, no matter how meaningless our efforts may feel at times. I hope this story inspires educators to "take up the task to maintain hope," even when our struggles may not result in the justice and change we hope for. We must dare to dream and struggle anyway.

Native Love

The pow wow had ended a few hours back. Somehow every year, we forget the immense amount of work it takes to put on a community event like this. There was only a handful of us left to pack up, put away the chairs, and clean the gym. Upon finishing, a group of Native youth were in a group talking, some on the ground, some sitting on the rail, one dangling from a tree. At once, they all started laughing. The laughter in that moment was medicine, infectious, the type of laughter that penetrates your chest and that often come from delirium. Some of the youth had been there since 9 p.m. and it was probably nearing midnight. For a fleeting moment as I looked at them, it was as if the last two years of our work together was right there, vivid, spilling out of their giggles and chiding remarks as they treated each other like siblings. For that moment, I was overwhelmed with joy and goodness, convinced that some of our efforts were leading to what Vine Deloria Jr. had hoped for education: the creation of "good people" (as cited in Demmert & Towner, 2003, p. 1).

In that moment as I listened to their laughter, I had a sensation that paralleled my experience of entering motherhood—my sense of self had expanded. These students—once strangers—now felt like kin. Their joy was my joy, their being was entangled with my own. I was sensing the relational network we had fostered; the connections between us all. Ojibwe writer Louise Erdrich once wrote, "Every Native American is a survivor, an anomaly, a surprise on earth. We were all slated for extinction before the march of progress. But surprise, we are progress" (as cited in Keene, 2014, p. 1). Overjoyed at the moment, I wanted to shout "*You* are what this work is about! *You* are miracles!" But I held back. I marveled at the ways these teenagers from three different high schools in the district could act like family, especially with all the drama in their lives. I didn't need to say anything to them because they didn't need me to affirm them in that moment; they had each other.

One of the youth was drawing on the white board we had used for our project that day. At this year's pow wow, I had asked some of the youth to help me with a photo project called Native Love, a project developed by the National Indigenous Women's Resource Center (NIWRC) designed to "raise awareness and help end violence against Native youth by empowering them to redefine Native Love" (NIWRC website, http://nativelove.niwrc.org/). With our camera, a white board, and dry erase marker, we walked around the pow wow explaining the project and asking people if they would like to participate. Underneath the words #NativeLoveIs ... we asked folks to provide their own definitions of love. We then took their picture as they held the white board. Nearly one hundred youth and elders, men and women, responded to the question. To see grown men and teenage boys answer with words like community, acceptance, family, and respect was a blessing, a "bendición" as one young man answered. Tradition. Fry Bread. Family. Heritage. Mom. Beautiful. Culture. Togetherness. Love. Nature. Kindness. Ceremony. Water. Children. Involvement. It was Native Love I was experiencing as those youth giggled, embodying and reflecting positive and healthy relationships.

It felt so hopeful and promising to witness these loving affirmations, and to be able to offer those beautiful words and images back to the community in a photo collage. With our limited budget, social media was the only way to share these images, but this "desire-based" project (Tuck, 2009), a chance for our community to develop "positive representations" of ourselves (Keene, 2015), circulated through likes, shares, and positive comments throughout the community.

My reflections on the project were complicated, however. Watching the young man doodle on the board as the youth talked to each other reminded me of the meaningful work we did. It felt important, for example, to walk around with a teenage boy and prompt him to explain the project to others. It felt important to spend time with a young girl as she listened to elders define love in empowering ways: appreciation, togetherness, the river, respect, my sons. There was wisdom in those words and I know it meant something for us to be a part of it. Yet that evening, I was also humbled. Troubled.

I had just taken a break from the project to help with honoring the graduates. The parent committee had just gifted the high school students their Pendleton stoles for graduation, an honor I hoped they would carry with them to their graduations, as the parent group fought hard for those rights. The community had just sat down after congratulating them in an honor song and everyone marveled at the tiny tots dancers who took the floor.

There was joy in the room. I sat on the outskirts of the dance floor, watching the tiny tots dance. I began talking with one mother who asked about my white board when I noticed her face was deeply bruised. As we both watched her daughter dance, she told me of the violent relationship she was in and was trying to escape. She was fearful, but strong for her daughter. He had recently crossed a line, she told me, and she was determined to leave him. She was staying at a friend's house, but looking for more support. I gave her my cell and told her about shelters and resources in the area. We were both crying. I held my white-board, and looked down at the words "Native Love is ..." I felt the weakness of the project crumble under the lived and real violence it was supposed to address. The children had finished dancing and her daughter approached us from the dance floor. The mother told her daughter about my project and her daughter said that she wanted to write something. The little girl, perhaps 5 years old, took the whiteboard from my hands and underneath the words "Native Love Is ...," in slow and purposeful childlike letters, she wrote, "my mama."

Notes

1 See Castagno & Brayboy's (2008) literature review, or the introduction for examples.
2 See Oyate's "Living Stories" for examples that occurred in this area, including Raven's story and Qala's story (http://oyate.org/index.php/resources/45-resources/living-stories).
3 Hawai'i is still an unceded sovereign Hawaiian kingdom, illegally annexed by the US (Goodyear-Ka'ōpua, 2013; Silva, 2004). Other unrecognized Native nations, such as the Muwekma Ohlone in California, or the Duwamish Tribe or Chinook Indian Nation in Washington, also argue that their lands remain unceded territory within the United States.
4 Washington's "Since Time Immemorial" Tribal Sovereignty Curriculum, or "Montana's Indian Education for All" curriculum are two online sites that provide a wealth of information and curriculum about Native sovereignty. With the passage of Senate Bill 13: Tribal History/Shared History the state of Oregon is hoping to be among those that emphasize tribal sovereignty as core knowledge in public schools.
5 One's citizenship in a tribal nation is based in law; an ancestral claim to Indigeneity establishes a connection through blood; a cultural claim may be justified through one's knowledge of Indigenous languages or ceremonies; or one may simply assert one's Indigeneity as a form of personal self-identification. These rationalizations might also overlap, as citizenship in a tribal nation (political/legal) may require demonstrated

ancestry (biological); or recognition by the federal government may need to be justified through ancestry (biological) and/or a nation's distinctiveness as a community (culture).

6   Some scholars argue that legal and political understandings of sovereignty, despite their limits, have and continue to be an effective form of advocacy for Native rights (Barker, 2005; Deloria, 1998; Wilkins, 1997). Others are concerned that sovereignty foregrounds Western constructions of nationhood and recognition (Alfred, 1999; Coulthard, 2014), opting instead to theorize practices of Indigenous cultural resurgence and notions of peoplehood (Alfred, 1999; Alfred & Corntassel, 2005; Corntassel, 2012; Holm, Pearson, & Chavis, 2003). Some have worked thoughtfully to "detach and *dethink* the notion of sovereignty from its connections to Western understandings of power and relationship and base it on indigenous notions of power" (Grande, 2015, p. 70), theorizing sovereignty as a spiritual, pedagogical, intellectual, and relational project that centers Indigenous families', lands', and knowledges (Grande, 2015; Teves, Smith, & Raheja, 2015). Still others have theorized the ideological and representational dimensions of sovereignty, such as "intellectual sovereignty" (Warrior, 1992), "American Indian intellectualism" (Cook-Lynn, 1996), "rhetorical sovereignty" (Lyons, 2000), or "visual sovereignty" (Raheja, 2010), among others.

7   See the following websites for examples of youth action: More than that (https://www. youtube.com/watch?v=FhribaNXr7A); Earth Guardians (http://www.earthguardians. org/xiuhtezcatl/); and *Rezpect Our Water* (https://www.youtube.com/channel/ UC4Xfw9SHGin9Eb-cQh4T1IQ).

References

20 U.S.C. § 6102(b). (2015). Every Student Succeeds Act (2015) Retrieved from https:// www.gpo.gov/fdsys/pkg/BILLS-114s1177enr/pdf/BILLS-114s1177enr.pdf.

Alfred, G. (1999). *Peace, power, righteousness: An indigenous manifesto*. Don Mills, ON: Oxford University Press.

Alfred, T., & Corntassel, J. (2005). Being Indigenous: Resurgences against contemporary colonialism. *Government and Opposition*, 40(4), 597–614.

Archibald, J. A. (2008). *Indigenous storywork: Educating the heart, mind, body, and spirit*. Vancouver: UBC Press.

Atwood, E. & López, G. R. (2014). Let's be critically honest: Towards a messier counterstory in critical race theory. *International Journal of Qualitative Studies in Education*, 27 (9), 1134–1154.

Barker, J. (2005). *Sovereignty matters: Locations of contestation and possibility in indigenous struggles for self-determination*. Lincoln, NE: University of Nebraska Press.

Bartolomé, L. I. (2008). Authentic cariño and respect in minority education: The political and ideological dimensions of love. *International Journal of Critical Pedagogy*, 1(1), 1–17.

Basso, K. H. (1984). "Stalking with stories": Names, places, and moral narratives among Western Apache. In E. Bruner (Ed.). *Text, play, and story: The construction and reconstruction of self and society* (pp. 19–55). Washington, DC: American Ethnological Society.

Beulieu, D., & Figueira, A. M. (2006). *The power of Native teachers: Language and culture in the classroom*. Tempe, AZ: The Center for Indian Education. Arizona State University.

Bell, D. (1980). Brown v. Board of Education and the Interest-Convergence Dilemma. *Harvard Law Review*, 93(3), 518–533.

Brandzel, A. (2016). *Against citizenship: The violence of the normative*. Urbana, IL: University of Illinois Press.

Brayboy, B. M. J. (2005). Toward a tribal critical race theory in education. *Urban Review: Issues and Ideas in Public Education*, 5, 425–446.

Brayboy, B., & Castagno, A. (2009). Self-determination through self-education: Culturally responsive schooling for Indigenous students in the USA. *Teaching Education*, 20(1): 31–53.

Brayboy, B. M. J., & McCarty, T. L. (2010). Indigenous knowledges and social justice pedagogy. In T. K. Chapman & N. Hobbel (Eds.), *Social justice pedagogy across the curriculum: The practice of freedom* (pp. 184–200). New York, NY: Routledge.

Brayboy, M. E., & Morgan, M. Y. (1998). Voices of Indianness: The lived world of Native American women. *Womens Studies International Forum*, 21(4), 341–354.

Brayboy, B. M. J., Fann, A. J., Castagno, A. E., & Solyom, J. A. (2012). *Postsecondary education for American Indian and Alaska Natives: Higher education for nation building and self-determination*. San Francisco, CA: Wiley Subscription Services.

Bruyneel, K. (2007). *The third space of sovereignty: The postcolonial politics of U.S.-indigenous relations*. Minneapolis, MN: University of Minnesota Press.

Byrd, J. A. (2011). *The transit of empire: Indigenous critiques of colonialism*. Minneapolis: University of Minnesota Press.

Calderón, D. (2009). Making explicit the jurisprudential foundations of multiculturalism: The continuing challenges of colonial education in US schooling for Indigenous education. In A. Kempf (Ed.), *Breaching the colonial contract: Anti-colonialism in the U.S. and Canada* (pp. 53–77). New York, NY: Springer.

Calderón, D. (2011). Locating the foundations of epistemologies of ignorance in normative multicultural education. In N. Jaramillo & E. Malewski (Eds.), *Epistemologies of ignorance in education* (pp. 105–127). Charlotte, NC: Information Age Pub.

Calderón, D. (2014a). Speaking back to manifest destinies: A land education-based approach to critical curriculum inquiry. *Environmental Education Research*, 20(1), 24–36.

Calderón, D. (2014b). Uncovering settler grammars in curriculum. *Educational Studies: Journal of the American Educational Studies Association*, 50(4), 313–338.

Case, E. (2017). A gift of dreams: For the senior class of Kanu o ka ʻĀina. Retrieved from https://hewahipaakai.wordpress.com/tag/mauna-kea/.

Castagno, A. E. (2014). *Educated in whiteness: Good intentions and diversity in schools*. Minneapolis, MN: University of Minnesota Press.

Castagno, A. E., & Brayboy, B. M. K. J. (2008). Culturally responsive schooling for Indigenous youth: A review of the literature. *Review of Educational Research*, 78(4), 941–993.

Chang, P., & RosiekJ. (2003). Anti-colonial antinomies: A case of cultural conflict in the high school biology curriculum. *Curriculum Inquiry*, 33(3), 251–290.

Charleston, M. G. (1994). Toward true Native education: A treaty of 1992. Final report of the Indian Nations at Risk Task Force. *Journal of American Indian Education*, 33(2), 7–56.

Chilisa, B. (2012). *Indigenous research methodologies*. Thousand Oaks, CA: Sage.

Clandinin, D., & Connelly, M. (1995). *Teachers' professional knowledge landscapes*. New York, NY: Teachers College Press.

Cochran-Smith, M. & Lytle, S. L. (1999). Relationships of knowledge and practice: Teacher learning in communities. *Review of Research in Education*, 24, 249–273.

Connelly, F., & Clandinin, J. D. (1999). *Shaping a professional identity: Stories of educational practice*. New York, NY: Teachers College Press.

Connelly, F. M., Clandinin, D. J., & He, M. F. (1997). Teachers' personal practical knowledge on the professional knowledge landscape. *Teaching and Teacher Education*, 13(7), 665–674.

Cook-Lynn, E. (1996). American Indian intellectualism and the new Indian story. *American Indian Quarterly*, 20(1), 57–76.

Cook-Lynn, E. (2001). *Anti-Indianism in North America: A voice from Tatekeya's earth.* Urbana, IL: University of Illinois Press.

Corntassel, J. (2003). Who is Indigenous? Peoplehood and ethnonationalist approaches to rearticulating Indigenous identity. *Nationalism and Ethnic Politics,* 9(1), 75–100.

Corntassel, J. (2012). Re-envisioning resurgence: Indigenous pathways to decolonization and sustainable self-determination. *Decolonization: Indigeneity, Education, & Society,* 1(1), 86–101.

Corntassel, J., & Witmer, R. C. (2008). *Forced federalism: Contemporary challenges to indigenous nationhood* (American Indian law and policy series). Norman, OK: University of Oklahoma Press.

Coulthard, G. (2014). *Red skin, white masks: Rejecting the colonial politics of recognition.* Minneapolis, MN: University of Minnesota Press.

Curry-Stevens, A., Cross-Hemmer, A. & Coalition of Communities of Color. (2011). *The Native American community in Multnomah County: An unsettling profile.* Portland, OR: Portland State University.

Delgado, R. (1989). Storytelling for oppositionists and others: A plea for narrative. *Michigan Law Review,* 87, 2411–2441.

Delgado, R. (1996). Rodrigo's eleventh chronicle: Empathy and false empathy. *California Law Review,* 84(1), 61–100.

Deloria, P. (1998). *Playing Indian.* New Haven, CT: Yale University Press.

Demmert, W., & Towner, J. (2003). *A review of the research literature on the influences of culturally based education on the academic performance of Native American students.* Portland, OR: Northwest Regional Education Laboratory.

Denetdale, J. N. (2006). Chairmen, presidents, and princesses: The Navajo Nation, gender, and the politics of tradition. *Wicazo Sa Review,* 21(1), 9–28.

Derman-Sparks, L., & the A.B.C. Task Force. (1989). *Anti-bias curriculum: Tools for empowering young children.* Washington, DC: National Association for the Education of Young Children.

Deyhle, D., & Swisher, K. (1997). Research in American Indian and Alaska Native education: From assimilation to self-determination. *Review of Research in Education,* 22, 113–194.

Dibble, N., & Rosiek, J. (2002). White-out: A connection between a teacher's white identity and her science teaching. *International Journal of Education and the Arts,* 5(3). Retrieved from www.ijea.org/v3n5/.

Dion, S. D. (2007). Disrupting molded images: Identities, responsibilities and relationships—teachers and indigenous subject material. *Teaching Education,* 18(4), 329–342.

Dion, S. D. (2008). *Braiding histories: Learning from Aboriginal peoples' experiences and perspectives.* Vancouver, BC: UBC Press.

Doerfler, J. (2015). *Those who belong: Identity, family, blood, and citizenship among the White Earth Anishinaabeg.* East Lansing, MI: Michigan State Press.

Executive Office of the President. (2014). *Native youth report.* Washington, DC: Executive Office of the President. Retrieved from https://www.whitehouse.gov/sites/default/files/docs/20141129nativeyouthreport_final.pdf.

Fine, M., & Barreras, R. (2001). To be of use. *Analyses of Social Issues and Public Policy,* 1(1), 175–182.

Forte, M. (2013). *Who is an Indian?: Race, place, and the politics of indigeneity in the Americas.* Toronto: University of Toronto Press.

Freire, P. (1970). *Pedagogy of the oppressed.* New York, NY: Seabury Press.

Garroutte, E. (2003). *Real Indians identity and the survival of Native America.* Berkeley, CA: University of California Press.

Goeman, M., & Denetdale, J. (2009). Guest editors' introduction: Native feminisms: Legacies, interventions, and Indigenous sovereignties. *Wicazo Sa Review*, 24(2), 9–13.

Goodyear-Ka'ōpua, N. (2013). *The seeds we planted: Portraits of a native Hawaiian charter school*. Minneapolois, MN: University of Minnesota Press.

Goulet, L., & Goulet, K. N. (2014). *Teaching each other: Nehinuw concepts and Indigenous pedagogies*. Vancouver: UBC Press.

Grande, S. (2004). *Red pedagogy: Native American social and political thought*. Lanham, MD: Rowman & Littlefield.

Grande, S. (2015). *Red pedagogy: Native American social and political thought* (2nd ed.) Lanham, MD: Rowman & Littlefield.

Grande, S., San Pedro, T., & Windchief, S. (2015). Indigenous peoples and identity in the 21st century: Remembering, reclaiming, and regenerating. In E. P. Salett, & D. R. Koslow (Eds.), *Multicultural perspectives on race, ethnicity, and identity* (105–122). Washington, DC: National Association of Social Workers Press.

Green, R. (1988). The tribe called Wannabee: Playing Indian in America and Europe. *Folklore*, 99(1), 30–55.

Grossman, P., Wineburg, S., & Woolworth, S. (2001). Toward a theory of teacher community. *Teachers College Record*, 103(6), 942–1012.

Hall, L. (2005). "Hawaiian at heart" and other fictions. *The Contemporary Pacific*, 17(2), 404–413.

Hart, M. (2010). Indigenous worldviews, knowledge, and research: The development of an Indigenous research paradigm. *Journal of Indigenous Voices in Social Work*, 1(1), 1–16.

Hermes, M. (2005a). Complicating Discontinuity: What About Poverty? *Curriculum Inquiry*, 35(1), 9–26.

Hermes, M. (2005b). "Ma'iingan is just a misspelling of the word wolf": A case for teaching culture through language. *Anthropology & Education Quarterly*, 36(1), 43–56.

Hirschfelder, A., Molin, P. F., & Wakim, Y. (1999). *American Indian stereotypes in the world of children: A reader and bibliography* (2nd ed.). Lanham, MD: Scarecrow Press.

Holm, T., Pearson, D. J., & Chavis, B. (2003). Peoplehood: A model for the extension of sovereignty in American Indian studies. *Wicazo Sa Review*, 18(1), 7–24.

hooks, b. (1992). *Black looks: Race and representation*. Boston, MA: South End Press.

Huhndorf, S. (2001). *Going native: Indians in the American cultural imagination*. Ithaca, NY: Cornell University Press.

Jacobs, M. (2009). *White mother to a dark race: Settler colonialism, maternalism, and the removal of indigenous children in the American West and Australia, 1880–1940*. Lincoln, NE: University of Nebraska Press.

Kalt, J. P., & Norman, D. K. (2015). *Universities and Indian country: Case studies in tribal-driven research*. Tucson: University of Arizona Press.

Kaomea, J. (2005). Indigenous studies in the elementary curriculum: A cautionary Hawaiian example. *Anthropology Education Quarterly*, 36(1), 24–42.

Keene, A. (2014). *"College pride, Native pride" and Education for Native nation building: Portraits of Native students navigating freshman year* (Unpublished doctoral dissertation). Harvard University, Cambridge, MA.

Keene, A. (2015). Representations matter: Serving Native students in higher education. *Journal Committed to Social Change on Race and Ethnicity*, 1(1), 101–111.

Kovach, M. (2009). *Indigenous methodologies: Characteristics, conversations and contexts*. Toronto: University of Toronto Press.

Ladson-Billings, G. (1998). Just what is critical race theory and what's it doing in a nice field like education? *International Journal of Qualitative Studies in Education*, 11(1), 7–24.

Lambert, V. & Lambert, M. (2014). Teach our children well: On addressing negative stereotypes in schools. *American Indian Quarterly*, 38(4), 524–540.

LaRocque, E. (2010). *When the other is me: Native resistance discourse, 1850–1990*. Winnipeg: University of Manitoba Press.

Lawrence, B. (2004). *"Real" Indians and others: Mixed-blood urban Native peoples and indigenous nationhood*. Lincoln, NE: University of Nebraska Press.

Lee, T. S. (2011). Teaching Native youth, teaching about Native Peoples: Shifting the paradigm to socioculturally responsive education. In A. F. Ball & C. A. Tyson (Eds.), *Studying diversity in teacher education* (pp. 275–293). Lanham, MD: Rowman & Littlefield.

Leonardo, Z. (2004). The color of supremacy: Beyond the discourse of "white privilege". *Educational Philosophy and Theory*, 36(2), 137–152.

Lomawaima, K. T. (1995). Educating Native Americans. In J. A. Banks & C. A. M. Banks (Eds.), *Handbook of research on multicultural education* (pp. 331–347). New York: Macmillan.

Lomawaima, K. T. (2008). Tribal sovereigns: Reframing research in American Indian education. In M. Villegas, S. R. Neugebauer, & K. R. Venegas (Eds.), *Indigenous knowledge and education: Sites of struggle, strength, and survivance* (pp. 183–203). Cambridge, MA: Harvard Educational Review.

Lomawaima, K. T., & McCarty, T. L. (2006). *"To remain an Indian": Lessons in democracy from a century of Native American education*. New York: Teachers College Press.

Lyons, S. R. (2000). Rhetorical sovereignty: What do American Indians want from writing? *College Composition and Communication*, 51(3), 447–468.

Lyons, S. R. (2010). *X-Marks*. Minneapolis, MN: University of Minnesota Press.

MacGill, B. (2016). A paradigm shift in education: Pedagogy, standpoint, and ethics of care. *International Journal of Pedagogies and Learning*, 11(3), 238–247.

Martinez, G. (2010). *Native pride: The politics of curriculum and instruction in an urban public school*. Cresskill, NJ: Hampton Press.

Million, D. (2014). There is a river in me: Theory from life. In A. Simpson & A. Smith (Eds.), *Theorizing Native Studies* (pp. 31–42). Durham, NC: Duke University Press.

Montana Office of Public Instruction. (2012). *Essential understandings regarding Montana Indians*. Indian Education Division. Retrieved from http://montanateach.org/resources/essential-understandings-regarding-montana-indians/.

Moreton-Robinson, A. (2000). *Talkin' up to the white woman: Aboriginal women and feminism*. St. Lucia, Qld: University of Queensland Press.

Moreton-Robinson, A. (2016). *Critical indigenous studies: Engagements in first world locations*. Tucson, AZ: The University of Arizona Press.

Morrill, A., Tuck, E., & the Super Futures Haunt Qollective. (2016). Before dispossession or surviving it. *Liminalities: A Journal of Performance Studies*, 12(1), 1–20.

Noddings, N. (1984). *Caring: A feminine approach to ethics & moral education*. Berkeley, CA: University of California Press.

Noddings, N. (2002). *Educating moral people: A caring alternative to character education*. New York, NY: Teachers College Press.

Noddings, N. (2005). *The challenge to care in schools: An alternative approach to education*. New York, NY: Teachers College Press.

Norman, D. K., & Kalt, J. P. (2015). *Universities and Indian country: Case studies in tribal-driven research*. Tucson, AZ: University of Arizona Press.

Oregon Department of Education. (2014). *State of Oregon Government to Government Agency Education Cluster Meeting Manual*. Retrieved from www.ode.state.or.us/opportunities/grants/nclb/title_vii/g2g-ed–cluster-meeting-manual-final-2014.pdf.

Paris, D. (2012). Culturally sustaining pedagogy: A needed change in stance, terminology, and practice. *Educational Researcher*, 41, 93–97

Parker, A. (1916). The social elements of the Indian problem. *American Journal of Sociology*, 22(2), 252–267.

Patel, L. (2016). *Decolonizing educational research: From ownership to answerability.* New York, NY: Routledge.

Pepper, F. (1990). *Unbiased teaching about American Indians and Alaska Natives in elementary schools.* Charleston, WV: ERIC Digest.

Pepper, F.Oregon Department of Education, Fuller, J., & Butterfield, R. (2014). *Indians in Oregon today: Oregon middle school—high school curriculum.* Salem, OR: Oregon Dept. of Education, Division of Special Student Services, Federal Programs.

Powers, K. M. (2006). An exploratory study of cultural identity and culture-based educational programs for urban American Indian students. *Urban Education*, 1, 20–49.

Raheja, M. (2010). *Reservation reelism: Redfacing, visual sovereignty, and representations of Native Americans in film.* Lincoln, NE: University of Nebraska Press.

Reese, D. (2007). The word "squaw" in SIGN OF THE BEAVER [Web log post]. October 27. Retrieved from http://americanindiansinchildrensliterature.blogspot.com/2007/10/word-squaw-in-sign-of-beaver.html.

Rifkin, M. (2014). *Settler common sense: Queerness and everyday colonialism in the American Renaissance.* Minneapolis, MN: University of Minnesota Press.

Rigney, L. (1999). Internationalization of an Indigenous anticolonial cultural critique of research methodologies: A guide to Indigenist research methodology and its principles. *Wicazo Sa Review*, 14(2), 109–121.

Robertson, D. W. (2015). Invisibility in the color-blind era: Examining legitimized racism against Indigenous peoples. *American Indian Quarterly*, 39(2), 113–153.

Rolón-Dow, R. (2005). Critical care: A color(full) analysis of care narratives in the schooling experiences of Puerto Rican girls. *American Educational Research Journal*, 42(1), 77–111.

RosiekJ., & Atkinson, B. (2005). Bridging the divides: The need for a pragmatic semiotics of teacher knowledge research. *Educational Theory*, 55(4), 231–266.

RosiekJ., & Atkinson, B. (2007). The inevitability and importance of genres in narrative research on teaching practice. *Qualitative Inquiry*, 13(4), 499–521.

Sabzalian, L., & Shear, S. (2018). Confronting colonial blindness in civics education: Recognizing colonization, self-determination, and sovereignty as core knowledge for elementary social studies teacher education. In S. Shear, C. M. Tschida, E. Bellows, L. B. Buchanan, & E. E. Saylor (Eds.), *Making controversial issues relevant for elementary social studies: A critical reader.* Charlotte, NC: Information Age Press.

Sadker, D. (2009). Some practical ideas for confronting curricular bias. Retrieved from www.sadker.org/curricularbias.html.

Said, E. (1978). *Orientalism* (1st ed.). New York, NY: Pantheon Books.

Said, E. (1993). *Culture and imperialism* (1st ed.). New York, NY: Knopf.

Sconiers, Z., & Rosiek, J. (2000). Historical perspective as an important element of teacher knowledge: A sonata-form case study of equity issues in a chemistry classroom. *Harvard Educational Review*, 70(3), 370–404.

Shulman, L. (1986). Those who understand: Knowledge growth in teaching. *Educational Researcher*, 15(2), 4–14.

Shulman, L. (2004). Just in case: Reflections on learning from experience. In L. Shulman & S. M. Wilson (Eds.), *The wisdom of practice: Essays on teaching, learning, and learning to teach* (1st ed.) (pp. 463–482). San Francisco, CA: Jossey-Bass.

Silva, N. (2004). *Aloha betrayed: Native Hawaiian resistance to American colonialism*. Durham, NC: Duke University Press.

Simpson, A. (2007). On ethnographic refusal: Indigeneity, "voice," and colonial citizenship. *Junctures*, 9, 67–80.

Simpson, L. (2011). *Dancing on our turtle's back: Stories of Nishnaabeg re-creation, resurgence and a new emergence*. Winnipeg: Arbeiter Ring Pub.

Slapin, B., & Seale, D. (1998). *Through Indian eyes: The native experience in books for children*. Los Angeles, CA: American Indian Studies Center, University of California.

Slapin, B., & Seale, D. (2003). *Through Indian eyes: The Native experience in books for children*. Berkeley, CA: Oyate.

Smith, L. T. (2012). *Decolonizing methodologies: Research and indigenous peoples*. (2nd ed.) London: Zed Books.

Smith, L. T. (2008). On tricky ground: Researching the native in the age of uncertainty. In N. Denzin, & Y. S. Lincoln (Eds.), *The landscape of qualitative research* (pp. 113–143). Los Angeles, CA: Sage Publications.

Solorzano, D. G., & Bernal, D. D. (2001). Examining transformational resistance through a Critical Race and LatCrit Theory framework: Chicana and Chicano students in an urban context. *Urban Education*, 36(3), 308–342.

Solórzano, D. G., & Yosso, T. J. (2002). Critical race methodology: Counter-storytelling as an analytic framework for education research. *Qualitative Inquiry*, 8, 23–44.

St. Denis, V. (2011). Silencing Aboriginal curricular content and perspectives through multiculturalism: "There are other children here." *Review of Education, Pedagogy, and Cultural Studies*, 33(4), 306–317.

Steinhauer, E. (2002). Thoughts on an Indigenous research methodology. *Canadian Journal of Native Education*, 26(2), 69–81.

Stewart-Harawira, M. (2013). Challenging knowledge capitalism: Indigenous research in the 21st century. *Socialist Studies: The Journal of the Society for Socialist Studies*, 9(1), 39–51.

Sturm, C. (2002). *Blood politics: Race, culture, and identity in the Cherokee Nation of Oklahoma*. Berkeley, CA: University of California Press.

Teves, S. N., Smith, A., & Raheja, M. H. (2015). *Native studies keywords*. Tucson, AZ: The University of Arizona Press.

Thompson, A. (1998). Not the color purple: Black feminist lessons for educational caring. *Harvard Educational Review*, 68(4), 522–554.

Tuck, E. (2009). Suspending damage: A letter to communities. *Harvard Educational Review*, 79(3), 409–428.

Tuck, E., & Yang, K. W. (2012). Decolonization is not a metaphor. *Decolonization: Indigeneity, Education and Society*, 1, 1–40.

Tuck, E., & Yang, K. W. (2014a). R-words: Refusing research. In D. Paris & M. T. Winn (Eds.), *Humanizing research: Decolonizing qualitative inquiry with youth and communities* (pp. 223–248). Thousand Oaks, CA: Sage.

Tuck, E., & Yang, K. W. (2014b). Unbecoming Claims. *Qualitative Inquiry*, 20(6), 811–818.

Turner, D. A. (2006). *This is not a peace pipe: Towards a critical indigenous philosophy*. Toronto: University of Toronto Press.

Valenzuela, A. (1999). *Subtractive schooling: U.S.-Mexican youth and the politics of caring*. Albany, NY: State University of New York Press.

Vaught, S. E., & Castagno, A. E. (2008). "I don't think I'm a racist:" Critical Race Theory, teacher attitudes, and structural racism. *Race, Ethnicity and Education*, 11(2), 95–113.

Veracini, L. (2011). On settlerness. *Borderlands e-journal*, 10(1), 1–17.

Villegas, A. M., & Lucas, T. (2002). Preparing culturally responsive teachers: Rethinking the curriculum. *Journal of Teacher Education*, 53(1), 20–32.

Warrior, R. A. (1992). Intellectual sovereignty and the struggle for an American Indian future. *Wicazo Sa Review*, 8(1), 1–20.

Weber-Pillwax, C. (2001). What is Indigenous research? *Canadian Journal of Native Education*, 25, 166–174.

Wilkins, D. (1997). *American Indian sovereignty and the U.S. Supreme Court: The masking of justice.* Austin, TX: University of Texas Press.

Wilson, W. A. C. (2006). Burning down the house: Laura Ingalls Wilder and American Colonialism. In D. T. Jacobs (Ed.), *Unlearning the language of conquest: Scholars expose anti-Indianism in America* (pp. 66–80). Austin, TX: University of Texas Press.

Wilson, S. (2008). *Research is ceremony: Indigenous research methods.* Black Point, NS: Fernwood Pub.

Wolfe, P. (2006). Settler-colonialism and the elimination of the native. *Journal of Genocide Research*, 8(4), 387–409.

INDEX